HISTORICAL DICTIONARIES
OF WAR, REVOLUTION, AND CIVIL UNREST
Edited by Jon Woronoff

HISTORICAL DICTIONARY
OF THE
BRITISH AND IRISH CIVIL WARS
1637–1660

MARTYN BENNETT

Historical Dictionaries
of War, Revolution, and Civil Unrest, No. 14

The Scarecrow Press, Inc.
Lanham, Maryland, and London
2000

SCARECROW PRESS, INC.

Published in the United States of America
by Scarecrow Press, Inc.,
4720 Boston Way, Lanham, Maryland 20706
http://www.scarecrowpress.com

4 Pleydell Gardens, Folkestone
Kent CT20 2DN, England

Copyright © 2000 by Martyn Bennett

British Library Cataloguing in Publication Information Available

Library of Congress Cataloging-in-Publication Data

Bennett, Martyn.
    Historical dictionary of the British and Irish Civil Wars,
1637–1660 / Martyn Bennett.
        p.   cm. — (Historical dictionaries of war, revolution, and
civil unrest : 14)
    Includes bibliographical references.
    ISBN 0-8108-3661-0 (alk. paper)
    1. Great Britain—History—Puritan Revolution, 1642–1660
Dictionaries.   2. Great Britain—History—Charles I, 1625–1649
Dictionaries.   3. Ireland—History—1649–1660 Dictionaries.
4. Ireland—History—1625–1649 Dictionaries. I. Title.
II. Series: Historical dictionaries of war, revolution, and civil
unrest : no. 14.
DA405.B344   1999
941.06′2—dc21   99-26024
                                                         CIP

Manufactured in the United States of America

∞™ The paper used in this publication meets the minimum requirements of
American National Standard for Information Sciences—Permanence of
Paper for Printed Library Materials, ANSI Z39.48–1984.

To Deborah Tyler-Bennett

Contents

Editor's Foreword

Most wars are fairly straightforward. If nothing else, you know who is on opposing sides, the aims of the war are relatively clear, there is a reasonably well-demarcated front, and if nothing else, you know who won. The situation for the British and Irish Civil Wars was not that simple. Those backing each side varied over time, and there was no end to turncoats shifting from side to side. This meant that the aims of the war varied as well, depending on the tides of war, depending also on who fought and directed it. There were regions that opted for one side or another, but even they had pockets of opponents, and counties, villages, and even families were divided. Most oddly, although the parliamentarians surely "won" the war, not too many years later there was a restoration of the defeated royalists. If that were the end of it, maybe this war would be forgotten. But it was impossible to forget that the people also had rights, that they could impose them on the rulers, that the rulers could be overthrown and even executed.

This *Historical Dictionary of the British and Irish Civil Wars* provides a guide to this far from straightforward, indeed often extremely complex and confusing period. It covers the run-up to the war and the aftermath; it provides information not only on the military and political aspects, but also the economic, social, and religious consequences. It includes brief entries on a broad array of persons, places, institutions, and military encounters. The chronology is precious in following events; the Introduction puts the entries and events in their context. This guide is not only helpful when reading general works like this, readers should have it on hand when delving into the vast, and growing, literature that is mapped out in the bibliography.

The author of this volume, Martyn Bennett, is one of the leading authorities on the British and Irish Civil Wars. He has taught about the war and the period, first at Loughborough and Leicester Universities, and presently as Reader in History at Nottingham Trent University. He has already written extensively, including several major works, among them *The English Civil War, 1640–1649* (1995) and *The Civil Wars of Britain and Ireland, 1638–1651* (1997). Dr. Bennett has also visited the sites of many battles, to understand them on the ground as well, resulting in *Travellers' Guide to the Battlefields of the English Civil War* (1990). This experience has placed him in an ideal position to write such a guide as this.

JON WORONOFF
Series Editor

Acknowledgements

I would like to thank my colleagues in the Forward Seventeenth Century Seminar in the History Section of Nottingham Trent University. Their unfailing help and comments enhanced this volume. I also wish to thank the Faculty of Humanities at the university under Dean Professor Stephen Chan for the sabbatical period in 1998, part of which was dedicated to completing the work for this dictionary. Finally, I wish to thank my partner, Dr Deborah Tyler-Bennett, to whom I have dedicated this work, for reading and commenting on the definitions here included.

Map

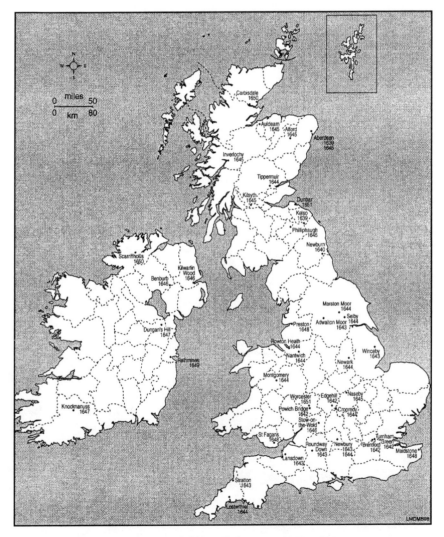

Map Battles of the Civil War, 1639–1651.

Chronology

1637   **23 July, Scotland:** Riots at St Giles, Edinburgh, as the new prayer book is read for the first time. **18 October, Scotland:** Opponents of Charles I's religious policy present the *Supplication and Complaint* to the king. **November to December, Scotland:** Opponents of the king form executive bodies, the Tables, to co-ordinate their action.

1638   **28 February, Scotland:** The National Covenant, binding the Scottish people together in defence of their kirk, is signed for the first time at St Giles, Edinburgh. **May, Scotland:** Charles I's cousin, the marquis of Hamilton, arrives in Scotland to represent the king. **21 November, Scotland:** The meeting of the General Assembly of the kirk that went on to disestablish the episcopate is held.

1639   **May, England:** Charles I assembles an army to attack Scotland. **4 June, Scotland:** A force of English troops led by the earl of Holland retreats after a clash with the Covenanter Army at Kelso. **11 June, Scotland:** Negotiations between the Scots and Charles I begin at Berwick. **19 June, Scotland:** Anti-Covenanter Scots are defeated at Aberdeen by the earl of Montrose. Negotiations at Berwick are concluded. **12 August, Scotland:** Meeting of the General Assembly. **31 August, Scotland:** The Estates session opened.

1640   **16 March, Ireland:** The Dublin Parliament votes four subsidies for Charles I. **13 April, England:** Parliament opens. **5 May, England:** Charles dissolves Parliament after it refuses to vote him taxes. **1 June, Ireland:** A new session of the Parliament begins to question the subsidies voted in March. **August, England and Scotland:** Forces gather on the borders in preparation for renewed war. **20 August, Scotland and England:** The Scots cross the border. **28 August, England:** The king's army is defeated at Newburn. Twelve peers petition the king for a new Parliament. **3 November, England:** Parliament meets. **11 November, England:** Root and Branch Petition is presented to Parliament. The earl of Strafford is arrested. **21 November, England:** The Archbishop of Canterbury is arrested.

1641 May, England: A plot in the army to rescue the earl of Strafford is exposed. **12 May, England:** Strafford is executed. **10 June, England:** Charles is presented with the Ten Propositions. **August, England:** Charles leaves London for Scotland. **14 August, Scotland:** Charles arrives in Edinburgh. **October, Scotland:** The Incident is exposed. **22 October, Ireland:** Rebels seize strongholds across Ulster, but fail to capture Dublin. **November, England and Scotland:** Parliaments begin organising to fight the rebels on Ireland. **23 November, England:** The Grand Remonstrance is sent to the king and published.

1642 5 January, England: Charles I fails in an attempt to arrest six of his leading opponents. **11 January, England:** The royal family leaves London. **March, Ireland:** Government forces go on the offensive. **11 March, England:** The Militia Ordinance gives power to Parliament to control the militia. **22 April, England:** The king is refused entry into Hull. **May, England:** The king begins issuing Commissions of Array to get control of the militia. **May, Ireland:** Scottish forces begin a major campaign in Ulster. **22 August, England:** The king raises his standard at Nottingham. **23 September, England:** The Battle of Powick Bridge is fought. **October, Ireland:** The Confederation of Kilkenny government is assembled. **23 October, England:** The Battle of Edgehill is fought. **12–13 November, England:** The king fails in his advance on London.

1643 January, Ireland: The king's representative, the marquis of Ormond, opens discussions with the Kilkenny government. **23 February, England:** The queen returns from Europe with arms and ammunition for the royalists. **March to April, England:** peace negotiations held at Oxford. **30 June, England:** The earl of Newcastle defeats the parliamentarians at Adwalton Moor in Yorkshire. **September, Ireland:** The Cessation ends fighting between the Confederation and the government forces. **September, England:** The English and Welsh Parliament is allied with the Scots in the Solemn League and Covenant. **6 September, England:** The Earl of Essex relieves Gloucester. **20 September, England:** Essex defeats the king's attempt to stop him from reaching London at the First Battle of Newbury.

1644 January, England: The king opens an alternative Parliament at Oxford. **16 January, England:** The Scottish Army of the Solemn League and Covenant invades England. **29 March, England:** Royalist attempts to conquer Southern England end with their defeat by Sir William Waller at Cheriton. **11 April, England:** Defeat at Selby in Yorkshire ends the marquis of Newcastle's attempt to hold back the Scots' invasion; he becomes besieged in York. **19 June, England:** Charles I defeats Waller at Cropredy

Bridge. **June, Scotland:** Alasdair MacColla and 1,600 Irish troops land in Scotland. **1 July, England:** Prince Rupert relieves York. **2 July, England:** Two parliamentarian armies and the Scots defeat Rupert at Marston Moor; the north falls into parliamentarian hands. **August, Scotland:** The marquis of Montrose joins forces with MacColla. **1 September, Scotland and England:** Montrose defeats Covenanter forces at Tippemuir; Essex's army surrenders to Charles I at Lostwithiel. **13 September, Scotland:** Montrose defeats Covenanters at Justice Mills, Aberdeen. **18 September, Wales:** Royalists in central Wales are defeated by Sir Thomas Myddleton at Montgomery. **26 October, England:** Three parliamentarian armies fail in their attempt to defeat the king at the Second Battle of Newbury.

1645 **February, England:** The New Model Army is created. **2 February, Scotland:** Montrose defeats the Covenanters at Inverlochy. **April, England:** The Self Denying Ordinance is passed by the House of Lords. **9 May, Scotland:** Montrose wins the Battle of Auldearn. **31 May, England:** Charles captures Leicester. **14 June, England:** Charles is defeated by Sir Thomas Fairfax at Naseby. **2 July, Scotland:** Montrose wins the Battle of the Bridge of Alford. **10 July, England:** Royalist forces under Lord Goring are defeated at Langport. **1 August, Wales:** Royalists defeated in Pembrokeshire at Colby Moor. **15 August, Scotland:** Montrose defeats the last home army at Kilsyth. **13 September, Scotland:** Montrose is defeated at Philliphaugh by part of the Army of the Solemn League and Covenant under David Leslie, which had returned from England. **23 September, England:** Charles is defeated at Rowton Heath near Chester. **1 November, Wales:** Welsh royalists defeated en route to Chester at Mold.

1646 **January, Ireland:** Charles's secret treaty with the Kilkenny government is exposed and then repudiated. This ends any chance of military support from Ireland. **3 February, England:** Chester surrenders to the parliamentarians. **14 February, England:** Royalists in the south-west are defeated by Fairfax. **21 March, England:** The last royalist army in the field is defeated at Stow on the Wold. **5 May, England:** Charles surrenders to the Scots besieging Newark. He orders his commanders to stop fighting and is taken by his captors to Newcastle. **5 June, Ireland:** Owen Roe O'Neill and the Ulster Army defeat the Scots under Robert Monro at Benburb. **July, England:** Parliament presents Charles with terms: the Newcastle Propositions; by the end of the year he rejects them. **4 August, Ireland:** Treaty between Ormond and Kilkenny is published by the Confederation. **1 September, Ireland:** Ormond Treaty repudiated by papal nuncio Rinuccini and Owen Roe O'Neill; signatories to the treaty excommunicated. Rinuccini creates a new Supreme Council.

1647   January, Ireland: Excommunications of September 1646 rescinded and a new Supreme Council composed of opponents of Rinuccini is created. **30 January, England:** The Scots hand Charles over to Parliament and leave the country. **March, England:** A radical political group, the Levellers, circulate the Large Petition calling for a new social and political settlement. **April, England:** Regiments of Horse begin to elect representatives known as Agitators to campaign for back pay and a new social settlement. They meet with Levellers. **4 June, England:** Cornet Joyce seizes the king from Holdenby House and takes him to the army at Newmarket. **14 June, England:** The army marches on London and sets out its opposition to Presbyterians in Parliament. **19 June, Ireland:** Ormond leaves Ireland and hands Dublin to Michael Jones and parliamentarian forces. **23 July, England:** The army leaders present treaty proposals known as *The Heads of the Proposals* to the king. **26 July, England:** Riots in London oblige Parliament to oppose the army. **4 August, England:** The army occupies outer London. **8 August, Ireland:** Leinster army defeated by Jones at Dungan's Hill. **October–November, England:** Radical proposals put forward by the army and by the Levellers and debated at Putney. **11 November, England:** Charles I escapes captivity. **13 November, Ireland:** Munster Army defeated by Lord Inchiquin's parliamentarian forces at Knockanuss. **15 November, England:** Mutiny at Ware in support of the Levellers defeated by Fairfax and Cromwell. **24 December, England:** Charles rejects treaty terms—The Four Bills —presented to him by Parliament. He has already signed a secret treaty, The Engagement, with the Scots. **December 25, England:** in Canterbury, London, and Norwich, riots held over the abolition of Christmas.

1648   22 February, Wales: Governor John Poyer refuses to hand Pembroke to New Model Army forces, which begins a rebellion in Wales. **10 April, Wales:** Poyer declares his support for the king. **28 April, England:** Scots seize Berwick on Tweed. **8 May, Wales:** Rebels defeated at St Fagins. **11 May, England:** Rebellion breaks out in Kent. **30 May–1 June, England:** Kentish rebels defeated by Fairfax. **4 June, England:** Rebellion breaks out in Essex. The rebels there are joined by fleeing Kentish rebels. **5 June, Wales:** Rebels in North Wales defeated at Y Dalar Hir. **20 June, England:** Fairfax surrounds Essex and Kentish rebels in Colchester. **8 July, England:** A Scottish army invades the north-west. **11 July, Wales:** Pembroke surrenders to Cromwell; rebellion in South Wales ends. **27 July, England:** Cromwell reaches Yorkshire and begins to track the Scots. **17 August, England:** Scots defeated by Cromwell at Preston. **29 August, England:** Colchester surrenders. **September, Scotland:** Opposition to the Engager party grows and attempts an advance on Edinburgh known as the Whiggamore raid. **26 September, Scotland:** Engager government collapses. **1 October, Wales:**

Rebellion in North Wales is crushed on Anglesey. **27 October, England:** Last attempt to negotiate with Charles I ends. **6 November, England:** Pride's Purge removes conservative M.P.s from the Commons.

1649 **19 January, Ireland:** Ormond and the Confederation establish a new treaty. **21 January, England:** Trial of Charles I opens at Westminster. **27 January, England:** Charles is sentenced to death. **30 January, England:** Charles is executed at Whitehall. **10 February, Scotland:** Charles I's son, Charles, is proclaimed king. **17 March, England:** The monarchy is abolished. **19 March, England:** The House of Lords is abolished. **1 April, England:** Digger Colonies established. **25 April, 5 May, England:** Women present petitions to Parliament for the release of Leveller prisoners. **15 May, England:** Leveller Mutiny put down at Burford. **11 July, Ireland:** Forces of the Ormond/Confederation alliance capture Drogheda. **2 August, Ireland:** Ormond defeated at Rathmines by Jones. **13 August, England:** Cromwell and the New Model leave England for Ireland. **11 September, Ireland:** Cromwell storms Drogheda. **12 October, Ireland:** Cromwell storms Wexford. **6 November, Ireland:** Owen Roe O'Neill died.

1650 **28 March, Ireland:** Cromwell captures Kilkenny. **10 April, Ireland:** Lord Broghill defeats the last of the alliance forces in Munster. **27 April, Scotland:** A small force of royalists led by Montrose is defeated at Carbisdale. Montrose had been sent to raise Scotland in the king's name, but is repudiated by Charles in negotiations with Edinburgh. **21 May, Scotland:** Montrose executed at Edinburgh. **26 May, Ireland:** Cromwell leaves Ireland. **21 June, Ireland:** The Ulster army destroyed at Scariffhollis. **26 June, England:** Fairfax resigns as commander in chief; Cromwell assumes command of the New Model. **July, Scotland:** An army is established to fight for Charles II. **26 July, Scotland:** Cromwell invades the country and reaches Dunbar. **3 September, Scotland:** The Scots defeated at Dunbar by Cromwell.

1651 **January–June, Scotland:** Cromwell falls ill and campaigning halts. **1 January, Scotland:** Charles II crowned. **March, England:** Ambassadors sent to The United Provinces suggest the unification of the Commonwealth and the Provinces: Proposals come to nothing. **June, Scotland:** Cromwell attempts to break Scottish defence lines. **July, Scotland:** Charles II dodges past Cromwell and invades England. **28 August, Scotland:** General Monck captures the Committee of Estates, the Scottish executive. **29 August, England:** Charles II encamps in Worcester as Cromwell closes in. **1 September, Scotland:** General Monck captures Dundee with great savagery. **3 September, England:** Cromwell defeats Charles II at Worcester. **16 October, Eng-**

land: Charles II escapes England for France. **27 October, Ireland:** Limerick, the last major stronghold in Ireland, surrenders to Henry Ireton. **7 November, Ireland:** Ireton dies at Limerick.

1652   12 February, Scotland: Union offered to Scotland. **21 April:** Union of Scotland and the Commonwealth announced. **May, Scotland:** The war comes to an end. **19 May, England:** Off the coast of Dover, Commonwealth and United Provinces fleets skirmish and open the war between the two countries. **12 August, Ireland:** The Act of Settlement, which moves Catholic landowners implicated in the war to west of the River Shannon, is put in place. **28 September, England:** Commonwealth fleet defeats United Provinces fleet at the mouth of the Thames. **30 November, England:** Commonwealth fleet defeated by the United Provinces off Dungeness.

1653   18–23 February, English Channel: United provinces fleet defeated. **4 March, Scotland:** The Glencairn rebellion breaks out in the Highlands. **20 April:** Cromwell dissolves the Parliament. **29 April:** A new Council of State created. **4 July:** The nominated Parliament, otherwise known as the Little Parliament or Barebones Parliament, meets. **12 December:** Parliament dissolves itself. **15 December:** The Instrument of Government accepted as the constitution of the Republic. The four united nations are now known as the Protectorate. **16 December:** Cromwell is appointed lord protector.

1654   5 April: War between the United Provinces and the Commonwealth ends. **September, Scotland:** The Highland rising defeated by Monck. **3 September:** The first Protectorate Parliament opens.

1655   22 January: The Parliament is dissolved. **8–13 March, England:** Isolated royalist rising in western England, generally referred to as Penruddock's rebellion, defeated. **May, Scotland:** The Glencairn Rebellion ends. **9 July, Ireland:** Henry Cromwell arrives in Dublin as commander of the army. **9 August:** Major generals appointed to administer England and Wales.

1656   17 September: The second Protectorate Parliament meets. **December:** James Naylor brought before Parliament for entering Bristol in the manner of Christ.

1657   January: The rule of the major generals ends. **6 May:** Cromwell agrees to accept the crown offered in the proposed new constitution, *The Humble Petition and Advice.* **8 May:** Cromwell, under pressure from the army, refuses the crown. **June:** Parliament sent into recess.

1658   **20 January:** Parliament resumes its sitting. **February:** Parliament dissolved. **3 September:** Cromwell dies. His son Richard becomes lord protector

1659   **27 January:** Richard's Parliament meets. **22 April:** Army regiments expel Parliament and the Protectorate is brought to an end. **5 May:** The Rump, or remains of the Long Parliament, is recalled. **1 August:** A royalist rising in Cheshire, called Booth's Rising, begins. **19 August:** Booth's rising is crushed. **13 October:** The Army expels the Rump. **November, Scotland:** George Monck and the regiments in Scotland declare their support for the Rump and begin to march southwards. **24 December:** The Rump is invited to resume its sitting.

1660   **2 February:** Monck arrives in London. **21 February:** Monck invites the M.P.s expelled in Pride's Purge (6 December 1648) to resume their seats. **16 March:** The Long Parliament dissolves itself. **25 April:** The Convention Parliament meets, and retires to hear from Charles II. **1 May:** The Declaration of Breda lays down Charles's terms for a Restoration of the monarchy. These are accepted. **8 May:** Charles is proclaimed king, the republic and the union of the nation come to an end. **26 May, England:** Charles returns.

Introduction

B etween 1637 and 1660 the British Isles were embroiled in a series of wars, rebellions, and revolutions that affected not only all the political and social institutions within them, but all of the people living there. When a large number of the people in Scotland rejected King Charles I's religious policy, they set in motion a series of rebellions that resonated throughout England, Wales, and Ireland and challenged the rule of the king. Radical changes in the political relationships within the four nations sparked a series of wars that brought far-reaching political revolution. By spring 1649 the king had been executed, the monarchy abolished in England and Wales, and a republic established. The 1650s saw Scotland and Ireland incorporated into the republic as the wars finally ended. The republic had a brief life—by 1660 it was ended and the monarchy restored, the united nation established in 1653 was again broken into its component parts, and the old institutions seemingly returned to pre-eminence.

Whilst the wars appeared to begin because of a religious dispute, the questions asked about the king's government ranged beyond his ambitions for a unified form of worship within his kingdoms. Debate over the nature of the relationships between the king and his three Parliaments evolved into major quarrels that prompted political revolutions in Scotland and England in 1638–40 and a rebellion in Ireland in 1641. In turn these developments prompted deeper questioning of political representation and the social structure. The wars that subsequently developed across the British Isles were fought on a range of issues that stretched beyond initial divisions and included religious, political, and racial conflicts that varied from country to country and region to region.

In 1637 the British Isles comprised four nations—England, Ireland, Scotland, and Wales. All except Wales had autonomous or at least quasi-autonomous political institutions, although they shared a monarch: Charles I. Wales had been incorporated into the realm of England by "acts of union" passed in the 1530s and 1540s.

The state religion in all four nations was Protestantism, but it varied in nature. In Scotland the church was Presbyterian, created during the absence from the country of the heir to the throne, Mary Stuart (1542–1561), and further developed independently of her during her reign (1561–1567). The kirk's hierarchy took the form of a pyramid with the parish at the base, the presbytery at the local level, the synod at the regional level, and the General Assembly at the apex. This kirk had been intended from the 1570s onward to be independent of the political state, but interference from King James VI prevented this aim from being fulfilled. King James had ensured the continuance of bishops within the church. This allowed for his personal involvement in the direction of the church through his appointment of bishops.

In England, Henry VIII had initiated the break from Rome during the 1530s and the church became thoroughly Protestant during the later years of his reign and that of Edward VI (1547–1553). Despite the brief reintroduction of Catholicism during the reign of Mary I (1553–1558), England had been Protestant for about a century by 1637. England's Protestant church had retained much of the structure of the Catholic church, including a hierarchy of bishops and two archbishops appointed by the reigning monarch. In turn the bishops controlled appointments to parishes and symbolised the relationship between the head of state and the church. England exported its Reformation church to Wales as a part of the "acts of union," which bound the states together. England also imposed its brand of Protestantism on Ireland during the colonisation process of the sixteenth and seventeenth centuries. Alongside this apparent unity of faiths was a series of other interpretations of God's relationship with his people.

In Scotland there remained a significant number of Roman Catholics, particularly in the Highland regions of central, northern, and western Scotland. In some ways religious differences were tied closely to wider cultural differences between Highland and Lowland societies including societal structures, dress, farming technique, and language.

In England too, there were Roman Catholics but these were a small minority in every region, although in upland regions and some northern counties their numbers were higher. The same was true of Wales, where the poverty of church livings had made it difficult to fill parish churches with Protestant ministers. England and Wales also had other groups of people who did not approve of the form of the state church. They referred to themselves as the Godly, particularly when being persecuted; contemporaries and historians tend to think of them as Puritans. Most Puritans, especially before the accession of Charles I in 1625, were encompassed within the church and saw change coming from within. However, there were groups that were essentially separatists and they established illegal congregations or gatherings in England and Wales especially after 1625.

Ireland's Protestant church never won the hearts and minds of the people and even as late as 1637 most of its members were incomers, Protestant settlers who had made Ireland their home since the sixteenth century. The lack of strict episcopal control had resulted in the parishes having ministers of a Puritan disposition and even, in Ulster, Presbyterian Scots in some parishes. Moreover, the Catholic church had strengthened its (illegal) presence in Ireland during the seventeenth century and by 1637 had bishops in place and was represented by a priest in almost every parish.

Charles I's accession to the throne in 1625 brought with it a series of political and religious conflicts. Charles, like his father James VI of Scotland who had become James I of England, Wales, and Ireland in 1603, believed in the Divine Right of Kings, that at its most extreme placed the monarch at the centre of the political world, responsible only to God. Unlike his father, Charles did not recognise that politics, even if inspired directly by God, was the art of the possible. James had trodden carefully in politics and religion; he was a participator who took a place in discussion and in debate sought to influence decision by argument. Charles was not a participator and sought to impose his decisions on his governments. Naturally this caused problems because it affected the new king's relations with his Parliaments in England (that also represented Wales), Scotland, and Ireland. It also brought to the fore religious issues, as the king was determined to reorder the church in the four nations by strengthening the episcopate. The king probably wanted identical systems of worship in each of the four nations and thereby sought to eradicate the individual nature of each of the churches.

Charles, with the support of his favourite, the duke of Buckingham, and through the work of agents like William Laud, who became Bishop of London in 1627, began to reform the nature of the church in England and Wales. Hitherto, the church had been largely Calvinist in nature, if not officially so. This had entailed the primacy of the pulpit from that God's word was interpreted for the people. It had also involved the belief in double predestination that divided the living and the dead into two groups, the elect and the reprobate. This division had been made before the Creation: the elect would be resurrected into eternal life at the end of the world, the reprobate were damned for eternity. No action and no amount of godly behaviour affected this selection. The seven sacraments, the rites of passage to heaven for the Catholic church, had no such meaning in a Calvinist church. Only a few were kept: baptism, for instance, marked a person's membership in Christ's church on earth, and communion was a commemorative and communal act, remembering the sacrifice of Christ (on behalf only of the elect), that brought the community together in that remembrance.

Charles rejected much of this. He wanted a faith in that receipt of sacraments together with a godly life ensured a soul's passage to heaven. This entailed a decline in the importance of the Word and thus the pulpit. This was matched by the reinstatement of the altar. Altars had previously been removed from churches when the sacraments declined in importance. Instead of being railed-off in a sanctified position at the east end of a church, altars had become communion tables set in "convenient" places. Often they had been placed in the centre of a church so that the congregation could gather around them at communion. Charles ended this practice. Communion tables were dragged back to the east end, draped in cloths and adorned with gilt chalices and candlesticks. The people were once again kept from them by rails. To many onlookers, this was worrisome because it looked like the Roman Catholic faith.

Furthermore, the king insisted that reinvigorated church courts ensured that ministers and congregations adhered to his instructions, and that all individuality within English and Welsh parishes was to be eradicated. These instructions were also sent out to the Church of Ireland, where the necessary machinery to enforce these rules was created by Deputy Lieutenant Thomas Wentworth and Bishop John Bramhall. The effect was to drive the Puritan-minded and the Scottish Presbyterian ministers out of the Church of Ireland. Charles's attempt to reform the kirk in Scotland had even more far-reaching consequences, that shall be referred to.

Politics during the reign of Charles I rapidly became problematic. The government of all four nations was essentially in the hands of an executive centred on the king over that no other body had control and in that no other body wielded much influence. The executive in each state was the council or Privy Council. Each of these—there were three—comprised the monarch's nominees. The Privy Council in Westminster, which governed England and Wales, worked with the king sometimes in attendance. The councils in Ireland and Scotland worked in his absence, with the monarch's place filled by a commissioner in Scotland and the lord deputy in Ireland. There was a Parliament in each of the three states: the one at Westminster consisted of an elected House of Commons and a hereditary House of Lords, comprised of aristocrats. In Ireland, a similar body existed in Dublin, but it could only debate bills approved previously by the English Privy Council. In Edinburgh the Estates met. This body included representatives of the clergy, the burghs (towns), the aristocracy, and the lairds (gentry) and was dominated by the Lords of the Articles, a form of steering committee that effectively debated and then framed legislation that the Estates voted on.

Before James VI became king of England in 1603, he had been an active member of the Lords of Articles, but his successor did not follow suit. Charles and his father held similar views about the nature of Parliaments, primarily using them as adjuncts to royal rule, called when necessary. Again, Charles and his father differed on practice, with James being subtle and amenable to debate, his son not. The Parliaments in Scotland and Ireland that met during Charles I's reign gave the impression that they were largely co-operative and complacent. In both cases this was the result of short-term effective management that plastered over some deep political cracks, rather than a true impression.

In Westminster, the good relationship between Charles and Parliament in 1625 soon foundered. The initial relationship had been based on Charles's and Parliament's dislike of King James's foreign policy, and Charles believed that he was manipulating Parliament rather than it being an equal partner with him in the attack on James. Parliament thought differently. When Charles came to the throne, his first Parliament quickly became aware of his real attitude. Fearing that the king was about to launch the country into a costly war, the Parliament tried to limit his financial capabilities, voting him customs duties for a year at a time rather than for life, as was customary. Protracted battles over finance in the late 1620s and constant questioning of the duke of Buckingham's stewardship of the military resulted in a series of dramatic disasters, added to developing fears over the king's religious policies. In late 1628 Parliament almost forced the king to recognise, in the Petition of Right, its central role in the levying of taxation, but in March 1629 the king dissolved Parliament, hoping not to have recourse to it again. Subsequently, a group of Members of Parliament (M.P.s) were arrested and sent to the Tower of London after they had prevented the dissolution for vital minutes by holding the speaker in his chair whilst a resolution opposing the king's religious policies was passed.

Charles began a process of executive government in England and Wales known as the Personal Rule. Parliaments did meet during the 1630s in Scotland and Ireland. In England and Wales, government was conducted entirely through the Privy Council, which attempted to tighten its grip on local authorities. Part of the impetus for this was the search for government finance. A series of long-abandoned measures were resurrected to bring money to the treasury: fines were raised for encroaching on royal forests, for failing to attend the coronation to be knighted, and so on. In 1635 Ship Money, an extraordinary coastal-defence tax, was collected despite there being no immediate threat to the nation. A year later the tax was extended to all counties regardless of their proximity to the sea, and the money used to rebuild the fleet. The intention was quickly clear: Ship Money became an ordinary tax. In 1637 a court case involving the refusal of John Hampden to pay his levy saw the king challenged over his failure to pursue finance through Parliament. The king's victory was narrow and many people took this as a moral justification for refusing to pay the levy, and default increased throughout the country. There seems to have been a fragility to the state that required only a catastrophe to fragment it.

Rebellions in Four Nations

Catastrophe came about in 1637. Charles's determination to enforce uniformity on his churches led him to strengthen the episcopal element in the kirk. At his much-delayed coronation in Scotland in 1633 he insisted that the Scottish bishops ape the English bishops he had brought with him. Moreover, the Englishmen were given precedence. To follow through this instruction in superiority, the king had his Scottish bishops draft a liturgy, a prayer book modelled on the alien *English Book of Common Prayer*. On 23 July 1637, this book was ready and was to be read from pulpits across Scotland. At St Giles, Edinburgh, the congregation was furious—to them this was a foreign doctrine at best, it was English at worst, and appeared to be popish. Folding stools were hurled at the dean. Crowds outside hammered on the doors. Across Scotland, ministers were attacked and churches stormed by angry men and women.

Charles's response was to treat this as an unwarranted rebellion. Even his loyal minister, the earl of Traquair, tried to convince him that the prayer book was a mistake, but to little avail. The Scottish council was packed with Charles's appointees, men with little personal authority or experience of government, there because Charles expected their elevation to power would ensure loyalty. As a result they had little sway with the wider political world and less with the Scottish people. Even if inexperienced in executive government, many had been wise enough to stay away from St Giles that Sunday, to avoid trouble and being associated with the prayer book.

As riots occurred across Scotland, members of the Council discussed the matter with leading opponents of the prayer book. Charles's refusal to discuss the matter in any meaningful way drove opponents to present him with a Supplication and Complaint in October 1637, which put the blame on the Scottish bishops. Charles reacted by threatening to arrest the supplicants, and hoped to end criticism by claiming direct responsibility for the prayer book; he believed that they would shy away from attacking the monarch. Instead, by February 1638, a National Covenant had been drafted. This Covenant was a reference to the 1581 Confession of Faith, which bound Scotsmen and women and James VI together in defence of the kirk. The Covenant went further, asserting that the religious changes imposed by James VI and Charles I were illegal because they contravened the basis of the kirk. The National Covenant was first signed at Edinburgh and then circulated throughout Scotland for men and women to sign at their own church doors.

The Covenanters demanded a General Assembly and Charles acceded, expecting his agents to be able to influence the choice of representatives. He even ordered that the General Assembly should meet at Glasgow, that he thought would circumvent opposition. Charles was hopelessly out of touch and his agents were not in control. The General Assembly, which met in November 1638, rejected the prayer book and abolished the office of bishop. The king's commissioner, the marquis of Hamilton, Traquair's replacement, failed to influence the assembly, and when he attempted to end the session by storming out he ran into a locked door. Even after Hamilton had managed to leave, the debates continued. Charles's reaction to his loss of control and influence was to prepare for war against his rebellious subjects.

By May 1639 an English and Welsh army gathered at the border. Elaborate plans for amphibious landings on the Scottish coast were drawn up and Hamilton prepared a fleet. In Ireland, where there was support for the Covenanters amongst the Presbyterian ministers in Ulster, Lord Deputy Wentworth imposed a series of oaths aimed at forcing Scots settlers to abjure the Covenant. At the same time, the marquis of Antrim, chief of the Clan MacDonald (known as MacDonnell in Ireland), proposed to take advantage of the situation. He offered to raise a clan army to invade western Scotland where his lost ancestral estates were situated and controlled by the Campbells. The Campbells, although led by the marquis of Argyll, a supporter of the king, were also associated with the Covenant through Argyll's heir, Lord Lorne. Wentworth suspected Antrim's motive and rejected the plan, preparing an Irish army instead, with Protestant officers and Catholic soldiers.

The first Bishop's War in 1639 was short. The amphibious landings were abandoned. Attempts to land at Aberdeen were called off when the earl of Montrose and a Covenanter Army captured the town. At the eastern border on 4 June, a section of the king's army was defeated in a skirmish near Kelso. This became something of a rout, and in its wake the Covenanters put forwards proposals for discussions. That summer a truce, the Pacification of Berwick, was negotiated, but all the while Charles I planned for war.

A new General Assembly of the kirk met in August and confirmed its predecessor's work. Later that same month the Estates also assembled, and they too confirmed the actions of the General Assembly. The Estates had been effectively controlled by Covenanters who had minimised the role of the king in influencing the selections of members, and steps were taken towards further controlling the business of the sessions. By the beginning of 1640, both the king and the Covenanters were preparing for renewed war.

Charles sought to improve the financial support for his government and war effort. He planned a two-pronged approach. Wentworth summoned a Parliament in Dublin, that he expected to manipulate into voting four subsidies for the king. In April a Parliament would meet at Westminster and was expected to follow suit. In March 1640 the Dublin Parliament met and all went according to plan, but the Westminster Parliament refused to discuss finance unless a series of grievances was addressed. The grievances were bound up with the collection of taxation in the 1630s, religious issues, and the way in that the 1629 Parliament had been closed. When he failed to influence the Parliament at all, Charles dissolved it on 5 May.

Plans for war went forward, but opposition to the king had developed in the wake of the Parliament. Soldiers mustered for the army went on the rampage, destroying altar rails and religious images, and people across the country began to refuse to pay taxation. Support for the Scots was to be found across England, where people who objected to the religious reforms of Archbishop Laud refused to pay for them to be imposed in Scotland. In Ireland, many Scots in Ulster refused Wentworth's oaths and left the country, leaving tracts of countryside untilled.

The war in the summer of 1640 saw the defeat of the king's army at the Battle of Newburn and the occupation of northern England by the Covenanter Army. This time peace negotiations were conducted on the Scots' terms. They demanded freedom for the kirk, but also wanted a Parliament at Westminster to confirm the terms. This gelled with calls within England and Wales for a new Parliament. With an army in occupation for that he was to provide pay, the king had no option but to accede. Parliament met on 3 November and the king's few supporters were overwhelmed.

Three Parliaments now worked in opposition to the king. The Dublin Parliament had met in the summer and began to unravel the financial arrangements it had put in place in March. It then went on to question the relationship between itself and the lord deputy and even questioned its subordination to the Privy Council in London. Moreover, Irish and Scots politicians presented evidence about Wentworth's government of Ireland and his planned invasion of Scotland. This was taken up by Westminster and in November Wentworth, now known as the earl of Strafford, was impeached and imprisoned along with Archbishop Laud.

As the Dublin Parliament began to deconstruct the government in Ireland, the Estates began to reduce the power of the king in Scottish government. The Westminster Parliament began to take apart the machinery of government that had sustained the Personal Rule. As well as impeaching Strafford and Laud, Parliament aimed its ire at ministers Lord Finch and Francis Windebank, who both fled to France to escape. Ship Money was abolished and forest fines were banned. Two acts prevented another period of Personal Rule: One established that there should be Parliaments at least every three years; the other made it impossible for Parliament to be dissolved without its own consent. In May 1641, against the background of a plot hatched amongst some of the king's army officers, Strafford was executed. This effectively settled the issues raised by the Personal Rule, but Parliament presented the king with Ten Propositions demanding a further role in government by having the right to nominate ministers and to have a say in foreign policy.

The king went to Scotland in the summer months of 1641 to ratify the Treaty of London, which had ended the war, and also to ratify the acts passed in the Estates, which diminished his role in Scottish government. The Estates had passed a series of measures that had been the inspiration for the Westminster Parliament's work during the spring. Charles also harboured hopes of nurturing a royalist party in Scotland that could overthrow the Covenanter government. The earl of Montrose, the Covenanter general, had become disillusioned with the Covenanter cause and had questioned the ambitions of the earl of Argyll (formerly Lord Lorne). By the time Charles went to Edinburgh, however, Montrose was imprisoned. An attempted coup d'état, known as the Incident, was exposed and Charles became implicated in it. With his attempts to overturn the Covenanter government in tatters, the king returned to London. Within days of his arrival news broke of a rebellion in Ireland.

The Irish Rebellion

In the wake of the successes at Edinburgh and Westminster, Catholic Irish and long-established English settler families began to press for similar changes at home. Autonomy for the Dublin Parliament was one aim, but others related to religious issues and the tenure rights of the Catholic population. Rights to practice their religion openly was a major demand and the king had tentatively suggested that it might be possible. The Catholic population too had insecure tenure on their estates having never been granted firm property rights because of their religion. These two issues were bound together and known as the Graces.

Given the king's powerlessness, the Irish felt able to press their cause. Although the Scots had secured the safety of the kirk, however, and the Welsh and English had freed themselves from Laud's reforms, religious rights for Catholics were not acceptable to the Protestant Parliaments in Edinburgh and Westminster. Frustrated groups began to discuss the possibility of a rising in Ireland, and exiled Irishmen became involved in these discussions. By October the discussions had crystallised into a plan to seize strongholds throughout Ulster and Dublin Castle.

On 22 October rebellion broke out, but although the forts in Ulster were captured by Sir Phelim O'Neill and others, Dublin remained in government hands. By November, rebellion had spread throughout Ireland and the Old English settlers had joined with the Catholic Irish rebels. The government forces managed to hold onto pockets around the Irish coast, but supplies and reinforcements were necessary if there was any possibility of remaining there. In Edinburgh and Westminster the governments began to discuss military and financial plans for reconquering Ireland. Whilst King Charles outwardly discussed these issues with the Westminster Parliament, he also plotted to seize prominent leaders. Charles was assured that there was now a significant group of M.P.s who supported him rather than his opponents.

In late November, after heated debate, Parliament had passed the Grand Remonstrance. This was a sort of petition that had set out the evils of the 1630s and the remedies that had been applied; finally, the remonstrance proposed further reforms. No sooner was this passed by the Commons than it was published. This broadcasting of Parliament's position was disliked by many M.P.s. Christmastide 1641 was a period of riots in London and Westminster by mobs supporting the aims of the Grand Remonstrance, and in particular the removal of the bishops from the House of Lords in a move similar to the exclusion of bishops from Scottish government. On 5 January Charles marched into Westminster to arrest five leading M.P.s and Lord Mandeville. This coup d'état, like that in Scotland the previous October, failed (the proposed victims had fled), and it provoked continued rioting that in turn drove the king and his family out of the capital.

Over the next months Charles and Parliament grew further estranged, agreeing only on the need to fund the war against the Irish rebels. The raising of an army to fight in Ireland drove the final wedge between the king and Parliament, however. It was felt that the king, implicated in an army plot and two coup d'états, could not be trusted if given the military command. He suggested he would have to go to Ireland, especially as the rebels there claimed to have the king's warrant for their rebellion. With the Militia Ordinance, Parliament took away the king's military powers in March. In April the king responded by trying to seize the arsenal deposited at Hull during the Bishop's War. He was denied entry into the city. In May Charles began the recreation of obsolete county-based commissions of array to regain control of the Trained Bands. Throughout the summer of 1642 both he and Parliament battled to raise armies, each hoping to overawe the other.

In Ireland the war had taken two turns of fortune. Money and troops had begun arriving in the spring. The marquis of Ormond took command of the English forces and began to make inroads into rebel territory in Leinster province. In eastern Ulster a Scottish army landed and took control of the region in May. As summer drew on, however, attention in England had turned inwards and the supply of resources to Ireland dried up as king and Parliament commandeered the money for their own use. War broke out in England and Wales in August.

Wars and Civil Wars, 1641–1653

War raged in the four nations for the next 11 years: In Ireland there was a constant state of war; in the other three nations war was more sporadic. Each war impinged on the others and all were closely related to the needs of Charles I, who sought to offset failure in one nation with success and resources from at least one of the others.

In England and Wales, the war that broke out in August 1642 began as both sides, royalists and parliamentarians, assembled field armies, first, to try and overawe their enemy, and then, second, to inflict military defeat in one cataclysmic battle. Neither scenario was to be enacted. By October the king had moved from his initial musters in the North Midlands towards London, whilst Parliament's commander in chief, the earl of Essex, moved westwards from the East Midlands to stop him. Scouting techniques were so underdeveloped that the king got between the earl and London, and then the two armies bumped into each other whilst searching for quarters. On 23 October 1643, the first major battle of the war in England took place at Edgehill. Partly due to the inexperience within the two armies, the battle was drawn and the war had to take on a new complexion.

After the king failed to press his attack on London in mid-November, both sides now began a fight for territory and the resources to maintain a nationwide war. The winter was spent in regional battles as local commanders began to seize castles and towns in that to establish garrisons. By the spring, the king controlled much of the south-west and north-east of England and had a significant presence in both the North and South Midlands. The royalists also held onto the vast majority of Wales. Parliament controlled all major ports, the south-east and the Lancashire and Cheshire area, as well as significant Midland areas of England, and a good proportion of Pembrokeshire in Wales. The king believed himself to be in a strong position within the country and as such did not take the opportunity to negotiate the end of the war, which arose in spring 1643.

Attempts to dislodge the royalists from their strongholds in the north, the south-west, and the South Midlands failed in the summer of 1643. In the south-west, parliamentarian general Sir William Waller, who had met with great success at the end of 1642, was defeated at Rowton Down in July. The earl of Essex's attempt to capture Oxford was curtailed in June, and that same month the earl of Newcastle defeated the Yorkshire parliamentarians Lord Fairfax and his son, Sir Thomas, and bottled them up in Hull. Both Parliament and the king sought outside help at this point. At first, Scotland remained aloof from the conflict in England and Wales. The Covenanters had offered to act as mediator but the king had rejected their approach. The leading parliamentarian, John Pym, had exploited the Scots' fear of the Catholic forces in Ireland. He suggested that the king was negotiating with the Irish, and that there might be Irish landings on the Scottish coast as a result of such discussions. He also hinted that if the king, who appeared to have the upper hand in England and Wales, were to win, then he might turn on Scotland.

The Development of the Wars

In Ireland, stalemate had developed after the funding from across the Irish sea had dried up. The English and Scots forces held significant areas of territory in Ulster (in Down and Antrim), around Dublin in Leinster, and around Cork and Youghal in Munster. There were also a few garrisons in Connacht held by the English. The Irish meanwhile had unified their forces and their administration. Provincial armies had been created from the disparate forces and generals appointed. A government was formed with an executive, the Supreme Council, and a legislative, the General Assembly, which consisted of elected representatives of the shires and boroughs. Each county had a council of its own that sent representatives to provincial assemblies. Despite this organisation, resources were few and the Catholic Confederation of Kilkenny was unable to defeat the English or Scottish garrisons and armies.

Negotiations with the English began in 1643, with the aim of getting royal recognition for the Catholic religion and for the property rights of the Catholic peoples. The king's representative, the earl of Ormond, was unwilling to make major concessions, but by September at least a cease-fire had been arranged. This Cessation allowed for the return home of the English forces sent to Ireland in 1642, and these men were co-opted as royalist forces. This in turn enabled Pym to show the Scots that he had been right about the suspected negotiations, and the Scots became convinced of the need to join the Westminster Parliament against the king. In 16 January 1644 the Army of the Solemn League and Covenant, named after the treaty between Edinburgh and Westminster, invaded north-east England. The English and Welsh people under the control of Parliament would fund the invading army and there would be consideration given to the creation of a Presbyterian church in England and Wales.

Even before the Scots crossed the border, the war had taken a different complexion. In September three royalist armies were weakened by fruitless attempts to capture the prominent parliamentarian strongholds of Hull, Gloucester, and Plymouth. Failure to capture any of them had wasted resources and reduced the numbers of effective soldiers through disease and injury. It took time to assemble the forces necessary to hold back the Scots, and in the end it was fruitless—defeat at the Battle of Selby on 11 April led to the collapse of the royalist hold on the north. The marquis of Newcastle and his once powerful army became bottled up in York. Royalist attempts to encroach on south-east England came to an end in the spring. Yet Parliament's attempt to capture Oxford again failed and a series of campaigns followed in that both Sir William Waller and the earl of Essex were defeated by the king. Waller's army had been caught in Oxfordshire and destroyed.

Essex had marched off into royalist territory in the far west only to be trapped and defeated at Lostwithiel in Cornwall at the beginning of September. On 2 July, the Northern Army and a rescue force led to its aid by Prince Rupert were defeated at Marston moor near York. With this defeat the royalists lost control of the north.

The king's victories in the south, and the failure of three combined parliamentarian armies to defeat him in the fall, temporarily offset the loss of the north. It also led to a false confidence that led some royalists to ridicule Parliament's reorganisation of its war effort and the creation of one field army from the three assembled in the autumn. This New Model Army was created in early 1645, and in June it defeated the king at Naseby and then set about conquering the south-west. Together, it and the Northern Association Army won the war during the summer of 1645. During the ensuing autumn and winter the New Model and local forces ended royalist resistance in the south of England, whilst the Northern Association forces and the Scots cleared the north and North Midlands of major royalist strongholds. In Wales, Welsh parliamentarians cleared the south of the country whilst Lancashire and Cheshire parliamentarians captured central and northern royalist strongholds.

Fighting had broken out in Scotland during 1644. Alasdair MacColla had led a force of Irish and Highland troops from Ireland to the Western Isles in July 1644. The Catholic Confederation hoped that this force would oblige the Scots to withdraw forces from Ulster; the marquis of Ormond, who lent support to the expedition, hoped that the Scots would withdraw forces from England. MacColla, who was of the MacDonald clan, probably hoped for both, but also had an eye for regaining clan land lost to the Campbells. In August 1644 MacColla was joined by the earl of Montrose, by now a fully fledged royalist. Montrose had a commission to raise the loyal Scots against the Covenanter government. Together, the two commanders embarked on a campaign that over the next year saw them defeat all the home armies the Edinburgh government sent against them. At Kilsyth, on 15 August 1645, Montrose defeated the last of these armies and Scotland appeared to be his to command. He summoned the Estates to Glasgow and began to receive tributes from politicians. Ironically, it was to be one of the early aims of the war that was to defeat Montrose. A section of the Army of the Solemn League and Covenant did leave England. On 13 September David Leslie and a section of the Scots Horse caught Montrose's men at Philliphaugh and destroyed them. The month-old royalist domination of Scotland was over: But guerrilla warfare was to continue in the country until 1647.

In Ireland, the king had sought a treaty not because he was able to accept any of the Confederation's demands, but because he needed their military help. Ormond, part of the Protestant group that hitherto controlled Ireland's political world, was unwilling personally to accept the freedom Catholics wanted for their faith. Charles sought to circumvent him by sending the earl of Glamorgan, a Welsh Catholic, to negotiate secretly with the Confederation. Glamorgan's terms were more acceptable at Kilkenny, but a papal representative, Giovanni Battista Rinuccini, arrived just before the terms were agreed. He was wary about the secret nature of the discussions and urged holding out for public acknowledgement. Before he could renegotiate the treaty personally with Glamorgan, a copy of the secret treaty fell into enemy hands. Upon the Westminster Parliament's horrified publication of the terms, Charles I repudiated them and Ormond arrested Glamorgan.

The Political Scene in England and Wales

Thus ended any chance the king had of rescue by his Irish subjects and this influenced his decision to surrender to the Scots in May 1646. Charles had not given up the idea of winning. He had surrendered to the Scots because he thought he could drive a wedge between them and their English allies. In the years since the Scots had crossed the border, several political developments had occurred within the parliamentarian cause. Political factions had developed at Westminster with differing war aims. The group named the War Party sought outright military victory to establish a position of strength from that to negotiate with the king. The Peace Party sought negotiation as a primary objective. A sort of middle group balanced between the two, trying to pursue effective aims without adhering to either extreme.

Overlapping these groups were rival religious interests, named Independents—who opposed the establishment of an overweening national church and favoured independent congregations—and the Presbyterians—who aimed at an English version of the kirk as a national church to replace the Church of England. The Independents tended to oppose the Scots and their involvement in the war and in the Westminster Council of Divines, which was debating the state of the church. There were Independents within each of the three groupings, but they were generally outnumbered by Presbyterians. The army contained a significant number of Independents, however, and in 1647 this was to provide significant muscle for the Independents in Parliament.

At the time of the king's surrender the Presbyterians still dominated Parliament, but Charles knew that if he paid court to the Scots he would provoke the army. He also knew that the Scots were suspicious of the New Model Army and that they believed the English Presbyterians to be weak in their determination to establish a Presbyterian church in England. Thus, for the next two years, he played one against the other. He refused to come to any hard-and-fast terms, rejecting the Newcastle Propositions sent to him by

Westminster. He encouraged the Scots to see the lack of reference to Scottish affairs in terms of a slight, and the tentative establishment of Presbyterianism as a sign of weakness. By January 1647 the Scots were tired of holding Charles and left him to the English.

The Reshaping of the Wars

In Ireland, the hard-line Catholics had managed by the autumn of 1646 to dominate the Supreme Council. Rinuccini had brought with him arms and money from Europe, and a good portion of this was distributed to the Ulster Army of Owen Roe O'Neill. With this aid O'Neill was able to defeat Robert Monro and the Scots at Benburb on 5 June 1646. The defeat was important because it was the end of the Scots' field army in Ulster, but it was also a lost opportunity in that O'Neill did not go on to destroy the army's bases in eastern Ulster. Instead, he and his forces marched south to provide the nuncio with the military might necessary to impose his will on the Supreme Council. A final attempt to come to terms with Ormond in the summer was swept aside and Rinuccini excommunicated the signatories of the treaty. With no chance of anything less than full freedom for the Catholic church in Ireland, Ormond handed Dublin over to the forces of the Westminster Parliament and went to England.

The rift between the Presbyterians and the Independents worsened during 1647. The advent of a radical political group, the Levellers, provoked a further widening of this gap. Even Parliament refused to consider the radical proposals put forward by the Levellers, who developed close relationships with radical representatives in the New Model Army, combining soldiers' grievances with calls for a radical political settlement. The Presbyterian-controlled Parliament was intent on disbanding the New Model and conscripting some of its soldiers into an army to be sent to Ireland. Soldiers opposed these moves because they would not receive full arrears of pay and because many of them were volunteers and felt they should not be subject to conscription.

They managed to get the support of the army leadership, and commanders Sir Thomas Fairfax and Oliver Cromwell led them in an advance on London. At first, Parliament made concessions and eleven of the most vociferous Presbyterians, who the army had singled out, left the House of Commons. However, the army was disliked by a significant number of Londoners who rioted, stormed Parliament, and demanded that it resist the New Model. The eleven members returned and Parliament tried to create a counterarmy. All of this determination faded away when Fairfax and the New Model reached the outskirts of the city. In the meantime, soldiers under Cornet Joyce seized the king and in July the army leaders presented him with a treaty, the Heads of the Proposals. At first, Charles let the Scots and English Presbyterians think that he favoured them because of the Proposals' refusal to privilege Presbyterianism. This encouraged both groups to step up discussions with him. In the end, Charles rejected the Heads.

The Levellers and the army radicals were angry that the leadership had discussed terms with the king at all. Both groups drafted more radical proposals. *The Case of the Army Truly Stated* and the Levellers' proposed constitution, *The Agreement of the People*, were discussed at Putney church with the army leadership in late October and early November. The radical proposals were moderated somewhat before acceptance, but the discussions were halted by the king's escape from Hampton Court. This threw both Parliament and the army into a panic; a meeting of several regiments at Ware was prohibited and angry scenes developed when some regiments turned up against orders. Presbyterians in Parliament rapidly drafted a series of Four Bills to present to the king and the Scots tried to persuade him to come to terms with them. At the very end of 1647 Charles signed a treaty with the Scots known as the Engagement, which entailed a Scottish army invading England on his behalf. The Westminster Parliament immediately voted to end negotiations with the king.

The Second Civil War and the Revolution

During the spring and summer of 1648 a Second Civil War was fought in England and Wales. Localised risings in Kent and Essex and in south and north Wales were defeated by the New Model Army, and in August the Scottish Army was defeated at the Battle of Preston. At the end of this war it was clear that the king was a major problem. Parliament, again under the sway of Presbyterians, reopened discussions with Charles, although more radical people wanted him brought to trial. The king's intransigence, based on his realistic hopes of forging an alliance with the Confederation of Kilkenny, drove more moderate army commanders such as Henry Ireton and Oliver Cromwell into supporting moves to try the king. Accordingly, on 6 December 1648, Parliament was purged of its Presbyterian membership by Colonel Thomas Pride and Lord Grey. The resulting Independent Commons created a High Court of Justice to try Charles. When the House of Lords objected, the Commons declared itself the supreme political body in the nation. In January 1649 Charles was tried and executed. In March the House of Lords and the monarchy were abolished and England and Wales became a republic and free state.

In Ireland, the alliance Charles had hoped for came about; the unity of purpose between Rinuccini and O'Neill had declined during 1648 and both became isolated. The nuncio's power in the Supreme Council declined and

O'Neill objected to the confederation allying itself to Protestants such as Lord Inchiquin and Ormond. For a good part of 1648, O'Neill had withdrawn from the Confederation and something of a civil war within the Catholic cause had been fought. Even after Charles's execution and the defeat of the Levellers at Burford had freed the Westminster Parliament from internal troubles, allowing it to contemplate dealing with Ireland, O'Neill delayed long before joining the alliance with Ormond. When he did, it was doubly too late: O'Neill was dying and Oliver Cromwell had landed in Ireland with the New Model Army. After storming Drogheda and Wexford in the autumn, Cromwell began to take control of Munster during the winter. By the spring of 1650 the New Model had captured central Ireland, and in the summer Protestant forces in Ulster defeated the Ulster Army at Scarriffhollis. When Cromwell returned to England in May 1650, the war in Ireland was confined to guerrilla and siege warfare in Connacht.

The hard-line Scots, who had been displaced from power by the those who had supported the Engagement, had returned to power after the defeat of the Engager Army at Preston. They had been helped in their return by the New Model Army under Cromwell. However, the execution of their king a few weeks later had angered the Edinburgh government, led by the Kirk Party. Discussions were opened with the king's heir, Prince Charles, and by May 1650 Charles sailed from exile in the United Provinces to Scotland. The Scots, led by the marquis of Argyll, were determined to ensure that the prince adhere to the Covenant and had him sign it before offering material help. Even so, the Kirk Party refused to allow any former royalists or Engagers to serve in the army created to take on the New Model Army.

English forces invaded Scotland on Cromwell's return from Ireland, and on 3 September defeated the Scots at Dunbar. Bad weather, disease, and lack of supplies prevented the victory from being completed during the winter, and Cromwell's own ill health further delayed campaigning in the first half of 1651. In the meantime, the Kirk Party had been split over the issue of creating a new army. Some of the Covenanters were willing to compromise and forge a new force from royalists and Engagers as well as the more spiritually pure. Moreover, Charles, after much delay to prevent his accruing more power, was crowned and he took charge of the new army.

As the New Model Army attempted to break through the defensive lines in east Scotland, the king and his army slipped past them and invaded England. By 15 August the army was at Wigan, but Cromwell was in pursuit. By the end of the month the king's army was lodged in Worcester and Cromwell was approaching the outskirts of the city. On 3 September the Scots and royalists were defeated and the king forced to flee and begin a long and tortuous flight to France.

The Republic of the Four Nations

In the wake of this the wars in Scotland and Ireland were ended and the new republic secured. In 1652 Scotland and Ireland were incorporated into the republic. Neither had any real option. Scots political leaders were offered the choice between incorporation into the republic and participation in a united government established at Westminster or being treated as a conquered nation. Ireland had no political leadership recognised by the conquering forces. Its citizens were divided into categories depending on their relationship with the Confederation of Kilkenny or the alliance with Ormond. Many of the gentry who were not executed, transported to the West Indies, or in exile were uprooted from lands in Leinster, Munster, or Ulster and shipped to smaller estates in Connacht, were they were ringed in by garrisons. Their former possessions were given to colonial settlers, including former soldiers.

The former principality of Wales was treated to special legislation that sought to ensure the propagation of godliness; Commissions were established to eject ministers of dubious reputation and put new men in their place. Schools were founded in a further attempt to introduce godliness and civility. Unfortunately, these measures were largely carried out by Englishmen, and many of the officials in charge, even if Welsh, were suspected of malfeasance and profiteering. In England, the Westminster Parliament never sufficiently dealt with army pay and other related issues. It also angered many by its reluctance to set a date for new elections. By April 1653 distrust had reached such a stage that Cromwell led a party of soldiers into Parliament and threw out the M.P.s. It was the beginning of Cromwell's time at the centre of the political world.

The republic embarked on a series of experiments designed to find a godly political state. The first attempt was to create an assembly that could decide the form of the future government. A Parliament was therefore created of representatives selected by the Council of State, which had itself been put in place by the army after the expulsion of the Long Parliament in April. This body was known as the Little or the Barebones Parliament; it comprised 140 men chosen from within their communities for their godly and moral tone. Within the Little Parliament there was a vocal contingent of Fifth Monarchists, for whom the business of earthly government could be seen in the short term as preparation for the Fifth Monarchy or the rule of Christ and his saints, which they believed to be imminent.

The Parliament first met on 4 July 1653 and discussed important issues such as the continued payment of tithes to support the church. It passed legislation on marriage and on imprisonment for debt. It also debated army funding, but its relationship with the army leadership, which had been instrumental in calling it into being, declined quickly. On 12 December a moderate faction of the M.P.s, frustrated at the failure to deal with major issues, connived to dissolve the Parliament. Just before the dissolution, John Lambert had drafted a constitution, the Instrument of Government, which created the Protectorate. In its finished form the Instrument established a state with a lord protector and a Council of State as the executive, with a regularly called Parliament representing the four nations.

Cromwell as lord protector was given wide-ranging powers, but was expected to work with both the Council and Parliament in consultative government. The relationship between the lord protector and the Parliament, which first met on 3 September 1654, was not a smooth one. Elections returned a contingent of what were to be called Commonwealthmen, who had been opposed to the expulsion of Parliament in April 1653. They defied instructions not to debate the nature of the new constitution. On 12 September the army purged the Parliament of the Commonwealthmen. Even after this, government and Parliament disagreed over religious toleration and taxation policy. When, in the early days of 1655, Parliament turned to discussing the militia, Cromwell dissolved it.

In March 1655 a small royalist uprising led by a former colonel, John Penruddock, broke out in south-west England. Although the uprising itself was supposed to be part of a wider movement orchestrated by the royalist secret organisation, the Sealed Knot, Penruddock's men were isolated and easily defeated. The uprising provoked the government into imposing a form of military rule on England and Wales, however. In 1656 the two countries were divided into eleven districts each under the supervision of a major general. The major generals were to oversee the imposition of a Decimation Tax on former royalists designed to finance the militia. Major generals were also to become involved in local government and to have a reforming effect on the traditional bodies still in place within the counties. The major generals participated in quarter-sessions courts and were to oversee elections. In the autumn of 1656 their involvement in elections caused great resentment across the country and their chosen candidates were rejected. This resulted in the election of a Parliament hostile to the major generals and antipathetic to the Protectorate. This second Parliament also disagreed with the government on religious and financial issues. In January 1657 Parliament's failure to ratify the Decimation Tax resulted in the demise of the major generals.

Renewed discussions on the nature of government led to the creation of a new constitution, framed by a section of the Parliament, and known as the *Humble Petition and Advice*. The *Humble Petition* was presented to Cromwell in late February 1657. Initially, this asked that Cromwell take the title of king and be allowed to choose his successor, and the lord protector seemed willing. Opposition from John Lambert and the army led to Cromwell rejecting the title of king, however, but he did accept the right to nominate his successor and a second Upper House of sixty-three members to be added to Parliament. The reformed Parliament continued to meet until June when it went into recess. It met again on 20 January 1658, but this time with members excluded in 1656 restored to it. When sections of the lower house seemed determined to try and seduce the army from its loyalty to the government, Cromwell dissolved it.

The Protectorate, although consisting of a legislature that embraced all four nations, was not seen as a collective of equals from north of the River Tweed or west of the Irish Sea. Scotland was administered almost as a dependency, despite the agreement made in 1652. Much of the judiciary was initially staffed by Englishmen and half the counties had English high sheriffs. Even the kirk had its appointments vetted by Englishmen. This was partly a result of the continued need for a large military presence there, but it belied any notion that Scotland was an equal partner. The Glencairn uprising in the Highlands that began during 1653 had resulted in concerted military action, General George Monck being sent to destroy the rebellion in 1654. By May 1655 it had been ruthlessly repressed at ground level whilst the leadership was treated leniently in order to secure later compliance in the Highlands. Most of the representatives for Scottish constituencies sent to the Little Parliament were English officers, but this had changed by the first Protectorate Parliament. Local government was also returned into Scots' hands, but candidates at home and at Westminster were subject to the approval of the Council.

In Ireland, since 1652 government was in the hands of a lord deputy as it had been under the monarchy. For five years this was Charles Fleetwood, but from 1657 Cromwell's son Henry held the post. There was a heavy military presence in place also, and this was felt particularly during the attempts to transport Catholic landholders to the west of the River Shannon. The programme failed to create a pattern of landholding analogous to England, where large estates tended to dominate. There were so many interest groups buying the confiscated land that the country remained one of relatively small landholders. As with Scotland, Ireland's representatives at Westminster were approved men, in this case vetted by the lord deputy. With regard to the religious aspirations of the people, after the initial persecution of Catholics in the wake of the war, attitudes were relaxed. Fleetwood had planned to complete the conversion of the country with schools and a well-funded ministry, but the financial will in London was lacking. From 1657 priests began to make their way to Ireland to reestablish their clandestine church. Henry Cromwell concentrated on developing the Church of Ireland and persecuted dissenting Protestants, especially Baptists and Quakers, rather than Catholics.

In accordance with the *Humble Petition and Advice*, Oliver Cromwell appointed his son Richard as successor. On 3 September 1658 the lord protector died. Oliver Cromwell's attempt to keep Richard free of the influences of the major competitors on the state had worked on one level: he could be seen as being genuinely above the existing political intrigues. On the other hand, Richard had neither a powerbase nor a set of allies on which he could depend. The Parliament, that met on 27 January 1659, fell prey to the attacks of the Commonwealthmen, who again questioned the basis of the constitution and the logistics of the expensive armed forces. Nevertheless, with electoral adjustments and some tampering with the membership of the Upper House, the constitution began to work.

The Commonwealthmen effectively killed the Protectorate, for in May 1659 the army, provoked by propaganda distributed by the Commonwealthmen, dissolved the House, expelled Richard from office, and reconvened the Long Parliament. Why the army believed that this Rump Parliament would be any more favourable is in question, but this was a period of great expectations. The Parliament was bombarded with radical petitions. Naturally this also provoked fears in some sections of society and provided wide-ranging support for a short-lived royalist uprising led by George Booth in August. In October 1659 the Rump Parliament was again expelled and government was in the hands of an army-dominated Council of Safety.

The republic was in free-fall. General Monck, from his Scottish powerbase, opposed the expulsion of the Parliament and purged his forces of opponents. Lambert marched the English forces to confront Monck, but the apparent solidarity in England, Wales, and Ireland crumbled. At the very end of December the Long Parliament reassembled, and in January Monck began a march southwards. By 11 February 1660, Monck, who had set out acting as a servant of the Parliament, ordered it to readmit the members who had been expelled in 1648 by Colonel Pride. The enlarged House of Commons dissolved itself on 16 March after establishing elections to a successor.

On 25 April 1660, a Convention Parliament of both Commons and Lords met at Westminster and decided to offer the republic to the exiled Charles Stuart. He responded on May Day with a conciliatory Declaration of Breda, that Parliament accepted. On 26 May 1660, the exiled prince returned to his kingdom and the three monarchies were resurrected. Whilst the king proclaimed a general amnesty for many, formalised as the Act of Indemnity and Oblivion, the regicides who had signed the death warrant for or officiated at the execution of Charles I were not to be spared. Eleven out of the forty-one survivors were executed. The bodies of Henry Ireton, Oliver Cromwell, and John Bradshaw were exhumed and displayed in mock executions.

For eight years the four nations had been forged into a united republic. Even if this was not a union of equals, it had created a political system that overlay all of the three monarchies. The Restoration set the clock back, untangling the revolution of 1648–49 and the union of 1652–53, reestablishing monarchical rule. By 1661 the clock had been put back beyond the revolutions of 1639–42, removing the constitutional changes that had limited the power of Charles I and bolstered Parliament's place in English, Welsh, and Scottish government.

Some things could not be changed. The collapse of the state church in 1642 had allowed for the development of many Protestant sects throughout the four nations. Although the Church of England was restored with often vicious vigour, religious pluralism was not eradicated. In Scotland the kirk was disestablished and the Covenanters persecuted, but Presbyterianism could not be destroyed completely. In Ireland, there was a well-established dissenting movement that could not be displaced by the recreation of the Church of Ireland and Presbyterianism remained strong in Ulster. Whilst political power was concentrated ever more strongly in Church of Ireland hands, the majority of the population remained Roman Catholic.

In political terms also, no amount of hard-line, ultra-royalist politics of the sort that categorised Charles II's second (or cavalier) Parliament could overturn history. The collective memory of the period 1637–60 may have been one of war and disorder. To some people it was also one of excitement, filled with possibilities for radical change. As with the Levellers after 1649, although the physical representation of republicanism had vanished after 1660, the ideas that brought a republic about and that it in turn engendered, did not. In many respects, the Restoration was something of a chimera.

The Dictionary

ᗌ A ᗍ

ABERDEEN DOCTORS. The Scottish city of Aberdeen was the first place to witness serious fighting during the wars. Some of the academics from the university, known as the Aberdeen Doctors, refused to sign the Covenant (q.v.) and persuaded the town not to do so too. In response a team of Covenanters (q.v.) was sent to debate the issue. The Aberdeen Doctors' stance was moderate; they did not find the episcopate to be forbidden by the Bible, but would not sign the Covenant because it was not sanctioned directly by the monarch or Scottish Privy Council, not because of theological differences or because they supported the episcopate fully.

Charles I (q.v.) took this opposition as an example of support and set out to exploit it. In 1639 and again in 1640 Aberdeen was to be the locus of anti-Covenanter risings and a proposed landing point for the king's forces. In 1639 the earl of Montrose (q.v.) defeated the marquis of Huntly's (q.v.) forces outside the city at the Bridge o[f] Dee. In 1644 Montrose, this time as a royalist (q.v.) lieutenant general, defeated the Covenanter forces from the city at the Battle of Justice Mills (q.v.).

ABJURATION, OATH OF. This oath was imposed on Catholics (q.v.) who were sequestered or active in the royalist (q.v.) cause. It required them to renounce the pope and the tenets of the Catholic church. Only if they abjured could they compound (q.v.) for their estates.

ADAMS, MARY (?–1652). A member of the Ranter (q.v.) sect who believed herself to be carrying the new Messiah. She committed suicide after the birth of a still-born child.

ADWALTON, BATTLE OF. Fought on 30 June 1643 in the vicinity of Adwalton and Drighlington between Leeds and Bradford in Yorkshire, this battle saw the forces of the marquis of Newcastle (q.v.) outmanoeuvre and then defeat the parliamentarian army under Lord Fairfax (q.v.)

and his son, Sir Thomas Fairfax (q.v.). This forced the Parliamentarians (q.v.) into hiding at Hull (q.v.), whilst Newcastle was able to dominate the West Riding of Yorkshire. Almost total control of the north-east of England meant that Newcastle was able to march south and drive the parliamentarian forces out of central Lincolnshire.

AGITATORS. During 1647, to represent the views of the rank and file at the General Council of the Army (q.v.), agitators or agents were elected by, first, the Horse (q.v.) regiments and then the Foot (q.v.) regiments of the New Model Army (q.v.), The agitators were important figures in the relationships between the army and the Levellers (q.v.) during the period June 1647 to December 1648.

AGREEMENTS OF THE PEOPLE. There were three *Agreements*. The first was drafted by the Leveller (q.v.) leaders and Agitators (q.v.) from the Army Regiments in the late summer and autumn of 1647. This first *Agreement* was presented to the General Council of the Army (q.v.) at the end of October at Putney Church. A good deal of the ensuing Putney Debates (q.v.) centred on the *Agreement*'s apparent call for democratic reform, which implied that every free man would have a vote regardless of status. This was rejected by the grandees (q.v.), in particular Henry Ireton (q.v.). The escape of King Charles I (q.v.) from Hampton Court brought these discussions to an end. A new *Agreement* was drafted after the Second Civil War, this time with the co-operation of Ireton and parts of the Army Council. This watered down the demand for an expanded electorate considerably, suggesting that anyone in receipt of wages would be ineligible for a vote. In any case the *Agreement* was presented to the Parliament (q.v.) in Westminster during the king's trial and therefore shelved. The third *Agreement* was drafted in the spring of 1649 and returned to a more radical, if now highly polished set of demands, for an expanded electorate, a unicameral assembly, and annual elections. The Leveller mutiny in May 1649 and its defeat at Burford (q.v.) led to the downfall of the *Agreement*.

AIRLIE, JAMES OGILVY, 1ST EARL OF (?1615–?1704). Airlie was an opponent of the Covenanters (q.v.) and was fined for his behaviour in 1639–40. In 1645 he allied himself to the marquis of Montrose's royalist (qq.v.) forces and was present at Montrose's victory at the Battle of Kilsyth (q.v.). He was also present at the defeat of the royalist forces at the Battle of Philliphaugh (q.v.).

ALDBOURNE CHASE, BATTLE OF. This skirmish, on 18 September 1643, halted the march of the earl of Essex (q.v.) towards London after his relief of Gloucester (September 6) (q.v.). The royalist (q.v.) army had pursued Essex after having been successfully diverted away from the earl's path. Eventually Prince Rupert (q.v.) intercepted Essex at Aldbourne Chase and forced him to turn back to Hungerford, whilst with the Foot King Charles I (qq.v.) entered Newbury, getting between Essex and London.

ALFORD, (BRIDGE OF) BATTLE OF. This battle was fought on 2 July 1644 between the marquis of Montrose's royalist (qq.v.) Scots and Irish army and the Covenanter Army of William Baillie (qq.v.). Baillie was attempting to keep Montrose from the Highlands (q.v.), where he would be able to find refuge, whereas Montrose sought to entrap Baillie to defeat the Covenanters before leaving the Highland region. Montrose had slightly more Horse (q.v.) than he had had at Inverlochy and Auldearn (qq.v.), and with these he launched an attack on Baillie. The royalists were not able to inflict defeat on the superior numbers of Covenanter Horse (q.v.), however, and were being pushed back when Montrose's Foot (q.v.) were able to fire on the Covenanter Horse, driving them off. The royalist Foot drove back their opponents in the centre of the field, and the sudden appearance of their baggage train gave the impression that reinforcements had arrived, and the Covenanters began a hasty retreat. Lord Gordon, Montrose's principle commander of Horse and main figure in the royalist Gordon family's support for Montrose, was killed late in the battle.

ANABAPTISTS. A term generally used as an insult against Baptists (q.v.) to tar them with the brush of social revolution. The German Anabaptist movement seemed to be a harbinger of great social upheaval, such as the Munster Commune of John of Leiden established in 1534. There were strong theological links between Baptists and Dutch Anabaptists after the First Civil War (q.v.) as both rejected the idea of a structured national church and infant baptism. They were in favour of pacifism, religious toleration and the separation of church and state.

ANCASTER HEATH, BATTLE OF. Royalist (q.v.) forces from Nottinghamshire and Lincolnshire, under Sir Charles Cavendish, defeated Lord Willoughby of Parham on 11 April 1644. Willoughby had tried to surprise a meeting of the Lincolnshire Commissioners of Array (q.v.) at a county meeting being held at Grantham designed to indict prominent county Parliamentarians for treason.

ANDREWS PLOT. This united royalists (q.v.), including Colonel Eusibius Andrews, and former parliamentarians such as Sir John Gell (q.v.), in an attempt to seize the Isle of Ely in the name of Charles II (q.v.), who was at this time negotiating with the Scots prior to going to Scotland. The plotters were arrested in March 1650 and Andrews was executed in August.

ANGLO-SCOTTISH WARS. *See* BISHOP'S WARS.

ANTE-COVENANTER. This term was given to any person who refused to sign the National Covenant (q.v.). It bound together moderate opponents and the more politically motivated opponents in an undistinguished body from whom additional levies were extracted to support the war effort of the Covenanters (q.v.).

ANTINOMIAN. The general principle that earthly laws and morals are subordinate to the laws of God. The doctrine of free grace, which entailed universal salvation, was seen to exonerate the truly enlightened from any divine retribution. The charge of antinomianism was levelled at several religious sects, such as the Baptists (q.v.) in an attempt to make them out to be in favour of dissolving social and moral bonds.

ANTRIM, RANDAL MACDONALD, EARL OF (1609–1683). Antrim was involved in the buildup to war between England and Scotland during the Covenant (q.v.) crisis of 1638–40. He proposed raising a force from his clan, the MacDonnells, in north-eastern Ireland and the MacDonalds in western Scotland and the Isles. This plan was discouraged by the lord deputy of Ireland, Viscount Wentworth (q.v.), who believed it to be impractical and ill-organised; he also suspected that it related more to Antrim's desire to seize former clan land from the Covenanter Campbells than it did from a wish to support Charles I (q.v.). Wentworth also realised that the support from the Catholic (q.v.) MacDonnells/MacDonalds would politically compromise the king.

In 1641 it appears that Antrim was involved in one of the plots that evolved into the Irish Rebellion (q.v.). He was captured just after the uprising began and details of his involvement began to emerge. However, Antrim escaped and assisted in the recruitment of Catholic Irish troops for service under his kinsman Alasdair MacColla (q.v.) who served with the marquis of Montrose (q.v.) in Scotland. Antrim made bargains with continental powers whereby he received arms and ships for his Scottish campaigns in return for supplying mercenaries. When Charles I surrendered in May 1646, Antrim defied orders to lay down arms and sided with the Catholic Confederation of Kilkenny (q.v.) against the marquis of Ormond's (q.v.) attempts to create a Catholic/royalist (q.v.) alliance.

When the English/Welsh army defeated the Confederation in 1649–53, Antrim changed sides and through judicious negotiation succeeded in getting into the British Republic's (q.v.) favour. After the Restoration (q.v.) in 1660 it only took him five years to secure his freedom and estates.

APOLOGY OF THE COMMON SOLDIERS. This was drafted and signed by the Agitators (q.v.) in spring 1647 and presented to the Parliament (q.v.) in Westminster on 28 April. It was later joined with the *Apology of the Soldiers to Their Officers* dated 3 May 1647. The original draft avoided wider political issues and concentrated on demands for back pay and treatment of the soldiers. Nevertheless the Agitators had been treated as criminals by Parliament on receipt of the Large Petition (q.v.). The second apology attempted to promote sympathy for the common soldiers' grievances from the officer corps in the light of Parliament's savage rejection of the original Apology.

ARGYLL, ARCHIBALD CAMPBELL, MARQUIS OF (1598–1661). Argyll emerged as a prominent leader amongst the Covenanters (q.v.) after the death of his father, who did not support the Covenant (q.v.). In the Covenanting cause Argyll saw the chance to advance the cause of the Clan Campbell and further secure his hold over newly acquired territory, the former lands of the Catholic MacDonalds. It was claimed by 1640 that Argyll wanted to depose Charles I (q.v.) and that marriage of his daughter into the Stuart family of the marquis of Hamilton (q.v.) suggested to some that he had ambitions for interfering in the succession.

Argyll remained at the centre of the Scottish government, but his prestige was severely damaged by the defeats inflicted on him by the marquis of Montrose (q.v.) at Inverlochy (q.v.) on 31 January 1645, and by the loss of clan lands to the army of MacColla (q.v.) and Montrose. After the Covenanter victory over the royalists (q.v.), Argyll was for a time eclipsed by the moderates, who came to terms with the captive king. During the period of the Engagement (q.v.) and the disastrous invasion of England in 1648, Argyll remained in the shadows. He re-emerged as part of the seizure of power by the Whiggamores (q.v.), and the uneasy alliance with Oliver Cromwell (q.v.) in 1648–49. Despite trying to control Charles II (q.v.) in 1650–51, Argyll and the extremists divided the leadership of the army and state, and were thus swept aside by the defeats at the Battles of Dunbar (1650) and Worcester (1651) (qq.v.). Argyll was reduced to negotiating with the Commonwealth (q.v.) to pass on part of the massive debts incurred during the wars since 1639. At the Restoration (q.v.), Argyll was singled out for exemplary treatment and executed.

ARMAGH. This county in the province of Ulster (q.v.) was the seat of the Church of Ireland and the Catholic (q.v.) primates of Ireland. In 1641–42 during the Irish Rebellion (q.v.) some of the atrocities of the rebellion took place in Armagh, including that at Portadown in November 1641, where 80–100 Protestants were massacred. In all, in sporadic and unplanned massacres, between 17.5 percent and 43 percent of the colonist population were killed in Armagh. The rebellion was then followed by a savage attack by the Scottish army, which took Newry on 5 May and burned Armagh the following day. The county was also the site of the Battle of Benburb (q.v.) in 1646.

ARMAGH, JAMES USSHER, ARCHBISHOP OF (1581–1656). The primate of Ireland from 1625, Ussher's belief that the pope was the Antichrist rather than an erring brother contributed in part to his being respected by Puritans (q.v.), who would otherwise have had little truck with a prelate. A writer of history and geography, Ussher's intellectual approach led him to propose a compromise settlement in the church in 1641. Whilst he castigated the Roman Catholic (q.v.) church, his attitude toward Protestant sects was more liberal. Although invited to the Westminster Assembly (q.v.), he, like many Anglican divines, did not attend. Usher was provided with a pension by the Westminster Parliament (q.v.) in 1643 and attended Charles I (q.v.) at his execution.

ARMY OF THE SOLEMN LEAGUE AND COVENANT. This army was raised in late 1643 in Scotland to send into England to assist the parliamentarians (q.v.) in the war against Charles I (q.v.). From January 1644 the army fought chiefly in the north of England except for a brief campaign in the midlands in 1645. The army fought at the Battle of Marston Moor (q.v.) in 1644 and at the final siege of Newark (q.v.). It was only in late January 1647 that the army finally left England and was disbanded.

ARMY PLOT. In April 1641 a group of officers from King Charles I's (q.v.) army stationed in the north of England drafted a petition calling for a halt to attacks on the episcopate (q.v.), and for adequate funds for army pay. The senior officers in the army refused to accept the petition, but the petitioners went on to suggest that the army move on London to rescue Thomas Wentworth, Earl of Strafford (q.v.). Plotters in London infiltrated the Tower of London and Queen Henrietta Maria (q.v.) made preparations to join Sir George Goring (q.v.) at Portsmouth (q.v.) and to hold the port in the king's name. Details of the plot were leaked to the Parliament (q.v.) in Westminster, however, which increased the guard at the Tower and prevented the queen from leaving London. The plot increased suspicion of the queen and doomed the earl of Strafford.

ARNOLD, RICHARD (?–1647). The Leveller (q.v.) martyr, alone amongst the three who were tried and found guilty of mutiny at Corkbush Field (q.v.) in 1647. Arnold had been in Richard Lilburne's regiment, which had attended the banned rendezvous in the days after the Putney Debates (q.v.) and the flight of King Charles I from Hampton Court (qq.v.).

ASHBY-DE-LA-ZOUCH. The castle at Ashby-de-la-Zouch belonged to the earl of Huntingdon, but from the end of 1642 it was garrisoned by his royalist (q.v.) son Henry Hastings, later Lord Loughborough (q.v.). The town was not only a base for Hastings's army but was the centre of the Leicestershire royalist Commission of Array (q.v.) and for the region's administration. The castle was attacked by Thomas, Lord Grey of Groby (q.v.) in January 1643, but remained in royalist hands throughout the First Civil War (q.v.). When Hastings laid down his arms at the beginning of March 1646, the castle's war-time defences were dismantled. The castle was partially destroyed from the end of 1648.

ASSESSMENTS. A variety of assessments were levied in the four kingdoms during the war and some will be found under their titles, contribution, monthlie maintenance, general applotment, monthly pay, and weekly assessment (qq.v.). There were sporadic assessments of a range of things necessary for the war, such as beds, bedding and linen, and horses, often made in conjunction with the civil and military authorities and the local representatives of government, constables (q.v.), factors, and baillies. Beds and bedding were levied from communities in the vicinity of garrisons for the use of the soldiers.

ASSOCIATIONS OF COUNTIES. In England and Wales both sides sought to combine counties to further the war effort by combining resources, manpower and taxation from a group of counties. Commanding officers, whether royalist (q.v.) colonel generals or parliamentarian (q.v.) major generals, were put in command of the military affairs. The Westminster Parliament's (q.v.) County Committees (q.v.) delegated members to form an association committee. The royalists may have centred co-operation on the high sheriffs, who were mandated to serve on the county-based Commission of Array (q.v.). Certainly there were some royalists who were members of more than one Commission of Array, for instance, Henry Hastings, Lord Loughborough (q.v.), sat on the Derbyshire and the Leicestershire Commission.

Associated counties met with mixed fortunes. The most successful parliamentarian association was the Eastern Association (q.v.), consisting of the counties of East Anglia and the south-east Midlands, and eventually embracing Lincolnshire too. Conversely, the East Midlands Association under Lord Grey of Groby (q.v.) was rendered ineffective by 1644 and sections of it were hived off by other associations. For example, Nottinghamshire became a part of the Northern Association (q.v.). This latter association was only able to become effective after the Battle of Marston Moor (q.v.) on 2 July 1644, when its creation was no doubt helped by the presence of the Army of the the Solemn League and Covenant (q.v.). Even so this association retained an independent parliamentarian army until 1647, as did the Western Association under Edward Massey (q.v.).

Royalist associations are harder to trace, but there certainly existed two in the Midland, one under Henry Hastings embracing Nottinghamshire, Derbyshire, Leicestershire, Staffordshire, and Rutland, and the other Warwickshire and Shropshire. Staffordshire and the latter counties as well as Herefordshire and Worcestershire became absorbed in the brief manifestation of the Marcher Association (q.v.), whereby the local gentry tried to protect their autonomy by forging new agreements with the king about taxation and other matters in 1645. This association collapsed in the face of royalist aggression before May 1645.

ASTLEY, SIR JACOB, LORD (1579–1652). Astley had continental military experience, and was involved in the organisation of King Charles I's (q.v.) army in the first of the Bishop's Wars (q.v.). In 1642 he was appointed sergeant major-general of the Foot (q.v.), and took over command when Prince Rupert and the earl of Lindsey (qq.v.) argued on the field at Edgehill (q.v.). He is famous for uttering the prayer, "O lord, thou knowest how busy I must be this day. If I forget thee, do not thou forget me." Astley was present at the Battles of Newbury I, 1643; Lostwithiel, 1644; Newbury II, 1644; Naseby, 1645; Rowton Heath, 1645; and Stow on the Wold, 1646 (qq.v.). He was ennobled in late 1644. In late 1645 he was sent to join Lord Loughborough (q.v.) in an attempt to keep open a route to Chester via the North Midlands, but went to Worcester once this became impossible. In March 1646 he was to bring his levies to Oxford, as they constituted the last army in the field. He was caught and defeated at Stow on the Wold on 21 March by Sir William Brereton (q.v.). At the end of the First Civil War (q.v.) he retired to Kent, where he died in 1652.

ASTON, SIR ARTHUR (?–1649). Aston gained military experience in the Polish army in the wars against the Turks, and during the 1630s served in the European wars on the side of the Protestant Gustavus Adolphus of Sweden, although he himself was a Roman Catholic (q.v.). He returned to England at the outbreak of the Bishop's Wars (q.v.) and was appointed sergeant major-general under Lord Conway in 1640.

Charles declined his services in 1642 on religious grounds, but when the parliamentarian Lord Fairfax (qq.v.) offered him an appointment, Prince Rupert (q.v.) stepped in and gave Aston command of a regiment of Dragoons (q.v.). In 1643 he became governor of Reading, until it surrendered in April, and then governor of Oxford (q.v.) in August. After losing a leg to gangrene, Aston was replaced by his deputy, Sir Henry Gage. He then, in some dudgeon, went to Ireland, where he was appointed governor of Drogheda (q.v.) by the marquis of Ormond (q.v.). He remained there until 1649 when Oliver Cromwell (q.v.) attacked and captured the town. In the ensuing fighting, Aston was beaten to death with his own wooden leg.

ATTAINDER, ACT OF. The opposition in the Parliament (q.v.) of Westminster centred its attacks on two of the principle figures from Charles I's Personal Rule (qq.v.), Thomas Wentworth, Earl of Strafford (q.v.) and Archbishop William Laud (q.v.). Wentworth was brought to trial first, in April 1641. He was charged with treason, on evidence assembled from English and Irish sources. Much of this evidence was flawed, however, being of dubious validity and moreover none of the individual charges constituted treason. As a result the trial stalled. The king's chief opponents instead drew up a Bill of Attainder, a mediaeval instrument which simply took rumours of guilt as proof of fact. This passed through both houses of Parliament (q.v.), although the Lords may have assented in the belief that the king would not sacrifice his friend and minister. By the time the attainder reached the king, however, he was in a precarious political position following the exposure of the Army Plot (q.v.), which had implicated Queen Henrietta Maria (q.v.). In order to save her from possible impeachment, Charles signed the Bill. Strafford was executed on 12 May 1641.

AULDEARN, BATTLE OF. Fought on 9 May 1645, this was the first of the earl of Montrose's (q.v.) battles in eastern Scotland, near Nairn. Montrose was being pursued by Sir John Urry's (q.v.) forces when he turned at bay and awaited attack. It has been recently argued that Urry caught Montrose off guard and that the battle was a confused affair with royalists (q.v.) being fed into the battle against the attacking Covenanter (q.v.) forces as they were roused and regrouped. Eventually Urry's attack was slowed and then halted. Once the Covenanter Horse (q.v.) had been defeated they retreated, colliding with the Foot (q.v.), and spreading panic throughout Urry's forces.

AXTEL, DANIEL (?–1661). Once a pedlar, Axtel rose from humble origins; in 1649 he was in charge of the guard at Charles I's (q.v.) trial. For undertaking this duty Axtel was executed at the Restoration (q.v.). As lieutenant colonel of John Hewson's (q.v.) regiment of Foot (q.v.), Axtel was involved in suppressing the Kentish revolt during the Second Civil War (q.v.). Axtell also served in Ireland from 1649, being present at Drogheda and Wexford (qq.v.). In 1650 Axtel became governor of the captured city and former seat of government, Kilkenny (q.v.).

↩ B ↩

BAGOT, RICHARD (1619–1645). Bagot was governor of Lichfield until being fatally wounded at the Battle of Naseby (q.v.). He originally served in Lord Paget/Richard Bolles's regiment, then formed his own regiments on being appointed governor in April 1643. His brother Harvey was his lieutenant colonel and then succeeded him as governor. His father, Sir Harvey, was a commissioner of array (q.v.) for Staffordshire.

BAILLIE, DR ROBERT (1599–1662). Baillie was a fairly moderate Presbyterian and minister at Kilwinnig in south-west Scotland. He became a supporter of the National Covenant (q.v.) after realising that the king was intransigent in his aims. In the early 1640s Baillie was a professor of divinity at Glasgow, but he was also one of the Scottish representatives at the Westminster Assembly of Divines (q.v.) from 1644. In the early 1650s Baillie saw that the widest possible base had to be created for Scotland to offer effective opposition to the threatened English conquest after the defeat at the Battle of Dunbar (q.v.) on 3 September 1650. Baillie kept a series of journals including his letters to and from prominent figures during the course of the wars and revolutions.

BAILLIE, WILLIAM. Baillie was one of the principle Covenanter (q.v.) generals assigned the task of defeating the earl of Montrose (q.v.) in 1645. He was defeated at the Battles of Bridge of Alford and Kilsyth (qq.v.).

BANBURY, OXFORDSHIRE. The town and castle were garrisoned by royalists (q.v.) in the wake of the Battle of Edgehill (q.v.). The relationship between the garrison and the town was particularly strained because of the town's reputation as a Puritan (q.v.) community. The three-month siege of July–October 1644 exacerbated matters, as did the destruction of parts of the town to strengthen the castle in 1645. At the end of the war, the townspeople gained permission to demolish the castle. Little trace of it remains.

BANKES, LADY MARY. In 1643–45 Lady Mary defended Corfe Castle in Dorset against local parliamentarian (q.v.) forces. Her husband, Sir John Bankes, was chief justice of the Bench of Common Pleas and accompanied King Charles I (q.v.) at Oxford (q.v.). In the early part of the war Lady Mary stocked the castle with ammunition and offered no direct defiance to the county parliamentarians. Eventually she was given a small garrison of 50 men by Prince Maurice (q.v). The first attack on the castle came on 23 June 1643, but after some days the siege ended in failure. The castle remained in Lady Mary's hands until December 1645 when it was besieged by regiments from the New Model Army (q.v.). The garrison was betrayed by one of the lieutenants who brought a party of parliamentarians into the castle pretending that they were reinforcements. The castle was demolished but its defenders were allowed to leave unmolested.

BAPTISTS. The Baptist movement had its origins at the beginning of the 17th century and rejected predestination and infant baptism. Salvation was dependent on grace and entry into a covenant with God had to be made of one's free will. By the 1640s two strands had emerged within the faith, General Baptists—who rejected predestination—and Particular Baptists—who did not. Both practised baptism by total immersion and thus attracted the nickname: Dippers. The Particular Baptists sought converts amongst the members of other Independent (q.v.) churches and engaged in public disputes with ministers of other churches, the General Baptists appealed to the mass of ordinary people through evangelical meetings and printed propaganda.

All members of Baptist congregations were regarded as equals and this outlook, amongst others, allied the General Baptists closely with radical political movements such as the Levellers (q.v.), who argued for religious freedom and limited toleration. The Particular Baptists publicly disavowed the Levellers in 1649. Equality was to some extent stretched across the gender divide, and many women, including Lucy Hutchinson (q.v.), became Baptists, drawn by this aspect. Conservatism inherent to the movement did not allow women to participate as speakers or ministers, however.

There was considerable hostility towards Baptists, who were seen as ignorant of Scripture and accused of undermining the patriarchal structure of society. They were often accused of being Anabaptists (q.v.), something that was so dangerous that the Particular Baptists accused the Levellers of Anabaptism in an effort to distance themselves from the movement and the implications of such an accusation. Whilst the movement prospered under the early Republican regimes of the 1650s, the advent of the Barebones Parliament (q.v.) undermined them somewhat because of the developing Fifth Monarchist (q.v.) movement, which drew some away from the Baptists' seeming complacency towards a more radical approach to Millenarianism (q.v.). For the remaining years of the republic, the Baptists remained enthusiastic for the benefits of toleration it brought. Nevertheless, the association with populism ensured that the Baptists were repressed by the Restoration (q.v.) regime.

BAREBONES PARLIAMENT. This was the nickname applied to the Little Parliament of 1653. Following Oliver Cromwell's (q.v.) expulsion of the Long Parliament (q.v.) in April, a new Parliament (q.v.) was created with nominees from all four nations of the British Isles. The Parliament met in July and sat until 12 December when it was dissolved by the moderate members, who were dismayed at its failure to deal with the war with the Dutch and army finance. Praise-God Barebones was the leader of a small extremist faction within the Parliament and opponents of the regime named the Parliament after him to associate it with his radicalism.

BASCOT HEATH, BATTLE OF. This was a small conflict, occurring on 23 August 1642, which was part of King Charles I's (q.v.) attempt to secure the county magazines in between his forces and London. It was also part of the local struggle between two Warwickshire landowners, Lord Brooke and the earl of Northampton (qq.v.), for control of the county. The royalists (q.v.), who were already pulling back from their attacks on Warwick and Coventry, were defeated by the parliamentarian forces that now included forces raised in Leicestershire and Buckinghamshire amassed to drive the royalists out of the South Midlands.

BASING HOUSE. This fortified mansion belonging to the marquis of Winchester (q.v.) was an important royalist (q.v.) base in the South. It was seen by Parliament (q.v.) as a nest of papists (q.v.), and became a particular target. The house was besieged by Sir William Waller (q.v.) in November 1643; failing to storm the house at the beginning of the month he tried again on 12 November, but withdrew three days later. In 1644 the house was the centre of King Charles I's (q.v.) attempts to supply his southernmost outposts, there and at Donnington Castle near Newbury. This campaign involved the second Battle of Newbury (q.v.). In 1645 the house was besieged for some months by local forces. On 8 October Oliver Cromwell (q.v.) and part of the New Model Army (q.v.) arrived before it. On 12 October after a summons had been rejected, the house was subjected to heavy bombardment and stormed at 6 A.M. the next day. The garrison and the family members inside were subjected to great brutality, the artists Wencelsas Hollar and Inigo Jones were roughly treated, and several priests murdered. The excuse given for this action was that the garrison was suspected of being Roman Catholic (q.v.).

BASTWICKE, JOHN (1593–1654). One of the pre-civil war radicals, Bastwicke's Presbyterianism (q.v.) attracted the support of young political enthusiasts such as John Lilburne (q.v.) in the 1630s. Bastwicke, along with Henry Burton and William Prynne (qq.v.), was prosecuted by the Star Chamber (q.v.) in 1637 for attacking the episcopacy (q.v.). All three were pilloried and had their ears cropped. The Long Parliament (q.v.) gained the release of all three, but Bastwicke was captured by the king at Leicester in July 1642, imprisoned again, and could not be released until the capture of Knaresborough Castle by parliamentarians (q.v.) in 1645. His Presbyterianism now divided him from his earlier radical supporters and pushed him further from the centre of the Revolution.

BATTEN, WILLIAM (?–1667). Batten served as the earl of Warwick's (q.v.) vice admiral in the parliamentarian navy throughout the First Civil War (q.v.). In 1645 his fleet captured Weymouth from the royalists (q.v.) but he was removed from command in September 1647 by the Independents in Parliament for not arresting some Presbyterian (qq.v.) members of Parliament. The appointment of Thomas Rainsborough (q.v.) as his replacement led to a mutiny in the fleet, which Batten took advantage of and, in 1648, he briefly went over to the royalist side. He returned to Parliament's side when Prince Rupert (q.v.) was given his command by Prince Charles (q.v.).

BAXTER, RICHARD (1615–1691). Baxter became a Presbyterian (q.v.) chaplain in the parliamentarian (q.v.) garrison at Coventry. In the 1630s he served churches in Dudley and Bridgenorth after his ordination, preaching to "dead-hearted" people, without the use of surplice or using the sign of the cross, before moving on to Kidderminster. From Coventry, Baxter visited the New Model Army (q.v.) after the Battle of Naseby (q.v.) and was horrified at the numbers of Independents (q.v.) in it. To try to work against the Independent tide in the New Model Army, he joined Colonel Edward Whalley's regiment as chaplain. Baxter was with the army at the Battle of Langport (q.v.). After the war he returned to Kidderminster, where he remained through the 1650s. Whilst he despised what he saw as Oliver Cromwell's (q.v.) usurpation, he admitted that some facets of the Republic (q.v.), which were diametrically opposed to his own religious outlook, did much good in the country. After the Restoration (q.v.) Baxter was persecuted for his adherence to Presbyterianism.

BEDFORD, FRANCIS RUSSELL, EARL OF (1593–1641). Bedford was a leading figure in the opposition to Charles I (q.v.) in the Parliament (q.v.) of 1640–41. He was the patron of John Pym (q.v.), who fronted opposition in the Commons (q.v.). Bedford was prominent amongst those signing the Petition of Twelve Peers in August 1641 calling for a Parliament. In early 1641, the king tried to bridge the gap between himself and his opponents by bringing some of them into the government. Rumours abounded that Bedford was to be made lord treasurer and Pym chancellor of the exchequer. Bedford died in May that year, however.

BELASYSE, JOHN, LORD (1614–1689). Belasyse fought for King Charles I (q.v.) at the Battles of Edgehill and Brentford (qq.v.) and served in the south until 1644. In February 1644 he was appointed governor of York (q.v.) and left in command of the royalists (q.v.) in Yorkshire. Lord Fairfax and Sir Thomas Fairfax's (qq.v.) campaign in West Yorkshire was simultaneous with a campaign on the Yorkshire coast, splitting Belasyse's forces. On 11 April 1644, Belasyse was defeated at the Battle of Selby (q.v.) causing the collapse of the earl of Newcastle's (q.v.) campaign against the Army of the Solemn League and Covenant (q.v.). Belasyse was captured at the battle and was exchanged only in 1645 when he was appointed governor of Newark (q.v.), which he surrendered on 6 May 1646. After serving the French monarch in the late 1640s, Belasyse became a member of the secret royalist organisation known as the Sealed Knot (q.v.) in the 1650s. At the Restoration (q.v.) his Catholicism left him open to accusations of involvement in the Popish Plot "exposed" by Titus Oates. In 1686 he became James II's first lord of the treasury.

BELTON (LINCS), BATTLE OF. The Midland parliamentarians (q.v.) failed in their second attempt to capture Newark (q.v.) in early May 1643, and then failed to intercept the ammunition Queen Henrietta Maria (q.v.) sent to Oxford (q.v.) that month. By the time East Anglian forces arrived to lend assistance, the convoy had gone. After occupying Grantham in Lincolnshire, Colonel Oliver Cromwell's and Captain John Hotham's (qq.v.) forces were attacked in the early evening of 13 May 1643. The fighting developed at nearby Belton. Whilst Cromwell's Horse (q.v.) met with some success, Hotham's soldiers did not fare so well. Although the royalists (q.v.) could not force Cromwell out of Grantham, the parliamentarians retreated to Lincoln the next day.

BENBURB, BATTLE OF. This battle, fought on 5 June 1646, demonstrated the fruits of Nuncio Rinuccini's (q.v.) material support for the Catholic Confederation of Kilkenny (q.v). The Confederation's general of Ulster, Owen Roe O'Neill (qq.v.), recruited seven new regiments of Foot (q.v.) and seven troops of Horse (q.v.) and went on the offensive in the province. This was the first time he was able to pay his entire army properly since the war. The Scots, under Robert Monro (q.v.), assembled their forces in County Armagh (q.v.), and O'Neill marched to Benburb. There he was attacked by Monro on 5 June. The battle lasted five hours before O'Neill launched an attack with fresh troops and routed the Scots. This was an important victory and the Scots were never able to act alone in the province because of the losses inflicted. Potential fruits were squandered, however, as O'Neill needed supplies and this occupied his time immediately after the battle. Moreover, in the wake of the victory, Rinuccini's faction enacted a coup d'état in Kilkenny, and required O'Neill's army to overawe the conservative Old English (q.v.). The Ulster Army marched southwards without taking control of the Scottish bases in central Ulster.

BIDDLE, HESTER (?–1696). Hester Biddle was a Quaker (q.v.) who pressed for women's rights in the wake of the revolution. In her pamphlets of 1655, *Woe to Thee City of Oxford* and *Woe to Thee town of Cambridge*, Biddle attacked the antiquated education at the two English universities. In 1659 she exhorted the women of London not to ignore responsibility for social welfare. During the 1660s she continued to attend Quaker meetings, where she preached. In 1662, after being arrested for preaching at a Quaker meeting, she reproached her judge, Richard Browne, for betraying his own past religious radicalism. She was not heard of again after her arrest in 1665 for preaching in the street.

BID(D)LE, JOHN (1615–1662). An Oxford (q.v.) graduate schoolmaster at Gloucester (q.v.), Biddle began to write on the nature of God. Even in the parliamentarian (q.v.) city of Gloucester, this was too radical to be tolerated and his manuscripts were seized. In his tracts, *Twelve Arguments Drawn out of the Scriptures* (1647) and *A Confession of Faith* (1649), Biddle denied the doctrine of the Trinity. Questioning the Trinity had been made punishable by death by an ordinance of 1648, but he was protected by his Independent (q.v.) friends. In 1652 the Act of Oblivion (q.v.) allowed him to surface again and his followers, Biddellians or

Unitarians, began to preach. He was imprisoned, and then banished to the Scilly Isles in 1655 for publishing a catechism. He was released in 1662, but was rearrested on his return to London. He died in prison.

BILLETING. The billeting or accommodation of soldiers and horses by civilian householders was regarded as an unacceptable practise by Charles I's (q.v.) 1628 Parliament (q.v.), which proscribed it in the Petition of Right (q.v.). During the Civil War, billeting was widespread both in urban and rural areas, arrangements were worked out between officers or quartermasters and community officials, such as constables (q.v.). The costs for one night were generally set in England and Wales at around 4d for a man or a horse. Most people were issued tickets (billets), which they were supposed to be able to submit later for payment. Costs were sometimes offset against the regular taxes, such as contribution, weekly assessment, monthlie maintenance, and general applotment (qq.v.), but this was not always possible. Billeting could also be imposed as a punishment for tardy payment of levies. It was certainly practised by the royalists (q.v.) in South Wales in 1645 and by the Edinburgh government during the 1640s.

BIRCH, COLONEL JOHN (1615–1691). A Presbyterian (q.v.) merchant in Bristol (q.v.) who, with the support of Sir Arthur Hesilrige (q.v.), rose to regimental command. He fought with Sir William Waller's (q.v.) army in 1644. In 1645 he became the governor of first Bath and then Bristol, after the latter was surrendered by Prince Rupert (q.v.). Later that year he captured Hereford from the royalists (q.v.). His Presbyterianism divided him from many of his colleagues in the New Model Army (q.v.), and by 1651 he had joined Charles II (q.v.), who was fighting at Worcester (q.v.) that year.

BIRMINGHAM. In the 1640s Birmingham was still a small Warwickshire market town, although some small-scale industrial production had begun. When King Charles I (q.v.) moved through the town in October 1642 some of the townspeople plundered his baggage train and sent captured goods to the parliamentarian (q.v.) garrisons at Coventry and Warwick. This action, and the continued parliamentarian sympathies of the town, ensured that the royalists (q.v.) would make some show of strength there when Prince Rupert (q.v.) marched through in April 1643. The townspeople had by this time thrown up earthworks outside Birmingham and Rupert faced some resistance when he arrived there on Easter Monday (3 April) 1643. Even when Rupert's men had forced their way into the town, fighting continued at Deritend. On the following day, fires were started around the town, probably by departing royalists. The actions of Prince Rupert became headline news, inspiring titles such as *A True Relation of Prince Rupert's Barbarous Cruelty against the Towne of Brumingham* and *Prince Rupert's Burning Love to England discovered in Birmingham's Flames*. As such the albeit exaggerated effects of the attack on Birmingham did the royalists no favours and gave proof to the myth of cruel cavaliers (q.v.) attacking honest civilians.

BISHOP'S WARS, THE. This term was given to the Anglo-Scottish Wars of 1639 and 1640. The name referred to the attempt by King Charles I (q.v.) to impose a prayer book on Scotland based on the *Book of Common Prayer* (q.v.). The Scottish service book was drafted by a commission of English and Scottish bishops. The first Bishop's War took place in the summer of 1639, but almost no fighting occurred. A detachment of English forces under the earl of Holland (q.v.) encountered part of the Army of the Solemn League and Covenant (q.v.) near Kelso on 4 June. Under the impression that they were vastly outnumbered, the English fled. This increased the impetus for negotiations, and the war was ended by the Pacification of Berwick. In 1640 the king went to war with the Scots again, this time the Scottish Covenanter (q.v.) army crossed the border, defeating the English and Welsh forces at the Battle of Newburn (q.v.), going on to capture Newcastle and occupy the north of England. The defeat led to the calling of a Westminster Parliament (q.v.)—the Long Parliament (q.v.)—and allowed the Scots to complete their political revolution.

BLAKE, ROBERT (1598–1657). Blake served as an M.P. in the Short and Long Parliaments (qq.v.) for his hometown of Bridgewater. He served in the defence of Bristol (q.v.) in 1643 and then as governor of Lyme. After the defeat of the earl of Essex (q.v.) at the Battle of Lostwithiel (q.v.), Blake held on to Taunton against the attempts by royalist (q.v.) forces to dislodge him. From 1649 onwards he served at sea, helping to restore order in the fleet after some of it had mutinied and joined Charles II (q.v.). Blake led the parliamentarian fleet against the royalist fleet under Prince Rupert (q.v.) during the war in Ireland. He defeated Rupert and Prince Maurice (q.v.) in Malaga Harbour after pursuing them into the Mediterranean, returning to blockade and capture the Isles of Scilly. He subsequently led the fleet against the Dutch, the Barbary pirates, and, in 1657, the Spanish. He died on the way home after destroying a Spanish treasure fleet. He was buried in Westminster Abbey, only to be exhumed at the Restoration (q.v.).

BLASPHEMY ACT (1650). Most of the legislation regarding blasphemy had become ineffective when the Court of High Commission (q.v.) was abolished in 1641. The 1650 Act against "several Atheistical, Blasphemous and Execrable Opinions" was aimed at the radical religious sects, such as the Ranters (q.v.), who disputed the basic tenets of the Christian faith. It particularly aimed its ire at antinomian (q.v.) beliefs and those who claimed divine inspiration for debauchery and drunkenness—in short the denial of the existence of sin. However the punishments to be meted out were similar to those imposed on vagrants, beggars, and bawds, the Act may be seen as being directed towards moral reformation as much as an attack on doctrine.

BLETCHINGTON HOUSE. This was a royalist (q.v.) satellite garrison in Oxfordshire. During Oliver Cromwell's (q.v.) campaign in the South Midlands in spring 1645, he defeated a party of Horse (q.v.) at Islip and pursued the retreating forces to Bletchington. Despite having no siege equipment, Cromwell summoned the house and the garrison surrendered without offering resistance. The seemingly precipitous surrender cost the governor, Colonel Francis Windebank, son of Secretary of State Sir Francis Windebank (q.v.), his life. He was tried by court martial at Oxford (q.v.) and shot.

BOLDON HILLS, BATTLE OF. Fought on 7–8 March 1644. The marquis of Newcastle (q.v.) attempted to bring Lord Leven's (q.v.) army into open battle in County Durham, something the Scots sought to avoid. Newcastle aimed to defeat the Scots before they progressed further into England after their invasion of 18 January 1644. At Boldon Hills, however, on 7 March Newcastle could not draw Leven out of a series of inaccessible positions. The next day heavy snow fell and Newcastle withdrew, driving off Scottish attempts to attack his rearguard.

BOLSOVER CASTLE. This castle in Derbyshire was one of the Midland homes of the marquis of Newcastle (q.v). It was garrisoned for King Charles I (q.v.) at the outset of the war by Captain Sigismund Beeton, a royalist (q.v.) from Henry Hastings, later Lord Loughborough's (q.v.), regiment. It surrendered to the parliamentarians (q.v.) in August 1644, but was briefly retaken by royalists from Newark (q.v.) the following summer, surrendering finally to Derbyshire parliamentarians in October 1645.

BOLTON (LANCS). Renowned for its Puritan (q.v.) or more strictly Presbyterian (q.v.) leanings, Bolton gained the nickname, "Geneva of Lancashire" (or "of the North"). In 1644 as Prince Rupert (q.v.) marched through Lancashire re-establishing a royalist (q.v.) presence en route to York (q.v.), he stormed the town on 28 May. As many as half the people there may have been killed: perhaps 800 civilians out of a population of 1,588. The prince sent the 16 colours captured at the siege to the Countess of Derby (q.v.) in her garrison at Lathom House (q.v.). The earl of Derby's (q.v.) involvement at the siege helped seal his fate: He was executed in the town in 1651 for his part in the Third Civil War (q.v.).

BOOK OF COMMON PRAYER. Based on Elizabeth I's adaptation of the second prayer book of Edward VI, the *Book of Common Prayer* contained the liturgy of the Church of England. This week-by-week calendar of services was required to be used in all places of worship in England and Wales. It also formed the basis of the prayer book drafted for use in Scotland in the 1630s, which led to rebellion there in 1637–40. In 1644 the Westminster Assembly of Divines (q.v.) designed a replacement, the *Directory of Public Worship* (q.v.), and the *Book of Common Prayer* was withdrawn. However, copies remained hidden in some parishes, enabling the prayer book to make a reappearance in 1660.

BOOK OF SPORTS (1618 and 1633). James VI (of Scotland) and I (of England, Wales, and Ireland) had attempted to end quarrels over which forms of games and pastimes were suitable after church on Sunday by issuing this book, including in it dancing, archery, maypoles, and morris dancing. It provoked hostile criticism then, but was attacked more vehemently when Charles I (q.v.) reissued it in 1633 and asked the clergy to ensure that its provisions were adhered to. Both kings believed that the book would keep people from antisocial behaviour such as drunkenness, and others, like the earl of Newcastle (q.v.), thought that it would keep the minds of the people from riot. On the other hand, critics of Charles's church attacked the book as a licence to ungodly behaviour on the Holy Day and it became the centre of dispute from its publication until the eve of the First Civil War (q.v.).

BOVEY TRACEY, BATTLE OF. While the New Model Army (q.v.) besieged Exeter, Prince Charles (q.v.) attempted to forge an army to attack it. As the royalist (q.v.) army began to assemble, however, on 9 January 1646 Oliver Cromwell (q.v.) attacked one section of it at its night quarters in Bovey Tracey. The royalists, caught by surprise, were defeated and lost 400 horses to the New Model. The defeat ended the prince's attempt to take on the New Model. In the wake of the catastrophe, the prince turned to Lord Hopton (q.v.), now in a form of retirement, to create a new army in the field.

BRADDOCK DOWN, BATTLE OF. Fought on 19 January 1642. Royalist (q.v.) forces under Sir Ralph Hopton (q.v.) were advancing into Devon, when Parliament's (q.v.) Western Army under the earl of Stamford (q.v.) was sent to stop them. Hopton was pushed back into Cornwall by Lord Ruthin's Plymouth (q.v.) forces. As Ruthin pursued Hopton into Cornwall he crossed Bodmin Moor. On 19 January, he detected what he believed to be straggling royalist troops to the east. He attacked them only to find that this was Hopton's main force, and that he had been lured into a trap. The startled parliamentarian forces were defeated and pursued into Lostwithiel (q.v.), over 1,200 were captured.

BRADFORD (YORKS). This town had strong links with Puritan (q.v.) thought imbued amongst its wool manufacturers and it resisted royalist (q.v.) control until it was captured after the Battle of Adwalton (q.v.) in June 1643. In March 1644 it became the centre of conflict and fell to the parliamentarians (q.v.) under John Lambert (q.v.) on 3 March. The Yorkshire royalists led by John Belasyse (q.v.) were under tremendous pressure to hold ground whilst the marquis of Newcastle (q.v.) was in the north trying to stem the advance of the Army of the Solemn League and Covenant (q.v.). Retaking Bradford was important if the royalists were to hold on to the West Riding of the county, but there were serious problems in the East Riding where garrisons at Driffield and Bridlington (q.v.) had fallen in February. An attempt to retake the town failed on 25 March, leaving Belasyse and the royalists deprived of a stronghold in the West Riding.

BRADSHAW, JOHN (1602–1659). A fairly obscure Cheshire lawyer, who after the First Civil War (q.v) had risen to be chief justice of Chester, Bradshaw was thrust into the centre of affairs when he was chosen as the president of the High Court of Justice (q.v.), which tried the king. His management of the court was not adept and King Charles I (q.v.) was able to dominate some of the proceedings. After the trial Bradshaw became the president of the first Council of State (q.v.), but as his relationship with Oliver Cromwell (q.v.) was poor, he did not play a prominent part in the Republican years. He died in 1659, but his body was exhumed from Westminster Abbey at the Restoration (q.v.)

BRAMPTON BRYAN (HEREFORDSHIRE). This parliamentarian (q.v.) garrison on the Welsh border proved an annoyance to royalist (q.v.) forces in the region, particularly those operating from Hereford and Abbey Cwm Hir in Radnorshire. The garrison was commanded by Lady Brilliana Harley (q.v.) from the outset of the war until her death on 31

October 1643. The garrison was besieged from 26 July 1643 to 9 September by Sir William Vavasour, and the siege only ended when the royalists were required at the siege of Gloucester (q.v.). The castle was besieged again in spring 1644 and fell after a three-week struggle.

BRENTFORD, BATTLE OF. Fought on 12 November 1642. Having garrisoned Oxford, King Charles I (qq.v.) belatedly marched towards London on 12 November following the Great Western Road, north of the Thames. Two regiments were stationed in the town, Lord Brooke's and Denzil Holles's (qq.v.). Behind them were amassing the London Trained Bands (q.v.) and the earl of Essex's (q.v.) army, which had marched back to London via Warwick, after the Battle of Edgehill (q.v.). Prince Rupert (q.v.) and the royalist Horse (qq.v.) crashed into the town, but were held up for some time by the two regiments, supported by a third, John Hampden's (q.v.), which arrived later in the day. Although the royalists eventually captured the town, the delay caused by the parliamentarian (q.v.) defence allowed for the assembly of the huge army at Turnham Green (q.v.), which was determined to keep the king out of London.

BRERETON, SIR WILLIAM (1604–1661). Brereton led early attempts to defeat the royalists (q.v.) in his native Cheshire. His tireless campaigning prevented the royalists from ever establishing a firm grip on the county. In spring 1645 he successfully interfered in the royalist control of Staffordshire, successfully capturing Wolverhampton and establishing a garrison at Stafford. He was prominent in attempts to capture control of North Wales, which would have isolated Chester and would have limited the potential for landing troops from Ireland in the area. As the royalist cause declined Brereton hemmed in the Chester garrison, besieging the town in spring 1645 and again in the autumn with help from Michael Jones (q.v.). Once the town surrendered in February 1646, Brereton set about reducing the remaining royalist garrisons in the Midlands, including Tutbury, Dudley, and Lichfield (q.v.). He defeated the last royalist Field Army at the Battle of Stow on the Wold (q.v.) in March 1646.

BRIDGEMAN, SIR ORLANDO (1606–1674). Bridgeman was an M.P. before the war and sat at the Oxford Parliament (q.v.) in 1644. During the First Civil War (q.v.) he served as the earl of Derby's (q.v.) commander in Cheshire, where he secured Chester for the royalists (q.v.) early in the war. During the winter of 1643–44 he was prominent in securing the region for the landing of troops from Ireland. This success marked his retirement from local active service and he went on to serve as an M.P. at Oxford (q.v.). In 1660 he presided over the trials of the regicides (q.v.)

BRIDLINGTON. A dual settlement in the East Riding of Yorkshire; one part was concentrated on the site of the old Augustinian Priory of St Mary, the other, Bridlington Quay, around a harbour at the mouth of the Gypsey Race. Queen Henrietta Maria (q.v.) landed here with arms and ammunition on 23 February 1643 after sailing from the United Provinces. Her party was bombarded from the sea after she landed, and the queen had to take shelter in the river valley, until her Dutch escort ships put themselves between the parliamentarian (q.v.) vessels and the quay. Her landing brought two advantages to the royalists (q.v) in the region: first, a supply of ammunitions and weapons, which allowed for the creation of a new army, formed to eventually escort the queen south with the rest of the weapons. Second, the queen's arrival led to the parliamentarian governor of Scarborough, Sir Hugh Cholmley, changing sides. This defection enabled the royalists to dominate the east coast down towards Hull (q.v.).

BRISTOL. The second port in the country, Bristol was in the hands of parliamentarian (q.v.) sympathisers at the outset of the war, but by the summer of 1643 was the central target of royalist (q.v.) campaigns in the west in spring and summer 1643. Following the royalist victory at the Battle of Roundway Down (q.v.) on 13 July, Sir Ralph Hopton (q.v.) occupied Bath, where he was joined by Prince Rupert and Prince Maurice (qq.v.). The initial summons to surrender Bristol was made on 24 July, but it was rejected by the governor, Nathaniel Fiennes (q.v.). On 26 July the royalists stormed the town. Led by Dorothy Hazard and Joan Batten, at one point a group of women in the town held up the royalist attack on the Frome gate when the soldiers lost heart; but at the end of the day Fiennes surrendered. Bristol then became the royalists' main seaport, and from March 1645 it was the centre of the devolved royalist administration of the south-west led by Prince Charles and his court.

In summer 1645, following the defeat of Lord George Goring (q.v.) at the Battle of Langport (q.v.), Bristol was threatened by the New Model Army (q.v.). By this time Rupert was the governor and he initially believed that, because the defences were improved and his garrison was larger than Fiennes's had been, he could hold the port for some months. By 28 August the New Model had closed in and taken one of the outlying forts. On 10 September the town was stormed. Whilst the storm was only partly successful, Rupert's forces were defeated and trapped and he sued for surrender that night. On 11 September the royalists left the city. The seeming precipitous surrender ended Rupert's role in the First Civil War (q.v.). Although he sought and was cleared by court martial of treasonable action, his uncle did not place trust in him again.

BRISTOL, JOHN DIGBY, EARL OF (1580–1653). Bristol, a former ambassador to Spain, fell out of royal favour after the failure of the attempted Spanish match in 1623. By 1642 he was back in King Charles I's (q.v.) council and with the king at the Battle of Edgehill (q.v.). After the battle Bristol advised against a direct march on London. During the winter of 1643–44, Bristol became involved in negotiations between the members of the Peace Party (q.v.)—who opposed the proposed Presbyterian (q.v.) church settlement, and the king, involving the retention of the episcopate (q.v.), but the removal of present incumbents. These negotiations faltered on the king's unwillingness to commit himself to them. Bristol retired from the centre of royalist politics the following spring.

BROOKE, ROBERT GREVILLE, LORD (1608–1643). Lord Brooke along with Lord Saye and Sele (q.v.), refused to assist King Charles I (q.v.) in the wars against the Scots, for which they were questioned at York. They objected to the king's attempt to alter the form of worship in the Scottish kirk (q.v.). Brooke produced a pamphlet attacking the episcopate (q.v.) in England, *A Discourse Opening the Nature of That Episcopacie which is Exercised in England.* In 1642 he raised a purple-coated regiment of Foot (q.v.) that included John Lilburne (q.v.) amongst its officers. With these troops Brooke contested control of Warwickshire with the earl of Northampton (q.v.) in the summer. The regiment fought at the Battle of Brentford (q.v.). Brooke was given command of the counties of Warwickshire and Staffordshire in 1642, and in March that year was killed as he tried to capture Lichfield (q.v.) from the royalists.

BROTHERLY ASSISTANCE. Also known as the Solemn League and Covenant (q.v.), this was the engagement between the Scots and the Parliament (q.v.) in Westminster in which the Scots agreed to invade the north of England in support of Parliament. It also applied to the financial provision that was made for the Army of the Solemn League and Covenant (q.v.). From November 1643 £30,000 per month was to be raised in England and Wales as a supplementary tax. John Pym (q.v.) had ensured that the first levy would reach Scotland as the Solemn League was signed in Edinburgh on 23 November 1643. The levy was raised in the form of a monthly forced loan on all communities within Parliament's control. The money was in serious arrears by the end of the First Civil War (q.v.).

BUNBURY, TREATY OF. This was a locally negotiated truce in Cheshire in 1642. The royalists' (q.v.) attempts to overrun the county stalled when local people under Henry Mainwaring of Kerchincham rose up in objection to locally imposed taxes. In December, Mainwaring welded these neutralists into a force that overran the east of the county, penning Sir Orlando Bridgeman (q.v.) in Chester. In response Bridgeman and Mainwaring negotiated a treaty at Bunbury on 22 December. Whilst King Charles I (q.v.) accepted this deal, as it bought the royalists time and secured their precarious hold on the west of the county, Parliament (q.v.) was angry at the treaty and dispatched Sir William Brereton (q.v.) to bring it to an end. His arrival in the area in mid-January 1643 ended the treaty.

BUNYAN, JOHN (1628–1688). Born into an artisan family in Elstow in Bedfordshire, during the First Civil War (q.v.), Bunyan fought for the parliamentarians (q.v.) from 1644, serving in Richard Cochayne's regiment in the garrison at Newport Pagnell. In 1647 he volunteered for service in Ireland, but his regiment did not get beyond Chester. In the garrison Bunyan was exposed to radical preachers, possibly even William Erbury and George Fox (qq.v.). In 1649 Bunyan's wife (about whom we know little, not even her name) introduced him to religious writings and he developed an Independent (q.v.) outlook, joining a congregation in Bedford. By 1657 he had been accepted as a preacher. From the beginning of the Restoration (q.v.) his radical position led to him being imprisoned. For most of the next 12 years Bunyan remained in Bedford Gaol, where amongst other writings he composed *Grace Abounding to the Chief of Sinners*, published in 1666, and *Pilgrim's Progress*, published in 1678.

BURFORD MUTINY. In May 1649, during the Leveller (q.v.) mutiny, Oliver Cromwell (q.v.) and the loyal New Model (q.v.) regiments fought at Burford. Whilst Levellers were losing sympathy amongst some previous supporters, including the Baptists (q.v.), they were able to take advantage of a schism in the army. As in 1647 this centred on the attempt to force veterans to serve in Ireland. The Levellers produced *The English Soldier's Standard,* which called for the recreation of the General Council of the Army (q.v.) and for the acceptance of the *Agreement of the People* (q.v.). They also questioned the moral rights of the English in Ireland. Some troops mutinied in London over arrears of pay, and as a result one of the soldiers, Richard Lockyer (q.v.), was executed outside St Paul's. A regiment en route for embarkation at Bristol (q.v.) refused to leave Salisbury. In Oxfordshire William Thompson (q.v.) gathered disaffected troops around him at Banbury (q.v.). Cromwell marched quickly from London surprising the rebels at Burford in the early hours of 14 May 1649. About 340 men were captured and sentenced to death: three, Cornet James Thompson (brother of William) and Corporals Church and Perkins (the Burford Martyrs), were shot in the churchyard on 17 May.

BURNHAM HEATH, KENT. During the Kentish Revolt, part of the Second Civil War (q.v.), the rebels and royalists (q.v.) mustered here before marching to London on 29 May 1648. The earl of Norwich (q.v.) was appointed commander. On 1 June, Norwich failed to assist the rebels at Maidstone (q.v.) when Thomas Fairfax (q.v.) stormed the town. Many of the rebels gave up the fight, but Norwich led the rest towards London, and failing to get into the city, sailed his forces across the Thames into Essex, where they headed for Colchester (q.v.).

BURTON, HENRY (1578–1648). Along with John Bastwicke and William Prynne (qq.v.), Burton was pilloried and cropped in 1637 for sedition. He was released from prison by the Long Parliament (q.v.). Unlike the other two, Burton had broader beliefs concerning toleration and became an Independent (q.v.), opposed to the Presbyterianism (q.v.) of his fellow sufferers. He believed that the Civil War marked the beginning of Armageddon and that the rebellion in Ireland was proof of this. In 1644 he published *Vindication of Churches Commonly Called Independent.*

BYRON, JOHN, LORD (1599–1652). Byron's most important role in the war was as field marshal of North Wales at the end of 1643. He took over from Lord Capel (q.v.), and with the assistance of Orlando Bridgeman (q.v.) and others prepared the area for the arrival of troops from Ireland. In January 1644 he set about the capture of Nantwich in Cheshire, but was defeated at the Battle of Nantwich (q.v.) on 25 January. The defeat resulted in the capture or dispersal of most of the troops shipped from Ireland thus far. Byron's position in the region crumbled. In the summer of 1644 Byron joined Prince Rupert's (q.v.) march for the relief of York (q.v.). At the Battle of Marston Moor (q.v.) Byron's precipitous action in leading the right flank of the royalist Horse (qq.v.) forward resulted in the defeat of that wing, and perhaps to the loss of the battle itself. Byron was brother to Sir Richard Byron (q.v.) and nephew of Sir Nicholas (q.v.). In 1646 he went into exile.

BYRON, SIR NICHOLAS (1600–?). Sir Nicholas was experienced in company command in Europe and was prominent in the early attempts by King Charles I (q.v.) to establish a military presence in the South Midlands. In 1643 he commanded the centre of the royalist (q.v.) army at the first Battle of Newbury (q.v.), where he and his nephew John led the successful attack on Round Hill. Earlier in 1643 he had served in Cheshire, and returned again at the end of the year. He was appointed governor of Chester in January 1644, but was captured before taking up the appointment. This marked the end of his military career.

BYRON, SIR RICHARD, SECOND LORD BYRON (1600–1679). Richard Byron served in the South Midlands before being appointed governor of Newark (q.v.) towards the end of 1643. His was a Nottinghamshire family and his three brothers also served on the royalist (q.v.) side. He survived a three-week siege in March 1644 and strengthened the town's defences afterwards. His career at Newark ended after the Battle of Denton in October 1646, when his forces and those of Lord Loughborough (q.v.) were defeated in Lincolnshire. In the 1650s he returned to the family homes at Strelley and Newstead.

↩ **C** ↪

CASTLEHAVEN, GEORGE T(O)UCHET, THIRD EARL OF (?1617 –1684). Castlehaven joined Charles I (q.v.) to fight in the first Bishop's War (q.v.) at Berwick, but when he offered to help fight the rebels during the Irish Rebellion (q.v.) his offer was refused because he was a Roman Catholic (q.v.); instead he was imprisoned in 1642. When he escaped, Castlehaven joined the Catholic Confederation of Kilkenny (q.v.). In 1644 he was appointed above Owen Roe O'Neill (q.v.) to command the campaign against Robert Monro (q.v.).

In 1646 Castlehaven changed sides and left Ireland with the marquis of Ormond (q.v.) in 1647, having advised handing Dublin to Parliament (qq.v.) rather than the confederates. He returned with Ormond in 1648, when Castlehaven was appointed to command the Horse (q.v.). He was present at the Battle of Rathmines (q.v.). From 1649 he was commander of the Army of Leinster (q.v.). Castlehaven fought in Ireland until 1651 when he left for Europe; there he fought in France and then in the Spanish army before returning to England at the Restoration (q.v.).

CATHOLIC. An adherent of the Church of Rome. Catholics formed the minority of the population in England, Wales, and and Scotland, where stringent laws were sporadically enacted to exclude or marginalise them. Open practice of the liturgy of the Catholic Church was forbidden. In Ireland Catholics were in the majority, but generally were similarly excluded from power and authority. Because of their apparent adherence to an outside power, the pope, Catholics were regarded as political and religious enemies of the state and therefore they were dealt with more harshly by the parliamentarians (q.v.).

CATHOLIC CONFEDERATION OF KILKENNY. This was the independent government of Ireland established in 1642 in the wake of several meetings of the clergy held at Kells in March. The clergy and leaders of the rebellion from the four provinces met at Kilkenny (q.v.) on 10 May 1642 and formed the Confederation. The Confederation was seen as a temporary expedient and accepted as quasi-legal, acting on behalf of King Charles I (q.v.) even though it was engaged in fighting the king's lieutenant, the marquis of Ormond (q.v.). The Confederation established a government structure consisting of a Supreme Council (executive) and a General Assembly (legislative), based on parliamentary precedent and an electoral system, whilst avoiding the title "Parliament" (q.v.).

Within the Confederation were several factions each with secular and religious elements: the Irish who had risen in 1641; returning exiled Irish; and Old English (q.v.). These factions did not always co-operate. In secular terms the returning exiles were asking for the return of lands confiscated after the Nine Years War, religious elements wanted a full, open, and restored Catholic (q.v.) church. The 1641 Rebels were more reluctant to demand full restorations of land, as some of them had benefited from confiscations, although they wanted a restored Church too. The Old English were less concerned with either element, seeking protection against the political and religious domination of the New English (q.v.) and the New Scots, and they actively sought terms with the king that would leave the Catholic church only covertly tolerated.

Despite these rifts the Confederation imposed order on the rebellion, appointing generals to the four provinces, holding a General Assembly from 24 October 1642, and instituting taxation—the general applotment (q.v.) and customs and excise (q.v.) levies. The Confederation factions were divided on their varying willingness to deal with Ormond. Whilst for the most time the Ormondist faction of the Old English dominated affairs, the more radical Irish faction was supported by the Nuncio Rinuccini (q.v.) and held sway from September 1646 following the king's defeat in England and Wales. This resulted in a refusal to compromise with the king who was in no position to agree to Rinuccini's terms. By 1648 the clerical faction's position was challenged, Rinuccini left Ireland, and the Confederation sided with Ormond. This grand alliance of royalists (q.v.) and Catholics was only powerful on paper and against the concerted attacks of first Michael Jones (q.v.) and then Oliver Cromwell (q.v.), who was in turn superseded by Henry Ireton (q.v.), the Confederation collapsed in the war of 1649–53.

CALLANDER, BATTLE OF. Fought on 13 February 1646. Under instructions from the marquis of Argyll (q.v.), refugee Campbells driven from their lands by Alasdair MacColla's (q.v.) forces were being led by James Campbell of Ardkinglas towards the Lowlands to be formed into a new regiment. On their way they captured the castle at Loch Dochart and received reinforcements from the Menzies and the Stewarts of Balquhidder. When they reached Callander, however, they were attacked by a small Highland force under James Grahame and John Drummond and were defeated.

CARBERY, RICHARD VAUGHAN, EARL OF (1600–1686). From a powerful family in Carmarthenshire, Carbery remains somewhat obscure, although he had served as an M.P. In March 1643 he took command of the royalist (q.v.) forces in south-west Wales, an area that avoided fighting into the summer of 1643 despite the armed presence of both sides. Using diplomatic rather than military means, Carbery conquered most of the parliamentarian (q.v.) strongholds in Pembrokeshire by the end of the year. However, a counterattack by Rowland Laugharne and John Poyer (qq.v.) had driven the royalists out of the county again by the end of spring 1644. Carberry was recalled to Oxford (q.v.) after trying to negotiate a local peace treaty and the parliamentarians went on to conquer Carmarthenshire and Cardiganshire. Carbery did not join the 1648 rising in south-west Wales and remained at peace with the Republican regimes.

CARY, MARY. Cary was a Fifth Monarchist (q.v.) who believed that the Civil Wars, and in particular the New Model Army (q.v.) were preparations for the millennium. She produced political tracts on the theme of millenarianism (q.v.), including *The Resurrection of the Witnesses*, averring that the army had from 5 April 1645 been the witnesses to God's overthrow of the beast that had terrorised the world since the beginning of the Rebellion in Ireland. She continued this theme into the 1650s in commentaries on *Daniel*, such as the *Little Horns Doom and Downfall* (1653), at a time when the little horn was being identified as Oliver Cromwell (q.v.), an agent of the last of the earthly monarchies. Whilst exhorting people to take up arms to fight for Sion, Cary took care to identify the nature of her Utopia, and it has been remarked that her vision was intensely female, granting a real, not purely spiritual equality to women, from whom burdens such as infant mortality would be removed.

CARBISDALE, BATTLE OF. Fought on 27 April 1650. The marquis of Montrose (q.v.), the newly appointed lieutenant general of Scotland, had gone to the Baltic States in 1649 to try to raise troops for a landing in Scotland. In the meantime Prince Charles (q.v.) succeeded in coming to terms with the Scots himself and abandoned Montrose. In March 1650 Montrose arrived at Kirkwall in Orkney. From there he crossed to Scotland landing near John O'Groats on 12 April. On 27 April he was attacked by Lieutenant Colonel Archibald Strachan and three troops of Horse (q.v.), a company of musketeers, and 400 local levies. Montrose's raw recruits were easily outclassed although his Danish troops put up a fight. Montrose was capture and later executed.

CAPEL, ARTHUR, LORD (1610–1649). Born in Essex, and educated at Cambridge University, Capel opposed the levy of ship money (q.v.) as M.P. for Hertfordshire in both the Short and Long Parliaments (qq.v.). After the execution of the earl of Strafford (q.v.), however, he shifted his allegiance and was ennobled in the summer of 1641. In 1642 he fought in the royalist (q.v.) army at the Battle of Edgehill (q.v.) and in 1643 was appointed to command Cheshire, the northern Marches, and North Wales. Whilst his command was marked with some success in its early days, by the fall of 1643 parliamentarians (q.v.) had made serious incursions into his command. In December his command was given to the marquis of Ormond (q.v.) who, as he was remaining in Ireland, ceded the operational control to John Byron (q.v.). Capel returned to Oxford (q.v.), where he remained until 1645 when he was sent into the west with Prince Charles (q.v.). In 1646 he fought alongside Ralph, Lord Hopton (q.v.) at the Battle of Torrington (q.v.). He then went into exile via the Isles of Scilly in France, but had returned to his estates by 1648. In June that year he joined the Essex rebels and ended up in the garrison at Colchester (q.v.). Taken prisoner at the surrender, Capel was tried and sentenced to death by the High Court of Justice (q.v.). He, the earl of Holland, and the duke of Hamilton (qq.v.) were beheaded on 9 March 1649.

CASE OF THE ARMIE TRULY STATED. Published in mid-October 1647, this pamphlet bridged Leveller and Agitator (qq.v.) demands and proposals for the settlement of the nation. The army commanders were castigated for having let the rank and file down and for having treated with King Charles I (q.v.) in the creation of the *Heads of the Proposals* (q.v.) without consulting them. The grandees (q.v.) were also criticised for seeming to have abandoned the cause of soldier's pay and conditions for which they had seemed to stand up in the summer of 1647. Whilst a fairly rambling document, possibly drafted by John Wildman and Robert Everard (qq.v.), the arguments in it were refined in the *Agreements of the People* (q.v.) issued a fortnight or so later.

CAVALIER. This was the nickname given to supporters of King Charles I (q.v.) as early as 29 December 1641, during the Westminster (q.v.) riots. Initially this was a reference to "cavaliero" Catholic (q.v.) Spanish soldiers. The royalists (q.v.) themselves took to using the name, however, endowing it with more romantic and loyal associations.

CESSATION. After the formation of the Catholic Confederation at Kilkenny (q.v.) in late 1642, attempts were made to forge an agreement between it and the forces under the marquis of Ormond (q.v.). The Confederation aimed at constructing a lasting peace guaranteeing some degree of religious freedom for the Catholic (q.v.) Irish, although within this broad aim lay the divergent objectives of the Old English (q.v.) and the Old Irish. King Charles I (q.v.) wanted to secure peace so that he could draw troops back from Ireland to assist him in England and Wales. Stalemate in the war during 1643 also provided impetus, and with the help of the earl of Clanricarde (q.v.), Ormond and the Confederates reached agreement on 15 September. The Cessation was not all embracing, the Scottish forces in the north continued fighting and Irish raids on territories ascribed to English garrisons caused trouble elsewhere. Nevertheless, the Cessation did free thousands of troops for the king and they were shipped to Bristol (q.v.), Chester, and North Wales at the end of the year. Within the Confederation the Old Irish, supported by the representatives of the pope, first Pier Francesco Scarampi and then Giovanni Battista Rinuccini (qq.v.), bridled against the agreement with Ormond as it embraced no guarantees on religious issues.

CHARLES I (1600–1649). Born in Dunfermline, the second son of James VI of Scotland, later became King James I of England and Ireland, Charles was heir to the three thrones after the death of his brother Henry in 1612. Charles had suffered rickets as an infant and was plagued with a stutter for most of his life, these ailments, it has been argued, left him insecure, and his sudden thrust into the role of heir put him into a position for which he was ill prepared. When Charles became king in 1625 his relationship with Parliament (q.v.) declined after a promising start. In 1623 Charles had been sent to Spain by his father to try to arrange a marriage with the infanta. He was, however, rebuffed. His failure made him the ally of an anti-Spanish Parliament. Financial problems beset his dealings with the English and Welsh Parliament, and the king dispensed with it temporarily at first and then in the long term from 1629, whilst he sought funding from a variety of obsolete means, including forest fines, exactions from wards of court, and new applications of traditional taxes such as ship money (q.v.).

Religious issues centred on Charles's promotion of William Laud (q.v.), misinterpreted as favoring Roman Catholicism (q.v.), which plagued his relationships with the Parliaments in England and eventually

Scotland, although the decision to strengthen Bishop's structures in the kirk (q.v.) angered the Scottish people most, driving them to open revolt by 1638. Only in Wales and Ireland did his rule remain intact until the 1640s, but in Ireland this was due to the rigorous rule of Thomas Wentworth, earl of Strafford (q.v.), which only temporarily suppressed opposition rather than ending it. The Bishop's Wars (q.v.) opened the floodgates of opposition and resulted in a political revolution in Scotland emulated in England and desired in Ireland. Against opponents in four nations Charles was powerless.

Nevertheless the king was a born conspirator and sought advantage in every relationship. He tried to overturn the Scottish Revolution in 1641, in the wake of the failed Army Plot (q.v.) in England, and sought to create an army ostensibly for use in Ireland, but probably intended for use against Parliament in early 1642. During the First Civil War (q.v.) Charles sought support from Ireland, first, in the form of troops sent there to quell the rebellion and then from Catholic Irish soldiers recruited by the Catholic Confederation of Kilkenny (q.v.). He also tried to destabilise Scotland through the military intervention of the earl of Montrose and Alasdair MacColla (qq.v.). In the end military defeat in England and Wales overcame all of his intrigues. In 1647–48, however, he sought to turn Scotland against England, and the English Independents (q.v.) against the English Presbyterians (q.v.), and to create an alliance with the Confederation that would have had the effect of alienating all other groups. His alliance with a section of the Scottish political elite, resulting in the Engagement (q.v.) and the Second Civil War (q.v.), ended in disaster and raised the issue of his trial.

At the end of 1648 Charles was brought from prison on the Isle of Wight to Westminster (q.v.) and in January 1649 put on trial before a High Court of Justice (q.v.). It was a show trial with one verdict and one sentence. Charles was found guilty of treason against the people of England (not the other nations) despite eloquent and stutter-free statements of law and right. On 30 January 1649, King Charles was executed in front of the Westminster Banqueting Hall. His political testimony, *Eikon Basilike* (q.v.), was published quickly and aided the conversion of the "man of blood" (q.v.) into a martyr.

CHARLES II (1630–1685). Born in 1630, Prince Charles was the eldest son of Charles I and Queen Henrietta Maria (qq.v.). From 1638 his tutor was the earl of Newcastle (q.v.). In 1641 he played his first overt political role, taking a plea from his father to the House of Lords (q.v.) asking for the life of Thomas Wentworth, earl of Strafford (q.v.), then under sentence of death, to be spared. Newcastle was replaced by a leading figure in opposition politics, the marquis of Hertford (q.v.), in an attempt to win public approval. Attempts in February 1642 to keep the prince under parliament's tutelage failed when the king snatched his son from Greenwich before a commission from Parliament (q.v.) arrived.

During the First Civil War (q.v.), with honorific commands, Charles accompanied his father. In 1645 he was given nominal command of the royalist (q.v.) forces in the west of England with a court of his own established at Bristol (q.v.). It was a short appointment and the command was swept away by the defeat of the king's forces across the country. Charles went into exile first in the Isles of Scilly and then Jersey before going to join his mother in France. During the Second Civil War (q.v.) the prince commanded the royalist fleet with little effect. In 1650 he went to Scotland, where after the defeat of the Scottish Army at the Battle of Dunbar (q.v.) he was crowned king of Britain. In 1651 he led a new army into England where it was defeated at Worcester (q.v.) on 3 September, a year after Dunbar. At six feet, the young king was unusually tall for his day, potentially making him easy to identify. A dramatic escape followed the Battle of Worcester, with the king being pursued through the West Midlands and the south before embarking for France. Charles Stuart remained in exile in France and the Netherlands for the remainder of the 1650s. Agents on both sides of the Channel plotted his return to the throne, with little success. In the end it was the internal collapse of the Protectorate (q.v.), which left Charles as the only candidate considered likely to bring stability to the British Isles, that restored Charles to the throne in 1660. His rule oversaw the sweeping away of the legacy of much of the previous 22 years, and the repression of dissenting sects. He reigned until 1685.

CHARLES, PRINCE. *See* CHARLES II.

CHERITON, BATTLE OF. Fought on 28 March 1644. In the winter of 1643–44 Sir William Waller (q.v.) had met with some success in defeating the royalists' (q.v.) attempts to approach London south of the Thames. In March the campaign began again with Waller on the offensive and Ralph, Lord Hopton (q.v.) determined to stop him. On 28 March Hopton drove off the musketeers that had been sent through Cheriton Wood by Waller overnight. Hopton was nominally under the command of Lord Forth (q.v.), who did want the whole army to attack Waller. This caution led to a gap developing between the royalist centre and the exposed right flank. Waller exploited this, driving back the royalists and forcing their eventual orderly retreat. Hopton's army was later drafted into the Oxford field army (q.v.).

CHIDLEY, KATHERINE. Chidley was an Independent (q.v.) who lived in London. From 1641 onwards she published tracts, including *The Justification of the Independent Churches to Christ*, supporting the independence of congregations. In *Good Counsell to the Petitioners for Presbyterian Government that they may declare their faith before they build their Church* (1645), she especially attacked the Presbyterians (q.v.) for not adhering to God's word. Through pamphlets she also entered into debate with Thomas Edwards (q.v.), author of *Gangraena* (q.v.), over the consequences of Independency. Members of her family were associated with the Leveller (q.v.) movement and it is widely thought that she was the author of the 1649 *Petition of Women*, which clearly linked women into the property-owning power nexus by pointing out that the *Petition of Right* (q.v.) had implications for women too.

CLANRICARDE, ULICK BURKE, 5TH EARL OF (1604–1657). An opponent of Thomas Wentworth, later earl of Strafford (q.v.) in Ireland during the 1630s, Clanricarde and his father were instrumental in defeating the lord deputy's plans for plantations in Connaght. Despite being a Catholic (q.v.), he served with the king's army in the Bishop's Wars (q.v.). Unlike many of his family Clanricarde opposed the Rebellion and tried to hold Galway County aloof from the ensuing war. King Charles I (q.v.) appointed him one of the commissioners to receive the Remonstrance of the Catholics of Ireland in 1643 and from then on he was a principal negotiator and from 1644 commander of the royalist (q.v.) forces in Connaght. Despite his unique position—a Roman Catholic loyal to the king, related to principal Confederates—Clanricarde was unable to secure a lasting settlement. In 1649 he fought alongside the marquis of Ormond (q.v.) and succeeded him as lord deputy in 1650. In 1652 he surrendered at Galway. For his protection of Protestants (q.v.) in 1641, he was allowed to live in England on his Somerhill estates in Kent.

CLARENDON, EDWARD HYDE, EARL OF (1600–1674). Hyde was educated at Oxford University and later became a lawyer. His circle of friends included John Culpepper and Lucius Carey, Viscount Falkland (q.v.). In 1640 Hyde was elected to both the Short and Long Parliaments (qq.v,) where there the three men opposed the government of Charles I (q.v.); Hyde sat on several committees examining facets of the Personal Rule (q.v.). He was involved in drawing up the charges against the Earl of Strafford (q.v.). In the second session of the Long Parliament, Hyde became alienated from the opposition movement and was so angered by the *Grand Remonstrance* (q.v.) that he assisted the king draft his response to it.

Although he was now working with the king, Hyde was not told of the plot to arrest the Five Members (q.v.). He then had to spend some time working on improving the king's image after the debacle. Hyde joined the king at York in the spring of 1642 and remained with the royalists (q.v.) throughout the First Civil War (q.v.). In 1645 Hyde was sent to the west to work with Prince Charles (q.v.), and after the war went in to exile with the prince. After the death of Charles I Hyde remained as a principle advisor to Charles and strove to stop the prince from making alliances with Presbyterian factions (q.v.) in England and Scotland during the 1650s, which might have tied him too closely to any one faction. In 1658 Hyde was appointed Lord Chancellor, a role he took up in earnest at the Restoration (q.v.) when he was also made Earl of Clarendon.

Clarendon was at the forefront of the Restoration political settlement but acquired many political enemies. In 1667 they succeeded in driving him from office and Clarendon spent the rest of his life in exile. Clarendon had begun gathering material for a history of the civil wars during the 1640s and had written parts of it during his first exile. After 1667 he began again to work on the book, which was finished by 1674. The work, *The History of the Rebellion and Civil Wars in England*, was not published until 1702–1704.

CLASSES, ACT OF. Passed through the Scottish Estates by the newly dominant Kirk Party (q.v.) in 1650, the Act prohibited supporters of the Engagement (q.v.) and the marquis of Montrose (q.v.) from holding office. The Act placed these people in various categories or classes according to their "guilt." The effect was to deprive government of experienced politicians and the army of veteran commanders at the point when conflict between Scotland and England became open war. The lack of experienced army personnel was partly responsible for the Scots' defeat at the Battle of Dunbar (q.v.) on 3 September 1650. The Act was repealed the following spring.

CLEVELAND, JOHN (1613–1658). Cleveland was born in Loughborough, Leicestershire and educated at Cambridge, where he became a tutor. In February 1645 Cleveland was ejected for royalism (q.v.), and accompanied Sir Richard Willys to Newark (qq.v.) as judge–advocate in the garrison there. He wrote several poems attacking the parliamentarian (q.v.) regime, including *Upon Sir Thomas. . . .*, which satirised the lowly status of parliamentarian local government. In prose too he attacked local officials describing county committeemen as "the relics of regal government, but, like holy relics he outbulks the substance whereof he is remnant. There is a score of kings in a committee. . . ." Cleveland was imprisoned at Yarmouth in 1655, but was released by Oliver Cromwell (q.v.). His collection of work, *Poems*, was published in 1656.

CLONMEL, COUNTY WATERFORD. Hugh O'Neill (q.v.) defended the town of Clonmel against Oliver Cromwell's (q.v.) forces in 1650. At a time when garrisons across the south were falling to the English army, O'Neill's victory demonstrated that there had been potential in the Catholic Confederation of Kilkenny's (q.v.) alliance with the royalists (q.v.). O'Neill's defence withstood a storm attempt on 9 May, causing heavy casualties amongst the English forces. That night, O'Neill and the army slipped out of the town, leaving Cromwell to unwittingly accept the surrender of the demilitarised town the day following.

CLUBMEN. The Clubman movement was essentially neutralist with antecedents in fall 1642, when counties such as Lincolnshire and Staffordshire, and towns like Leicester, attempted to remain aloof from the war. Clubmen and women had fairly conservative aims, the orderly prosecution of the war with an end to indiscriminate taxation, the preservation of episcopacy (q.v.) and the Protestant religion, and agreement between King Charles I and Parliament (qq.v.) along the lines of the "political settlement" of 1641. In addition to these general grievances there were specific causes that may have been the inspiration behind the risings: in Worcestershire there was anger at the appointment of a Catholic (q.v.) nobleman to the leadership of the Marcher Association (q.v.); in Herefordshire, additional levies were unpopular; and in the south-west, the depredation of unruly soldiers.

COAT AND CONDUCT MONEY. This refers to the countrywide taxation in England and Wales used to support the Trained Bands (q.v.), when they were required in active service outside their home shire or in foreign campaigns. The levy covered the costs of food, arms, ammunition, and uniforms whilst the levies were being escorted (conducted) to musters where the treasury would take over. At the end of hostilities the tax would be repaid. There was widespread opposition to the tax during the Bishops' Wars (q.v.), which exacerbated the general taxation problems caused by ship money (q.v.). Opposition to the levy was also raised in the Short Parliament (q.v.).

COLBY MOOR, BATTLE OF. Fought on 1 August 1645. In spring 1645 the royalists (q.v.) in South Wales had driven their opponents back into Pembrokeshire. Defeat in England resulted, however, in the withdrawal from Wales of some of King Charles's (q.v.) forces under Sir Charles

Gerard (q.v.). The parliamentarian Rowland Laugharne (qq.v.) went on the offensive and defeated the royalists at Colby Moor near Haverford-west.

COLCHESTER, ESSEX. In 1642 the town was the scene of an attack by the populace on the home of the Lucas family, prominent local royalists (q.v.), which included Sir Charles (q.v.), a future general, and Margaret, the future Duchess of Newcastle (q.v.). In 1648 the town was subjected to a siege for almost 11 weeks. Remnants of the failed royalist risings in Kent and Essex made their way to the town and were immediately sur-rounded by Thomas, Lord Fairfax and the New Model Army (qq.v.). The besieged hoped for relief from either the royalist fleet under Prince Charles (q.v.) or the Engager Army (q.v.) under the duke of Hamilton (q.v.), which invaded England in July. In the end the fleet could not reach the mouth of the river Colne and Hamilton was defeated at the Battle of Preston on August 17 by Oliver Cromwell (q.v.). The townspeople were reduced to desperate straits, the army's horses and then domestic pets, rats, and so on became food. Fairfax refused to let the royalists evacuate the town's women and children, driving them back into the town when they were herded out of the gates. When the royalists surrendered, Fair-fax's council of war ordered that Sir Charles Lucas and Sir George Lisle (q.v.) be shot for breaking a previous parole. A third man, Bernard Gas-coine, was reprieved because of his Italian birth.

COMMISSION FOR THE PROPAGATION OF THE GOSPEL IN WALES. Established by the Act for the Better Propagation of the Gospel in Wales passed on 22 February 1650, the commission consisted of 71 members, 28 of whom were responsible for the north and 43 for the south. The commission was charged with removing unsuitable ministers from Welsh parishes and replacing them with men considered "godly." In three years 278 men were ejected. Far fewer were recruited and itinerant ministers had to be employed to serve vacant parishes. Elementary schools were also set up in Wales under the auspices of the commission.

COMMISSIONS OF ARRAY. Commissions of Array had their origins in the 13th century when they had been used to raise troops. During the 16th century, the county-based Commissions of Array fell into abeyance to be replaced by the Lieutenancy. Charles I (q.v.) resurrected them in the Second Bishops' War (q.v.) to circumvent the need to repay coat and con-duct money (q.v.), an obligation that could not be afforded in 1640. In 1642 there was a similar problem over payment of the troops Charles pro-posed to raise, but since the Militia Ordinance (q.v.) of March, Parliament (q.v.) controlled the mechanism of raising troops through the lord lieutenants (q.v.). The first commission of that year was directed to Lancashire at the end of May, most followed that of Leicestershire on 11 June. Parliament declared the issue of such commissions to be illegal and their enactment was fraught with difficulties and for the most part they failed in their immediate intent—the marshalling of the Trained Bands (q.v.). Commissions of Array were reinvigorated later in the year, becoming the principal county body charged with maintaining the royalist (q.v.) war effort throughout the First Civil War (q.v.).

COMMITTEE FOR THE ADVANCE OF MONEY. This committee, based at Haberdasher's Hall, London, was created in November 1642 to collect money for the parliamentarian (q.v.) cause at 8 percent interest. The levies were based on the fifth and twentieth levies (q.v.), at one-fifth of personal estate and one-twentieth of real estate. The principal levies collected by the committee included the weekly assessment (q.v.) until the beginning of 1645, when it was superseded by the monthly pay (q.v.). The committee could distrain goods in cases of default. The committee existed until 1655 with collections of military levies at the core of its purpose.

COMMITTEE OF BOTH KINGDOMS. Developed from the Committee of Safety (q.v.) in February 1644 to perform some executive duties in the wake of the entry of the Scots into the war in England and Wales. This committee met in Derby House, London. The committee directed military affairs south of the border; although perhaps it should have dealt also with the war in Scotland from 1644 onwards, it did little in this arena. In 1645 the committee exercised a heavy hand on the New Model Army (q.v.) during the siege of Oxford (q.v.), until King Charles I's (q.v.) capture of Leicester (q.v.) forced it to relax its grip. The committee became the Committee for Irish Affairs when the war ended south of the Scottish border and later was once again named the Committee of Safety.

COMMITTEE FOR COMPOUNDING WITH DELINQUENTS. This committee, located at Goldsmith's Hall, London, was established in 1644 to take responsibility for negotiating the recovery of property and estates belonging to royalists (q.v.), and from 1648 onwards, Roman Catholics (q.v.) with estates and so on worth £200 or more.

COMMITTEE OF ESTATES. This body replaced the Scottish Privy Council (q.v.) as the executive body of government during 1640–41 and again during the period of the Solemn League and Covenant (q.v.) from 1643 until the defeat of the Scots at Worcester (q.v.) in 1651. The membership of the committee was selected by the Estates (q.v.), and the committee continued sitting when the Estates were not in session. The last Committee of Estates was captured at Alyth, by the English army in August 1651, and the following year Scottish government was remodelled by the English Republic (q.v.).

COMMITTEE OF SAFETY. Created in the early days of the First Civil War (q.v.), this executive committee originally combined military and civilian matters and offered advice to the lord general, the earl of Essex (q.v.). By 1643 its exact role had become blurred, it failed to maintain proper communications between itself and the county committees (q.v.). By the end of 1643 it was packed with supporters of Essex, who strove to support the earl against criticism of his handling of the war. In 1644 the Committee of Safety was enlarged to become the Committee of Both Kingdoms (q.v.). The Committee of Safety was revived in 1648.

COMMONS, HOUSE OF. *See* PARLIAMENT.

COMMONWEALTH. England and Wales became a commonwealth and free state on 19 May 1649. Scotland and Ireland were incorporated into this body between then and 16 December 1653, when the Little or Barebones Parliament (q.v.) was dissolved and the Protectorate (q.v.) established.

COMMONWEALTHMEN. Name given to opponents of the army's role in dissolving the Rump and Barebone's Parliaments (qq.v.) and of Oliver Cromwell's (q.v.) powers as protector during the later Protectorate (q.v.) parliaments. Principal commonwealthmen included Edmund Ludlow, Henry Marten, and Sir Arthur Hesilrige (qq.v.), men who had been at the heart of the creation of the Republic (q.v.) in 1649–50 but who were now effectively excluded from the first Protectorate Parliament, as they were intent on debating the constitution, the Instrument of Government (q.v.). The commonwealthmen were instrumental in bringing down the Protectorship of Richard Cromwell (q.v.) in 1659 but failed to win many seats in the 1660 elections to a Convention Parliament.

COMPOSITION. This term refers to the sum of money based on estate value, paid by former royalists (q.v.), who wished to have sequestration (q.v.) removed from their estates. *See also* Compounding.

COMPOUNDING. The act of paying to the Committee for Compounding with Delinquents (q.v.) a specific fine based on a fixed proportion of an estate determined by the payer's involvement with the royalist (q.v.) cause after surrender or capture. Officers or administrators could be fined one-sixth the value of their estate. Major royalists could compound by being fined one-third or a half of their estates.

CONSTABLES. At the lower levels of English and Welsh county government were high or chief constables in charge of a district within a county, such as a hundred or wapentake. These officials communicated orders and instructions from a range of county administrators, including the sheriffs, justices of the peace, and lord lieutenants, to the parish-based petty constables. Petty constables were faced with the blunt edge of military finance, they had to allocate and collect taxation and were responsible for billeting soldiers on their communities. Surviving constables' accounts are a valuable source used to examine the financial burden of the Civil War.

CONTRIBUTION. This was the royalists' (q.v.) main weekly levy imposed throughout areas that they controlled in England and Wales. Income from contribution was to be the main source of money that supplied the garrisons and field armies. Allotments were made by the commissioners of array (q.v.), who also allocated its distribution amongst the garrisons in their county, possibly using proportions established in ship money (q.v.) collections. Traditional county divisions such as hundreds and wapentakes were used in the process of allocation. Garrisons were also responsible for collecting the levies on a regular basis from constables (q.v.). Contribution was collected in cash and in goods, with goods tending to be the smaller part of the collection, often a third of the value of the whole sum. Contribution collection broke down in many areas as the royalist cause waned, although in some areas, including that around Lichfield (q.v.) in Staffordshire, collections remained efficient up until the end of 1645.

COOTE, SIR CHARLES (?–1661). Son of the Sir Charles killed during the Irish Rebellion in 1642, Coote led the Protestant forces in north-west Ireland having raised Horse (q.v.) in Connacht in 1643. Coote's Roscommon garrisons bridled uneasily under the Cessation (q.v.) and frequently broke the terms of the treaty. In 1645 Coote joined the parliamentarians (q.v.) and was appointed their president of Connacht. He captured Sligo (q.v.) in June of that year and a string of other castles in the north. These he held throughout the 1640s despite the onslaughts of Owen Roe O'Neill (q.v.) in 1647. By 1648 Coote was president of Ulster (q.v.), and during O'Neill's separation from the Catholic Confederation of Kilkenny (q.v.) Coote and his former enemy tried to come to terms to defeat the Scots in Ulster, by this time enemies to the English Parliament (q.v.), to the Confederation, and to O'Neill. The truce benefited neither and Owen Roe returned to the Confederation and its alliance with the marquis of Ormond (q.v.), whilst the English Parliament censured Coote. In 1650 Coote's forces defeated the Ulster army at the Battle of Scariffhollis (q.v.) in County Donegal. Owen Roe O'Neill's son, Henry O'Neill (q.v.), was captured and executed on Coote's orders, and the Ulster army's commander, Ever MacMahon, Bishop of Clogher, was captured days later and hanged later that year, again on Coote's orders.

CORKBUSH FIELD, WARE. This was the site of the mutiny by regiments influenced by the Levellers (q.v.) in November 1647. In the wake of the collapse of the Putney Debates (q.v.), which in turn followed the escape of King Charles I (q.v.) from Hampton Court (q.v.), the Levellers sought to put their radical programme before the common soldiers. The army command declared against the meeting and only two regiments turned up in defiance of them. Thomas, Lord Fairfax and Oliver Cromwell (qq.v.) persuaded the regiments to return to duty and ripped the copies of the Leveller's *Agreement of the People* (q.v.) from the soldiers' hats. The ringleaders were tried for mutiny and sentenced to death. After drawing lots, one man was shot. This failure soured relations between the army and the Levellers, but did not end it, as it is possible that the escape of the king so threatened the peace that the soldiers saw that his defeat was more important than a new constitution.

COTES, BATTLE OF. Fought on 17–18 March 1644. Whilst Sir John Meldrum (q.v.) besieged Newark (q.v.) his Horse (q.v.) regiments attempted to prevent any relief attempt by Leicestershire royalist (q.v.) forces. After a skirmish north of Leicester (q.v.) on 16 March, the parliamentarians (q.v.) took possession of the east end of an important bridge over the River Soar at Cotes a day later. Royalists took up position on the opposite bank and skirmishing ensued on 17 March. A day later the parliamentarians, under Sir Edward Hartopp, drove the royalists off and occupied Loughborough. During the day at Ashby-de-la-Zouch, Lord Loughborough (qq.v.) sent more regiments towards Loughborough town and Prince Rupert's (q.v.) forces began to arrive at Ashby. Hartopp withdrew from Loughborough and Cotes, possibly because of the increasing numbers of royalists arriving, leaving the bridge free for Prince Rupert and Lord Loughborough's relief force to head quickly to Newark.

COUNCIL OF STATE. The first council was established as the executive in February 1649, and was consistently reformed and reconstituted after the dissolution of the Rump Parliament (q.v.) in 1653 by the Barebones Parliament (q.v.), and then during the Protectorate (q.v.). The Council was central to John Lambert's Instrument of Government (qq.v.) and a powerful check on the lord protector (q.v.). Under the second Protectorate constitution, the Council of State became far more dependent on Oliver Cromwell (q.v.) and subordinate to him.

COUNTY COMMITTEES. From late 1642 onwards, Parliament (q.v.) began to structure its war effort in each county. At the centre of this structure lay the county committee, comprised of men drawn from the gentry, preferably with experience in county administration. The general committees, sometimes referred to as militia committees, developed a series of subcommittees to deal with excise (q.v.) and accounts. Regional associations (q.v.) had committees made up of representatives from the county committees involved. County committees remained in place into the early 1650s.

COVENANT. *See* NATIONAL COVENANT.

COVENANTERS. This term could be applied to Scots who had signed the National Covenant (q.v.). Usually it was more strictly applied to the politically active signatories throughout the period 1638–60 and sometimes to the soldiers serving in the Scottish armies during the Bishop's Wars (q.v.) of 1639–40. The term could also be applied to English and Welsh signatories of the Solemn League and Covenant (q.v.) from 1644 onwards.

CRAWFORD, LAWRENCE, MAJOR GENERAL (1611–1645). Crawford served in the Eastern Association (q.v.) army and was one of Oliver Cromwell's (q.v.) principal critics, especially after his failure to defeat the royalists (q.v.) at the second Battle of Newbury (q.v.). Like the army commander, the earl of Manchester (q.v.), Crawford was a Presbyterian (q.v.); he accused Cromwell of radical religious and social intent. In the latter months of 1644, the argument led in part led to the Self Denying Ordinance (q.v.) and the creation of the New Model Army (q.v.). Crawford was killed at the siege of Hereford in 1645.

CROMWELL, HENRY (1628–1674). Whilst too young to have participated in the wars of the 1640s, Oliver Cromwell's (q.v.) youngest son, Henry, had risen to the rank of colonel by 1654, when his father sent him to examine the state of government in Ireland. In 1655 he was appointed major general in Ireland and in 1657, lord deputy. His rule in Ireland was marked by a period of attempted reconciliation between the new regime and the Protestant settlers known as the New English (q.v.). This marked the reversal of a phase when, under General Charles Fleetwood (q.v.), the radical religious elements in the army had striven for thorough godly reform in Ireland. After the Restoration (q.v.) he was allowed to go into retirement at Wicken in Cambridgeshire.

CROMWELL, OLIVER (1599–1658). Cromwell was born in Huntingdon and educated at the Free School there and later at Sidney Sussex College, Cambridge, although he did not take a degree. He married Elizabeth Bouchier in 1620. He sat as M.P. for his hometown in 1628. His financial fortunes declined in the early 1630s and his position in Huntingdon's governing classes was ended. Within a few years his fortunes revived through inheritances, although by this time he had moved to Ely. By the end of the 1630s he identified himself with the radical religious outlook and so became part of the opposition to the Short and Long Parliaments (qq.v.) of 1640. From the beginning of the latter, Cromwell's opposition to King Charles I (q.v.) became apparent and he was appointed to many important committees and campaigned for the release of John Lilburne (q.v.).

Cromwell's first military action was his prevention of the king's attempt to commandeer Cambridge University silver plate. Cromwell stopped the majority leaving the town and seized Cambridge castle's ammunition. Cromwell raised a troop of Horse (q.v.) later that summer, and although he was not on the field at the Battle of Edgehill (q.v.), he was prominent in actions in the following spring and summer in the east and north Midlands. That fall he was instrumental in destroying the royalist (q.v.) hold on much of Lincolnshire; he participated in the royalist's defeat at the Battle of Winceby (q.v.) on 11 October 1643. Cromwell reached an important point in his career when he was made lieutenant general of the Eastern Association Army (q.v.) under the earl of Manchester (q.v.). It was as leader of the Horse that he played a crucial part in the defeat of Prince Rupert and the marquis of Newcastle at Marston Moor (qq.v.) in July 1644. His role in the Newbury (q.v.) campaign in October and November that year was not as glorious as his work on the field. The resulting arguments between Cromwell and his commander led to an important political victory at the turn of the year when the New Model Army (q.v.) was created and the Self Denying Ordinance (q.v.) removed Manchester and the earl of Essex (q.v.) from command. The ordinance could also have removed Cromwell from command but he was, at Sir

Thomas Fairfax's (q.v.) insistence, appointed lieutenant general of the New Model. In 1645 he played a major part in the defeat of the royalists at the battles of Naseby, Langport, and at Bristol (qq.v.).

After the First Civil War (q.v.), Cromwell and Fairfax (q.v.) defended their soldiers against the attacks made on them by the Presbyterian-dominated House of Commons (qq.v.), which already regarded Cromwell's Independent (q.v.) tendencies as a threat. Even so, Cromwell held out against attempts by the Levellers (q.v.) and their sympathisers in the army for military support for radical political change. In 1648 Cromwell defeated the uprisings in Wales and then destroyed the Scots invasion force at the Battle of Preston (q.v.) on 17 August. Cromwell remained at the siege of Pontefract (q.v.) whilst his son-in-law, Henry Ireton (q.v.), and others devised and executed the purge of the House of Commons, but he returned in time to throw himself behind the trial and execution of the king.

Cromwell led the English forces sent to Ireland in August 1649 that perpetuated the brutalities of the war there by instigating massacres at Drogheda and Wexford (qq.v.), justified by misplaced claims of blood-guilt. On his return from Ireland, Cromwell took over command of the army from Fairfax and defeated the Scots, who were now in league with Charles II (q.v.), at the Battle of Dunbar (q.v.) on 3 September 1650. Exactly one year later Charles II's army was defeated by Cromwell at the Battle of Worcester (q.v.).

Cromwell again entered the political arena, defending the interests of the army. By 1652 he was convinced that the Parliament (q.v.) should dissolve itself but he was still considering a wide range of options, including a monarchy. By the time the Parliament began to discuss the nature of the new constitution, Cromwell and the officers had serious reservations and on 20 April he marched into the house with a detachment of soldiers and ended the session. Over the next weeks, Cromwell, with a small council of officers and politicians, managed the country whilst the Council of Officers devised an expedient constitution. This involved a nominated assembly of 140 members that would in turn devise a more lasting structure. This Little Parliament or Barebones Parliament (q.v.), lasted five of its projected 16 months. Moderate members opposed to the radical actions of a section of the assembly resigned, handing their powers to Cromwell.

Under the Instrument of Government (q.v.) of December 1653, Cromwell became lord protector (q.v.). In the Protectorate (q.v.) his powers were extensive, if generally restricted by having to work with the Council of State (q.v.) or Parliament. He held two Parliaments in his short rule, and relations were not always harmonious, sometimes because of disagreements over the nature of the constitution, especially in 1657 when a faction sought to offer him a crown. His work with the Council was thorough and exacting; he was conscientious in ensuring consular government. His premature death in 1658 prevented the thorough healing of bonds within the state at large and the polity—too much still rested upon him as the only person able to bridge the gap between the army and the political world. Five years was too short a time.

CROMWELL, RICHARD (1626–1712). Unlike his younger brother, Henry (q.v.), Richard Cromwell did not take up a career in the military. Much of his early life was sedentary and centred on study and the life of a country gentleman in Hampshire. Only in 1657, when Oliver Cromwell (q.v.) secured the nomination of his successor, was Richard brought into the government and appointed to the Council of State (q.v.), although even at this stage he was not accorded any powers. On the death of Oliver Cromwell in 1658 it was accepted that Richard would be the successor and he became the second lord protector (q.v.). His rather conservative surroundings in Hampshire where a Presbyterian (q.v.) church settlement was much in evidence promised something similar to his brother Henry's settlement in Ireland. Henry forged a working relationship between the Protestant gentry and the new regime at the expense of the religious radicals. The problem with this was that it alienated many of his father's allies in the army. The result was that when Richard's Parliament (q.v.) clashed head on with the army over pay and taxation he was powerless to control either, he had to accede to army demands that Parliament be dissolved, and in May he went into retirement and the Protectorate (q.v.) came to an end. Like his brother, he was largely untroubled during the Restoration (q.v.), although he left England in 1660. He returned to the country at the end of the century.

CROPREDY BRIDGE, BATTLE OF. Fought on 28 June 1644. The Oxford (q.v.) garrison came under increasing pressure from the earl of Essex and Sir William Waller (qq.v.) in the spring of 1644 following the defeat of Ralph, Lord Hopton at the Battle of Cheriton (qq.v.). By May, Reading and Abingdon were in Parliament's (q.v.) hands. King Charles I (q.v.) took charge of the army himself, and marched out of Oxford, threatening Waller's lines of communications at Abingdon before dramatically turning about and heading for Worcester (q.v.). Waller followed and Essex, glad to be free of his rival, set off for the south-west to tackle Prince Maurice (q.v.). The king dragged Waller across the Midlands before doubling back again to Banbury (q.v.), where he waited for Waller to return from Gloucester. On 28 June the royalist (q.v.) army set off north along the east bank of the River Cherwell with Waller once again trailing them on the west bank. At Cropredy, Waller seized his chance to defeat the straggling royalist forces and crossed the river at two points. His plan was to defeat the scattered sections of the king's army before they could unite, but unfortunately for him, his attempts to cross the river were themselves held up and his army could not unite on the other bank. Instead his forces were defeated and driven back over the Cherwell, and in the next few weeks Waller's army disintegrated.

➷ D ➷

D'AVENANT, SIR WILLIAM (1606–1668). Oxford (q.v.)-educated poet and dramatist who authored *The Wits* (1636), *Unfortunate Lovers* (1643), and masques during the 1630s. D'Avenant was implicated in royalist (q.v.) plots and fled to France. He returned to England with Henrietta Maria (q.v.) in 1643 and served at the siege of Gloucester (q.v.). He went again to France in 1645. In 1650 he was arrested at sea en route to Virginia and imprisoned in the Tower. Released in 1652, possibly through the influence of John Milton, he was imprisoned again in 1659 for involvement in George Booth's uprising that year. After the Restoration (q.v.), D'Avenant formed The Duke's Theatrical Company.

DAVIES, LADY ELEANOR (1590–1652). One of the period's most prolific prophetesses, she predicted the death of the Duke of Buckingham and the birth of Charles II (q.v.), but from 1633 began to foretell the death of Charles I (q.v.), which ended her court celebrity. During the 1640s and 1650s, although crippled by debt and periodic imprisonment, Lady Eleanor continued to publish her prophesies, and began to predict the millennium (millenarianism [q.v.]), having in 1648 hailed Oliver Cromwell (q.v.) as a "splendid sun." By 1650, in *The Appearance or presence of the Son of Man*, she seems to have predicted that a female deity would bring peace to the earth and associated herself with that deity.

DECIMATION TAX. A levy charged on former royalists (q.v.) in the wake of Pennruddock's rebellion in spring 1655. Royalists' estates were charged at one-tenth their value and the money was to be used for militia payments by the major generals (q.v.).

DECLARATION, THE. In June 1647, as Parliament (q.v.) and the army continued to become estranged, the New Model Army (q.v.) drew up this document calling for Parliament to be purged of its most vigorous opponents, including Denzil Holles (q.v.), who had drafted the Declaration of Dislike (q.v.), and for further remodeling of the present house. Parliament rejected The Declaration on 24 June, but as the army approached and a more conciliatory declaration was drafted, the 11 Presbyterian (q.v.) members left Westminster (q.v.).

DECLARATION OF DISLIKE. Drafted by Denzil Holles (q.v.), one of the Presbyterians (q.v.) in the House of Commons (q.v.), this document was targeted by the New Model Army (q.v.) in March 1647 as a rejection of the Petition of the Officers and Soldiers of the Army (q.v.). The declaration was only withdrawn after the army had marched closer to London and had issued The Declaration (q.v.) forcing eleven members of the Commons, including Holles, to flee Westminster.

DECLARATION OF THE GENERAL COUNCIL OF THE ARMY. This document, drafted in mid-January 1649, offered the General Council of the Army's (q.v.) support for the Four Bills (q.v.) passed by Parliament (q.v.) as a basis for negotiation with King Charles I (q.v.) the previous month. However, it also contained the warning that the settlement of the kingdom would go on with or without the king.

DELINQUENT. A term applied by royalists and parliamentarians (qq.v.) in England and Wales to their respective enemies. The term could be applied to both those active in service to the other side, and to those who simply supported one of the sides or was suspected of doing so.

DENBIGH, BASIL FIELDING, EARL OF (c.1608–1674). Son of the royalist (q.v.) commander killed at the storm of Birmingham (q.v.), he fought at the Battle of Edgehill (q.v.) for Parliament (q.v.). In 1643 Denbigh became commander of the associated counties of Shropshire, Staffordshire, Worcestershire, Warwickshire, and Northamptonshire. Doubts over his loyalty delayed his assuming command. When he did, in 1644 he pinned down the south Staffordshire royalists, but he did not work well with Sir William Brereton (q.v.) and they had rival factions on Staffordshire's County Committee (q.v.). His command came to an end in 1644 and he became a commissioner for the Treaty of Uxbridge (q.v.). Whilst not participating in the trial of Charles I (q.v.), Denbigh did serve on the Council of State (q.v.) from 1649–51. By the end of the decade he had become a royalist.

DERBY, JAMES STANLEY, SEVENTH EARL OF (1607–1651). As Lord Strange, he attended King Charles I at York (qq.v.), before attempting to storm Manchester in July, for which he was later accused of being the first to foment war. Again in October, now as the earl of Derby, he tried and failed to take the town. Nevertheless. his forces soon controlled Lancashire, but Manchester still stood out against the royalists (q.v.). His dominance of the area was short-lived, however, and he was defeated at the Battle of Whalley Bridge (q.v.) in the spring of 1643. In 1644 he assisted Prince Rupert's (q.v.) campaign in Lancashire, but thereafter left England, retiring to his estates on the Isle of Man, whilst his wife Charlotte Tremoille, Countess of Derby (q.v.), defended Lathom House (q.v.). Derby rejected any terms and in 1651 joined Charles II's (q.v.) campaign in England. He was captured at the Battle of Wigan Lane (q.v.), and tried for treason and beheaded in Bolton (q.v.).

DERBY, CHARLOTTE TREMOILLE, COUNTESS OF (1599–1664). During 1644 the countess defended Lathom House (q.v.) in Lancashire from parliamentarian (q.v.) attacks. She also was able to make attacks on the parliamentarian control in the county. In the spring of 1644 she defied Sir Thomas Fairfax's (q.v.) call to surrender. In June 1644 Prince Rupert (q.v.) deposited all of the colours captured in his recent campaign at the house as he progressed through Lancashire. The countess later joined her husband, the earl of Derby (q.v.), on the Isle of Man and was reputedly angry that it was surrendered to Parliament (q.v.) after her husband's capture.

DERBY HOUSE. The London home of the earl and countess of Derby (q.v.), this mansion was taken over for use by Parliament (q.v.) as the meeting place and offices of the Committee of Both Kingdoms (q.v.). The house gave rise to the committee being referred to as the Derby House Committee.

DERING, SIR EDWARD (1599–1644). This was a man of apparently vacillating opinions. He introduced the Root and Branch Petition (q.v.) into the Commons (q.v.) in 1641, but later defended the episcopacy (q.v.). In January 1642 he had been expelled from the Commons for publishing his speeches, some of which attacked John Pym (q.v.). In 1642, at the height of the spring crisis, whilst King Charles I (q.v.) was attempting to seize Hull (q.v.), Dering, M.P. for Kent, was associated with the Kentish Petition (q.v.). For this action he was impeached. He was to join the royalist (q.v.) forces once war broke out. In 1644 Dering left the royalist forces and compounded (q.v.) and took the National Covenant (q.v.); however, he died before regaining his estates.

D'EWES, SIR SIMONDS (1602–1650). One of the most consistent diarists of the 1640s Parliament (q.v.). D'Ewes, M.P. for Sudbury, was a moderate and a Presbyterian (q.v.) from a divided family. His brother, a royalist (q.v.) lieutenant colonel, was killed during the earl of Essex's (q.v.) attack on Reading in April 1643. D'Ewes joined the Peace Party (q.v.) in the Commons (q.v.) in late October 1642 in proposing peace negotiations in the wake of the Battle of Edgehill (q.v.), and he pressed the case again nearer Christmas that year. In August 1643, having witnessed the harsh treatment meted out to the women peace petitioners at Westminster when two women were killed, he savagely criticised their treatment in his diary. D'Ewes' Presbyterianism resulted in his expulsion from Parliament at Pride's Purge (q.v.) in December 1648.

DIGBY, GEORGE, LORD (1612–1677). Digby was in the House of Commons (q.v.) until his involvement with the Army Plot (q.v.) in 1641. After betraying the plan to Parliament (q.v.), he was readmitted and then sat in the House of Lords (q.v.). He was expelled in 1642 and became part of the royal court, where he was an enemy of Prince Rupert (q.v.), an animosity he was able to exercise in his position as gentlemen of the bedchamber to King Charles I (q.v.). In 1645 he took the field, leading the Northern Horse (q.v.) into the north of England to try and resurrect royalist (q.v.) fortunes. He was defeated at Carlisle Sands. In 1649 he was banished by Parliament and went into exile in France.

DIGGERS. In March 1649 the first colony of True Levellers (q.v.) established themselves at St George's Hill, London, on wasteland that was formerly the property of Charles I (q.v.). They began to farm the land and held all things in the colony in common. The Digger writers Gerard Winstanley and William Everard (qq.v.) stated the aims of the movement in *The True Leveller's Standard Advanced*, in which they claimed to be returning the earth to the "common treasury" established by God whereby mankind would have dominion over animals but not over each other, and that the produce of the land would be earned by the "sweat of our brows." They saw this change as happening through example, rather than by force. The landowners living near them regarded them as a threat and began to disrupt their colonies through use of the law and hired thugs. Within a year the colonies at St George's and Cobham, and perhaps all of the others scattered through the Midlands and the Home counties, had been abandoned. The Digger philosophy had roots in pantheism and in agrarian utopianism; the colony near Wellingborough showed the potential for the movement to aid practically the rural dispossessed and unemployed.

DIRECTORY OF PUBLIC WORSHIP. In January 1645 the *Book of Common Prayer* (q.v.) was abolished, and the *Directory*, drawn up by the Westminster Assembly of Divines (q.v.), established in its place. The *Directory* was essentially a self-help guide, which did not seek to establish anything but suggestions for services. After a slow introduction, perhaps only 10 percent of the country's parishes bought copies. In August 1645 parishes were again instructed to buy copies of the *Directory* and to hand in for destruction the old service books, although many were still tardy in doing this, even in areas where Parliament (q.v.) held sway. Some places continued with the old liturgy throughout the 1640s and 1650s, even in London.

DIVINE RIGHT. The belief that monarchs ruled by the will of God alone was supported in differing ways by James VI and I and his son Charles I (q.v.). This was an absolutist theory that suggested that the monarch was the fountain of all power and justice. Power therefore descended from those above: monarchs governed by God's will, magistrates and other lesser governors by the monarch's will. This could place a monarch above the law in certain contexts, raising the spectre of tyranny, a charge later levelled at Charles I in his trial. There was no role in this model for any ascending power, which left an elective chamber in Parliament (q.v.) in an ambivalent position and which probably coloured Charles's perception of the need to rule with the aid of Parliament at all.

DOBSON, WILLIAM (1611–1646). Dobson trained as an artist at the studio of William Peake, who was the son of the sergeant painter to James VI and I. After his apprenticeship he lived near the surveyor of Charles I's (q.v.) paintings and gained familiarity with the works of Titian, Van Dyke, Veronese, and Tintoretto in the royal collection. It is possible that Van Dyke introduced him to the king. It is not known how Dobson came to join the court at the king's Oxford (q.v.) capital during the war, but he was there by the end of March 1643. There he painted a succession of royalists (q.v.)—Prince Rupert, Prince Charles (Charles II), Lord Byron, and Sir Charles Lucas (qq.v.)—as well as Charles I himself. His later portraits show evidence of meagre resources. He remained in Oxford until the surrender and then returned to his London home, but by the end of the year he was dead.

DONNINGTON CASTLE. The castle in Berkshire, near Newbury, was one of Oxford's (q.v.) satellite garrisons established by the royalists (q.v.). In the fall of 1644 it was embroiled in the parliamentarian (q.v.) campaign to block any attempt that King Charles I (q.v.) might make on

London and the king's attempt to defend Oxford's southern approaches. In late October 1644 the king arrived at Donnington with supplies and as he paused there his army was attacked by parliamentarian forces in what was to be the second Battle of Newbury (q.v.). After the battle the castle was attacked by the earl of Manchester (q.v.), but the king returned on 9 November with more supplies and to retrieve the guns deposited there after the battle.

DORISLAUS, ISAAC (1595–1649). A Dutch professor of ancient history at Cambridge, dismissed for lecturing on the ascent of power, favoured by Lord Brooke (q.v.). When the High Court of Justice (q.v.) assembled, Dorislaus drafted the charge against King Charles I (q.v.). During the trial he served with the prosecution. Dorislaus was one of the first victims of royalist (q.v.) revenge, being murdered in The Hague four months after the trial of Charles I.

DOWNES, JOHN. Downes, M.P. for Arundel, interrupted the trial of Charles I (q.v.) asking whether he and his fellow judges should listen to the king's arguments. The court adjourned briefly and Downes was subdued and acquiesced in the subsequent progress of the trial. Downes signed the death warrant. He subsequently served on the Council of State (q.v.) in 1651 and again in 1659. He was imprisoned in Newgate at the Restoration as a regicide (qq.v.).

DRAGOONS. Dragoons were mounted infantry who used horses in order to reach places of strategic or tactical importance rapidly, as at the Battle of Edgehill (q.v.) when King Charles I's (q.v.) dragoons seized flanking hedges before the battle began. Once the fighting started, however, dragoons generally fought on foot. They were lightly protected by a buff coat and were accoutred similar to the Horse (q.v.), although armed with a musket, which may even have been a matchlock (q.v.) rather than a more sophisticated weapon. In periods when horses were in short supply the dragoons may well have found themselves without, as the Horse had a higher priority. Dragoons were organised into companies, and for much of the war could be found tagged onto a colonel's Horse regiment no more than company strength. A regiment of 1,000 was created for the New Model Army (q.v.) and under Colonel John Okey (q.v.) it charged the royalist (q.v.) army flank at the Battle of Naseby (q.v.).

DRAKE. An artillery piece firing a cannon bullet weighing three pounds. The cannon barrel was four feet long.

DROGHEDA. A port in County Louth besieged early in the Irish Rebellion (q.v.) by Colonel MacMahon and the O'Reillies, and defended by Lord Moore. The earl of Ormond (q.v.) relieved the town before the year was out and it remained in English hands throughout the war. In 1649 the town was a garrison held for the alliance of the royalists (q.v.) of Ormond and the Catholic Confederation of Kilkenny (q.v.).

When Oliver Cromwell (q.v.) arrived in Ireland in late August 1649 he struck out north towards Drogheda, and on 2 September he besieged the town. On 11 September Drogheda was stormed. In the fighting that ensued, the governor, Sir Arthur Aston (q.v.), was beaten to death with his own wooden leg and his soldiers were refused quarter. Civilians and priests were also murdered in large numbers. Cromwell justified the massacre on the grounds that the people of Drogheda were Catholics (q.v.) tainted with the bloodguilt of the 1641 massacres. In fact they had of course held out against the rebellion; earlier in the decade, the soldiers also had been a part of the bastion of Protestant colonists holding out in Munster. In 1649 Drogheda was already imbued with the myths and ignorance that obscured the English view of Ireland. In terms of the numbers killed, the massacres there and at Wexford (q.v.), when compared to the scale of the killing in the Irish wars, were not extraordinary, but the memory of these two tragedies has remained the greatest stain on Cromwell's character.

DUBLIN. The capital of English government in Ireland was the intended centre of the Irish Rebellion (q.v.) of 1641, but the attempt to capture the town and castle was betrayed. Dublin became the centre of resistance to the Rebellion and remained in English hands throughout. With its extensive international trading links and its deep water port at Ringsend, Dublin was also the point of departure for those fleeing Ireland, but also for imports of troops, ammunition, and supplies from England. Dublin was attacked by the forces of the Catholic Confederation of Kilkenny (q.v.) in 1646 and again in 1647 when the Irish forces were defeated at the Battle of Dungan's Hill (q.v.). In 1647 the marquis of Ormond (q.v.) handed the city to the English Parliament's (q.v.) forces under Michael Jones (q.v.). In 1649 Ringsend was the landing point for the New Model Army (q.v.) under Oliver Cromwell (q.v.).

DUNBAR, BATTLE OF. Fought on 3 September 1650. When the Scottish political elite accepted Charles II (q.v.) as king, a war with England and Wales became inevitable. A new army was created, but no Engager (q.v.) veterans or royalists (q.v.) could serve, and the army was rather lacklustre and inexperienced. Nevertheless, when the New Model Army (q.v.) under Oliver Cromwell (q.v.), now the commander in chief of the Commonwealth (q.v.) forces invaded Scotland, David Leslie (q.v.) held the advantage. Without adequate supplies, the New Model succumbed to illness and the army withered away. Leslie moved to cut the New Model off from England and placed himself on Doon Hill south of Dunbar. Cromwell launched an attack on him on 3 September, however, which paralysed the Scots' left whilst rolling up the right flank and centre; some 10,000 men were captured and 3,000 killed. In the wake of this defeat, Charles II and the Kirk Party (q.v.) agreed on a more moderate stance, allowing for the enlistment of Engagers and royalists in the new army, which went on to invade England in the campaign that ended at Worcester (q.v.) in 1651.

DUNGAN'S HILL, BATTLE OF. Fought on 8 August 1647. Michael Jones (q.v.) had set out from Dublin (q.v.) to attack Thomas Preston (q.v.), the general of the Leinster Army of the Catholic Confederation of Kilkenny (qq.v.), on 1 August. Preston had been conducting a relaxed campaign around Dublin for some weeks and at the end of July laid siege to Trim. As Jones approached, Preston left Trim and headed slowly towards Dublin, Jones followed and caught him at Dungan's Hill. After a battle lasting two hours, Jones's superiority in Horse (q.v.) defeated Preston. The Irish forces' casualties were high and Preston lost all of his artillery. The battle cost the Confederation the initiative in Leinster, and left the English with secure possession of what would become their bridgehead into Ireland, Dublin.

∽ **E** ∽

EASTERN ASSOCIATION. From the end of 1642 Parliament (q.v.) began to organise associations of counties under the military command of major generals (q.v.). The Eastern Association, consisting of the counties of East Anglia, Norfolk, Suffolk, Essex, Cambridgeshire, the Isle of Ely, Hertfordshire, and Huntingdonshire, was formed on 20 December 1642, and was to be the most successful association. As much as with any other factor, success lay in the absence of either long-lasting royalist (q.v.) garrisons or a significant invasion of its territory. The assessments (q.v.) raised paid for the creation in July and August 1643 of an army under the command of the earl of Manchester (q.v.), which, having secured the region's boundaries and taken military possession of much of Lincolnshire, which was added to the association in late 1643, marched northwards in May 1644 to assist in the siege of York (q.v.). After the surrender of York on 16 July 1644, Manchester marched south and captured large swathes of royalist territory in the North Midlands, before being summoned south for the campaign that ended in the second Battle of Newbury (q.v.) and King Charles I's (q.v.) relief of Donnington Castle (q.v.). In the wake of this debacle, the Eastern Association Army was absorbed into the New Model Army (q.v.), its commander was retired, but the second in command, Oliver Cromwell (q.v.), went on to be the second in command in the new army. In August 1645 the king's depleted army occupied Eastern Association territory for the only time during the First Civil War (q.v.), before moving westwards towards Hereford.

EDGEHILL, BATTLE OF. Fought on 23 October 1642. The principal aims of the two opposing commanders, King Charles I and the earl of Essex (qq.v.), in autumn 1642 were fairly simple: the king aimed to march on his capital, and Essex wanted to stop him. The king marched from his base at Shrewsbury in early October, whilst Essex busied himself creating garrisons across the South Midlands, between Coventry and Hereford. Whilst he was thus engaged, the king bypassed Essex and got between him and London. Poor scouting techniques resulted in the two armies colliding at Kineton in Warwickshire on the night of 22–23 October.

The next day, the king's army attacked Essex at the foot of Edgehill. The two armies were evenly matched with 12,000–14,000 men apiece, but the king's superiority in Horse (q.v.) saw initial royalist (q.v.) charges drive off both wings of the parliamentarian (q.v.) army. The actions of Essex's Foot (q.v.) and a small reserve of Horse, which was able to have a disproportionate effect because of the absence of the royalist Horse, which had left the field in pursuit of fleeing opponents, prevented defeat. The battle was fought to a standstill and the two armies faced each other overnight. On 24 October Essex withdrew north, but later dashed down to London to hold the king back at the Battles of Brentford (q.v.) and Turnham Green (q.v.).

EDWARDS, THOMAS (?–1647). Edwards was a London-based Presbyterian (q.v.) minister who had been dismissed from Cambridge in the 1630s for unacceptable political views. In 1644 he published *Antapologia*, but his principal contribution to the period was his *Gangraena or a Catalogue of many of the Errours Herisies and Blasphemies and Pernicious Practices* of 1646. Edwards was concerned that the freedom which had come about as the result of the collapse of the Church of England had allowed for the development of a wide range of religious sects and ideas propagated by uneducated preachers; for him, religious toleration was the greatest of evils as it would lead to atheism. He particularly identified the New Model Army (q.v.) as the location of many of these groups, but warned that sectaries were spreading their heresies into the north and west. He was associated with Robert Baillie (q.v.), who shared his vision of religious anarchy. He reported on a wide range of religious heresies as well as one political one, which included the suggestion that the English had no right to interfere in the affairs of Ireland. In 1647, the year of his death, he was heavily involved in the attempt by Parliament (q.v.) to create an army in London to oppose the New Model. *See also Gangraena.*

EIKON BASILIKE. Just over a week after the execution of Charles I (q.v.) on 8 February 1649, this book was published; translated, its title means, the royal image or the image of the king. It was supposedly a compilation of the king's writings during his years of imprisonment since the First Civil War (q.v.), probably made by Dr John Gauden and published by Richard Royston. The book contested the principles behind Parliament's (q.v.) war on the king, it acknowledged mistakes, but suggested that the king had constantly sought God's guidance in an effort to undermine the presumed godly principles espoused by his enemies. The book tried to stress the king's honesty in his dealings in a series of meditations and prayers. Whilst such an argument was difficult to support, if not impossible, the book went into 30 editions within the year and the image manufactured within it began to confer on Charles the status of a martyr.

ELEVEN MEMBERS. In the summer of 1647 the New Model Army (q.v.) marched on London during its confrontation with Parliament (q.v.) over issues of pay, indemnity from war-time actions, and service in Ireland. The Presbyterian (q.v.) majority was in a difficult position. The army wanted its arrears, dating back almost a year, but around England and Wales there was growing dissatisfaction with the continued heavy burden of taxation. Attempts to capitalise on this discontent and build up a Presbyterian army from officers and men cashiered at the creation of the New Model Army (q.v.) or from the disbanded Western Army, backed by Thomas Edwards (q.v.) failed. The New Model identified 11 principal opponents in the House of Commons (q.v.) including Denzil Holles (q.v.). On 16 June the army presented the demands to the Commons, but the 11 men withdrew voluntarily. This weakened the Presbyterian hold on Parliament and allowed the New Model to press its claims successfully, leading to back pay and the exception of volunteers from service in Ireland.

ENGAGEMENT, THE (1647). In May 1646 Charles I (q.v.) surrendered to the Covenanter (q.v.) army at Newark (q.v.). For the next seven months the Scots attempted to come to terms with the king, but in January 1647 in exasperation the Scots handed King Charles I to the Parliament (q.v.) in Westminster. For the next year relations between the Scots and Westminster became increasingly strained; the victory of the New Model Army (q.v.) over the Presbyterian (q.v.) faction at Westminster further estranged the two nations. At the same time in the Estates (q.v.) the royalist (q.v.) faction gained some strength. By the end of the year two factors had convinced the Scottish commissioners treating with the king at Hampton Court (q.v.) that settlement with him was preferable to settlement with a Westminster dominated by the Independents (q.v.). Although Charles kept his options open and refused to flee to Scotland, the commissioners signed the Engagement with him on 26 December 1647. This committed him to an experiment with a Presbyterian system in England in return for military intervention in England by the Scots on his behalf. The result was the invasion of England in 1648, which comprised a major component of the Second Civil War (q.v.).

ENGAGEMENT, THE (1650). The oath of loyalty to the Commonwealth (q.v.) imposed on all adult men in face of the war against Charles II (q.v.) and Scotland.

ENGAGERS. Adherents, especially in the Estates (q.v.), to The Engagement (q.v.) signed by Charles I (q.v.) and the Scottish commissioners in December 1647.

ENGLAND'S NEW CHAINS DISCOVERED. In the wake of the trial of Charles I (q.v.), John Lilburne (q.v.) presented a petition to Parliament (q.v.) that attacked the arbitrary nature of its actions since Pride's Purge (q.v.) and the establishment of the High Court of Justice (q.v.). At the same time it was an appeal to the Rump Parliament (q.v.) to re-establish the rule of law. *England's New Chains Discovered* was the published version of this petition. Essentially Lilburne was suggesting that the execution of King Charles I, far from freeing the country from tyranny, had simply seen one tyrant (the king) replaced by another (Parliament, particularly the army). The pamphlet marked further deterioration in the relationships of Parliament, the army, and the Levellers (q.v.) in the wake of Parliament's failure to debate the second *Agreement of the People* (q.v.) and the army's failure to commit itself to its role in the Westminster Debates. When he published a second part, widening his attack to embrace the Council of State (q.v.) in April 1649, Lilburne and others were imprisoned in the Tower. He had provided Parliament with a pretext for the arrest of the principal Levellers in a bid to prevent Leveller-inspired disturbances. The mutiny that followed and ended at Burford (q.v.) was inspired by the belief in the new tyranny detailed in *England's New Chains Discovered.*

EPISCOPACY. In essence the rule of the church through a hierarchical chain with the pope and cardinals at the top and the priests at the bottom. The system had its origins with St. Peter and authority was conveyed through the "apostolic succession," the "laying on of hands," which began with St Peter and linked each priest with that original action. The Protestant Reformation interfered with this link, but did not break it, the head of the Protestant church in the British Isles was the remaining monarch who governed the church through bishops. The churches in the four nations were intrinsically different. The Anglican church was the oldest, that in Wales was imposed as part of the Acts of Union of the 1530s, which turned Wales into a provincial principality. The Church of Ireland was part of the English colonial process there, which was unsuccessful in winning the hearts and minds of the people. The Scottish church had developed without a monarch to guide the process and thus established the Presbyterian (q.v.) system.

Both Charles I (q.v.) and his father, James VI and I, attempted to reintroduce and then bolster the role of the episcopate in the kirk (q.v.). Charles's attempt to unify practices in Scotland with those in England and Wales inspired rebellion and the signing of the National Covenant (q.v.), which in turn escalated the estrangement of the Scots from their king, which resulted in the Second Bishop's War (q.v.). In England too the episcopate came under attack in the 1630's, not initially on principle but on the grounds of opposition to the policies of William Laud (q.v.) and the arminians. From 1640 onwards and during the First Civil War (q.v.), however, attacks on episcopacy developed from issues of form into an attack on its fundamental structure and the episcopate was abolished in England and Wales. In Ireland the Protestant episcopate was swept aside following the Irish Rebellion (q.v.), although initially the rebels had declared themselves openly opposed only to puritan (q.v.) factions within the church and to Scottish Presbyterians in Ulster (q.v.).

ERBURY, WILLIAM (1604–1654). An Oxford graduate who was forced out of his Cardiff living in 1638, having been accused of being a schismatic. During the First Civil War (q.v.) he served as chaplain in Sir Philip Skippon's (q.v.) regiment. Erbury rejected predestination, which opened him to attack by Thomas Edwards (q.v.).

ESSEX, ROBERT DEVEREAUX, 3RD EARL OF (1591–1646). Son of Elizabeth I's former favourite, the title, which was lost at his father' execution in 1601, was restored to Robert in 1604. In 1613 Essex was the centre of a scandal when his wife, Francis Howard, succeeded in getting the marriage annulled on grounds of Essex's inability to consummate the union, after the divorce Francis went on to be the centre of a further scandal involving murder. Essex divorced his second wife, Elizabeth Paulet, for adultery. Essex gained experience in military service in Europe and in 1639 was appointed second-in-command of the English forces during the Bishop's Wars (q.v.).

Essex thereafter sided with Parliament (q.v.) in its attacks on King Charles I's (q.v.) rule, and in July 1642 was appointed commander in chief of the forces raised by Parliament. It has been argued that Essex's role was seen as much greater than that of a military leader and that his position was compared to that of a regent in charge of a minor or incapacitated monarch. He was likened by some to John the Baptist, the herald of a future leader. He did prove something of a disappointment, partly because of his lethargy and limited strategic sense. In October 1642, while supposedly blocking the king' advance on London, Essex let his enemy slip by and fought the Battle of Edgehill (q.v.), with the king between himself and the capital. He did, however, outpace the king and interpose himself between the royalists (q.v.) and London, slowing and then turning back the king's advance at the Battles of Brentford and Turnham Green (qq.v.).

In 1643, after capturing Reading and approaching the king's capital at Oxford (q.v.), Essex was struck with inertia, until the siege of Gloucester (q.v.). With an enhanced grasp of strategy, Essex out-played the king and reached Gloucester on 8 September 1643. On his return journey, however, Essex was overtaken by the king and again at the first Battle of Newbury (q.v.) had to fight with Charles' army between himself and London. This time he defeated the king and proceeded to London. His laxness during the summer has persuaded Parliament to create independent armies under the earl of Manchester and Sir William Waller (qq.v.), much to Essex's chagrin. During the spring of the following year Essex and Waller again attempted to close in on Oxford but failed to have any lasting effect. When the king marched out of the capital in May, Essex and Waller parted company, the latter pursuing the king around the Midlands, the former setting off to the west. After the king had defeated Waller at the Battle of Cropredy Bridge (q.v.), he followed Essex westwards. By August the earl was trapped in Cornwall and at the Battle of Lostwithiel (q.v.) his army was caught, the Horse (q.v.) broke out of the trap, Essex escaped by sea, but the Foot (q.v.) was captured.

This defeat marked the end of Essex's independent command, the three principal parliamentarian armies in the south (Essex's, Manchester's, and Waller's) were brought together in the autumn, but the divided command led to the bungling of the second Battle of Newbury (q.v.) in October 1644. This in turn led to the arguments in Parliament out of which came the Self Denying Ordinance (q.v.), which deprived all three commanders of their posts and spawned the New Model Army (q.v.). Although both Essex and Manchester were given posts on the Committee of Both Kingdoms (q.v.), which initially entailed directing the New Model Army, Essex's military career was at an end. He died shortly after the end of the First Civil War (q.v.).

ESTATES. The Scottish Parliament was traditionally composed of the three estates of clergy (which effectively meant the representatives of the Scottish Episcopacy [q.v.]), nobility, and representatives of the burghs and counties. In 1640, following the Scottish political revolution of 1638–40, the clerical estate was abolished and the later two groups were acknowledged as three distinct estates. Additionally, the revolution had seen the demise of the steering committee, the Lords of the Articles, which had prepared legislation and presented it to the assembled estates. Since 1623 the Lords of the Articles had been dominated by royal appointments and had thus become a tool of the monarch, which stifled debate and reduced the role of the legislature to voting on issues without debate. The Lords of the Articles were therefore replaced by a series of tables representing the three estates and the kirk (q.v.). A fifth table formed the executive body. By 1640 the Estates had also established the mechanisms by which they would meet every three years at the least, with or without a summons being issued by King Charles I (q.v.).

The very balance of power between the king and the estates had been radically changed, minimising the king' control and reducing him to the role of a cipher, as his approval was no longer deemed necessary for an act to become law. This point was hammered home in summer 1641 when the king was forced to approve his own diminution. There were 18 sessions of Parliament held between June 1640 and June 1651. The estates were dominated by the Covenanters (q.v.), although royalists (q.v.) were able to influence affairs following the end of the First Civil War (q.v.) in England and Wales. This state of affairs allowed for the signing of the Engagement (q.v.) with Charles in late 1647, which provoked the Second Civil War (q.v.) in 1648. Following the defeat of the Engagers (q.v.) a reinvigorated Kirk Party (q.v.) faction dominated the Estates until their defeat in the war against England in 1651–52.

EVERARD, ROBERT. A Leveller (q.v.) in the New Model Army (q.v.) who participated in the Putney Debates (q.v.) in October and November 1647. Everard was involved in the Burford Mutiny (q.v.) but may have stayed in the army until 1651. Between 1649 and 1652, Everard published several pamphlets that supported the Baptist (q.v.) tenets of adult baptism, and the Ranters' (q.v.) views on original sin.

EVERARD, WILLIAM. It is possible that William Everard first appeared in the period as a spy for the parliamentarian (q.v.) scoutmaster-general, Sir Samuel Luke (q.v.). It is also possible that he was the same man who, then an agitator (q.v.), was arrested at the Corkbush Field (q.v.) mutiny and later cashiered from the New Model Army (q.v.). In March 1643 Everard was with the Digger (q.v.) colony at St George's Hill where he spoke with Thomas, Lord Fairfax (q.v.), who believed him mad. Everard contributed the *True Levellers' Standard Advanced* (q.v.) with Gerard Winstanley (q.v.). Thereafter he left the colony and possibly joined in the mutiny at Burford (q.v.) in May 1649, laying low afterwards. In the 1650s he was committed to the Bridewell prison for apparent insanity.

EXCISE. Taxes on home-produced goods were regarded as worthy of emergency taxation in England and Wales during the 17th century. By 1643 it was clear that direct taxation was not producing the required income, and in July Parliament (q.v.) enacted an excise tax. Offices were established in London, and major market towns and subcommittees were appended to the county committees (q.v.) in parliamentarian (q.v.) territory. In 1644 King Charles I's (q.v.) Oxford Parliament (q.v.) enacted a similar process, but as it came into effect just as the royalist (q.v.) cause suffered a major downturn in fortune its effectiveness was limited. For Parliament excise proved the second largest source of income after the weekly assessment (q.v.). Excise taxes proved unpopular, especially as they were extended from luxury items to foodstuffs. Riots ensued in Chester against the royalist excise in 1645 and Derby women prevented collection there for several months that same year. The continuation of the excise taxes after the First Civil War (q.v.) prompted riots at Smithfield, London, and elsewhere in 1647. Excise was not abolished at the Restoration (q.v.).

⤔ **F** ⤔

FAIRFAX, LADY ANNE. Married to Sir Thomas, later 3rd Baron Fairfax of Cameron (q.v.), Lady Anne was one of the only people to publicly denounce the trial of Charles I (q.v.) in 1649. At the first public session of the trial, when her husband's name was read, she called out "He hath more wit than to be here." At the last public session, when the king was sentenced, as the charge was read out in the name of the people of England, Lady Fairfax yelled "Not half, not a quarter of the people of England. Oliver Cromwell (q.v.) is a traitor!" As the muskets of the court guards were levelled at her, she was hustled out of the public gallery. Lady Anne was perhaps reflecting somewhat the concern of her husband, but her public display surpassed his preparedness to intervene at all. These were her views, not his.

FAIRFAX, FERDINANDO, 2ND BARON FAIRFAX OF CAMERON (1584–1648). Ferdinando Fairfax saw some military action on the continent and later served as an M.P. for Boroughbridge in Parliament (q.v.) during the 1620s. In 1640 he represented Yorkshire; his Scottish title did not debar him from a seat in the Commons (q.v.). With prominent land-holding interests in the West Riding of Yorkshire, the Fairfax family was associated with the cloth-making and finishing trades of that area. Lord Fairfax and his son Sir Thomas, later 3rd Baron Fairfax (q.v.), became the natural leaders of King Charles I's (q.v.) opponents in Yorkshire, and Parliament sent Lord Fairfax to observe the king at York (q.v.) in summer 1642. Upon the outbreak of the First Civil War (q.v.) father and son attempted to take control of the county and were embroiled in a struggle with the earl of Newcastle (q.v.) from late 1642 until the summer of the following year when they were defeated at Adwalton Moor (q.v.).

Lord Fairfax was bottled up in Hull (q.v.), but taking advantage of first the earl of Newcastle's failure to capture the port in fall 1643 and then the invasion of the Covenanter (q.v.) Army in January 1644, he went on the offensive in Yorkshire whilst his son fought in Lincolnshire and then in the north-west. Reunited by April 1644, the Fairfaxes defeated the Yorkshire royalists (q.v.) at the Battle of Selby (q.v.), which precipitated the collapse of the royalist north. At the subsequent siege of York the Fairfaxes were joined by the Scots and then by the earl of Manchester and the Eastern Association (qq.v.) army. Although he initially fled the field at Marston Moor (q.v.), on 2 July 1644, Lord Fairfax was able to take advantage of the defeat of Prince Rupert (q.v.) and construct a North Association, which he commanded until the Self Denying Ordinance (q.v.) ended his public role. He died of blood poisoning in 1648.

FAIRFAX, SIR THOMAS, 3RD BARON FAIRFAX OF CAMERON (1612–1671). Like his father, Ferdinando, 2nd Baron Fairfax (q.v.) before him, Sir Thomas served on the continent, after first attending Cambridge

University. Also, like his father, he served King Charles I (q.v.) in the Bishop's Wars (q.v.). By 1642 he was opposed to the king's actions and presented him with a petition during the rally on Heyworth Moor near York in June when the king was attempting to marshal public support. When the king refused to take the petition, Sir Thomas thrust it into his bridle. During the First Civil War (q.v.) Sir Thomas served as his father's second in command and was responsible for most of the parliamentarian (q.v.) successes in Yorkshire before the Battle of Adwalton (q.v.) in 1643.

Whilst his father was governor of Hull (q.v.), Sir Thomas took the Horse (q.v.) regiments and served in Lincolnshire alongside Oliver Cromwell (q.v.) in fall 1643. He then crossed the Pennines in winter, having dodged the earl of Newcastle's, Northern Army (qq.v.) in the Midlands, to assist Sir William Brereton (q.v.) in defeating Lord Byron (q.v.) at the Battle of Nantwich (q.v.) in January 1644. During the Battle of Marston Moor (q.v.), Sir Thomas's quick action assisted greatly in the defeat of the royalists (q.v.). After the surrender of York, Sir Thomas assisted his father in the mopping up operations in York. When the Self Denying Ordinance (q.v.) forced the reconstruction of Parliament's (q.v.) military command, however, Sir Thomas was appointed commander in chief of the New Model Army (q.v.) with Oliver Cromwell as his second. Fairfax led the army to victory at the Battles of Naseby and Langport (qq.v.) and captured Bristol (q.v.) and finally Oxford (q.v.).

After the First Civil War, Fairfax was swept up in the political battles of words between the army and the Presbyterian (q.v.) faction in Parliament. Whilst Fairfax stood up for the rights of the soldiers and took their part in petitions and during the march on London, he did not agree with their political alliance with the Levellers (q.v.) and ruthlessly suppressed support for them when it threatened his control of the army.

During the Second Civil War (q.v.) Fairfax commanded the section of the New Model that defeated the Kentish Rebels and then besieged Colchester (q.v.). Although appointed to the commission that established the trial of the king, Fairfax played a minimal role at the outset and then disappeared from view, whilst his wife, Lady Anne Fairfax (q.v.), demonstrated public opposition. He gave up command of the army during 1650 when asked to lead it against Scotland; Cromwell assumed command. During the Commonwealth and Protectorate (qq.v.) Thomas, Lord Fairfax since the death of his father in 1648, remained distant. He assisted in facilitating the Restoration (q.v.) but played no major public role between the surrender of Colchester and his death in 1671.

FALKLAND, LUCIUS CARY, VISCOUNT (1610–1643). Falkland was one of the intellectuals who formed the Great Tew Circle, which he hosted at his country seat, where they discussed, amongst other things, ecumenicalism in the years before the war. He was associated with King Charles I' s (q.v.) faction in Parliament (q.v.) in the early 1640s where he was M.P. for the Isle of Wight, after initially favouring the prosecution of the earl of Strafford (q.v.) and the abolition of ship money (q.v.). Pressure in Parliament to alter the fundamentals of the Church of England pushed Falkland towards the king's position and in January 1642 he was appointed secretary of state to the king. After Parliament's rejection of conciliatory proposals carried from York to Westminster (qq.v.) by Falkland, the viscount threw himself into the royalist (q.v.) camp and served in the king's army at the outbreak of the First Civil War (q.v.).

Falkland fought at the Battle of Edgehill (q.v.), but at the siege of Gloucester (q.v.) a year later was disconsolate with the thought of the internecine nature of the war. His death at the first Battle of Newbury (q.v.) days later was ascribed to a suicidal desire to end his part in the war. His death saddened the king, but left his friends, especially Sir Edward Hyde, devastated.

FANSHAWE, LADY ANNE (1625–1680). In 1644 Anne Harrison married Sir Richard Fanshawe, the secretary of state for war to Prince Charles (q.v.), in the garrison at Oxford (q.v.). Lady Fanshawe accompanied her husband into exile at the end of the First Civil War (q.v.), but they both returned in 1646 to compound (q.v.) for the family estates. They visited King Charles I (q.v.) whilst he was a prisoner at Hampton Court (q.v.) in 1647. In 1648 Sir Richard became treasurer to the royalist (q.v.) fleet based in Ireland. Lady Anne joined him there in 1649 after the execution of the king. They both fled the country in 1650 and went to Spain, thence to France. Whilst Lady Anne returned to England, her husband went on to serve Charles II (q.v.) in Scotland before being captured. The couple eventually lived in retirement during the 1650s, but Sir Richard received preferment at the Restoration (q.v.). Lady Anne kept a diary or journal of the years from the beginning of the Civil Wars to 1672, and later compiled these into a memoir for her surviving children, which provided a useful eyewitness account of the war in three of the four nations of the British Isles.

FAST SERMONS. On fasting days initiated in February 1642 by King Charles I (q.v.), sermons of a political–religious content were preached in London. Initially these fasts were acts of self-sacrifice intended to intercede with God for the swift end to the Irish Rebellion (q.v.) that were to be held on the last Wednesday of every month. Parliament (q.v.) commandeered their use as a means of unifying London behind its cause during the First Civil War (q.v.).

FIENNES, SIR NATHANIEL (1607–1669). Fiennes was the second son of the oppositionist Lord Saye and Sele (q.v.) and represented Banbury in the Short Parliament (q.v.) and again in the Long Parliament (q.v.), where he opposed the episcopate (q.v.). In the First Civil War (q.v.) he fought at the Battles of Powick Bridge and Edgehill (qq.v.) before becoming governor of Bristol (q.v.) in 1643. His surrender of the town to Prince Rupert (q.v.), after an assault on 26 July 1643, resulted in a court martial that sentenced him to death, despite Prince Rupert's offer to clear him. The earl of Essex (q.v.) secured his freedom and he went abroad, returning only after 1646.

Prince Rupert's surrender of Bristol in 1645 demonstrated the difficulties faced in holding Bristol and Fiennes was restored to honour and appointed to Parliament's (q.v.) Army Committee in 1647. He believed that the Treaty of Newport (q.v.) offered a real chance for peace and was thus excluded from Parliament at Pride's Purge (q.v.) in December 1649. He stayed out of politics until the mid-1650s, when he served in several Protectorate (q.v.) parliaments, becoming one of the new lords created by Oliver Cromwell (q.v.) in 1658. Fiennes's political career ended with the Restoration (q.v.).

FIFTH AND TWENTIETH LEVIES. Taxation levied at the rate of one-fifth of personal estate and one-twentieth of real estate. This proportion formed the basis of Parliament's (q.v.) levy, the weekly assessment (q.v.), in the First Civil War (q.v.).

FIFTH MONARCHISTS. A sect that believed in the imminence of Christ's kingdom, the Fifth Monarchy, which would follow the collapse of the other four: Babylon, Egypt, Rome, and the Roman Catholic Church. The Civil Wars were interpreted as the violent end of the latter. The apogee of the Fifth Monarchists, who numbered amongst them Colonel Thomas Harrison (q.v.), came in 1653 with the Barebones Parliament (q.v.), when they were able to influence central government politics. The failure of the millennium (millenarianism [q.v.]) to begin in 1655 or 1656 led many Fifth Monarchists to shift from a passive stance to an active and violent propagation of the new kingdom and the belief that Oliver Cromwell (q.v.) was an agent of the fourth monarchy rather than one of the saints destined to rule on Christ's behalf. This prompted the risings of Thomas Venner (q.v.) in 1656 and 1661.

FINCH, SIR JOHN, LORD (1584–1660). Speaker in the House of Commons (q.v.) during the Parliament (q.v.) of 1628–29, Finch was held in his chair by Denzil Holles and William Strode (qq.v.) to prevent him from dissolving Parliament on 2 March 1629 whilst declarations against arminianism were passed by acclamation. Finch served as a chief justice during the 1630s and was involved in the trials of William Prynne, John Bastwicke, and Henry Burton (qq.v.). In 1640 Finch was appointed lord keeper and on 13 April made the king's speech at the opening of the Short Parliament (q.v.), the first since he had been held down in the speaker's chair. When the Parliament refused to levy taxation before addressing grievances, Finch was sent to exhort both houses to action. Given that he was under investigation for his role in the 1629 dissolution, he was hardly accorded much attention. During the first session of the Long Parliament (q.v.) Finch was impeached for his past support of ship money (q.v.) and his persecution of religious dissidents, charges levelled by Lord Falkland (q.v.). Finch did not wait to be arrested, but fled to the Netherlands in December 1641.

FIRELOCK. A type of flintlock musket in which a spark ignited the main charge by means of a flint striking metal when the trigger was pulled. Since this required no lighted matchcord as did the matchlock (q.v.) musket, it was safer to use, being less prone to unintentional ignition. For this reason, the firelock was often carried by those in charge of munitions. Its convenience made it appropriate for Horse (q.v.) troops also.

FIRST CIVIL WAR. This term denotes the period between summer 1642 and spring 1646, during which time a war was fought in England and Wales. The first act of the war is often considered to be the raising of the standard at Nottingham (q.v.) on 22 August 1642, the last being the surrender of King Charles I (q.v.) to the Scots at Newark (q.v.) on 6 May 1646. Fighting had broken out in Yorkshire, Lancashire, and Warwickshire before the standard was raised, however. Moreover, the war in England and Wales continued in certain areas after the king's surrender, with garrisons surrendering throughout the following summer, and Harlech Castle (q.v.) fighting on until 1647. The war in Scotland continued into 1648, and that in Ireland saw renewed vigour after the war in England and Wales had officially ended.

FIVE MEMBERS, THE. John Hampden, Sir Arthur Hesilrige, Denzil Holles, John Pym, and William Strode (qq.v.) were the five intended House of Commons' (q.v.) targets of Charles I's (q.v.) attempted coup d'état of early January 1642. All five of the M.P.s had a long history of opposition to the king's government, stretching back over a decade. By January 1642 they were perceived as the leaders of the House of Commons' opposition. Along with Viscount Mandeville, later the earl of Manchester (q.v.), the five members were charged with treason on

4 January. On the following day, accompanied by the elector palatine and 300 armed men, the king marched to St. Stephen's Chapel where the Commons assembled at Westminster (q.v.), and leaving his guard at the door, entered the chamber, took up his seat (the speaker's chair), and demanded the surrender of the five men. They had remained in the house until the last minute, slipping away by boat as the king arrived. The speaker refused to cooperate by pointing out the five men, declaring that he had neither "eyes to see nor tongue to speak in this place but as the house is pleased to direct me," a reflection of what one of the five, Denzil Holles, had shouted at Speaker Sir John Finch (q.v.) as he and Strode held Finch in his chair at the dissolution of Parliament in 1629.

This ignominious failure was followed by the king and his family's flight to Hampton Court (q.v.) and the eventual rift between the king and Parliament that resulted in the king going north to York (q.v.). For the M.P.s, it raised the spectre of the consequences of failure and made some of them more determined to press on with the reformation of government.

FLEETWOOD, CHARLES (1618–1692). The brother of a royalist (q.v.), Fleetwood served in the earl of Essex's (q.v.) lifeguard at the Battle of Edgehill (q.v.), and fought at the first Battle of Newbury (q.v.) and later in the Eastern Association (q.v.) army of the earl of Manchester (q.v.). He was an Independent (q.v.) and went on to command a regiment of the New Model Army (q.v.) at the Battle of Naseby (q.v.). His inclinations drove him to side against Parliament (q.v.) during the conflict between it and the army in 1647. During the Second Civil War (q.v.) he was involved in the siege of Colchester (q.v.). By 1650 he was lieutenant general of the Horse (q.v.) and served at the Battle of Dunbar (q.v.). In 1651 he was appointed to the Council of State (q.v.) and then became commander in chief in Ireland, marrying the widow of Henry Ireton (q.v.), Bridget Cromwell, daughter of Oliver Cromwell (q.v.). In 1654 he became lord deputy in Ireland. By 1655 he was back in England and participated in the "rule" of the major generals (q.v.), commanding the eastern counties. When Richard Cromwell (q.v.) refused to accede to the needs of the army, Fleetwood was prominent in overthrowing him and thus assisted in sowing the seeds of the Restoration (q.v.), although he lingered too long in his defence of the Republic (q.v.) to be rewarded by Charles II (q.v.). He lived in retirement at Stoke Newington. His second wife, Bridget, died in 1662, and he married Mary Hartopp, widow of a Leicestershire parliamentarian cavalry colonel.

FOOT. A term used to denote the infantry. Organised into regiments, theoretically composed of 1,200 men, regiments of Foot in England, Wales, and Ireland were usually much smaller until the creation of the New Model Army (q.v.). The armies of the Covenanters (q.v.) were usually up to size at the outset of campaigns. Regiments of Foot consisted of both lightly armoured musketeers armed with a musket (q.v.), and armoured pikemen armed with an 18-foot-long pike (q.v.). These should have been in the proportion of 2:1, but in many cases, especially in the English and Welsh forces at the commencement of the war, were often 1:1 because of the shortage of muskets. By 1646–47, in the Catholic Confederation of Kilkenny (q.v.) armies in Ireland, the desired ratio had been achieved and the same is perhaps true for England and Wales. In Scotland the preferred ratio was 3:2, but in 1650 shortages left it at 2:3. In English armies regiments were composed of companies of varying size, but most consisted of around 100 men, whilst the colonel's, lieutenant colonel's, and major's companies were larger. In Scottish regiments all companies were theoretically the same size, but that size changed throughout the war years from between 93 and 121 in 1642, to a standard 80 in 1646, and 108 in 1650. During formal battles regiments were grouped into brigades or tertios, theoretically of three regiments, but depending on the size of regiments, the brigades consisted of as many as made the appearance of an effective force. In a set battle the regiment drew up with its pikemen in the centre and the musketeers on each flank, in ranks six deep.

FORCED LOANS. This was a means by which the monarch could raise money, often in emergencies. The money was to be repaid at the public rate of interest, which was 8 percent in the 1640s. In 1627 King Charles I (q.v.) imposed a Forced Loan on the country that provoked widespread opposition. As a result of this reaction, Parliament (q.v.) sought tighter control of the raising of finance and drew up the Petition of Right (q.v.) in 1628, pressuring the king into agreeing that Parliament should be involved in the taxation process. Although Charles went on to ignore this agreement during the 1630s, his opponents continued to use the Petition of Right as a precedent for its claim to a role in financial affairs, and people of all ranks saw it as their means of protection from arbitrary taxation.

FORLORN HOPE. Consisting of chosen musketeers from several Foot (q.v.) regiments, the Forlorn Hope served as skirmishers in front of the main army, firing at the enemy to reduce moral and attempt to break the coherence of an attacking force. On being attacked, they returned to the safety of their own (or the nearest) regiment.

FORTESCUE, SIR FAITHFUL (1581–1666). After service in Ireland after the Irish Rebellion (q.v.), Fortescue returned to England to raise soldiers for the war. His troop of Horse (q.v.) was co-opted into Parliament's (q.v.) army during the summer of 1642, however, and he was also commissioned to be lieutenant colonel of the earl of Peterborough's Foot (q.v.). At the Battle of Edgehill (q.v.) Fortescue and his troop changed sides as the battle began, signalling to Prince Rupert (q.v.) their intention by firing pistols into the ground and ripping off their orange sashes. This action certainly undermined the confidence of the left wing of the earl of Essex's (q.v.) army, which was subsequently driven from the field.

FORTH, PATRICK RUTHVEN, EARL OF (1573–1651). Although born in Scotland, Ruthven spent much of his life on the continent in the Swedish armies, achieving the rank of colonel of Horse (q.v.) by 1618. He was much prized by Gustavus Adolphus. In 1638 he returned to Britain and was made muster master of Scotland as part of Charles I's (q.v.) attempt to militarise supporters in opposition to the Covenanters (q.v.). He was ennobled in 1639 as Baron Ruthven of Ettrick. Ruthven was appointed governor of Edinburgh Castle during the Second Bishop's War (q.v.). He held the castle throughout the war despite constant attack and food and water shortages, surrendering only on 15 September 1640.

Ruthven returned to the continent in 1642 and brought back 22 officers; together they joined the king at Shrewsbury. For this he was named earl of Forth. He was given command of the royalist (q.v.) army at Edgehill (q.v.), an action that incensed the nominal commander Lord Lindsey (q.v.), who then went on to be killed at the head of his own regiment during the battle. Forth urged a direct attack on London after Edgehill. Although overruled, he was prominent in the attack on Brentford (q.v.) on 12 November 1642, for which he was made Earl of Brentford.

In September 1643 Forth was injured at the siege of Gloucester (q.v.). In the following year he was given nominal command of the army Ralph Lord Hopton (q.v.) led in the south. The divided command, despite the best will in the world, led to some confusion and probably played a role in the royalists' defeat at the Battle of Cheriton (qq.v.). Forth remained on service during the next year, being replaced as commander in chief by Prince Rupert (q.v.) in 1645. He then was part of Prince Charles's court in the west and went into exile with the prince. In 1649 he gathered arms for the royalist cause and returned to Scotland with Charles II (q.v.) in 1650, but was not allowed to serve in the army. He died in 1651 at Dundee.

FOUR BILLS. These four bills comprised the last formal offer of a treaty made by Parliament to King Charles I (qq.v.). The bills effectively consolidated the proposals discussed at the various negotiations since the

Treaty of Uxbridge (q.v.) in 1645. The first bill placed control of the militia in the hands of Parliament for 20 years; the second renounced the king's anti-Parliament denunciations since 1642; the third renounced war-time ennoblements, such as those of the earl of Forth, Lord Hopton, and Lord Loughborough (qq.v.); and the fourth ended the king's remaining control of the means of summoning and dispensing with Parliaments. If these terms were agreed on, then other issues, including the establishment of a Presbyterian (q.v.) church system, would be negotiated.

These bills angered the Scots, who particularly disliked the relegation of religious issues, and they sought to influence the king to refuse the terms. The king played Parliament and the Scottish commissioners off each other during December 1647 and eventually agreed on terms with the Scots, signing the Engagement (q.v.), before rejecting the Four Bills. This prompted Parliament into passing the Vote of No Addresses (q.v.), and led to Scotland's invasion of England in the Second Civil War (q.v.) in 1648.

FOX, GEORGE (1621–1691). Fox was born in Leicestershire, the son of a weaver. It would appear that during the First Civil War (q.v.) Fox travelled the country seeking some form of divine explanation for the events he witnessed. As a result of his discussions with ministers and his constant dialogue with God, Fox rejected the Presbyterian (q.v.) system being imposed on England. He had begun to preach just after the war and by 1649 was imprisoned for a fight that developed in a Nottingham church after a dispute with the minister. From his preaching developed the Society of Friends, referred to as Quakers (q.v.) by observers who witnessed their passionate testimonies to divine inspiration. Fox spent the 1650s travelling throughout England and Scotland.

During the 1660s he tried to convince King Charles II (q.v.) that the Quakers should be allowed toleration, when in fact they were persecuted across Britain and Ireland. Fox was variously imprisoned in Lancaster, Scarborough, and Worcester (qq.v.) during the 1660s and 1670s, although he was able to spread his message in Ireland, America, and the West Indies.

↩ **G** ↪

GANGRAENA. This three-volume work was produced by Thomas Edwards (q.v.) during 1646. The first volume was a catalogue of the heresies of the sects that were springing up in the wake of the collapse of the Church of England. Edwards sought a Presbyterian (q.v.) approach to church structure, rather than what he saw as the anarchy of the gathered churches (q.v.) and unlicensed and ill-educated preachers. Edwards called for further evidence of these malpractices and volumes two and three contained correspondence from readers of the first volume about practices they had seen or heard of as well as more material assembled by Edwards himself.

GATHERED CHURCHES. A term applied to congregations that came together because of shared religious approaches. These were the basis of the Independent (q.v.) approach to worship and the postwar restructuring of the church in England and Wales.

GEDDES, JENET (OR JANET). A figure of almost mythical status, Geddes is popularly accredited with starting the entire period of war and revolution. When the Scottish version of the *Book of Common Prayer* (q.v.) was being read for the first time in Scottish churches on 23 July 1637, Geddes was alleged to have hurled her small portable cutty stool at the dean of the cathedral in his adjacent pulpit, denouncing his popish text. Jenet Geddes may not have thrown this stool, although such a person did live in Edinburgh and some 22 years later held a lucken booth in the market outside the west face of the cathedral. No contemporary evidence exists to indicate that it was she who threw the stool. References to her were only made some time after the event. Even so, she had become a potent revolutionary figure. Today in the cathedral stands on the north side of the nave a sculpture of the stool by Merilyn Smith in the name of Scottish women. Nearby, a few yards from the pulpit, is a plaque that reads:

> Constant oral tradition affirms that near this spot a Brave Scotchwoman Janet Geddes on 23 July 1637 struck the first blow in the great struggle for the freedom of conscience which after a conflict of half a century ended in the establishment of civic and religious liberty.

There seems to be little doubt that women were involved in the stool-throwing that day, and alternative names for the first to hurl her stool include Barbara Hamilton, the wife of Edinburgh merchant John Mearn. Women were involved in the planning stages of that day's riots and the riots that ensued.

GELL, SIR JOHN (1593–1671). Gell, a lead-mine lessee, was high sheriff of Derbyshire in 1636 and at the end of his term of office proposed that the county could actually pay more than it had in that year's levy. In 1642 he was given a baronetcy, but sided with Parliament (q.v.). In October 1642 he led troops borrowed from the garrisons at Hull (q.v.)

and Sheffield into Derbyshire and occupied the town and county for Parliament, driving out small royalist (q.v.) forces and going on the offensive against the royalists in neighbouring Leicestershire. In March 1643 he captured Lichfield (q.v.) and fought at the Battle of Hopton Heath (q.v.). Although at the end of that year he lost control of the county, he held onto Derby throughout the war and mopped up royalist garrisons in the region throughout 1644–45.

Gell became disillusioned with the cause as his arrears of pay grew and in 1645 he tried to divert the excise tax (q.v.) for the use of the county. He remained important to the county committee (q.v.) until the end of the First Civil War (q.v.), although his management of it led to serious political divisions within the committee; in addition, the election of his brother Thomas to Parliament in the 1645 Recruiter Elections (q.v.) was considered dubious. Disgruntled with his treatment by Parliament, Gell eventually threw in his lot with the region's royalist factions and was bound up in a plot in 1649. He was arrested and sentenced to life imprisonment in 1650, but in 1653 was pardoned and lived in retirement in London until his death.

GENERAL APPLOTMENT. This was the general levy established by the Catholic Confederation of Kilkenny (q.v.) to fund the war. Levies were collected within each parish and administered by the county committees (q.v.) and the provincial committees. Little material regarding the grass-roots-level collections is available, but it is clear that collection was probably continuous from much of the country not affected by fighting, even if in reduced amounts.

GENERAL COUNCIL OF OFFICERS. Established in August 1647 by the high command of the New Model Army (q.v.) to replace the Council of War, this council drafted the Heads of the Proposals (q.v.) offered to King Charles I (q.v.) in October of that year.

GENERAL COUNCIL OF THE ARMY. Established in July 1645, the council was formed of agitators (q.v.) elected by the regiments of the New Model Army (q.v.) and elected officers. The council was established to deal with the threats being made by the Presbyterians (q.v.) in Parliament (q.v.) to disband much of the army without pay and to send other sections to Ireland. As a result, the army presented a united face, enabling it to overcome its opponents and forcing the Eleven Members (q.v.) to leave the House of Commons (q.v.). The council was also the body that debated the *Agreement of the People* at the Putney Debates (qq.v.) during October–November 1647.

GERARD, SIR CHARLES (1618–1694). Gerard succeeded Lord Carbery (q.v.) as commander in South Wales in 1644. Gerard's being Catholic (q.v.) ensured that he was an unpopular figure and his control of royalist (q.v.) actions in the region prompted popular uprisings, culminating in the creation of the Peace or Peaceable Army (q.v.) in the late summer of 1645. Gerard abandoned the royalist cause after Prince Rupert (q.v.) had been deprived of command by Charles I (q.v.) after the surrender of Bristol (q.v.).

GLAMORGAN, EDWARD SOMERSET, EARL OF (1603–1667). Son of the Roman Catholic earl of Worcester (qq.v.), who was probably the richest man in England and Wales. At the outbreak of the First Civil War (q.v.), whilst still Lord Herbert of Raglan, he raised royalist (q.v.) forces in South Wales with Lord Carbery and Lord Hertford (qq.v.). By 1643 Glamorgan was lieutenant general for south-east Wales and the county of Herefordshire. His attack on Gloucester (q.v.) in February and March failed, and on 25 March his army was defeated at the Battle of Highnam (q.v.) by parliamentarian (q.v.) general Sir William Waller (q.v.), which left Monmouthshire open to invasion. On 15 April Herbert attempted to reconstruct his war effort, but abandoned his lieutenants and sought help in Oxford (q.v.) just as Waller returned to the area. Hereford fell to Waller. Although his rank saved him from censure, Herbert's personal authority was at an end; he retained nominal command and was in the field until autumn.

At the beginning of 1645 Lord Herbert was raised in the peerage to the earl of Glamorgan and sent to Ireland to treat directly with the Catholic Confederation of Kilkenny (q.v.) without informing the Marquis of Ormond (q.v.) of his true purpose. He arrived in July and began negotiating for an army of 20,000 to be sent to England and Wales in return for conceding satisfaction of religious demands, something Ormond had refused to negotiate. More radical members of the Confederation wanted public acknowledgement of the treaty, urged on by Cardinal Rinuccini (q.v.), the nuncio; Old English (q.v.) representatives wanted the security of a treaty with Ormond, even if religious issues were unsatisfactorily dealt with. In the end, the treaty was exposed when a copy of it fell into parliamentarian hands after the death of the Archbishop of Tuam in a skirmish in early 1646. Ormond, believing the earl to be acting against the interests of the crown because of the previously unacceptable conditions offered to the Catholics (q.v.), immediately arrested Glamorgan on a charge of treason, only to be convinced of the fact he was working for the king. Glamorgan continued to try and work for military aid for the royalist cause in England and

Wales, only to be disowned by Charles I (q.v.) when the king surrendered to the Scots in May 1646.

GLENHAM, SIR THOMAS (c.1595–1649). Born in Suffolk and educated at Oxford University, Glenham served as an M.P. in the early Parliaments of King Charles I (qq.v.); he also served in military expeditions in the late 1620s. In August 1642 Glenham served as military advisor to the earl of Cumberland, who was left in charge of royalist (q.v.) affairs in Yorkshire. In 1644 Glenham commanded the efforts to prepare northern England for the invasion of the Scots. After the Battle of Marston Moor (q.v.) he was given the governorship of York (q.v.), but had little option other than to surrender on 16 July 1645. He then took over at Carlisle, where he held out against the Scots until 28 June 1645. Thereafter he joined the king's army, and succeeded Sir William Legge as governor of Oxford (q.v.), which he held until 26 June 1646. Although he paid composition (q.v.) for his estate after the First Civil War (q.v.), in 1648 he took part in the Second Civil War (q.v.) and in the capture of Carlisle. The circumstances of his death are unknown.

GLOUCESTER, SIEGE OF. This city was regarded as the gateway to southern Wales and was garrisoned by the earl of Stamford (q.v.) in December 1642 to prevent recruits from South Wales from joining the king. Stamford's lieutenant, Colonel Edward Massey (q.v.), remained there as governor. In August 1643 Gloucester became the centre of royalist (q.v.) attempts to complete the conquest of South Midland and southern Marcher counties. From 10 August to 5 September the king besieged the city with the Oxford Field Army (q.v.). The city was considered so important that the earl of Essex (q.v.) was sent to its rescue with Parliament's (q.v.) main army. He raised the siege at the beginning of September and sent in the much-needed supplies before turning back towards London. The royalists chased him and got between Essex and London. At the Second Battle of Newbury (q.v.) the king failed to defeat Essex and he was able to continue to London, where he received a hero's welcome. Gloucester was not placed under close siege again. It is possible that the siege of Gloucester was responsible for the royalists' losing the initiative during the latter months of 1643.

GORING, GEORGE, LORD (1608–1657). Goring had served in Europe before returning to England to receive an appointment as governor of Portsmouth in 1639. He then served in both Bishop's Wars (q.v.). In 1641 he formulated the Army Plot (q.v.) but betrayed his fellow conspirators to Parliament (q.v.). He betrayed Parliament at the outbreak of the war and tried to hold Portsmouth for the king, only to flee to France when it became clear that he did not have the support of the town.

In 1643 he returned to England and became lieutenant general to the earl of Newcastle (q.v.). He was captured in May 1643 at the Battle of Wakefield (q.v.), but secured an exchange after nine months in the Tower. He rejoined the Northern Army (q.v.) and led the Horse (q.v.) into Nottinghamshire when Newcastle had to return from the north to defend York (q.v.) in April 1644. From there he joined Prince Rupert's (q.v.) march into the north and was present at the Battle of Marston Moor (q.v.). During the battle he succeeded in defeating and driving from the field the parliamentarian and Scottish right wing, but could not overcome the collapse of the royalist right and was defeated by the remainder of the Scots and East Anglian Horse.

In August 1644 Goring was appointed lieutenant general of the Horse in the Oxford Field Army (q.v.) after Lord Wilmot (q.v.) had been dismissed. He then participated in the Battle of Lostwithiel and the second Battle of Newbury (qq.v.). For much of the winter and spring of 1644–45 Goring was preoccupied with the siege of Taunton (q.v.). He was recalled to the field army in the early stages of the Naseby (q.v.) campaign, although he was sent back to Taunton before the king had left the Midlands. After the Battle of Naseby, for a time he had the most powerful royalist army in existence and Sir Thomas Fairfax (q.v.) moved south-west to deal with him. Goring was defeated at the Battle of Langport (q.v.) on 10 July 1645. He then left the country. Goring served in the English components of the Spanish army during the 1650s and died in Madrid.

GRAND JURIES. In normal circumstances these bodies examined the nature of cases brought to the quarter sessions (q.v.) of the assize courts. The jury's purpose was to ascertain whether the cases were sufficient to be prosecuted before the court or not. In the months before the First Civil War (q.v.), grand juries became the forum for discussions about the political crisis and for drafting and signing of petitions to King Charles I and Parliament (qq.v.). Even during the war the juries had some importance, forcing Charles to reestablish his war effort in Worcestershire, Shropshire, Herefordshire, and Staffordshire along lines more acceptable to the gentry of the counties.

GRAND REMONSTRANCE. In late summer 1641 the impetus for further political change in the nature of government in England and Wales was waning and King Charles I's (q.v.) apparent conciliation seemed to some to have ended contention. John Pym (q.v.) and his supporters, however, did not believe the king could be held to the agreements that had been wrung out of him, nor did they believe that the power structure had been changed sufficiently to rule out the monarch's being able to rule without Parliament (q.v.) in the future. They set about drafting the *Grand Remonstrance*, a document in three parts. First to be outlined were the "evils" of the king's Personal Rule (q.v.), such as ship money (q.v.), and religious innovations were rehearsed. Second, the actions taken by Parliament to end those "evils" were described. Finally, the problems and suggested remedies that remained were set out: these included a role for Parliament in appointing ministers of the crown, Parliament's involvement in the direction of foreign policy, and the right of Parliament to direct the education of the monarch's children.

The House of Commons (q.v.) debated the *Remonstrance* fiercely when it was presented in November. Even in the wake of the Irish Rebellion (q.v.), which seemed to confirm Pym's assertion that the country was still under threat, there seemed little impetus for further change: Unity was called for. The debate lasted 17 hours and in the end it was passed by only 11 votes, although a greater majority was reached in the debate on publishing the document, even though some commentators were clearly unhappy at making public this contentious examination of the problems within the political structure. The king's response in December was conciliatory, being drafted by some of the moderate M.P.s, including Sir Edward Hyde (q.v.). He acknowledged and indicated approval for the changes already undertaken, but also suggested that the further demands were unreasonable and that they worked against traditional precepts of government. Whatever good this approach did the king was swept away, however, when he attempted to arrest the Five Members (q.v.) in January 1642.

GRANDEES. This was the name by which the senior commanders of the New Model Army (q.v.), including Thomas, Lord Fairfax, Oliver Cromwell, and Henry Ireton (qq.v.), were referred to by the Levellers (q.v.) and radicals in the army. The term was an insult, suggesting that the army leaders had assumed an unwarranted superiority, and was applied as relations between the junior officers and rank and file in the army declined from late 1647 onwards.

GRANTHAM, BATTLE OF. Fought on 13 May 1643. Oliver Cromwell (q.v.) was part of a region-wide attempt to capture Newark (q.v.)—a major royalist (q.v.) garrison on the Nottinghamshire–Lincolnshire border. His forces and those from Lincolnshire under John Hotham (q.v.) scouted the area around Newark and then returned to Grantham. They had been followed, however, and as night fell royalists (q.v.) attacked the outposts. Cromwell abandoned Grantham and turned on his attackers at Belton, and in a confusing night fight drove off his opponents, extricated himself successfully, and retreated to Lincoln.

GRENVILE, SIR BEVILL (1596–1643). An Oxford-educated Cornishman from Kellygarth, Grenvile was a friend of Sir John Eliot and an opponent of the king until the First Bishop's War (q.v.) in 1639. Grenvile was an active commissioner of array (q.v.) in summer 1642 and joined Ralph Hopton's (q.v.) army. He fought at the Battle of Braddock Down and Stratton (qq.v.). In June 1643 Grenvile joined Prince Maurice's (q.v.) army and was with it at the Battle of Lansdown Hill (q.v.). In leading an attack up the hill against Sir William Waller's Foot (qq.v.), Grenvile was hit with a pole-axe and died the following day.

GRENVILE, SIR RICHARD (1600–1658). The younger brother of Sir Bevill Grenvile (q.v.). He fought in Ireland after the Irish Rebellion (q.v.), but in 1643 was shipped home after the Cessation (q.v.) and, landing at Liverpool, joined the parliamentarians (q.v.) and was appointed lieutenant general to Sir William Waller (q.v.). On 3 March 1643, however, he fled to Oxford (q.v.) and betrayed all his general's plans. He was then appointed lieutenant general to Ralph Hopton (q.v.). He attacked Plymouth (q.v.) on several occasions and was involved in the defeat of the earl of Essex (q.v.) at the Battle of Lostwithiel (q.v.) in 1644. Grenvile attracted hostility from supporters of both sides for his brutality—in October 1644 he had wanted to murder all the members of the Saltash garrison after he had captured the town. This has been explained as a result of his experience of war in Ireland, although an alternative cause may be the execution of his illegitimate son, caught whilst working as a spy in Plymouth a few weeks earlier.

In 1645 he was involved in Lord Goring's siege of Taunton (qq.v.), although he did not work well with any commander. In January 1645, having recommended that Hopton be called out of semiretirement to lead the royalist forces in the south-west, he refused to serve under him. Prince Charles (q.v.) had Grenvile arrested and placed in Launceston prison. Parliament refused to grant Grenvile a pardon at the end of the war and he went into exile.

GROBY, THOMAS, LORD GREY OF (1623–1657). Son of the earl of Stamford (q.v.) and Leicester M.P., Grey of Groby was only 19 or 20 when appointed to command Parliament's (q.v.) association (q.v.) of East Midland counties. He proved a cautious commander, concerned with strengthening his own territorial hold in Leicestershire before acting on his wider duties. Untrue allegations were made by Sir John Gell (q.v.) that Grey abandoned the siege of Ashby de la Zouch (q.v.) in January 1642 because of groundless rumours that Prince Rupert (q.v.) was approaching. Rupert was advancing towards Ashby and Grey placed his forces in Rupert's way. The prince turned west before reaching Grey's men because he heard that the siege had been raised. Even so, Grey's leadership was uninspired, and his association failed to achieve headway in the face of Lord Loughborough's (q.v.) determined campaigns. By the time Parliament achieved superiority in the East Midlands in the summer of 1644, the association had been broken up and Grey had retired from the scene.

On 6 December 1648, Grey assisted Colonel Thomas Pride (q.v.) in excluding the Presbyterian (q.v.) members of the House of Commons (q.v.). Pride's Purge (q.v.) paved the way for the trial of King Charles I (q.v.). Grey was a member of the High Court of Justice (q.v.) and his is the first signature on Charles I's death warrant after that of the court president, John Bradshaw (q.v.). Grey became a Fifth Monarchist (q.v.) during the 1650s and became politically estranged from his father. He died before succeeding to his father's title of Stamford.

⇜ H ⇝

HACKER, FRANCIS (?–1660). In East Bridgeford near Nottingham, Hacker served in the Leicestershire parliamentarian (q.v.) forces and on the county committee (q.v.) from 1643. He was captured at a fight at Melton Mowbray (q.v.) in 1644, but was exchanged later in the war, becoming a colonel of Horse (q.v.). In 1649 he officiated at the execution of Charles I (q.v.) for which, at the Restoration (q.v.) he was arrested and executed.

HACKER, ROWLAND (?–1674). Brother of Francis Hacker (q.v.) and also of East Bridgeford in Nottinghamshire. First a captain in royalist Richard Byron's Horse (qq.v.). He then became a major in Henry Hastings's (q.v.) Horse, governor of the short-lived garrison at Trent Bridge, and then at Wiverton House near Newark (q.v.).

HAMBLEDON HILL, DORSET. On 4 August 1645, a gathering of 2,000 Clubmen (q.v.) was attacked by the New Model Army (q.v.). These clubmen were from Dorset and Wiltshire, and unlike their colleagues in Somerset, opposed the entry of the New Model into their territory, their political sympathies resting more with King Charles I (q.v.). Oliver Cromwell's (q.v.) attack on the Clubmen ended any hopes of converting them into a royalist (q.v.) peoples' army.

HAMILTON, JAMES STEWART, DUKE OF (1606–1649). A cousin of Charles I (q.v.), Hamilton acted as the king's commissioner in Scotland from 1637, where he tried to mediate between the king and the Covenanters (q.v.). His failure to moderate the king's approach meant that his mission could not succeed, and he became embroiled in the king's military plans during the Bishop's Wars (q.v.). During 1640–41 Hamilton signed the Covenant and his daughter married the leader of the Covenanters, the marquis of Argyll (q.v.). In October that year, Charles, who now counted Hamilton an enemy, countenanced the plot to kidnap Hamilton and his brother, which became known as the Incident (q.v.). During the First Civil War (q.v.) Hamilton tried to keep the Covenanters from siding with the Parliament (q.v.) in Westminster, but failed. Charles had him imprisoned in England. Upon his release, Hamilton successfully steered the Scottish Estates (q.v.) towards the king's cause, exploiting the growing mistrust of the influence of the Independents (q.v.) in the English and Welsh Parliament (q.v.). Hamilton secured the treaty, known as the Engagement (q.v.), with the king and in July 1649 led the Engager (q.v.) army into England. This force was defeated at the Battle of Preston (q.v.) by Oliver Cromwell (q.v.) and Hamilton was captured. In 1649 Hamilton was tried by the High Court of Justice (q.v.) and executed.

HAMILTON, WILLIAM STEWART, 2ND DUKE OF (?–1651). Brother of the first Duke of Hamilton (q.v.), known then as the Earl of Lanark, he served as Scottish secretary in the early 1640s, when he, with his brother, signed the Covenant (q.v.). He was also targeted for kidnap in the Incident (q.v.), but was warned and went into hiding. During the 1640s Lanark continued to participate in the executive of the Estates (q.v.) despite his conservative or royalist (q.v.) leanings. In 1648–49 he supported his brother's moves in taking the Scots into the Engagement (q.v.). In the wake of defeat in the Second Civil War (q.v.) Lanark's power declined and he lost his place in government. He then joined the royalist exiles in Holland.

Hamilton's fortunes rose again following Charles II's (q.v.) voyage to Scotland in 1650, but more particularly after the defeat at the Battle of Dunbar (q.v.) had weakened the power of the Kirk Party (q.v.). After his brother's execution, Lanark became the second duke of Hamilton and fought with Charles II's army at the Battle of Worcester (q.v.), where he was fatally wounded.

HAMPDEN, JOHN (1594–1643). Hampden was from Great Hampden in Buckinghamshire, educated at Oxford University and a cousin of Oliver Cromwell (q.v.). He served as an M.P. during the 1620 Parliaments of King Charles I (qq.v.), but came to prominence in 1636–37 when he refused to pay a ship money (q.v.) levy of 20 shillings. Hampden was defended by Oliver St John (q.v.), and the defence was based on the notion that whilst the king could decide to levy emergency taxes in times of danger, as was claimed in relation to ship money, normally taxation was the responsibility of Parliament. Hampden contested that since the first levy of ship money there had been ample time for Parliament to have been called and levied ordinary taxation. Seven of 12 judges assembled from the prerogative courts to try the case sided with the king, a verdict that was to encourage opposition to the tax rather than lessen it.

In the Short Parliament (q.v.) Hampden was placed on the committee to investigate ship money. In the Long Parliament (q.v.) Hampden was initially a moderate who did not want to see the earl of Strafford (q.v.) executed by Act of Attainder (q.v.). However, this position was undermined when, with the king in Edinburgh during the autumn of 1641, he witnessed the king's apparent involvement in The Incident (q.v.), and it was clear that the king regarded him as a dangerous enemy. In January 1642 Hampden was one of the Five Members (q.v.) Charles tried to arrest.

When the war broke out in England, Hampden raised a regiment of Foot (q.v.). This regiment served in the very last moments of the Battle of Edgehill (q.v.) when it was attacked as it arrived in Kineton village. It also served at the Battle of Brentford (q.v.). In the summer of 1643 Hampden urged the earl of Essex (q.v.) to attack Oxford (q.v.), but was mortally wounded at the Battle of Chalgrove Field. It is believed that the course of the subsequent war and revolutions would have been different had he lived. Hampden's integrity was recognised by both sides.

HAMPTON COURT. Originally build by Thomas Wolsey, the palace came into the hands of Henry VIII. Charles I (q.v.) and his family fled to the palace after the failure to arrest the Five Members (q.v.). During the summer of 1647, when the New Model Army (q.v.) moved on London, King Charles I was lodged at Hampton Court. Here negotiations were reopened following the king's rejection of the Heads of the Proposals (q.v.) with which he had been presented by the leadership of the army. On 11 November, after long negotiations with Scottish commissioners, Charles I escaped and fled to Carisbrooke on the Isle of Wight.

HARLECH CASTLE. Harlech was seized early in the war by royalists (q.v.) and was held by them throughout the war. By June 1646 it was one of the handful of castles still holding out against Parliament's (q.v.) conquest of Wales. The castle, under its governor William Owen, did not surrender until 15 March 1647, the last garrison outside Scotland to do so in the First Civil War (q.v.).

HARLEY, LADY BRILLIANA (1600–1643). Brilliana who had been born in the United Provinces town of Brill, married Sir Robert Harley (q.v.) in 1623. Brilliana was associated with the Puritan (q.v.) or "godly" community of Herefordshire and viewed the policies of the Archbishop of Canterbury William Laud (q.v.) with alarm. As factions developed across the country in 1641–42, Brilliana Harley was almost the sole exception in the Herefordshire social elite, which was predominantly royalist (q.v.). When war broke out in 1642 Brilliana set about the protection of her home Brampton Bryan (q.v.). The county was of major strategic importance in the links between Wales and England, and the garrison became important. After the spring 1643 campaigns of Sir William Waller (q.v.) in Herefordshire ended with his abandonment of Hereford in April, the county was, with the exception of Brampton Bryan, a royalist county. In the summer of that year the royalists decided to remove this last obstacle. The garrison was besieged from July 26 by Sir William Vavasour with around 700 men. With a garrison of 50 musketeers and 50 civilians, Brilliana defended the castle for seven weeks against military assault and even royal intervention. The siege was lifted on 9 September when Vavasour was directed to join the main royalist army in an attack on the earl of Essex (q.v.). Unfortunately the siege had strained Brilliana's health and she died on 31 October.

HARLEY, SIR ROBERT (1579–1656). From Brampton Bryan (q.v.) in Herefordshire, Harley served the county in Parliament (q.v.) in the early years of James VI and I, again in the 1620s, and again in the Long Parliament (q.v.). He had served as master of the mint from 1626–35 under the patronage of his father-in-law Lord Conway, father of his third wife, Brilliana Harley (q.v.). His political and religious views centred on opposition to Archbishop William Laud's (q.v.) policies but he harboured a desire to act as a royal official in his own county as a justice of the peace and deputy lieutenant.

By 1640 Harley was an opponent of King Charles I's (q.v.) government and attacked the Council of Wales and the Marches (q.v.) for its power over the English shires bordering Wales, as part of the attack on the prerogative courts. During the First Civil War (q.v.), Harley became associated with John Pym's (q.v.) Middle Group, which wanted vigorous prosecution of the war to negotiate from a position of strength. His attraction for the Presbyterian (q.v.) church system and his affinity for the Scots colored his attitude to the New Model Army (q.v.) in the postwar years. By 1647 his desire to disband the army led to the demand by the army that he be excluded from Parliament as one of the Eleven Members (q.v.). Pride's Purge (q.v.), which saw Harley briefly imprisoned as well as the subsequent execution of the king in 1649, ended Harley's political career and he went into retirement until his death.

HARQUEBUSIERS. By the time of the civil wars this was an outmoded term for lightly armed cavalry or Horse (q.v.). The term derived from the firearm, the harquebus, a short-barrelled matchlock (q.v.) musket that had been replaced by the carbine by the 1640s. By 1640 the armour worn by an harquebusier consisted of a three-barred or lobster-pot helmet, the latter name deriving from the sometimes articulated rear-neck guard, back and breast plates, and an armoured elbow-gauntlet for the rein-holding left arm. Many regiments wore a buff coat instead of this armour.

HARRISON, THOMAS (1616–1660). Harrison was a radical amongst the officers of the New Model Army (q.v.), and an M.P. from 1645 onwards. He commanded a regiment from 1647, having previously served as major to Charles Fleetwood (q.v.). His radicalism ensured that Harrison sought to bring the army and the Levellers (q.v.) closer together, and his regiment turned up at the Corkbush Field (q.v.) rendezvous with the *Agreement of the People* (q.v.) in their hats. During the Second Civil War (q.v.) Harrison's regiment fought the Scots' Engager (q.v.) army in the north. In December 1648 Harrison escorted Charles I to Westminster (qq.v.) for his trial and sat as part of the High Court of Justice (q.v.). He also signed the king's death warrant. In the early 1650s Harrison rose to the rank of major general (q.v.) and commanded forces in the south-east. He was present at the Battle of Worcester (q.v.) the following year.

By this time Harrison was associated with the Fifth Monarchists (q.v.) and having participated in the expulsion of the Rump Parliament (q.v.) in April 1653, sat as the leader of the Fifth Monarchists in the Barebones Parliament (q.v.). When he opposed the establishment of the Protectorate (q.v.), Harrison was dismissed from the army and was imprisoned during the following year. He was then laid low by ill health and played no further role in politics. In 1660 he was singled out for retribution. He was the first of the regicides (q.v.) to be executed.

HASELRIGG. *See* HESILRIGE.

HASTINGS, HENRY. *See* LOUGHBOROUGH, LORD.

HEADS OF THE PROPOSALS. This was the proposed treaty drawn up by the leadership of the New Model Army (q.v.) and presented to Charles I (q.v.) in July 1647. The proposals were fairly generous, and did not impose a Presbyterian (q.v.) system on England or Wales. There was to be a biennial Parliament (q.v.) with an executive made up of the king and a Council of State (q.v.) whose members would be chosen by Parliament. Parliament would be fully involved in foreign and military affairs, as had been demanded in the Ten Propositions, *Grand Remonstrance*, and the Nineteen Propositions (qq.v.). The Church of England was to remain disestablished, but the Covenant (q.v.) would not be imposed. There was to be an act of indemnity for parliamentarians (q.v.), and the massive list of proscribed royalists (q.v.) contained in the Newcastle Propositions (q.v.) was scaled down. The king was to be debarred from military power for only 10 years.

Despite the generosity of these terms, which annoyed the army rank and file and the Levellers (q.v.), the king rejected them in an attempt to again divide his enemies. The Heads of the Proposals had been essentially an Independent (q.v.) document, and the king now saw his chance to appeal to the Presbyterians (q.v.) and to the Scots; his discussions with the latter eventually led to the signing of the Engagement (q.v.).

HELMESLEY CASTLE. In the north Riding of Yorkshire, this castle initially represented a part of the royalist (q.v.) hold on the north of England, but following the Battle of Marston Moor (q.v.) it became a symbol of the royalist determination to hold on to the small pockets of territory in the north. It was placed under siege in August 1644 and surrendered to John Lambert (q.v.) on 22 November that year.

HENDERSON, ALEXANDER (1583–1646). Minister of Leuchars in Scotland, in 1638 he was responsible, with Archibald Johnston (q.v.) of Wariston for drafting the Covenant (q.v.). In the wake of the Covenanters' defeat of King Charles I (q.v.) in the Bishop's Wars (q.v.), Henderson became the king's chaplain. Henderson failed to get the king to seek the assistance of the Scots in 1642 and in 1643 drafted the Solemn League and Covenant (q.v.) establishing the alliance between Scotland and the Parliament (q.v.) at Westminster. Henderson became one of the Scottish commissioners present at the Westminster Assembly of Divines (q.v.), and assisted in the creation of the *Directory of Public Worship* (q.v.). He was influential in trying to press the king to accept a Presbyterian (q.v.) system at the Treaty of Uxbridge (q.v.) discussions of 1645, and again after the king's surrender at Newark (q.v.), when Charles allowed Henderson to accompany him to Newcastle (q.v.).

HENRIETTA MARIA, QUEEN (1609–1669). Born the sixth child of Henri IV, Henrietta was married by proxy to Charles I (q.v.) in 1625. Their marriage was stormy for the first few years, and only became affectionate and stable following the death of the duke of Buckingham in 1628. Henrietta introduced some French customs into the English court, including the participation of women in masques, which offended John Bastwicke (q.v.) so much. It was her Catholicism (q.v.) and the way that her marriage treaty allowed her to exercise in public that offended many. In the period of crisis—1640–42—the queen was involved in the Army Plot (q.v.). There was a danger in early 1642 that her behaviour was about to prompt Parliament (q.v.) into impeaching her and Charles sent her abroad to raise money for arms by selling the crown jewels.

On 23 February 1643, she landed at Bridlington (q.v.) Quay with a large cache of arms that was in part used to create an army of her own; the army escorted the rest of the munitions southwards in June 1643. On her way to join the king she used her army to support Lord Loughborough (q.v.) in threatening the garrison at Nottingham and then attacking and capturing Burton on Trent. She resided at Oxford (q.v.) until spring 1644 when the city was threatened by the armies of Sir William Waller and the earl of Essex (qq.v.). Heavily pregnant, the queen moved to Exeter, but when the attack on Oxford failed and Essex, on a whim, decided to march into the west, she was placed in danger again. The child was born in June, but the queen, herself very ill, had to leave it behind as she was evacuated to France; the child joined her in 1646. Henrietta remained in France until the Restoration (q.v.). In the 1650s she attempted to influence the court of her son Charles II (q.v.) with little success; nevertheless she maintained a powerful faction of royalist (q.v.) exiles around her. She visited England twice during his reign, but died in France.

HERBERT, LORD. *See* GLAMORGAN, EARL OF.

HERTFORD, WILLIAM SEYMOUR, MARQUIS OF (1587–1660). Privy counsellor to Charles I (q.v.) from 1641 onwards, he was present at York (q.v.) in 1642 until being sent into the south-west to raise forces. He commanded the army he raised with Ralph Hopton (q.v.) in the summer of that year. Upon being driven from Somerset and his garrison at Sherbourne Castle in early September 1642, Hertford took the Horse (q.v.) across the Bristol (q.v.) Channel into south Wales whilst Hopton retreated with the Foot (q.v.) into Cornwall. In Wales Hertford galvanised Lord Carberry and Lord Herbert (qq.v.) and raised forces in south Wales counties. With these forces he forced the parliamentarian earl of Stamford (qq.v.) to withdraw his troops from Worcester (q.v.) and Hereford. This grip in the southern Marcher counties (q.v.) did not last and Hertford's forces were defeated by Sir William Waller (q.v.) during the spring. Hertford was able to exact some revenge, for it was he and Prince Maurice (q.v.) who brought Horse from Oxford (q.v.) on 13 July, which enabled Hopton's royalist (q.v.) forces to defeat Waller at the Battle of Roundway Down (q.v.). Hertford was from then on mainly involved in the court at Oxford and was present at the Treaty of Uxbridge (q.v.) negotiations.

HESILRIGE, SIR ARTHUR (1601–1661). Of Noseley in Leicestershire, his father was one of the Five Knights arrested for their opposition to the forced loans (q.v.) of the 1620s. Hesilrige interrupted the collection of ship money (q.v.) in his county during the 1630s. Elected M.P. for Leicester in the Short and Long Parliaments (qq.v.). Hesilrige was a leading figure in the attempts to dismantle Charles I's (q.v.) government; he introduced the Act of Attainder (q.v.) against Thomas Wentworth, earl of Strafford (q.v.) in 1641. His leading role was acknowledged when Charles attempted to arrest him as one of the Five Members (q.v.) in January 1642. In the First Civil War (q.v.) Hesilrige raised a troop of armoured Horse (q.v.) nicknamed "the Lobsters" because of their dated three-quarter armour. The Lobsters served with Sir William Waller's (q.v.) forces in the south-west and were involved in his defeat at the Battle of Roundway Down (q.v.) in 1643 and in Waller's victory at the Battle of Cheriton (q.v.) in 1644.

Hesilrige was a member of the Committee of Both Kingdoms (q.v.) and was a religious Independent (q.v.). In 1648 he opposed Pride's Purge (q.v.) and the subsequent trial and execution of Charles I. His essential Republicanism led him to take a place on the Council of State (q.v.). He was a leading figure in the Rump Parliament (q.v.) during the early 1650s and saw it as more than the stopgap others perceived it to be. The expulsion of the Parliament and the establishment of the Protectorate (q.v.) was therefore anathema to him and Hesilrige became identified as one of the Commonwealthmen (q.v.) opponents of Oliver Cromwell (q.v.). Although elected to the first Parliament under the Instrument of Government (q.v.) Hesilrige was excluded at the door of the house by troops for debating the new constitution. He was also elected to the Parliament of Richard Cromwell (q.v.) and after the collapse of the Protectorate he returned to the House of Commons (q.v.) with the Rump Parliament in 1659. Hesilrige seems not have stood for election to the Convention Parliament (q.v.) in 1660 and was imprisoned at the Restoration (q.v.). He died in the Tower of London.

HEWSON, COLONEL JOHN (?–1662). Hewson rose to command what had been John Pickering's regiment of Foot (q.v.) in the parliamentarian New Model Army (qq.v.). He was an Independent (q.v.) in religious affairs, but did not favour the political radicalism of the Levellers (q.v.). In 1648–49 he drafted the army's justification for moving on London, and then participated in the High Court of Justice (q.v.), which tried Charles I (q.v.) and then signed his death warrant. From 1649 his regiment served with the army in Ireland at Drogheda (q.v.). After the Restoration (q.v.) Hewson went into exile and died in Holland.

HIGH COMMISSION, COURT OF. This was the supreme court of the Church of England established by Henry VIII, which examined church affairs and maintained the Reformation church. It could also be used as a means of ensuring conformity to a style of church governance, however, and in the 1630s was the tool with which Archbishop William Laud (q.v.) sought to bring about his desire of order and conformity. The church was also able to effect censorship of the press. The association with Laud prompted the Long Parliament (q.v.) to abolish the court in July 1641. This had the effect of allowing for the burgeoning of an unfettered press in England and Wales.

HIGH COURT OF JUSTICE. This court was established on 1 January 1649 to try King Charles I (q.v.). It was presided over by John Bradshaw (q.v.). The court consisted of 150 commissioners drawn from Parliament (q.v.) and local government in England and Wales, although many of the nominees, including Thomas, Lord Fairfax (q.v.) refused to attend. The court held public sessions from 21 January and Charles I was sentenced to death on 27 January. The court later tried Lord Capel, the duke of Hamilton (qq.v.), and others captured at the end of the Second Civil War (q.v.).

HIGHLANDS/HIGHLANDERS. The inhabitants of the Highland region of north, west, and central Scotland as well as the west coast islands. These Gaelic-speaking clans included some who were firmly attached to the Catholic (q.v.) faith and those, such as the Macdonalds, who had strong links with north-east Ulster (q.v.). However, the Campbells, led by the principal Covenanter (q.v.), the marquis of Argyll (q.v.), were also Highlanders. There were distinct cultural as well as language differences between the Highlanders and the residents of the lowlands; their mode of dress was still a more traditional use of the kilt and their farming systems were more heavily dependent on pasture farming. In the Civil Wars the Highlanders assembled by the marquis of Montrose (q.v.) were fighting as much for their own social, political, and religious agenda as for King Charles I (q.v.); indeed, neither the king nor his father, James VI, had shown much sympathy towards the Highlanders, who they both saw as lawless and disorderly. The same reasons for fighting could be levelled at the Covenanter clans under Argyll. In the 1650s the Protectorate (q.v.) adopted a conciliatory attitude to the Highlands in pacified areas, but acted cruelly against clans associated with disorder.

HIGHNAM, BATTLE OF. This battle, fought on 23 March 1643, ended the control of the Marcher counties (q.v.) established by Lord Herbert and Lord Hertford (qq.v.) in the spring of 1643. Sir William Waller (q.v.) went on the offensive in March. He defeated the royalists (q.v.) under Lord Herbert at the Battle of Highnam in Gloucestershire and then two days later ended the royalists' siege of Gloucester (q.v.). This opened up south Wales to invasion, but after initially pursuing the royalists into Monmouthshire, Waller turned northwards and, in the face of his advance, the royalist command in Herefordshire collapsed. Hereford was occupied shortly afterwards.

HILL OF CROFTY. On 3 December 1641, representatives of the Catholic (q.v.) Irish Rebels led by Rory More met Old English (q.v.) representatives at the Hill of Crofty near Drogheda (q.v.), a town where English forces were under siege. The aim was to bring together these two groups, in the light of the general blame being attached to all Catholics by the executive in Dublin (q.v.). The meeting was a success. Leading former loyalists like Viscount Mayo were won over and a remonstrance setting out the rebels' belief that a "Puritan" (q.v.) faction was subverting King Charles I's (q.v.) government and church in Ireland, was drafted.

HILTON, BATTLE OF. Fought on 23 March 1644, this was one of the attempts made by the royalist (q.v.) commander in the north, the marquis of Newcastle (q.v.), to bring the Scottish Army of the Solemn League and Covenant (q.v.) to battle as it advanced into northern England in 1644. The army had invaded England on 18 January 1644 and successfully avoided being engaged in a fight. By 23 March, the Scots had been forced to retreat to Sunderland on the River Wear after the Battle of Boldon Hills (q.v.). At Hilton, however, although the Scots suffered heavy casualties, they could not be drawn into a major battle. Their advance continued slowly until the defeat of the Yorkshire royalists at the Battle of Selby (q.v.), when the marquis of Newcastle had to retreat southwards leaving the roads open to the Scots.

HOBBES, THOMAS (1588–1679). Hobbes's political philosophy enabled the Civil War to be seen as the result of humankind's factious state. This he set out in his work, *Leviathan*, published in 1651. He observed the Civil Wars from Paris, where he had fled in 1640, having been a resident at the home of the earl of Devonshire and sometimes at that of the earl of Newcastle (q.v.) before the war. Much of his philosophical work was dedicated to the prevention of civil wars through the imposition of monumental state authority, often identified as a monarchy, supported by rational obedience. Such obedience would preclude the development of factious religious sects, which by the 1660s he blamed for the civil wars. Hobbes's view of a monarchy did not accord with that of the Stuarts, however, as it did not allow for Divine Right (q.v.). When he presented *Leviathan* to Charles II (q.v.) in 1651, he angered the royalists (q.v.) and so fled to London. *Leviathan* did not offer grounds for Parliament's (q.v.) claims to authority either, but Hobbes practised what he had preached and remained obedient to the leviathans of the Commonwealth and Protectorate (qq.v.). At the Restoration (q.v.) Hobbes was accorded a pension by Charles II.

HOLDENBY HOUSE, NORTHAMPTONSHIRE. When at the end of January 1647 the Scottish forces left England, they handed King Charles I (q.v.) over to the Parliament (q.v.) at Westminster. The king was escorted southwards and by spring was lodged at Holdenby. On 3 June he was seized from there and taken to the rendezvous of the New Model Army (q.v.) at Newmarket by Cornet George Joyce (q.v.) and a troop of Horse (q.v.).

HOLLAND, HENRY RICH, EARL OF (1590–1649). Holland played little role in the first stages of the First Civil War (q.v.), indeed he had an ambiguous position. As a Puritan (q.v.) he had connections within the oppositionist groups, his brother was the earl of Warwick (q.v.), but he was part of Queen Henrietta Maria's (q.v.) household. He had played a major part in the humiliation of the English forces at Kelso in 1639 during the first Bishop's War (q.v.) when he precipitated retreat. In London in late 1642 he was involved in the defence of the town on the eve of the Battle of Turnham Green (q.v.), but was prominent in the Peace Party (q.v.). In the middle of 1643 he joined King Charles I (q.v.) and fought at the first Battle of Newbury (q.v.), but then returned to Parliament (q.v.) out of pique when passed over for an appointment to the king's bedchamber.

In 1648 he led a force determined to relieve the royalists (q.v.) besieged in Colchester (q.v.) but was defeated and captured at St Neots. He was tried before the High Court of Justice (q.v.) along with Lord Capel and the duke of Hamilton (qq.v.). He was executed on 9 March 1649.

HOLLES, DENZIL (1598–1680). Second son of the 1st earl of Clare and brother to the second earl, Holles was a noted member of Parliament (q.v.) in the 1620s when he represented a Cornish seat. He played little part in Parliament until March 1629, when he joined Sir John Eliot and others in holding the speaker, John Finch (q.v.), in his chair preventing the dissolution of Parliament until after several resolutions against church reform had been passed. For this he was imprisoned, but unlike Eliot, William Strode, or Benjamin Valentine (qq.v.) Holles was released after apologising. In 1640 Holles was elected to both the Short Parliament and the Long Parliament (qq.v.), and was one of the Five Members (q.v.) Charles I (q.v.) attempted to arrest in January 1642.

During the First Civil War (q.v.) Holles rose to prominence in the Peace Party (q.v.), whilst after the war this and his Presbyterianism (q.v.), marked him as an enemy of the New Model Army (q.v.) and he became one of the Eleven Members (q.v.) forced to leave Parliament during the summer of 1647. He then fled to France. In the early 1650s he worked on behalf of Charles II (q.v.), although he returned to England in 1654 where his son sat in the Protectorate (q.v.) parliaments. Holles returned to Parliament himself when George Monck (q.v.) recalled all the secluded members of the Long Parliament. At the Restoration (q.v.) Holles again returned to Parliament and was made Baron Holles of Ifield in 1661.

HOPKINS, MATTHEW (?–1647). This self-styled witchfinder-general was able to exploit the dysfunction of the civil war period in East Anglia to further his reputation for detecting witches for a fee. Hopkins came to prominence in 1645 in Essex when involved in the Manningtree witch trials. He was involved in the trial of hundreds of women and thus in their judicial murder in 1645–46 from which he made over a thousand pounds. He published *The Discovery of Witches*, a highly derivative pamphlet, in 1647. Hopkins's death is something of a mystery: according to his assistant John Stearne, he died peacefully, but it is also possible that he too was hanged for witchcraft after his methods were challenged.

HOPTON, SIR RALPH, LORD (1598–1652). A graduate of Oxford University, Hopton fought in the army of the elector palatine at the Battle of the White Mountain in 1620. He and his friend William Waller (q.v.) escorted Elizabeth, the Queen of Bohemia and sister to the future Charles I (q.v.), to Breslau. Knighted in 1626 and M.P. in the 1626 and the 1628 Parliament (q.v.), by the 1640s he was a moderate opponent of the king. By 1642 he had sided with the king and became second in command to Lord Hertford (q.v.) in the south-west. He became the leading royalist (q.v.) general in that area and defeated the earl of Stamford's (q.v.) forces at the Battles of Braddock Down and Stratton (qq.v.).

His old friend Waller defeated Hopton at the Battle of Lansdown Hill (q.v.). During Waller's ensuing siege of Devizes, Hopton sprung a neat trap by sending for reinforcements from Oxford (q.v.), which secured victory at the Battle of Roundway Down (q.v.) on 13 July. He became deputy governor of Bristol (q.v.) that month after Prince Rupert (q.v.) had captured the city, and was made Lord Hopton of Stratton in the fall. In the spring of 1644 he was placed under the command of Lord Forth (q.v.), and the problems of divided command in part led to their defeat by Waller at the Battle of Cheriton (q.v.) on 29 March. Their army was then incorporated into the Oxford Field Army (q.v.) and Hopton was given command of the artillery and sent with Prince Charles (q.v.) to the west as part of the prince's council.

The collapse of the royalist (q.v.) cause in the west was exacerbated by Lord Goring's (q.v.) behaviour. Hopton took control, but defeat was inevitable and at the Battle of Torrington (q.v.) he was defeated by Sir Thomas Fairfax (q.v.). Hopton went into exile, joining Prince Charles's fleet in 1648. In 1650 he led a small fleet sailing off the coast of his native Cornwall, but his opposition to Charles II's adoption of Presbyterianism (q.v.) prevented his involvement with the campaigns of 1650–51. He died in Bruges.

HOPTON HEATH, BATTLE OF. Fought on 19 March 1643. In an attempt to capture Stafford for Parliament (q.v.), following the capture of Lichfield (q.v.) in early March, Sir William Brereton and Sir John Gell (qq.v.) assembled their forces on nearby Hopton Heath. Royalist forces under Henry Hastings and the earl of Northampton (qq.v.), camped around Stafford, rushed out to meet them. With an army consisting principally of Horse (q.v.), the royalists charged onto the heath and with successive attacks drove the parliamentarian (q.v.) army off the field. Northampton was killed during the fighting, and Gell attempted, but failed, to swap his body for the artillery lost during the battle. The victory secured the royalist position in the county and Lichfield was recaptured the following month by Hastings and Prince Rupert (q.v.).

HORSE. The common term for cavalry, mounted troops that fought on horseback. There were two principal types: the cuirassier, such as the "Lobsters" created by Sir Arthur Hesilrige (q.v.), which died out during the war; and the Harquebusier (q.v.). The battlefield tactics of the Horse had undergone dramatic changes in Europe on the eve of the Civil War. The Horse had previously been used to rapidly bring concentrated firepower to bear on the enemy, however, King Gustavus Adolphus had instead used the combined weight and speed of charge to break enemy formations. At the Battles of Powick Bridge and Edgehill, Prince Rupert (qq.v.) used this method successfully and thus set the pattern for cavalry tactics in the war. It was a method improved upon by Oliver Cromwell (q.v.) and others who urged the retention of discipline and order after a charge to enable effective fighting in subsequent actions, as opposed to the disorganised melee and pursuit that followed Rupert's initial charges at Edgehill and in later battles.

At the outset of formal pitched battles, the Horse would be assembled in bodies on either side of the Foot (q.v.) arranged in the centre. The second in command of an army, the lieutenant general, was normally the commander of the Horse. Horse troops were expensive as the billeting charges of Horse and man were double that of a man at around 4d each a night. In the initial stages of the war troopers were expected to provide their own mounts and thus were of fairly high social status such as husbandmen.

HOTHAM, SIR JOHN (c.1585–1645). Hotham served in European wars in the 1620s and played a role in government in Yorkshire in the 1630s where he incurred the animosity of Thomas Wentworth (q.v.). He served as M.P. for Beverley in Charles I's (q.v.) early Parliaments (q.v.) and again in the Short and Long Parliaments (qq.v.), by which time he opposed the king and in 1641 gave evidence against Wentworth at his trial. By April 1642 Hotham had been appointed governor of Hull (q.v.), which by this time was a depository for much of the magazine from the Tower of London moved there during the Bishop's Wars (q.v.). Hotham defied Charles I when he requested entry to the town, and was proclaimed a traitor by the king. Attempts were made during the summer to seduce Hotham from Parliament, but he held out, defying a siege in July.

By 1643 Hotham and his son, John (q.v.), were seriously considering changing sides, and entered into secret negotiations with the earl of Newcastle and Queen Henrietta Maria (qq.v.). In the summer, the two Hothams were arrested and sent to the Tower of London. Their correspondence with Newcastle came to light after the Battle of Marston Moor (q.v.), confirming their guilt. They were tried and Sir John was executed on 2 January 1645.

HOTHAM, JOHN (1622–1645). Son of Sir John Hotham (q.v.), the younger Hotham was the most active leader of the parliamentarian (q.v.) forces in the summer of 1642, attacking royalist (q.v.) strongholds across the county from his father's base at Hull (q.v.). It is possible that he did not like being subordinated to the command of Lord Fairfax (q.v.) and his son, Sir Thomas Fairfax (q.v.), even though he was appointed lieutenant general of Horse (q.v.). Certainly, by the spring of 1643, he thought of changing sides alongside his father, and discussed the matter at Bridlington (q.v.) Quay with Queen Henrietta Maria and the earl of Newcastle (qq.v.). His forces served in Lincolnshire that spring, and his fellow parliamentarians at Nottingham became suspicious of him, as he appeared to be corresponding with the royalist garrison at Newark (q.v.). John Hotham was arrested in June but escaped and fled to Hull, where he was again arrested and with his father sent to the Tower. He was tried in November 1644 and executed on 1 January 1645.

HOUSE OF COMMONS. *See* PARLIAMENT, ENGLISH.

HOUSE OF LORDS. *See* PARLIAMENT, ENGLISH.

HULL, KINGSTON UPON. A major fishing and trading port on the River Hull, the town became important as the landing point for soldiers shipped from southern England during the Bishop's Wars (q.v.), and the repository of the magazine from the Tower of London. On 23 April 1642, Charles I (q.v.) attempted to gain entrance to the town, but the governor, Sir John Hotham (q.v.) defied him, marking the willingness of Parliament's (q.v.) supporters to defy the king's will. In July Hull was besieged by the king's army led by the earl of Lindsey (q.v.). Hotham flooded the area around the town, and on 27 July captured the royalist (q.v.) headquarters, after which the siege ended. During the rest of the year Sir John's son, John Hotham (q.v.), used the town as a base for successful military operations in Yorkshire.

In the summer of 1644, as a result of the success of the earl of Newcastle's (q.v.) forces in Yorkshire, Hull, having survived the Hotham's attempts to betray it, became the only major centre of parliamentarian activity in the north-east of England, and a refuge for all parliamentarian forces in the area. On 2 September 1643, Newcastle besieged the town with 16,000 men, but the governor, Sir John Meldrum (q.v.), defied the besiegers successfully for six weeks with help from sea-borne forces led by Thomas Rainsborough (q.v.). Newcastle abandoned the siege on 12 October after a seven-hour battle, but his forces had been severely depleted by disease. This contributed to their ineffectiveness in dealing the final blow to Parliament's cause in the north, and to Newcastle's inability to lead his army southwards. From that time on Hull's position became secure, although the end of the war brought no relief from royalist pirates preying on east coast fishing.

HUMBLE PETITION AND ADVICE. In 1656 Oliver Cromwell's (q.v.) second Parliament (q.v.) presented him with the *Humble Petition and Advice*, requesting that the constitution adopted at the outset of the Protectorate (q.v.), the *Instrument of Government* (q.v.), be altered. One provision was that the lord protector (q.v.) become a king; this Cromwell rejected and the modified *Humble Petition* was passed by Parliament on 25 May 1657. The protector could now choose a successor, and the power of the Council of State (q.v.) (to be renamed the Privy Council [q.v.]) was reduced by the creation of a second house filled with lifelong members nominated by the protector.

HUMBLE PETITION OF DIVERS WEL AFFECTED PERSONS. In September 1648, in the wake of the Second Civil War (q.v.), the Levellers (q.v.) presented this conciliatory petition to Parliament (q.v.) after Parliament had again opened negotiations (the Treaty of Newport [q.v.]) with King Charles I (q.v.). Whilst the petition was milder than the addresses made to Parliament by the Levellers in 1647, it nevertheless asked that they render the House of Lords (q.v.) and the king politically impotent, call annual Parliaments, and other provisions set out in the *Agreement of the People* (q.v.) drawn up a year earlier. The Levellers were hoping to forestall any agreement with the king that would exclude themselves or the army. The House of Commons (q.v.) was polite in its reception of the petition, but did little to put it into effect, something that prepared the way for the political revolution at the end of the year as demands for action against the king became more vocal.

HUMBLE REPRESENTATION OF THE GENERAL COUNCIL OF THE ARMY. In the wake of the Corkbush Field (q.v.) mutiny, the commanders of the New Model Army and the General Council of the Army (q.q.v) presented the Parliament (q.v.) with this petition, on 7 December 1647, calling for secure funding for the armed forces.

HUNTING OF THE FOXES, THE. This Leveller (q.v.) tract accused the grandees (q.v.), the high command of the New Model Army (q.v.), namely, Thomas, Lord Fairfax, Oliver Cromwell, and Henry Ireton (qq.v.), of betraying the people. The pamphlet may have been written by Richard Overton or John Lilburne (qq.v.) or by both men and was published on 21 March 1649. The pamphlet openly accused Cromwell and the others of planning the events that occurred after the removal of King Charles I (q.v.) from Holdenby House (q.v.) in order to seize power. The tone and inference in the pamphlet clearly indicates that the Levellers expected a clash with the army. That clash did come in May with the Burford (q.v.) Mutiny.

HUNTLY, GEORGE GORDON, MARQUIS OF (?–1649). Huntly was the prominent royalist (q.v.) in north eastern Scotland. During the Bishop's Wars (q.v.) it was Huntly who led opposition to the Covenanters (q.v.) in Scotland. In the Civil Wars of 1644–47, however, Huntly was slow to join the marquis of Montrose's (q.v.) army because it had been Montrose, as a Covenanter general, who had defeated Huntly in 1639. Huntly was also opposed to the involvement of Catholic Highlander (qq.v.) and Irish troops. Huntly's sons did join Montrose and eventually Huntly was drawn into the conflict. In 1647 he was captured and, in 1649, executed.

HURRY, SIR JOHN. *See* URRY, SIR JOHN.

HUTCHINSON, JOHN (1615–1664). Born the son of Sir Thomas Hutchinson of Owthorpe in Nottinghamshire, John was too young when war broke out to have filled the offices in county government that his father, a justice of the peace and M.P., had. Nevertheless, as war broke out in 1642 he and his wife, Lucy Hutchinson (q.v.), and his brother, George, became the centre of parliamentarianism (q.v.) in Nottinghamshire. John Hutchinson, with help from Sir John Gell (q.v.), seized Nottingham Castle in November 1642 and held it throughout the war, surviving several major attacks on it and the town. In 1646 Hutchinson became M.P. for the town and sat in judgement on the king in the trial of 1649; he signed the death warrant. During the commonwealth (q.v.) he was on the Council of State (q.v.), but his antipathy towards Oliver Cromwell (q.v.) led to obscurity during the Protectorate (q.v.).

Hutchinson returned to county government, being justice of the peace in the mid-1650s and high sheriff of Nottinghamshire in 1658–59. In 1660 he was elected to the Convention Parliament. At the Restoration he was allowed to remain free, but in 1663 he was arrested on little or no evidence of involvement in a plot to overthrow Charles II (q.v.). Hutchinson remained in prison at Sandown Castle until his death in September 1664 despite the efforts of his wife and several former enemies to secure his release.

HUTCHINSON, LUCY (1620–after 1675). Lucy Hutchinson remained in the garrison of Nottingham throughout the war, where she used medical skills learned from her mother to tend the wounded of both sides. She supported her husband's (John Hutchinson's [q.v.]) political stance when he took up the parliamentarian (q.v.) cause. She studied the Baptist (q.v.) faith and introduced it to her husband just after the First Civil War (q.v.), much to the displeasure of Nottingham's Presbyterian (q.v.) clique. Lucy Hutchinson worked on her husband's behalf as an agent, both in the Commonwealth (q.v.) and again in 1660, when she was active in securing his freedom. In 1663, when he was arrested, she tried to secure his release, personally meeting with Secretary of State Henry Bennet.

After John's death, Lucy, herself a writer of poetry and translator of Lucretius, set about creating a biography of her husband, to set his character before the world and his family. The *Memoirs of the Life of Colonel Hutchinson* remains one of the greatest works dealing with the Civil Wars and revolutions. Lucy Hutchinson explored the causes of the war, examined the motives of the participants on both sides, exposed hypocrisy, and traced the rise of Oliver Cromwell (q.v.) as part of her attempt to give her husband's role in this part of history its due credit. Her Republicanism and her love for John Hutchinson spills over at times, but never defeats her broader purpose.

HYDE, SIR EDWARD. *See* CLARENDON, EARL OF.

$\backsim$ | $\backsim$

IMPEACHMENT. During the years of monarchical government, ministers of state were chosen by the monarch. Parliament (q.v.) had no say in this choice. The only way Parliament could deal with an unpopular or bad minister was by impeachment, charging the minister with crimes such as treason before the House of Lords (q.v.). Impeachment was used against Thomas Wentworth, earl of Strafford (q.v.), in 1640–41.

IMPRESSMENT. This was the conscription of soldiers employed by both sides from 1643 onwards as the armies began to shrink. The royalist commissioners of array (qq.v.) and the parliamentarian county committees (qq.v.) were in charge of impressment. In 1645 Sir Thomas Fairfax (q.v.) was given powers to impress men to complete the recruitment of the New Model Army (q.v.). The Levellers (q.v.) opposed impressment and forbade governments its use in the *Agreement of the People* (q.v.).

INCHIQUIN, MURROUGH O'BRIEN, LORD (?–1674). Inchiquin was a Protestant Gaelic Irishman at the head of the O'Brien clan, and initially defended southern Munster against the rebels. Inchiquin took over command of the Munster Protestant forces in May 1642. He had been governor of Cork to that date. He initially observed the Cessation (q.v.) of 1643 and went over to England. King Charles I (q.v.) failed to make him the president of Munster, however, and after the defeat of the royalists (q.v) at the Battle of Marston Moor (q.v.), he returned to Munster and led his garrisons at Cork, Youghal, and Duncannon and his forces in revolt against the king and the Cessation. He was particularly brutal in his treatment of the Catholic (q.v.) Irish, and expelled all of them from Cork and Youghal after his return.

In 1647 Inchiquin received supplies from England, which enabled him to go on the offensive in Munster and on 13 November defeat the Catholic Confederation of Kilkenny (q.v.) forces at the Battle of Knocknanuss (q.v.), which in turn led to the seizure of most of the province. During 1648, however, Inchiquin's position deteriorated and he was cornered at Cork. In response he changed sides again and joined the Confederation in April. In 1649 Inchiquin joined the attack on Dublin (q.v.), but before the Battle of Rathmines (q.v.) he returned south to deal with a possible landing by English troops there. In 1650 Inchiquin, having supported the alliance of the Confederation with the marquis of Ormond (q.v.), left Ireland. He became a member of Charles II's (q.v.) exiled council, returning to Ireland in 1663.

INCIDENT, THE. In the summer of 1641, Charles I (q.v.) went to Edinburgh to ratify the Treaty of London (q.v.) and to approve the recent acts of the Estates (q.v.). He also had a secret agenda, that of trying to create a royalist (q.v.) party from disaffected Covenanters (q.v.) and others. A plan was hatched to kidnap prominent Covenanters, who included the marquis of Hamilton (q.v.) and his brother, as the prelude to a coup. The plot was betrayed by John Urry (q.v.) and Hamilton and the others went into hiding, leaving the king to claim ignorance of the plot: he was not believed. However, it was in no one's interest to expose the rift in government between the king and the Covenanters, and although an investigation was launched, the Incident was allowed to fade from view.

INDEMNITY AND OBLIVION, ACT OF. This Act, passed by Charles II (q.v.) at the Restoration (q.v.), was intended to allow a legal pall of forgetfulness to fall over the actions of the vast majority of former parliamentarians (q.v.). It did not embrace the regicides (q.v.) and leaders of the Kirk Party (q.v.), such as the marquis of Argyll or Archibald Johnston (qq.v.). Former royalists (q.v.) wryly commented that the Act granted indemnity to the king's enemies and oblivion to his friends.

INDEPENDENTS. After the collapse of the Church of England, there were two opposing views as to what would follow. Presbyterians (q.v.) wanted a reconstructed church on principles similar to the kirk (q.v.), but Independents (q.v.) wanted there to be no overall system, rather that congregations should be independent except for local groupings by mutual consent. The Independents, or Congregationalists as some call them, had important support in the army, rather than in Parliament (q.v.). The king sought to exploit the factions in Parliament to his own advantage, but failed to accept the Heads of the Proposals (q.v.), a treaty drafted by two of the leading Independents: Oliver Cromwell and Henry Ireton (qq.v.). In 1648 the decision to bring the king to trial was expedited by the Independents.

INSTRUMENT OF GOVERNMENT. This constitution established the Protectorate (q.v.) after the dissolution of the Barebones Parliament (q.v.). It created a unicameral assembly, with an executive consisting of a lord protector and a Council of State (qq.v.). The Instrument provided for triennial Parliaments (q.v.), which would draw members from all four nations. The constituencies in England and Wales were based on those established in the *Agreement of the People* (q.v.) and voting was open to those who owned or held land worth £200 per annum. Borough franchise was left as it then stood with the system varying from borough to borough. The Council was appointed by the first Instrument and the members were selected by the Council and the lord protector (q.v.) from names submitted by Parliament. Parliament had to approve of the officers of state put forward by the Council or protector before they could take office. The Instrument was debated by Parliament, which sought to alter sections of it. In 1656 the Instrument was replaced by the constitution of the *Humble Petition and Advice* (q.v.).

INTERREGNUM. The general name for the period between the reigns of Charles I and Charles II (qq.v.), that is, 1649–60. It is a problematic term: royalists (q.v.) believed there was no gap; in other words, Charles II reigned from the moment his father was dead, and indeed the young king was crowned in Scotland in 1651. The term could only be used retrospectively, as Republicans did not intend there ever to be another reign.

INVERKEITHING, BATTLE OF. Fought on 20 July 1651. As Charles II (q.v.) reconstructed the Scottish army using former royalists and Engagers (qq.v.), David Leslie (q.v.) faced the New Model Army (q.v.) regiments under John Lambert (q.v.), which occupied southern Scotland. Leslie was attempting to hold the English forces south of the Forth and protect his base at Stirling. In the battle 2,000 Scots were killed and the English forces pressed on into Fife and the Scottish Midlands, capturing Perth on 2 August. Lambert's advance northwards left the roads open for Charles II to take his forces southwards into western England.

INVERLOCHY, BATTLE OF. Fought on 2 February 1645. The marquis of Argyll (q.v.) personally led the forces dispatched to defeat the marquis of Montrose's (q.v.) army of Highlanders (q.v.) and Irishmen. He pursued them through the Great Glen in January 1645, but on 1 February they turned on him and after hazardous marches across the mountains began to attack Argyll's army during the night. The battle was very brief and murderous. The Irish forces grouped on Montrose's left advanced close to the Covenanter (q.v.) Army, firing before attacking with pike (q.v.) and sword, and this was mirrored by the Irish troops on the right led by Alasdair MacColla (q.v.), and finally by Montrose's centre composed of Highlanders (q.v.). In the face of this assault the Covenanter forces fled, pursued by Montrose's army, which slaughtered as many as it could catch. Montrose's army then marched on to capture Elgin. His defeat of Argyll and his capture of Elgin influenced many northern Scottish gentry to join Montrose, it also severely dented Argyll's prestige.

IRETON, HENRY (1611–1651). Born in Attenborough, south of Nottingham, and educated at Oxford University, Ireton served in the army of the earl of Essex (q.v.) during the Edgehill (q.v.) campaign of 1642. He returned to the county later that year and became part of the county committee (q.v.) there, alongside John Hutchinson (q.v.). In 1643 he served alongside Oliver Cromwell (q.v.) in Lincolnshire and went on to become Cromwell's deputy governor of the Isle of Ely. Cromwell and Ireton both served in the earl of Manchester's Eastern Association (qq.v.) Army and went on to the New Model Army (q.v.) in 1645. Ireton became commissary general.

At the Battle of Naseby (q.v.) Ireton commanded the parliamentarian (q.v.) left wing of Horse (q.v.), and though initially defeated by Prince Rupert (q.v.), was able to lead a section of his forces in an attack on the advancing royalist Foot (qq.v.). This proved to be a major contribution to the victory over King Charles I (q.v.). Later in 1645 and during 1646, he served with the New Model in the south-west and later at the siege of Oxford (q.v.). In June 1646 he married Oliver Cromwell's (q.v.) daughter Bridgit. He became M.P. for Appleby in October, and became a member of the Independent (q.v.) faction, opposed to the Presbyterian (q.v.) group with which he argued. In 1647 he sided with the army in its dispute with Parliament (q.v.) and drafted the Heads of the Proposals (q.v.) with Sir Thomas Fairfax (q.v.) and Cromwell. At the Putney Debates (q.v.) Ireton eloquently defended the relationship between property ownership and political rights. After the Second Civil War (q.v.) Ireton became more radical, understanding that the king could not be trusted to agree to a lasting peace. He discussed more radical settlements with the Levellers (q.v.), whom he had opposed at Putney, and pressed for the purge of Presbyterians in Parliament as a step towards bringing the king to trial. Ireton signed the death warrant at the end of the trial.

In mid-1649 Ireton went to Ireland as Cromwell's second in command and took over when his father-in-law left. He continued the war against the Catholic/royalist alliance (qq.v.) until his death of a fever at Limerick (q.v.) on 29 November 1649.

IRISH REBELLION. The term applied to the rising of 22 October 1641, when the Irish Catholics (q.v.) seized prominent towns across Ulster (q.v.) and attempted to capture Dublin (q.v.). The Rebellion spread across the country during the rest of the year, embracing the Old English (q.v.) as well as the Irish themselves. By the summer of 1642 the Rebellion had become something of a war for political equality with England, Wales, and Scotland and for religious freedom, if not for true independence. Later in the war there was a call for full independence from Charles I (q.v.) backed by the clerical party and the papal nuncio, Cardinal Rinuccini (q.v.). The Irish Rebellion sparked the war in England and Wales, by giving the king the opportunity to raise arms, an issue that helped drive a wedge between him and Parliament (q.v.). Also, because certain of the rebels including Phelim O'Neill (q.v.) claimed to have a commission from the king empowering them to rebel, it heightened suspicion of Charles I.

⇝ **J** ⇜

JERMYN, HENRY LORD (1604–1684). A member of Queen Henrietta Maria's (q.v.) household. In 1633, for his part in a duel, Jermyn was temporarily banished from the court. In 1641 Jermyn was involved in the Army Plot (q.v.). When the queen left England, Jermyn accompanied her to Europe in 1642. He returned in 1643 and served in her army. Again, when the queen fled England in 1644, Jermyn accompanied her. Jermyn was in favour of King Charles I (q.v.) making an advantageous deal with the Catholic Confederation of Kilkenny (q.v.) in 1645, although he later held the view that the king, defeated in England and Wales, should enlist the aid of Scottish and English Presbyterians (q.v.). He remained influential in the queen's circle throughout the interregnum (q.v.).

JOHNSTON OF WARISTON, SIR ARCHIBALD (?–1663). Johnston, a lawyer, was one of the architects of the Scottish revolution of 1638–40. It was he along with Alexander Henderson (q.v.) who drafted the National Covenant (q.v.) in 1638, which gave form to the Scots' opposition to Charles I's (q.v.) religious policy. Wariston's diary is one of the most valuable insights into the mind of a 17th-century "revolutionary," setting forth clearly the operation of his mind and his belief that revolutionary action was indeed the only way to preserve the covenant between the Scottish people and God. Johnston was one of the few people who told the king to his face that he was playing for time during the negotiations at Berwick after the first Bishop's War (q.v.). In the 1640s Johnston remained at the centre of politics in Scotland, but was circumvented during the period of the Engagement (q.v.). He was firmly associated with the Kirk Party (q.v.) and the marquis of Argyll (q.v.). Johnston returned to prominence again in 1649 when he was a most assiduous member of the Parliamentary Interval Committee, which acted as an executive during the intervals between sessions of the Scottish Estates (q.v.).

In the 1650s Johnston was drawn into the controversy between the Resolutioners and the Protesters (qq.v.) in Scotland, which had developed from the conflict in 1650–51 when the Resolutioners sought to increase military strength through opening the armed forces up to those formerly involved in the Engagement. Wariston was a Protester, a hard-liner opposed to any alliance with the "ungodly" and he represented this before Oliver Cromwell (q.v.) in debates in 1656–57, a debate won in the end by the Protesters. In 1657 Wariston was entrusted with Scottish affairs by Cromwell and was made a member of the second chamber established by the *Humble Petition and Advice* (q.v.). In 1659, after the fall of the Protectorate (q.v.), Johnston was appointed to the Council of State (q.v.). At the Restoration (q.v.) he was forced to flee to France. He was captured and eventually returned to Edinburgh, where he was tried and executed in 1663.

JONES, MICHAEL (?–1649). Jones led forces in the Northern Marches (q.v.) in the First Civil War (q.v.) and in 1645 was chiefly responsible for besieging Chester, where on 24 September he defeated the royalist (q.v.) army at the Battle of Rowton Heath (q.v.). In 1647 he was sent to Ireland to receive Dublin (q.v.) from the hands of the marquis of Ormond (q.v.) and thereby became the principal commander of the English forces in the country. He defended Dublin from siege forces led by Thomas Preston and Owen Roe O'Neill (qq.v.) and in August 1649, prior to Oliver Cromwell's arrival, defeated the Catholic Confederation of Kilkenny's (q.v.) forces at the Battle of Rathmines (q.v.). Jones died during the subsequent campaign.

JOYCE, CORNET GEORGE. Joyce was a cornet in Sir Thomas Fairfax's (q.v.) regiment of Horse (q.v.) and was an agitator (q.v.) elected by his troop during 1647. On 3 June 1648, Joyce led a party of Horse to Holdenby House (q.v.), seized King Charles I (q.v.) from his guards, and escorted him to the New Model Army (q.v.) at Newmarket. Joyce always claimed to be acting on behalf of his troops and fellow agitators in capturing the king, although Oliver Cromwell and Henry Ireton (qq.v.) have been accused of putting him up to it. Certainly Cromwell knew of the plan as Joyce visited his London home two days before reaching Holdenby House. Joyce eventually reached the rank of captain in Edmund Whalley's Horse.

JUSTICE MILLS, BATTLE OF. Fought on 13 September 1644. The marquis of Montrose and Alasdair MacColla (qq.v.) attacked the Covenanter (q.v.) army south of Aberdeen, having approached the town from Dundee. Much of the fighting took place around the upper and lower Justice Mills on the How Burn. Montrose advanced across the burn's valley towards Aberdeen and after a battle of some two hours defeated the government force and pressed on into Aberdeen.

JUSTICES OF THE PEACE (J.P.). Justices were appointed annually to the commission of the peace for a county and were the principal law offers in the provinces and boroughs. There were J.P.s in each county of England, Wales, and Ireland; the number of J.P.s on the bench varies from county to county, but the most were found in England. J.P.s were in the process of being introduced into Scotland throughout the period. The majority of them were there because of their social status and the "understanding" of the local community, which their standing brought. On each bench there was a quorum of members with legal training, at least one of whom had to be present at each meeting of a county's quarter sessions (q.v.). In England and Wales both Charles I and Parliament (qq.v.) attempted to keep control of the J.P.s and new commissions were issued periodically by both sides, although in most counties (Cornwall was one exception) quarter sessions were in abeyance between 1642 and 1646. In Ireland attempts to control the initial Irish Rebellion (q.v.) were hampered by the involvement of many J.P.s.

JUXON, WILLIAM, BISHOP OF LONDON (1582–1663). President of St John's College Oxford in 1621, following William Laud (q.v.). He also followed Laud as bishop of London after Laud became Archbishop of Canterbury in 1633. Juxon also served as lord treasurer from 1638, increasing suspicion of the role of the church in secular government, but he was generally respected throughout the church despite his Laudian credentials. He was Charles I's (q.v.) chaplain and accompanied him on the scaffold in 1649, where Charles gave him his star of the garter and his last word: "remember." At the Restoration (q.v.) he resumed following in Laud's footsteps and was appointed to Canterbury.

∽ **K** ∾

KENTFORD HEATH. The New Model Army (q.v.) held a rendezvous at Kentford Heath in Suffolk on 4–5 June 1647, in the wake of the seizure of King Charles I (q.v.) from Holdenby House (q.v.) by Cornet George Joyce (q.v.). Here the soldiers drew up a petition against the Presbyterian (q.v.) majority in Parliament (q.v.). The Presbyterians were held responsible for refusing to settle the issues of pay and for trying to enforce the disbandment of the army and the enlistment of soldiers for service in Ireland. This was one of the early blows in the campaign, which saw the army single out the Presbyterian leadership, the so-called Eleven Members (q.v.).

KENTISH PETITION. This petition was drawn up at the March assizes at Maidstone by Sir Edward Dering (q.v.) and his supporters. The petition sought to present a different view than the one drawn up by Sir Michael Livesey and a Puritan (q.v.) clique that supported Parliament (q.v.). The petition was moderate and heavily localist, although it dealt with the dubious legality of the Militia Ordinance (q.v.), and expressed a desire to retain the episcopal structure of the church and the *Book of Common Prayer* (q.v.). The authors of the petition, Dering and Justice Thomas Malet amongst them, were arrested before the petition was presented to Parliament. The petition was burned by the common hangman by order of Parliament.

KILKENNY. An Irish county town developed in the thirteenth century by Norman settlers. In 1642 the united Irish rebels established their capital at Kilkenny, where the Supreme Council and the General Assembly met. Kilkenny served as the capital of the Catholic Confederation (q.v.) until 1651. On 27 March 1650, Kilkenny was besieged by Oliver Cromwell (q.v.) and the New Model Army (q.v.). After initial defiance, the town was surrendered following a successful attack.

KILSYTH, BATTLE OF. Fought on 15 August 1645. After news of King Charles I's (q.v.) defeat at the Battle of Naseby (q.v.) reached Scotland, it became important that the marquis of Montrose (q.v.) lead his forces closer to England to aid the royalists (q.v.) there. Having defeated General William Baillie (q.v.) at the Bridge of Alford (q.v.), Montrose headed south towards Glasgow. He was pursued by Baillie and the marquis of Argyll (q.v.). On 15 August Montrose turned to face his pursuers at Kilsyth. As the Covenanter (q.v.) forces set about a flanking action, Montrose's forces attacked their centre. When the earl of Airlie's (q.v.) forces turned the flanking Covenanter Horse (q.v.) back, the Covenanter forces began to break. When the reserve forces failed to support the centre, Baillie and Argyll's army began to collapse. In the pursuit that followed, the last Covenanter army was destroyed. In the wake of Kilsyth, Montrose summoned a meeting of the Estates (q.v.) at Glasgow. Prominent Covenanters began to waver and drift over to him. This period of success was short lived. A portion of the Army of the Solemn League and Covenant (q.v.) was brought back to Scotland under David Leslie (q.v.) and it defeated Montrose and Alasdair MacColla (q.v.) at the Battle of Philliphaugh (q.v.).

KINGSTON, ROBERT PIERREPOINT, EARL OF (1584–1643). Although one of the most powerful figures in Nottinghamshire, Kingston remained aloof from the conflict of 1642, even though his heir, Henry Lord Newark was heavily involved. Kingston was accused of being too mean to support King Charles I (q.v.). Kingston was brought into the war as royalist (q.v.) commander in Lincolnshire under the earl of Newcastle (q.v.) in 1643. He was captured at Gainsborough when the town was taken by Oliver Cromwell (q.v.) and Lord Willoughby of Parham in July 1643. Kingston was being shipped along the Trent to Hull (q.v.) as prisoner when the boat was fired upon by royalist forces. Kingston was cut in two by a cannon ball. According to Lucy Hutchinson (q.v.), he had said the year before that "When I take armes with the king against the parliament, or with parliament against the king, let a cannon bullet devide me between them."

KINTYRE. This area of the Scottish west coast was a sensitive and strategic one given its proximity to Ireland. In the early seventeenth century there were unsuccessful attempts to establish plantations of Lowlanders there to break the cultural hegemony of the Gaelic or Highland (q.v.) population. Part of the motivation for the MacDonalds' support of the earl of Montrose and Alasdair MacColla's (qq.v.) Scottish campaigns was due to their desire to regain lost MacDonald lands in Kintyre. After King Charles I (q.v.) had ordered them to lay down arms, it was here that the forces of the earl of Antrim (q.v.) and MacColla held out against the marquis of Argyll's (q.v.) forces and then those of the Army of the Solemn League and Covenant (q.v.) until the summer of 1647. The devastation in the area caused by the prolonged war was great, and resulted in depopulation. This enabled the Campbells under Argyll to plant Lowland settlers onto the empty lands and continue the process of breaking down the Gaelic and Catholic (q.v.) hold on the region.

KIRK. The general name for the Protestant Church of Scotland as established after the Reformation. The kirk was organised regionally with the paroach (parish) at the local level, followed by the classis or groups of parishes, and then regional synods. At the apex was the General Assembly, established to administer the Protestant church during the reign of Mary, Queen of Scots (1542–1567).

KIRK PARTY. The Kirk Party developed from the hard-line Covenanter (q.v.) leadership in the Scottish government. They split from other Covenanters over the issue of the Engagement (q.v.); those who became the Kirk Party could not agree with this treaty with Charles I (q.v.). The marquis of Argyll (q.v.) was the central figure in the Party. After the collapse of the Engager (q.v.) invasion of England, the Kirk Party took over the government of Scotland and enjoyed the support of the majority of the ministers of the kirk (q.v.). The Kirk Party, whilst aiming for a radical overhaul of society, found itself in uneasy alliance with Prince Charles (q.v.) after the execution of Charles I. Defeat at the Battle of Dunbar (q.v.) discredited the party and its attempts to build an army without enlisting former royalists or Engagers (qq.v.). The Kirk Party's hold on power collapsed in the face of the continued English invasion of Scotland and pressure from royalists within Scotland. A hard-line faction of the Remonstrants (q.v.) or Protesters continued to refuse to compromise with the broader sweep of Covenanters.

KNOCKNANUSS, BATTLE OF. Fought on 13 November 1647. In the wake of Michael Jones's (q.v.) arrival in Ireland, the English Parliament's (q.v.) forces went on the offensive. In the autumn, Lord Inchiquin's (q.v.) forces in Munster attacked the Catholic Confederation's (q.v.) garrisons in the province, capturing Dungarvan and Cashel. Lord Taffe's army assembled to meet the challenge at Knocknanuss Hill. Inchiquin attacked from the lower ground after an artillery bombardment, sending Horse (q.v.) up the hill to attack Taffe's left flank. After two hours of heavy fighting, Inchiquin's reserve Horse attacked Taffe's right flank and drove the Catholic forces from the hill. The battle destroyed the Munster Army and left much of the province open to Inchiquin's forces.

KNOLLYS, HANSARD. In 1641, Knollys, a minister in Lincolnshire, wrote and published *A Glimpse of Sion's Glory*. The pamphlet claimed to see the second coming presaged in the tumultuous events of the past few years.

⇜ **L** ⇝

LAGAN ARMY. A combined army of Scots and English soldiers operating in Ulster (q.v.) from September 1647 and nominally under the command of George Monck (q.v.). The two sectional commanders were Sir Charles Coote and Robert Monro (qq.v.). Monck, having once been a part of the English forces stationed in Ireland in 1642–43, could not ensure the loyalty of his two juniors and in any case part of the Scots forces in Ulster accepted the Engagement (q.v.) with Charles I (q.v.) taking several prominent Ulster garrisons with them. Monck therefore had to expend considerable time retaking them.

On 21 June 1650, Coote and his section of the Lagan Army defeated the Ulster Army under Bishop Clogher at the Battle of Scarriffhollis (q.v.) in County Donegal. The Ulster Army had been the last field army of any consequence left to the royalist and Catholic (qq.v.) coalition led by the marquis of Ormond (q.v.).

LAMBERT, JOHN (1619–1684). Lambert began his Civil War career with Lord Fairfax's (q.v.) forces in Yorkshire. When the New Model Army (q.v.) was created Lambert moved into it with Sir Thomas Fairfax (q.v.). In 1647 Lambert became associated with the agitators (q.v.).

In 1648 Lambert was stationed in the north with two regiments of Foot (q.v.) and four of Horse (q.v.) to shadow the march of the Engager (q.v.) army as it moved southwards through Lancashire. He joined Oliver Cromwell (q.v.) at Wetherby after Cromwell had defeated the risings in south Wales. Together they crossed the Pennines and attacked the marquis of Hamilton (q.v.) in the rear as he crossed the Ribble at Preston. The Battle of Preston (q.v.) saw the destruction of the Engager army.

In 1650 Lambert accompanied Cromwell to Scotland and played a major role in the defeat of David Leslie (q.v.) at the Battle of Dunbar (q.v.). The following year he again shadowed a Scottish army, this time that of Charles II (q.v.), as it progressed through Lancashire. By mid-August 1651 Lambert was ahead of the king. Lambert fought at the Battle of Worcester (q.v.). In 1653 he was responsible for the creation of the Instrument of Government (q.v.), the constitution of the Protectorate (q.v.). His influence in the Protectorate declined in later years, but he remained implacably opposed to any regime that paid little attention to the army or that seemed to undermine the aims of the republic. In 1660 Lambert led a last-ditch attempt to save the republic (q.v.) from the tide of acquiescence that paved the way for the Restoration (q.v.), but his uprising was defeated near Edgehill in Warwickshire. He was imprisoned for the rest of his life by Charles II.

LANGDALE, SIR MARMADUKE, LATER LORD (1598–1661). This Roman Catholic (q.v.) Yorkshireman refused to collect ship money (q.v.) when high sheriff of Yorkshire in 1639. But in 1642 he raised troops for King Charles I (q.v.) on the outbreak of the First Civil War (q.v.). He became a part of the earl of Newcastle's Northern Army (qq.v.) and with the Northern Horse (q.v.) defeated the Scots' Army of the Solemn League and Covenant (q.v.) at Corbridge in February 1644. At the Battle of Marston Moor (q.v.) the following July he served under Lord Goring (q.v.). With a section of the Northern Horse he made his escape with Prince Rupert (q.v.) after their defeat at the battle, and served with the Oxford Field Army (q.v.) during late 1644.

In February 1645 Langdale led the Northern Horse on a lightening campaign through the Midlands in which he defeated parliamentarian (q.v.) forces at the Battle of Melton Mowbray (q.v.), and freed Newark (q.v.) from enemy forces that had hemmed in the garrison, before achieving his main goal of defeating Lord Fairfax (q.v.) and relieving the siege of Pontefract (q.v.). On his return southwards, Langdale rejoined the Oxford forces and accompanied them on the campaign that led to the capture of Leicester (q.v.) at the end of May. At the subsequent Battle of Naseby (q.v.), Langdale's forces were swept from the field by Oliver Cromwell (q.v.). Langdale remained with the king's field army and was defeated at the Battle of Rowton Heath (q.v.) in September. A month later, under the command of Lord Digby (q.v.), Langdale and the Northern Horse marched north to try a break for Scotland to reach the marquis of Montrose (q.v.). This small force was defeated at Sherburn in Elmet and although it reached Dumfries was driven back and defeated on the sands near Carlisle.

Langdale left England and went to France via the Isle of Man. In the Second Civil War (q.v.) he joined the Engager Army (q.v.) and marched into England. Defending the marquis of Hamilton's (q.v.) rear at the Battle of Preston (q.v.), Langdale was defeated by Cromwell, and captured. He escaped captivity in a series of disguises. Langdale served with European forces during the 1650s but was not embroiled in the royalist (q.v.) uprising because his Catholicism was offensive to Charles II's Presbyterian (qq.v.) allies, although he was ennobled in 1658. Langdale's war-time debts precluded a high profile at the Restoration (q.v.) and he could not afford to attend the coronation in April 1661. He died on 5 August that same year.

LANGPORT, BATTLE OF. Fought on 10 July 1645. Having defeated King Charles I (q.v.) at the Battle of Naseby, Sir Thomas Fairfax (qq.v.) led the New Model Army (q.v.) southwards to deal with Lord Goring's (q.v.) army in the south-west. Goring quickly moved northwards to try and join the king's remaining forces near Bridgewater. Fairfax set off in pursuit. Goring tried to lure Fairfax away from his line of march by sending Major General George Porter (q.v.) off towards Taunton, but Porter was caught and defeated at Ilchester, leaving Goring to face Fairfax at Langport. Goring put his forces into a strong position on rising ground on the west bank of the river Wagg Ryhne. Fairfax had to cross a ford and drive up a narrow lane to reach Goring's position, but with superior artillery he was able to silence the royalist (q.v.) guns guarding the ford, and after Oliver Cromwell (q.v.) and the Horse (q.v.) pushed across the river, Fairfax then had time to send his Foot (q.v.) over the river and defeat Goring.

LANSDOWN, BATTLE OF. Fought on 5 July 1643. Sir William Waller (q.v.) and his army had been sent into the south-west following the defeat of the earl of Stamford (q.v.) at the Battle of Stratton (q.v.) to hold back the royalist (q.v.) advance into Somerset. Waller placed himself on the defensible heights at Lansdown blocking the road to Bath, where on 5 July Sir Ralph Hopton (q.v.) attacked him. Initial attacks failed, but when Waller tried to drive his attackers off after they had temporarily withdrawn, his Horse (q.v.) under Sir Arthur Hesilrige (q.v.) was defeated. Hopton tried again. Despite long and costly attacks on Waller's fortified position the Cornish Foot (q.v.) could make little impression, moreover, the popular and skilled royalist commander Sir Bevill Grenvile (q.v.) was killed in the assault. Hopton had to withdraw. Although Waller too withdrew and left the road to Bath open, he had kept his army in good condition, whereas the royalists had suffered a high number of casualties. In the course of the retreat Hopton was seriously wounded when an idiot put his lighted matchcord into a barrel of gunpowder nearby. The royalist forces withdrew to Devizes and Waller quickly besieged them there.

LARGE PETITION. Drafted by William Walwyn (q.v.) in March 1647, this petition set out the Leveller (q.v.) programme in a comprehensive manner. The degree of organisation was sophisticated; the petition was sent out into each London parish and then taken around, ward by ward, for signatures. The petition was addressed to the House of Commons (q.v.) as if it were the sole representative of the people, although it did not specifically call for the abolition of the House of Lords (q.v.). The Commons did not debate the Large Petition until May when they ordered that it be burned by the common hangman.

LATHOM HOUSE. The Lancashire seat of the earl and countess of Derby (q.v.), Lathom became a royalist (q.v.) beacon in the county after their defeat at the Battle of Whalley (q.v.) in April 1643. The garrison was commanded by the countess, and in January it was placed under siege by Sir Thomas Fairfax (q.v.) in an attempt to clear the county of all royalists. The siege continued for several months during which time the countess led a spirited defence. It ended only when Prince Rupert (q.v.) led his army through the county preparatory to marching on York (q.v.). The countess was relieved of her command at this point, although the castle fought on until December 1645.

LAUD, WILLIAM, ARCHBISHOP OF CANTERBURY (1573–1645). Son of a Reading clothier, Laud's natural talents secured him a good education and advancement through the church. Laud professed to oppose the seemingly prevalent Calvinist modes in the Church of England current at the beginning of the seventeenth century. He found ready support from Charles I (q.v.) and when Charles became king Laud was favored, becoming bishop of London in 1628 and Archbishop of Canterbury. Laud and the king used their patronage to place like-minded men, usually referred to as arminians, into dioceses and parishes as well as in the two universities. It is debatable whether Laud was an arminian, and his changes to church liturgy and form have often been referred to as "Laudian" as a recognition of their distinctive stamp. The term is also used to describe his supporters.

Laud probably saw himself as bringing order and stability to a church that had undergone years of reforms, which had resulted in a latitudinarian approach to forms of worship, clerical attire, and church fabric. Laud believed in the sanctity of the sacraments and the role of the individual in his or her salvation, he rejected the predestination of Calvinism. His changes necessitated a shift in emphasis in liturgy from the Word of God to the Body of God. This then had a concomitant effect on the layout of the church. The pulpit was reduced in importance whilst the communion table was raised in status and moved altar-wise to the east end of the church and railed off to mark its importance as the locus of the sacraments.

To opponents with long memories or a working knowledge of Roman Catholic (q.v.) form, Laud's alterations looked suspiciously Catholic in tone. Laud refused to see the church of Rome as apostate, but instead regarded it as an erring brother in Christ; his apparent laxity in prosecuting Catholics contrasted with his harsh dealings with Puritans (q.v.) like John Bastwicke, William Prynne, and Henry Burton (qq.v.). Opposition to arminian policies had grown in strength within Parliament (q.v.) during the late 1620s, and by the 1630s Laud became the centre of criticism. Moreover, his role on the Privy Council (q.v.) smacked of meddling in politics and his leadership of the commission investigating encloses suggested undue interference with property. Laud became the centre of hostility in Scotland in 1637 following his influence in drafting the Scottish prayer book.

In late 1641 Laud was impeached (q.v.) and imprisoned in the Tower by the Long Parliament (q.v.). His reforms and then the episcopacy (q.v.) itself were dismantled whilst he languished. At the end of 1644, as Parliament's war effort flagged and the parliamentarians (q.v.) engaged in soul-searching and acrimonious disputes, Laud was remembered, tried, and executed on 10 January 1645. His death speech emphasized his and his master's repugnance for the church of Rome's errors, disappointing those who had portrayed him as the arch supporter of the pope.

LAUGHARNE, ROWLAND (?–1676). During the First Civil War (q.v.) Laugharne was a parliamentarian (q.v.) commander based in Pembroke, which was, for much of the war, an enclave surrounded by royalists (q.v.). In 1645 Laugharne began to seriously impinge on royalist control of south Wales, driving eastwards across the country. In June that year he was defeated and driven back into Pembrokeshire by Charles Gerrard (q.v.). Laugharne turned the tables on 1 August when he defeated the royalist forces at the Battle of Colby Moor (q.v.) near Haverfordwest. From this victory Laugharne went on conquer south Wales in alliance with the popular uprising against the royalists in the fall of 1645.

During the spring of 1646 it was Laugharne who dealt with Sir Edward Carne's revolt in south Wales, and in 1647 he again was involved in stemming the Glamorganshire revolt when some 2,000 men marched on Llandaff. Laugharne defeated the rebels when they moved onto Cardiff. Yet, by the early months of 1648, Laugharne was a resentful man. He did not approve of the New Model Army's (q.v.) role in political developments and resented the favoritism shown to its men and officers. When his colleague Colonel John Poyer (q.v.), governor of Pembroke, and his men went into rebellion, Laugharne's own forces, instead of disbanding as ordered, drifted to Pembroke. Laugharne raced back to Wales from London to take part in the rebellion that was swiftly commandeered as part of the royalist uprisings of that summer; the rebellion accompanied the invasion of England by the Engager Army (q.v.). Laugharne was defeated at St Fagin's by Colonel Horton on 8 May, and then pursued to Pembroke by Oliver Cromwell (q.v.). He held out until 11 July. Laugharne was court-martialled and sentenced to death. He and Poyer were allowed to throw dice, however. Laugharne won his life. In 1660 he was awarded a pension by Charles II (q.v.).

LEATHERHEAD MUTINY. During the process of creating the New Model Army (q.v.), several regiments from the earl of Essex's (q.v.)

forces based in Surrey were detailed to serve under Sir William Waller (q.v.) in February 1645. The troops had developed the same antipathy towards Waller as their commander had. As a result they mutinied rather than serve under Waller.

LEDBURY, BATTLE OF. Fought on 22 April 1645. In spring 1645 Prince Rupert and Prince Maurice (qq.v.) set about reconstructing the royalist (q.v.) presence in the Marcher (q.v.) counties bordering Wales. One of the problems was that forces from Edward Massey's (q.v.) Western Army forces from Gloucester were raiding the southern marches. On 22 April Rupert caught part of Massey's force in the Worcester town of Ledbury. After a series of street fights, Massey was driven from the town. The defeat curtailed his activities.

LEICESTER. This Midland town was the site of one of the earliest attempts to raise forces for King Charles I (q.v.). Henry Hastings (q.v.) raised men from his father's mines under the authority of the Commission of Array (q.v.) and led them to Leicester on 23 June 1642. Once there, however, he met with vigorous opposition and he failed to mobilise the Trained Bands (q.v.) At the beginning of 1643 the town tried to persuade Hastings and his local opponent, Lord Grey of Groby (q.v.), to leave the town free of troops. Grey soon occupied the town and it became a parliamentarian (q.v.) garrison for all but two weeks of the First Civil War (q.v.).

At the end of May 1645 the king led his forces to the town and besieged it. On 30 May the town was bombarded by Prince Rupert (q.v.) and in the early hours of the next day the royalist (q.v.) forces stormed Leicester. The small garrison and the men and women of the town fought for two hours to keep the royalists out. Tiles and slates were hurled from rooftops as the king's army neared the town centre, but in vain. Leicester was then handed to Henry Hastings, now Lord Loughborough, as his new headquarters. He began recruiting his forces anew and set about repairing the town and developing its fortifications. Two weeks later the king was defeated at the Battle of Naseby (q.v.) and the defeated royalists fled into Leicester. The New Model Army (q.v.) arrived in their wake and set about surrounding the town. The defensive works were not complete and there were still gaping holes in the walls where Rupert had battered them. Loughborough had little option but to surrender, although through a series of deceptions he got many of the fit soldiers and their horses out of the town first and secured the release of the wounded in the town. Leicester again became a parliamentarian garrison and the base for Parliament's (q.v.) attempts to defeat Lord Loughborough for the rest of the First Civil War.

LEINSTER, ARMY OF. After the reorganisation of the rebel war effort was effected by the creation of the Catholic Confederation of Kilkenny (q.v.), the forces in each province were formed into an army with a general appointed to command each one. Each army was also responsible to the respective provincial councils. The Leinster Army was placed under the command of Sir Thomas Preston (q.v.). Preston reorganised the forces of the Leinster Army along continental lines and within months was able to go on the offensive and close in on Dublin (q.v.) by early 1643.

The Leinster Army also served in Munster against Lord Inchiquin (q.v.) when he changed sides in 1644 and again in Connacht in 1646. The Leinster Army was a major component of the force that besieged Dublin in the autumn of 1646. The two armies, Preston's and Owen Roe O'Neill's Army of Ulster (qq.v.), did not co-ordinate their offensive and in November the siege was abandoned. On 7 August 1647, the Army of Leinster was defeated at the Battle of Dungan's Hill (q.v.) by Michael Jones's (q.v.) English and Welsh parliamentarian (q.v.) army and destroyed. Remains of the Leinster Army continued to fight as part of the Confederation forces under the marquis of Ormond (q.v.) in the summer of 1649, when it shared in the defeat at the Battle of Rathmines (q.v.).

LENTHALL, WILLIAM (1591–1662). An Oxford University graduate and lawyer, from 1640 Lenthall was M.P. for Woodstock in the Short and the Long Parliaments (qq.v.). He was speaker of the House of Commons (q.v.) in 1642 when King Charles I (q.v.) attempted to arrest the Five Members (q.v.). The speaker was traditionally supposed to represent the monarch, but when Charles demanded the Five Members, Lenthall, borrowing from Denzil Holles's (q.v.) assertions in 1629, informed him that the speaker was the agent of the Commons. Lenthall was an Independent (q.v.), and the object of resentment in the London riots of 1647.

In the 1650s he served as M.P. for Oxfordshire and again as speaker of the Long Parliament before its dissolution by Oliver Cromwell (q.v.). He was to serve in the role again when the Rump Parliament was summoned at the fall of the Protectorate (qq.v.). Lenthall supported George Monck and the Restoration (qq.v.).

LESLIE, ALEXANDER. *See* LEVEN, LORD.

LESLIE, DAVID (?–1682). Leslie had fought in the European wars like his commander in the Army of the Solemn League and Covenant (q.v.), the Earl of Leven (q.v.). He was appointed commander of the Horse (q.v.) for the invasion of England in 1644. At the Battle of Marston Moor (q.v.) he seconded Oliver Cromwell (q.v.) on the allies' left flank. Whilst

Cromwell was off the field having a wound dressed, Leslie continued the defeat, pursuing the royalist (q.v.) forces opposing him. Relations between the Scots and their English allies were soured by the London press's concentration on Cromwell's role at the expense of Leslie. In August 1645 Leslie was dispatched from the Scottish army at Hereford to go northward to deal with the threat posed by the earl of Montrose (q.v.) in Scotland. In September Leslie defeated Montrose at the Battle of Philliphaugh (q.v.). After the end of the First Civil War (q.v.), Leslie led the campaign against the royalist forces first in north-eastern Scotland and then on the west coast and the Scottish Isles, wars that he pursued with some brutality.

Leslie did not join the Engagers (q.v.) in 1648, but in 1650 he sided with Charles II (q.v.) and commanded the army at the Battle of Dunbar (q.v.). Leslie was also a part of the army that Charles II led into England in 1651. He commanded a contingent of Foot (q.v.) at the Battle of Worcester (q.v.). He was captured and imprisoned in London until the Restoration (q.v.).

LEVELLERS. This radical group developed during late 1646 after the First Civil War (q.v.). There were four principal theorists behind the movement: John Lilburne, William Walwyn, Robert Overton, and John Wildman (qq.v.). There were other important figures also: Colonel Thomas Rainsborough and Edward Sexby (qq.v.), as well as Katherine Chidley and Elizabeth Lilburne (qq.v.). Together, the group, with political and religious beliefs as diverse as radical Presbyterianism (q.v.) in the 1630s to the broadest possible religious toleration and campaigns against injustice, began to develop the notion that only democratic principles could fully justify the efforts undertaken to defeat Charles I (q.v.). The name "Levellers" was an insult, meant to suggest that they wanted to level estates and make people equal. In the *Remonstrance of Many Thousand Citizens*, Levellers suggested the abolition of the monarchy and the House of Lords (q.v.), and later in 1646 Lilburne attacked the Presbyterian domination of the House of Commons (q.v.). By 1647 the Levellers were proposing reforming the entire political system in the Large Petition (q.v.), which was addressed to the Commons as if it were the sole representative of the people.

During 1647 the Levellers allied themselves with radical factions in the army, and historical debate centres on this relationship. The questions surround the issue of the extent to which the Levellers prompted army radicalism or whether sections of the army were radicalised beforehand. Also, the problem arises of how much the Levellers were dependent on army support for their subsequent rise to importance. In October 1647 the

Levellers published their constitutional proposal, *The Agreement of the People* (q.v.), which was subsequently debated with the General Council of the Army (q.v.) at the Putney Debates (q.v.). Support for the *Agreement* in the army was muted after Sir Thomas Fairfax and Oliver Cromwell (qq.v.) put down the Corkbush Field (q.v.) mutiny; support for the *Agreement* also faltered during the Second Civil War (q.v.).

By the autumn of 1648, the Levellers, with widescale support in some sections of the army, again proposed radical solutions to the political entanglements and entered into discussions with an erstwhile opponent, Henry Ireton (q.v.), together drafting a second *Agreement*. This was set aside by the Commons during the trial of Charles I. Although originally supporting the abolition of the monarchy, the Levellers were concerned with the potential for one tyranny—the king's, to be replaced by another—the grandees' (q.v.). In May 1646 a third *Agreement* was published, prompting a mutiny that was put down at Burford (q.v.). Thereafter, as a movement the Levellers went into political decline, although the activists continued individual efforts to reopen wider debate on the revolution. Some, particularly Lilburne, were considered to be political threats and faced periodic arrest and imprisonment.

LEVEN, ALEXANDER LESLIE, LORD (1580–1661). Leven was a man of continental military experience, having served under Sweden's Gustavus Adolphus, when he was appointed commander of the Army of the Covenant (q.v.) in 1639. In 1640 he led the invasion of England and defeated King Charles I's (q.v.) forces at the Battle of Newburn (q.v.) in August. In 1641 Charles was obliged to ennoble his conqueror in Edinburgh during the ratification of the Treaty of London (q.v.).

In the summer of 1642 Leven took command of the Scottish forces fighting in Ulster (q.v.). There, in a brutal campaign, Leven cleared County Antrim of rebel forces before returning to Scotland, leaving his command to Robert Monro (q.v.). In late 1643 Leven was appointed commander of the Army of the Solemn League and Covenant (q.v.). With this army he invaded England in January 1644. For three months Leven avoided being drawn into battle by the royalist (q.v.) forces of the earl of Newcastle (q.v.). Following Newcastle's retreat after the Battle of Selby (q.v.), he participated in the siege of York (q.v.).

At the Battle of Marston Moor (q.v.) Leven fled the field in the company of the English commanders Lord Fairfax and the earl of Manchester (qq.v.) when a royalist (q.v.) victory appeared likely, leaving their seconds to reverse their fortunes and ensure victory. Leven remained in the north of England with his army for much of the rest of the war, although he led it southwards to Hereford in the summer of 1645, and into

Nottinghamshire to besiege Newark (q.v.) later that same year. In May 1645, on behalf of the allied forces involved in the siege of Newark, Leven received King Charles I's surrender. Almost immediately Leven led the army north to Newcastle (q.v.) with the king as prisoner. In January 1647 Leven led the army home. He did not associate with the Engagers (q.v.) and took up arms against them at the end of 1648, being involved in the Whiggamore (q.v.) raid. He likewise did not get involved with the first campaigns of Charles II (q.v.) in 1650, but later that year he was captured by the English forces and imprisoned.

LICHFIELD, STAFFORDSHIRE. An important market town, Lichfield was garrisoned at the end of 1642 as the earl of Chesterfield fled from his small Bretby garrison, having being chased out by Sir John Gell (q.v.). In early March 1643 the town was besieged by Lord Brooke (q.v.), who was killed in the early days of the siege. The town quickly fell to Gell. The local royalist (q.v.) commander, Henry Hastings (q.v.), enlisted first the help of the earl of Northampton (q.v.) with whom he fended off further attacks on Staffordshire royalist strongholds, and then the help of Prince Rupert (q.v.), and together in late April they besieged the town and on 21 April ensured its surrender. Lichfield remained an important royalist garrison until 10 July 1646.

LILBURNE, ELIZABETH. Elizabeth married John Lilburne (q.v.) in 1640 after his release from prison. She became politically active sometime around 1643, when she sought and obtained her husband's release from Oxford (q.v.) prison. She campaigned for his release after the House of Lords (q.v.) imprisoned him again in 1646. Her most public campaigning seems to have taken place in early 1649 when, with Katherine Chidley (q.v.), she strove for the release of all Leveller (q.v.) leaders and presented the Petitions of Women to Parliament (q.v.) on 24 April and the second on 5 May. Elizabeth Lilburne continued to campaign for the release of her husband throughout the 1650s when he was imprisoned by the various republican regimes.

LILBURNE, JOHN (1615–1657). The younger son of a gentleman, Lilburne was imprisoned in 1638 for importing the banned writings of William Prynne and John Bastwicke (qq.v.). He was released only when Oliver Cromwell (q.v.) raised his case in the Long Parliament (q.v.). Lilburne enlisted in Lord Brooke's (q.v.) regiment, and was captured and imprisoned under sentence of death at Oxford (q.v.). His wife, Elizabeth Lilburne (q.v.), organised his release and he later served as a dragoon (q.v.) commander in the Eastern Association (q.v.) Army and fought at the Battle of Marston Moor (q.v.) in 1644. His initial favouring of the Independents (q.v.) made him Presbyterian (q.v.) enemies, notably the earl of Manchester (q.v.), and he left the army because he would not take the Covenant (q.v.). He was imprisoned briefly in 1645 largely through the instigation of his former associates Prynne and Bastwicke who could not tolerate his advocacy of religious freedom. His developing radicalism also brought conflict with Cromwell, however. Lilburne became a prominent figure in the Leveller (q.v.) movement and drafted many of their pamphlets attacking Parliament and then the army leadership. In 1645 he had met William Walwyn (q.v.) and together they drafted the Leveller critiques of the Westminster Assembly of Divines (q.v.) and of the political system in England and Wales. Lilburne was imprisoned again in 1646 for attacking the earl of Manchester, who by this time was speaker of the House of Lords (q.v.). This kept him incarcerated whilst the *Remonstrance of Many Thousand Citizens* was being organised.

In 1649 Lilburne opposed the execution of King Charles I (q.v.) and the trials of prominent royalists (q.v.) by the High Court of Justice (q.v.) because he saw them as evidence of a new tyranny, a view expressed in his pamphlet, *England's New Chains Discovered* (q.v.). During the mutinies of 1649, Lilburne was in prison whilst his wife, Elizabeth, campaigned for his release, organising petitions and demonstrations with Katherine Chidley (q.v.).

After the decline of the Leveller movement, Lilburne joined in other political campaigns, Fenland drainage disputes in Lincolnshire, and arguments against companies and monopolists. In 1652 he was exiled for campaigning against Sir Arthur Hesilrige (q.v.). On being allowed back into England, he refused to declare loyalty to the Protectorate (q.v.) and was again imprisoned. Lilburne joined the Quakers (q.v.). He died just after his release from prison in 1657.

LILBURNE, ROBERT (1613–1665). Robert was the elder brother of John Lilburne (q.v.). He rose to a colonelcy in the New Model Army (q.v.) and became a friend of John Lambert (q.v.). His regiment mutinied at Corkbush Field (q.v.) in support of the Levellers' *Agreement of the People* (q.v.). In 1649 he sat on the High Court of Justice (q.v.), which tried King Charles I (q.v.) and he signed the king's death warrant.

In 1651–52 Lilburne served in Scotland. He was an M.P. for the East Riding of Yorkshire in the 1656 Protectorate Parliament (qq.v.). Lilburne opposed moves to bring about the Restoration (q.v.) and sided with Lambert's attempt to save the Republic (q.v.). He was imprisoned at the Restoration.

LILLEY, WILLIAM (1602–1681). An astrologer who began to publish works in the late 1630s. By 1644 Lilley was producing prophetic pamphlets as well as what were to become annual almanacs. Lilley's reputation soared when he published *The Starry Messenger*, which predicted a great parliamentarian (q.v.) victory on the day of the Battle of Naseby (q.v.). He was associated with attempts to help Charles I (q.v.) during his imprisonment in 1647–48 although he himself was in the employ of Parliament (q.v.).

During the 1650s Lilley published a book on the effects of eclipses, which he claimed to be a work of science. Late in life Lilley studied medicine and was licensed to practice when he was 68.

LIMERICK. This city fell to the rebels in 1642 and was, for the majority of the war in Ireland, a garrison for the Catholic Confederation of Kilkenny (q.v.). Limerick remained one of the few garrisons to hold out against Lord Inchiquin (q.v.) after the Battle of Dungan's Hill (q.v.) in 1647. In 1648–49 the city acted as a base for the royalist (q.v.) navy led by Prince Rupert (q.v.). It was too strong for Oliver Cromwell (q.v.) to attack in 1649 and did not come under siege from English forces until 14 June 1651. The city held out for four and a half months before surrendering to Henry Ireton (q.v.) on 27 October. Ireton died there a month later.

LINDSEY, ROBERT BERTIE, EARL OF (1582–1642). One of the prominent Lincolnshire aristocrats, Lindsey had seen service in European wars since he was a young boy. Lindsey was a keen royalist (q.v.) and raised troops from his Lincolnshire and Nottinghamshire estates in the summer of 1642. He was appointed general in chief of King Charles I's (q.v.) army in 1642 but was only effectively the commander of the Foot (q.v.) regiments. He was involved in a dispute with Prince Rupert (q.v.), technically his junior, who was known to desire independence, just before the beginning of the Battle of Edgehill (q.v.). Rupert and Lindsey favoured different formations for the Foot regiments on the field. When the king sided with Rupert, Lindsey lay down his command and went to the head of his regiment of Foot. He was mortally wounded during the battle and died shortly afterwards.

LISLE, SIR GEORGE (?–1648). Lisle served with King Charles I's (q.v.) field army. At the Second Battle of Newbury (q.v.) he led the defence of Shaw House, which was attacked by the earl of Manchester's (q.v.) forces. His defence of the house—he rushed around in shirt sleeves to ensure that he would be seen by his troops in the gathering dusk—was determined and successful. In May 1645, after the capture of Leicester (q.v.), with the rank of lieutenant general, Sir George was given command of the Leicestershire forces under Lord Loughborough (q.v.). He led a tertia at the Battle of Naseby (q.v.).

In 1648, during the Second Civil War (q.v.), Lisle was involved in the siege of Colchester (q.v.), with his former commander, Loughborough. After the surrender of the town, Lord Fairfax (q.v.) claimed that Lisle and Sir Charles Lucas (q.v.) had broken the terms of parole granted to them in the First Civil War (q.v.). Along with Sir Bernard Gascoigne, Lucas and Lisle were tried and shot.

LITTLE DEAN, BATTLE OF. Fought on 11 April 1643. Following the Battle of Highnam (q.v.), where he defeated the Herefordshire royalists (q.v.), Sir William Waller (q.v.) pursued his opponents into Wales. Prince Maurice (q.v.) moved into his rear, forcing Waller to return from Wales into Gloucestershire. Maurice brought him to battle at Little Dean and defeated him.

LITTLETON, LORD EDWARD (1589–1645). An Oxford University-educated barrister, Littleton, with estates in Staffordshire and Shropshire, had a career in north Wales and then entered Parliament (q.v.). He helped draft the Petition of Right (q.v.) of 1628. In the 1630s, however, he was taken into King Charles I's (q.v.) government, becoming solicitor general in 1634 and chief justice of the common pleas in 1640. In 1641 he became lord keeper of the great seal. The following year he was courted by Parliament as the estrangement between it and the king developed. Parliament had some success in persuading Littleton that Charles I had acted illegally in summoning the law courts to join him at York (q.v.). He left London in May, however, having sent the great seal ahead of him to York, removing thereby the instrument enabling enactment of legislation. He remained at Oxford (q.v.) during the First Civil War (q.v.), receiving one of the honorary doctorates of law awarded in 1643. Littleton was colonel of a regiment based in Oxford. He died in August 1645.

LLYWD, MORGAN (1619–1659). An Independent (q.v.) who served with the New Model Army (q.v.) in the 1650s as a chaplain. He had already founded a congregation in Wrexham in 1646. Llywd was the author of poetry and prose tracts. He was also involved in the 1650s in the Commission for the Propagation of the Gospel in Wales (q.v.).

LOCKYER, ROBERT (1626–1649). Lockyer served in Colonel Edward Whalley's regiment of Horse (q.v.) and in 1647 was elected as an agitator (q.v.) for the regiment. He was involved in the Corkbush Field mutiny (q.v.). In April 1649, whilst the principal Levellers (q.v.) were imprisoned, Lockyer was involved in a fracas at the Bull Inn, London, which centred on army pay. The grandees (q.v.), worried by the potential for a renewed potent link between the army and the Levellers, came down hard on the perceived leaders. Lockyer was tried and executed. His funeral was one of the largest Leveller demonstrations in London, with thousands of citizens bedecked with sea-green ribbons, the Leveller emblem.

LONDON, TREATY OF. This treaty brought an end to the 1640 Bishop's War (q.v.). Charles I (q.v.) had wanted peace agreed on before a Parliament (q.v.) could sit in England, but the Scots insisted on the treaty being negotiated in London and on it being ratified by a Parliament (q.v.) at Westminster. During the period whilst the treaty was discussed, the Army of the Covenant (q.v.) remained encamped in northern England. Charles I went to Edinburgh in August 1641 to sign the treaty, and to confirm the constitutional changes undertaken by the Estates (q.v.). He used the journey as a cover for trying to develop a royalist (q.v.) faction in Scotland, a plan that resulted in the Incident (q.v.).

LONG PARLIAMENT. The name was coined to distinguish the Parliament (q.v.) that sat from 3 November 1640 onwards from that of its brief predecessor that year, the Short Parliament (q.v.). The Long Parliament sat until April 1653, although it was heavily purged many times, of royalists (q.v.) in 1642, of Presbyterians (q.v.) in 1647 and 1648. In the summer of 1642 the Long Parliament took on itself the sole right of government, judging the king to be incapable of acting as the head of the executive. From January 1649 the Parliament consisted only of the House of Commons (q.v.) but was expected then to devise a new constitution, although it showed little inclination to do so.

The remaining members of the Long Parliament House of Commons were summoned at the end of the Protectorate (q.v.), when they were more commonly referred to as the Rump Parliament (q.v.).

LORD LIEUTENANT. From the late 1580s, lord lieutenants were permanent features of local government in charge of the Trained Bands (q.v.). The lieutenants were court appointed and generally members of the aristocracy; the everyday running of the militia was undertaken by their appointed deputies. The lieutenancy's involvement in disarming recusants and in other issues of local government during Charles I's Personal Rule (qq.v.) resulted in the office being treated with suspicion by parliamentarians (q.v.). The Long Parliament (q.v.) initiated investigations into the office, but with the onset of serious conflict with the king left the office intact. The Militia Ordinance (q.v.) replaced the incumbents with its own nominees. The lord lieutenants were initially the centre of the county committees (q.v.) but the duties of the office were generally absorbed by the committees and the lieutenancy went into a decline until reinvigorated at the Restoration (q.v.).

LORD PROTECTOR. This title had been used in England to denote a guardian appointed to govern in the interests of an underage monarch, such as Edward VI. The title was given to the head of state under the Instrument of Government (q.v.) in 1653. The first holder of the title was Oliver Cromwell (q.v.). The second and last was Richard Cromwell (q.v.). The *Humble Petition and Advice* (q.v.) effectively made the post hereditary by giving Oliver Cromwell the right to nominate a successor.

LORDS, HOUSE OF. *See* PARLIAMENT.

LOSTWITHIEL, BATTLE OF. Fought between 30 August and 2 September 1644. After the earl of Essex (q.v.) had marched into the southwest, King Charles I (q.v.) followed him. By August 1644 Essex was trapped on the Fowey peninsula and the king's army was moving in. At 3 A.M. on 31 August Essex had Sir William Balfour lead the 2,000 Horse (q.v.) in a breakout towards Plymouth (q.v.). Balfour managed to get past the royalist (q.v.) Horse under the earl of Cleveland, who could only follow him through the night. Balfour lost only 100 men on the way to Plymouth. Essex then began moving the Foot (q.v.) down the peninsula in the hope of removing them by sea. In the summer rain Essex's artillery was left behind on boggy roads. By the afternoon of 1 September most of Essex's Foot was drawn up on the earthworks of the ancient Castle Dore, with Sir Philip Skippon (q.v.) managing to hold off royalist attacks with the rearguard just south of Lostwithiel. When royalist forces got between the River Fowey and Essex's army the likelihood of evacuating the army faded.

Essex abandoned his army and took a fishing boat down the river to join the parliamentarian (q.v.) fleet sailing off the coast. Skippon had to surrender the Foot on the following day. Although disarmed the Foot were quickly released and allowed to march to Plymouth, where they joined the Horse and their commander. Parliament (q.v.) questioned Essex's actions, but he was able to point out that apart from the loss of arms and ammunition, he had been able to extricate all of the Horse fully armed and the Foot regiments had also got away to fight again. For the royalists this victory, coupled with that at the Battle of Cropredy Bridge (q.v.) seemed to offset the disaster in the north at the Battle of Marston Moor (q.v.).

LOUGHBOROUGH, HENRY HASTINGS, LORD (1609–1667). In 1642 Henry Hastings was one of the first people to put the Commission of Array (q.v.) into practise. He raised Horse and dragoons (qq.v.) during the summer of 1642 and worked with Prince Rupert (q.v.) during August and September, raiding the home of the parliamentarian earl of Stamford (qq.v.). Hastings served with Charles I's (q.v.) field army and fought at the Battles of Powick Bridge and Edgehill (qq.v.). After serving at the Battles of Brentford and Turnham Green (qq.v.), Hastings was sent back to his native county to establish Ashby-de-la-Zouch (q.v.) as a base for royalist (q.v.) activity and to challenge the control over the North Midlands being established by Sir John Gell and John Hutchinson (qq.v.). Hastings was made colonel general of Nottinghamshire, Derbyshire, Leicestershire, Rutland, and Staffordshire at the end of February 1643. He stabilised royalist control over the area with the help of the earl of Northampton (q.v.) and Prince Rupert in spring 1643 and the earl of Newcastle (q.v.) during the summer and fall. In October 1643 Hastings was ennobled as Lord Loughborough and given the rank of lieutenant general. By the end of the year, Hastings had established eight major and sixteen minor garrisons in his region, but he did not control any of the important county towns.

In 1644 strains on his command, such as the drain of troops to join the earl of Newcastle's attempt to halt the advance of the Army of the Solemn League and Covenant (q.v.), reduced Hastings effectiveness and Newark (q.v.) came under siege. Prince Rupert helped defeat the besiegers and the situation was stabilised somewhat, but the campaign, which ended with the royalist defeat at the Battle of Marston Moor (q.v.), had involved Loughborough in a huge commitment in resources and soldiers. Royalist garrisons in the Midland fell and Loughborough's power declined. There was a revival in fortunes during the spring of 1645 and the capture of Leicester (q.v.) seemed to herald a reversal of fortune. Sir George Lisle (q.v.) was attached to his command with the rank of lieutenant general of Leicestershire. Defeat at the Battle of Naseby (q.v.) ended this promise. Loughborough's power continued to decline and by the end of the year only the major garrisons, Lichfield (q.v.), Dudley, Tutbury, Newark and Ashby-de-la-Zouch, were left in royalist hands. In February 1646 Loughborough opened negotiations with the parliamentarians at Leicester.

In the Second Civil War (q.v.) Loughborough served as commissary general of the royalist garrison at Colchester (q.v.). When the garrison surrendered he was sent as a prisoner to Windsor Castle. Loughborough was named as one of the Seven Great Delinquents and probably faced trial before the High Court of Justice (q.v.). On the eve of King Charles I's execution, however, Loughborough escaped from Windsor.

During the 1650s Loughborough spent much of the time in Holland. He was a founding member of the Sealed Knot (q.v.) and at times entered England in disguise. His active involvement with royalist plots declined after 1655. At the Restoration (q.v.), Loughborough returned to England and was appointed lord lieutenant (q.v.) of Leicestershire. He lived in London at Loughborough House and died in early 1667.

LUCAS, SIR CHARLES (1613–1648). Lucas was born in Colchester (q.v.) and was the brother of Margaret, later marchioness and then duchess of Newcastle (q.v.). Lucas fought with Prince Rupert (q.v.) in the early stages of the First Civil War (q.v.). In early 1644, as part of the royalists (q.v.) response to the invasion of the Army of the Solemn League and Covenant (q.v.), Lucas was given power to raise a body of Horse (q.v.) drawn from Midland garrisons to head north. Lucas joined the marquis of Newcastle's (q.v.) army in Northumberland. After the Battle of Selby (q.v.) Newcastle retreated to York (q.v.) and the Horse, under Lord Goring (q.v.), was evacuated southwards. In June 1644 these forces joined with Prince Rupert in the march to relieve York.

At the Battle of Marston Moor (q.v.), Lucas served with Goring's Horse and attacked the flank of the parliamentarian Foot (qq.v.). After the defeat Lucas stayed with Prince Rupert's forces. In 1645 he fought at the Battle of Naseby (q.v.), and in 1646 he was second in command to Lord Astley (q.v.) at the Battle of Stow on the Wold (q.v.).

In the Second Civil War (q.v.) Lucas was involved in the Essex uprising and as it imploded he ended up at his home town of Colchester. At the end of the siege Lord Fairfax (q.v.) claimed that Lucas, along with Sir Bernard Gascoigne and Sir George Lisle (q.v.), had broken the terms of earlier parole agreements. After a court-martial, Lisle and Lucas were shot.

LUDLOW, EDMUND (1617–1692). Ludlow took up arms for Parliament (q.v.) at the Battle of Edgehill (q.v.) and entered the Long Parliament (q.v.) in the Recruiter Elections (q.v.) of 1646 as M.P. for Wiltshire. He was involved in the New Model Army's (q.v.) battles with Parliament (q.v.) in 1647. In 1648, after the Second Civil War (q.v.), he urged the purging of the Presbyterians (q.v.) in Parliament and in 1649 sat at the trial of Charles I (q.v.) and signed the death warrant.

Ludlow served in Ireland as a commissioner from 1650 until 1655 and took command of the army there briefly after the death of Henry Ireton at Limerick (qq.v.). Ludlow opposed the creation of the Protectorate (q.v.) and argued with Oliver Cromwell (q.v.), although he served in Richard Cromwell's (q.v.) Parliament in 1659. Later that year he sat again as part of the Rump Parliament (q.v.). Unlike many of the Commonwealthmen (q.v.) who had opposed Cromwell, Ludlow fled the country at the Restoration (q.v.) despite initially securing his liberty. His attempt to return to England in 1689 after the Glorious Revolution failed to win the approval of William III and Mary. Ludlow's memoirs were published in 1698.

LUKE, SIR SAMUEL (1603–1670). Luke served as M.P. for Bedford in both of the 1640 Parliaments (q.v.) and joined the earl of Essex's (q.v.) army in 1642 as a commander of dragoons (q.v.). He fought at the Battles of Edgehill (q.v.) and Chalgrove Field. From 1643 he served as scoutmaster general to Essex's army. His letterbooks from this period contain a good deal of important information about the running of the army's information networks.

LUNSFORD, SIR THOMAS (1610–1653). Lunsford was a violent man, who spent the years 1633–37 as an outlaw after an assault on Sir Thomas Pelham. Having been pardoned, he served in the Bishop's Wars (q.v.). Almost an archetypal macho cavalier (q.v.), Lunsford's very presence in London provoked widescale protests. In 1641 Charles I (q.v.) appointed him lieutenant of the Tower of London. The act was seen as a military threat to the city, reminiscent of the Army Plot (q.v.), and he was quickly replaced. During the apprentice demonstrations of December 1642, it was the presence of Lunsford at Westminster with armed thugs masquerading as royal guards that gave rise to the term "cavalier." Lunsford commanded a regiment during the First Civil War (q.v.). He left the country in 1646. By 1649 he was in Virginia, where he died.

LYME. This Dorset port (now Lyme Regis) was an important possession for the parliamentarians (q.v.) in the south-west. It was particularly important during the summer of 1644 when it tied down Prince Maurice (q.v.) in a pointless siege. The town was relieved on 15 June 1644 by the advance of the earl of Essex (q.v.) into Cornwall during the campaign that culminated in the Battle of Lostwithiel (q.v.).

↝ M ↜

MacCOLLA (or MacDONNELL or MacDONALD), ALASDAIR (?1605–15–1647). The son of Coll Ciotach, Alasdair MacColla was born into the Clan Ian Mor, as the Clan Donald underwent further decline. The advent of the Scottish Rebellion gave the MacDonald clan the opportunity to regain some of their status, as their principal opponents, the Campbells, led by the marquis of Argyll (q.v.), had signed the Covenant (q.v.). Thus, under the leadership of the clan chief, Ranald MacDonald, earl of Antrim (q.v.), the McDonnells, Clan Ian Mor included, began to stress their loyalty to Charles I (q.v.). MacColla was present in Ulster (q.v.) when the Irish Rebellion (q.v.) broke out, although initially the area of North Antrim where he was remained quiet and the regiment raised to defend the Scottish settlers was composed of both Protestants and Catholics (q.v.).

This harmony was soon broken, however, by Catholic sympathy towards the Irish Catholics in rebellion and by Protestant antipathy towards the Catholic companies in the regiment. On 2 January 1642, Alasdair MacColla led the Catholic companies in an attack on the Protestant companies at Portnaw that precipitated the spread of the Rebellion to Antrim. When Covenanter forces arrived in Antrim, MacColla joined Sir Phelim O'Neill's (q.v.) army and its vain attacks on the Lagan Army (q.v.) under Sir Robert Stewart (q.v.), and he was wounded at the Battle of Raphoe.

In late 1642 MacColla sided with Lord Leven (q.v.) and briefly turned against the rebels with whom he had worked. When he again sided with the Irish, he seems not to have received employment, and he was not heard from for a year. In late 1643 MacColla was part of an expeditionary force sent to the Isles, ostensibly to engage in a war against the Covenanters who had by this time sided with the English Parliament (q.v.), but also to regain lost MacDonald lands, part of the long-term ambitions of both MacColla and Antrim. In the summer of 1644 this had become a campaign on the mainland and in late summer he was joined by the marquis of Montrose (q.v.). Together, Montrose and MacColla augmented the Irish and Highland (q.v.) forces MacColla had with him and began the campaign that saw them defeat successive Covenanter forces at the Battles of Tippemuir, Auldearn, Bridge of Alford, and Kilsyth (qq.v.).

After the royalist defeat at the Battle of Philliphaugh (q.v.), Mac-Colla continued the fight in the Campbell lands of Argyll for almost two years, defying the king's order to lay down his weapons, which Montrose reluctantly obeyed. In 1647 MacColla returned to Ireland, where he was killed at the Battle of Knocknanuss (q.v.) in Munster.

MacDONALD, ALASDAIR. *See* MacCOLLA, ALASDAIR.

MacDONNELL, ALASDAIR. *See* MacCOLLA, ALASDAIR.

MACROOM, BATTLE OF. Fought on 10 April 1651. Lord Broghill defeated the last of the royalist (q.v.) field armies in Munster at Macroom. The forces were led by the bishop of Ross, who was captured and executed.

MAIDSTONE, BATTLE OF. Fought on 1 June 1648. The Kentish rebels and royalist (q.v.) forces hastily raised gathered in Maidstone at the end of May 1648. Their rebellion was one of the major risings that constituted the Second Civil War (q.v.). The New Model Army (q.v.) was divided in two, with Oliver Cromwell (q.v.) dispatched to deal with the risings in south Wales, while Sir Thomas, now Lord Fairfax (q.v.), marched into Kent. He attacked the rebels in Maidstone on 1 June. The battle lasted much of the day and consisted of vicious street fighting. Many of the fleeing royalists made it across the River Thames into Essex, where they joined the rebels there. With Fairfax in pursuit they set out for Colchester (q.v.).

MAJOR GENERALS. In the wake of Penruddock's (q.v.) Rising in 1655, Oliver Cromwell (q.v.) imposed a period of military rule on England and Wales. He divided the two countries into eleven districts, each of which was presided over by a major general. Although the main functions were to oversee the use of the decimation tax (q.v.) to finance and command the militia, the major generals also participated in other local government affairs. This alienated them from significant sections of the community. Their involvement in the parliamentary elections of 1656 (which they had persuaded Cromwell to call) ensured their being loathed by the communities over which they were supposed to preside. In early 1657 Parliament (q.v.) abolished the decimation tax and with it the major generals. Their period of rule is generally seen as one of military government, out of keeping with the rest of the Protectorate (q.v.).

MALIGNANTS. A general term used by both sides in England and Wales to describe their opponents. The term was suggestive of their criminal tendencies.

MALPAS, BATTLE OF. Fought on 25 August 1644. It was at this battle that Sir William Brereton (q.v.) caught up with and defeated a section of the royalist Horse (qq.v.) in Cheshire and drove them out of the county. These forces had been in the north-west of England since the defeat at the Battle of Marston Moor (q.v.).

MAN OF BLOOD. After the Second Civil War, Charles I (qq.v.) was being held increasingly responsible for the state of the kingdom. He was seen to be guilty of the deaths of those in the Second Civil War at a time when many held that God had judged against him in the First Civil War (q.v.). His defeat in the Second Civil War was seen as confirmation of God's judgement. Thus Charles was said to be a "man of blood," essentially one who, to assuage the nation's guilt, had to be brought to trial and have his blood shed as retribution and to ensure the spiritual survival of the nation.

MANCHESTER, LANCASHIRE. This developing market-and-industrial town is often said to be the place where the First Civil War (q.v.) began. When the earl of Derby (q.v.), then known by his title Lord Strange, tried to take possession of the magazine on 15 July 1642, he was opposed by the townspeople, who were renowned for their Puritan (q.v.) sympathies. In the fighting, Richard Perceval, a linen weaver, was killed. The royalists (q.v.) were driven out. Derby besieged the town in September of that year, but even after a 10-week blockade was unable to capture it. At the earl's trial in 1651 he was accused of spilling the first blood of the war—Perceval's blood.

MANCHESTER, EDWARD MONTAGU, 2ND EARL OF (1602–1671). Montagu served as M.P. for Huntingdonshire in the 1620s. He accompanied the future Charles I (q.v.) to Spain in 1623 when he went to try to win the hand of the Spanish infanta. During the 1630s Montagu became estranged from the court and was moving in Puritan (q.v.) circles with oppositionist former M.P.s like John Pym (q.v.).

Following the conferring of an earldom on his father, Montagu became Viscount Mandeville and in the 1640s was in the House of Lords (q.v.). He was able to put into effect his opposition to the king's policies to such an extent that when Charles sought the arrest of the Five Members (q.v.), Mandeville's was the sixth name and the only member of the Lords the king sought to arrest. In 1642 Mandeville raised a regiment, but it fled the field at the Battle of Edgehill (q.v.) and was disbanded soon after. In November he succeeded to the title earl of Manchester and was involved in the peace process instituted over the winter. By the following August Manchester was commander of the Eastern Association (q.v.) Army with Oliver Cromwell (q.v.), a distant relative, as his second. Manchester led his forces at the Battles of Winceby, Marston Moor, and the Second Battle of Newbury (qq.v.). The quarrel between Manchester and Cromwell resulted in the Self Denying Ordinance (q.v.), which in turn resulted in Manchester losing his command. He was appointed to the Committee of Both Kingdoms (q.v.), which allowed him some input into military affairs, as it had power over the New Model Army (q.v.). Manchester's affiliation to the Presbyterian (q.v.) Party ensured his eclipse from 1647 onwards and he was opposed to the trial of Charles I, although he was appointed chancellor of Cambridge University during the Republic (q.v.). In the late 1650s he worked towards the Restoration (q.v.) of the monarchy and was rewarded in 1660. Manchester became a privy councillor (q.v.). He later became a member of the Royal Society.

MARCHER ASSOCIATION. Unlike the associations (q.v.) formed by King Charles I or Parliament (qq.v.), the Marcher Association was formed by the gentry of the counties it embraced. Discussions amongst the gentry of the counties of Herefordshire, Worcestershire, Staffordshire, and Shropshire in late 1644 and early 1645 had centred on the need to keep order in their respective counties and ensure that the taxation burden was kept regular and used principally in the counties themselves. From these discussions grew the demand that the counties associate and raise troops for the defence of the association, led by men appointed by the leaders of the association. Charles I was almost forced to accede completely. The king did manage to impose Prince Maurice (q.v.) as leader of the association forces and gain some of the soldiers raised by the association for service in the main field army, but otherwise the region's gentry had their own way. The effectiveness of the association was limited by the fall of much of Shropshire to the parliamentarians (q.v.) in the summer of 1645 and by the overall decline in royalist (q.v.) fortunes.

MARCHER COUNTIES. This term relates to the English counties bordering Wales, Gloucestershire, Herefordshire, Shropshire, and Cheshire, and to some of their neighbouring counties, Worcestershire and Staffordshire. These counties were governed, along with Wales by the Council of Wales and the Marches (q.v.), although successful legal challenges to the council had diminished its powers over the English shires. During the First Civil War (q.v.) several of these counties formed the Marcher Association (q.v.).

MARCHES. A term that usually refers to the border area of England and Wales, but this could also refer to the counties on the borders of England and Scotland. *See also* Marcher Counties.

MARSHALL, STEPHEN (1594–1655). The son of a Huntingdonshire glover, Marshall went to Cambridge University and became vicar of Finchingfield. In 1636 he was reported for not conforming to Archbishop William Laud's (q.v.) reforms. A friend of John Pym (q.v.) and proponent of the Root and Branch Petition (q.v.), Marshall, as preacher at St

Margaret's, Westminster (q.v.), preached before Parliament (q.v.) on the eve of the First Civil War (q.v.). When Charles I (q.v.) fled from London after the attempt to arrest the Five Members (q.v.), Marshall preached on the theme of Judges 5:23 "Curse ye Meroz," urging that no one stand aside from the forthcoming struggle as it was the Lord's work. In 1642 he became an army chaplain. He was a delegate to Scotland in 1643, but as the war progressed he became an Independent (q.v.) and afterwards opposed the Presbyterians (q.v.), who dominated Parliament. He therefore sided with the New Model Army (q.v.). However, he was also appointed chaplain to Charles I at Holdenby House (q.v.) by Parliament and he vigorously opposed the trial and execution of the king. In the 1650s he became a minister at Ipswich and one of the Triers and Ejectors. His body, buried at Westminster, was exhumed at the Restoration (q.v.).

MARSTON MOOR, BATTLE OF. Fought on 2 July 1644. In order to relieve York (q.v.), which had been under siege since late April 1644, Prince Rupert (q.v.) raised an army in the Midlands to supplement his own forces and led it north through Lancashire. He crossed the Pennines and relieved the city on 1 July. On the following day he advanced on the rearguard of the retreating Scottish and parliamentarian (q.v.) armies. In all three armies, the Army of the Solemn League and Covenant (q.v.) under Lord Leven (q.v.); the Yorkshire parliamentarians under Lord Fairfax and his son, Sir Thomas Fairfax (qq.v.); and the Eastern Association Army under the earl of Manchester (qq.v.), besieged the city. In response to Rupert's approach, these forces turned to face him. Rupert drew up his army north of the Tockwith to Long Marston road and awaited the forces of the earl of Newcastle (q.v.) to join him from York. As Newcastle's army continued to arrive on the field during the early evening, the parliamentarians and Scots attacked. After a tactical error by Lord Byron (q.v.), the royalist Horse (qq.v.) on the right flank was caught in rough ground by the Scots Horse under David Leslie (q.v.) and the Eastern Association Horse under Oliver Cromwell (q.v.). The royalists on this flank were defeated and began to retreat. On the opposite flank the reverse had happened with Lord Goring (q.v.) catching the parliamentarian Horse in difficult terrain and inflicting defeat on them. The three allied commanders at this point fled the field, leaving their seconds to lead their forces.

Sir Thomas Fairfax was able to ride around the rear of the royalist army in disguise and inform Leslie and Cromwell of the state of the parliamentarian right flank. Cromwell then led Eastern Association Horse around the royalist rear and attacked Lord Goring, who was now caught on the same ground where he had defeated Fairfax earlier; he too was defeated. With both wings defeated the royalist Foot (q.v.) was now exposed to the onslaught of the allied Horse. Whilst it had held the parliamentarian and Scots Foot to a standstill, it could now no longer hold out and a retreat began.

Regiments of white-coats from the Northern Army (q.v.) held out in enclosed fields on the route to York allowing time for much of the army to escape before they were almost wiped out. The battle resulted in the collapse of the royalist hold on the north, Prince Rupert led his forces westwards, Newcastle laid down his command and York was again besieged.

MARTEN, HENRY (1602–1680). At the outset of the Civil Wars, Marten had the distinction of being one of the very few Republicans in Parliament (q.v.). He opposed the levies for the wars with Scotland in 1640 and became M.P. for Berkshire in the Short Parliament and the Long Parliament (qq.v.). He supported the Bill of Attainder (q.v.) against the earl of Stafford (q.v.), and from the outset of war in 1642 he wished to go beyond the bounds aimed at by most of King Charles I's (q.v.) opponents. John Pym (q.v.) had Marten imprisoned in 1643 for calling for the king's deposition. He served in military command, being governor of Reading in 1642 and Aylesbury in 1644. He opposed the alliance with the Scots, and whilst not being a religious man, opposed the Presbyterian (q.v.) influence they had in England.

In 1647 he proposed the Vote of No Addresses (q.v.) to curtail negotiations with Charles I and won the support of the Levellers (q.v.) and the army. Others shifted towards Marten's position as the 1640s progressed and some joined him in the High Court of Justice (q.v.), which tried the king in 1649. In the Commonwealth (q.v.) Marten served on the Council of State (q.v.), but his opposition to Oliver Cromwell (q.v.) ensured that he went into obscurity with the establishment of the Protectorate (q.v.) and he was imprisoned for debt in 1655–57. Marten had been a signatory to the death warrant, but escaped execution at the Restoration (q.v.) despite being tried for treason. He was, however, imprisoned and he died in Chepstow Castle 20 years later.

MARTIN MARPRIEST. This pseudonym was adopted by Richard Overton (q.v.), the future Leveller (q.v.), for the authorship of several satirical tracts criticising the Westminster Council of Divines (q.v.) during the First Civil War (q.v.). In the pamphlets, which deliberately recalled the work of the pseudonymous Elizabethan author Martin Marpriest, Overton created a range of characters including Sir Simon Synod, Sir John Presbyter, and Mr Persecution. Overton's principal targets were the Presbyterians (q.v.) and their refusal to accept any degree of religious toleration.

MARVELL, ANDREW (1621–1678). Educated in his hometown of Hull (q.v.) and at Cambridge University, Marvell travelled widely in Europe during the First Civil War (q.v.). He had friends amongst both royalists and parliamentarians (qq.v.), and dedicated poems to the royalist poet Lovelace and to the nephew of royalist General Lord Loughborough (q.v.). From 1650–52 he was tutor to Thomas Lord Fairfax's (q.v.) daughter at Nun Appleton where he wrote *Upon Appleton House*. In 1653 John Milton appointed him assistant secretary for foreign tongues in the Protectorate (q.v.) government and in 1657 he worked in the Latin secretaryship, again with Milton. Already an experienced poet before the 1650s, Marvell wrote several verses dedicated to national figures, including Thomas Lord Fairfax, and to Oliver Cromwell (q.v.). The best known of the latter is perhaps *An Horatian Ode upon Cromwell's return from Ireland* of 1650, often said to be the best English political poem, in which he commented upon the execution of King Charles I (q.v.). He also composed *Upon the death of His late highness the Lord Protector* in 1658. He sat in the last Protectorate Parliament (qq.v.).

At the Restoration (q.v.) he was elected M.P. for Hull, and remained a critic of monarchical government and the intolerance of the restored church. He advocated a republic again in the 1670s, although Charles II (q.v.) loved his satirical work calling for toleration. Marvell's most beautiful verse, such as *To His Coy Mistress*, must be set alongside his entire literary output of satire and polemic.

MASSEY, SIR EDWARD (?1617–19–?1674–75). Massey, a Cheshire man, may have been in service in Europe before returning to fight in the Bishop's Wars (q.v.). Initially in 1642 he joined King Charles I in York (qq.v.) but then took up the lieutenant colonelcy in the earl of Stamford's regiment of Foot (qq.v.). In the autumn campaign of that year he accompanied his regiment into the south-west and was eventually given command of the garrison at Gloucester (q.v.), which he held for the whole of the First Civil War (q.v.), holding out against a close siege in the autumn of 1643. By the end of the war as a major-general he commanded the Western Association (q.v.) Army.

From 1646 Massey represented Gloucester in Parliament (q.v.) and was a Presbyterian (q.v.). It was his religious beliefs that influenced officers to refuse to serve under him when he was appointed in 1647 to command forces destined for Ireland. He was impeached (q.v.) as one of the Eleven Members (q.v.) in 1647. Massey fled to Holland and when he returned after Pride's Purge (q.v.) in 1648 he was arrested. On his escape to Holland he joined Prince Charles Stuart (q.v.) and served in the campaigns of 1650 in Scotland. At the Battle of Worcester (q.v.) in 1651 he was wounded and captured. Although imprisoned in the Tower, Massey again escaped to Holland, where he was an active royalist (q.v.) plotter. In 1659 he was involved in the attempted royalist risings but was captured. Again he escaped the country. From 1660, when he was knighted at the Restoration (q.v.), Massey sat as M.P. for Gloucester until his death.

MATCHLOCK. The firing mechanism of a musket. When the trigger was pulled, a metal claw holding a piece of smouldering matchcord was lowered into a small pan containing fine-ground gunpowder. When this powder fired, it ignited the main charge through a small hole in the barrel.

MAURICE, PRINCE (1621–1652). Younger brother of Prince Rupert (q.v.), Maurice accompanied his brother to England in 1642, having likewise served in Protestant forces in Europe. He raised a regiment of Horse for Charles I (qq.v.) and fought at the Battles of Powick Bridge and Edgehill (qq.v.). Maurice led a small army in the West Midlands in the spring of 1643 and defeated Sir William Waller (q.v.) at the Battle of Ripple Field (q.v.) on 13 April. Later that year he fought alongside Ralph, Lord Hopton (q.v.) at the Battle of Lansdown (q.v.) and was instrumental in the royalist (q.v.) victory at the Battle of Roundway Down (q.v.).

Prince Maurice served in the west for the rest of that year, capturing Exeter and Dartmouth, but failed to make inroads against Lyme. In 1644 he was at the Battle of Lostwithiel (q.v.) and fought at the Second Battle of Newbury (q.v.). In 1645 he commanded the Marcher Association (q.v.) counties and had important success in restoring royalist positions there. He fought at the siege of Leicester and the Battle of Naseby (qq.v.) in the summer, and remained with the king's army that year. After his brother's surrender of Bristol (q.v.), Maurice took his part and went into exile with him. In the Second Civil War (q.v.) Maurice embarked on a naval career, continuing into the early 1650s with the royalist fleet, such as it was. He was drowned when his ship sank in 1652.

MELDRUM, SIR JOHN (1585–1645). Meldrum, a Scot, had extensive experience in wars on the continent before the Civil Wars. He was also involved in the settlement of his fellow Scots in Ulster (q.v.). He refused to serve King Charles I (q.v.) when summoned to York (q.v.) in 1642, citing the monarch and his father's ingratitude for past services. He took reinforcements to Hull (q.v.) during the siege in July 1642 and later that year fought at the Battle of Edgehill (q.v.). Having served in the south, in early 1643 he was sent to Nottingham (q.v.), where he took charge of the Horse (q.v.). He assisted again at Hull during the marquis of Newcastle's (q.v.) siege, which he helped bring to an end. He then teamed up with Sir

Thomas Fairfax (q.v.) and together they captured Gainsborough. In February 1644 Meldrum besieged Newark (q.v.) for some three weeks before being defeated outside the town by Prince Rupert and Lord Loughborough (qq.v.) on 21 March. He was able to assist the Fairfaxes at the Battle of Selby (q.v.), but when he was then sent to try and oppose Prince Rupert's march through Lancashire, he had little success. He fought at the Battle of Montgomery (q.v.) in September alongside Sir William Brereton (q.v.). In February 1645 he took over the siege of Scarborough (q.v.). He died there in July.

MELTON MOWBRAY, LEICESTERSHIRE. This small market town was twice embroiled in fighting. In November 1643 the Leicestershire county committee (q.v.) attempted to hold a meeting there. The royalist (q.v.) forces from Belvoir Castle attacked and drove off the military escort, capturing several members of the committee, including Sir Arthur Hesilrige's (q.v.) brother.

When Sir Marmaduke Langdale (q.v.) led the Northern Horse (qq.v.) northwards in 1645 to relieve the siege of Pontefact Castle (q.v.), he was intercepted on 25 February by Sir Edward Rossiter. Langdale drove the parliamentarian (q.v.) forces off and proceeded on his way.

MERCURIUS AULICUS. Printed at Oxford (q.v.) and sometimes in London, this was the principal official royalist newsbook (qq.v.). In January 1643 Charles I (q.v.) appointed John Berkenhead and Peter Heylin as joint editors. This octavo paper was published on a Sunday to allow for Oxford copies to reach London in time for the Tuesday carriers to take it throughout the country. It was sometimes printed in runs of 5,000 copies per issue and could be sold openly in the streets of London, as it was not covered by bans on proclamations. It was not until as late as January 1645 that a concerted effort was made to stop the London printer Richard Royston from printing the newsbook in the capital.

The newsbook reflected the views of the king and his close advisors, rather than any broader royalist position. The filler sections of glib counterblast against parliamentarian (q.v.) papers came to dominate the paper as royalist fortunes waned.

MERCURIUS BRITANNICUS. The primary objective of this parliamentarian newsbook (qq.v.) was the rebuttal of information printed by the royalist (q.v.) newsbook *Mercurius Aulicus* (q.v.). *Britannicus* was published in London.

MERCURIUS MILITARIS. This newsbook (q.v.) was published by John Harris. It was the newsbook of the New Model Army agitators (qq.v.).

MERCURIUS POLITICUS. This was the principal official newsbook (q.v.) of the 1650s. It was published in London every Thursday, and contained foreign and domestic news; from 1655 another edition with additional material was published each Monday. The editor was a former royalist (q.v.), Gilbert Mabot. By the mid-1650s the newsbook had begun to carry a widening range of advertising.

MERCURIUS RUSTICUS. In May 1643 the royalists (q.v.) established a second Oxford-based newsbook (q.v.), *Rusticus*, to concentrate on printing stories of the misdeeds of the parliamentarian (q.v.) armies and the atrocities committed by them. Nineteen issues dealt with such stories and a separate series dealt with parliamentarian attacks on churches and cathedrals. The editor himself was an ejected clergyman, Bruno Ryves; his editorials reflected those if the editors of *Mercurius Aulicus* (q.v.). The newsbook declined after March 1644, although collected editions were published from 1646 onwards.

MIDDLE GROUP. During the First Civil War Parliament (qq.v.) divided into factions. The most prominent of these were the War Party and the Peace Party (qq.v.). Research suggests that there was a third group that John Pym (q.v.) sought to use to manipulate the interests of the other parties so as to present a united front against King Charles I (q.v.). The Middle Group supported the earl of Essex (q.v.) but did not seek to alienate the other generals by so doing. The Middle Group was held together after Pym's death by Oliver St John (q.v.), but it fragmented at the end of 1644.

MIDDLETON, JOHN, LATER 1ST EARL (1619–1674). A Scottish soldier of continental experience, Middleton joined the Covenanter Army (q.v.) in 1639. He later served in the army of the Solemn League and Covenant (q.v.), and was second in command to David Leslie (q.v.) when in September 1645 he led part of the army back from England to take on the marquis of Montrose (q.v.). Middleton was at the subsequent Battle of Philliphaugh (q.v.).

During 1646–47 Middleton was involved in the Highland (q.v.) campaigns against Montrose and Alasdair MacColla (q.v.). He was one of the few senior Covenanter (q.v.) officers to accept the Engagement (q.v.) and fought at the Battle of Preston (q.v.) in the Second Civil War (q.v.) as lieutenant general of the Horse (q.v.). He joined the forces raised in 1650–51 by Charles Stuart (q.v.) and fought at Worcester (q.v.) in 1651, where he was captured. He escaped from the Tower of London and in 1654 was fighting in the Highlands with a small royalist force, until defeated by George Monck (q.v.).

Middleton was made an earl by Charles Stuart whilst in exile. At the Restoration (q.v.) he was initially in the king's favour, he represented the king at the Estates (q.v.), and was governor of Edinburgh Castle. He fell under suspicion of treason and bribery in 1661, however, and was deprived of office. He ended his life as governor of Tangiers.

MIDDLEWICH, CHESHIRE. There were two battles fought at this small market town. On 13 March 1643, Sir William Brereton (q.v.) defeated the forces of Sir Thomas Aston (q.v.). Aston had sought to increase royalist (q.v.) control outwards from the city of Chester and had enlisted the help of Midland royalist, Henry Hastings (q.v.). Aston's defeat allowed Brereton to move out of the county and assist in parliamentarian (q.v.) attempts to take control of Staffordshire to the south.

In December 1643 the newly installed Field Marshal John, Lord Byron (q.v.) sought to dominate Cheshire with the aid of reinforcements from Ireland following the Cessation (q.v.), in order to better control the area where further troops could be brought into England and Wales. He began to eliminate Brereton's garrisons. On 26 December Byron defeated Brereton's forces at Middlewich. Brereton was driven into Lancashire to where Sir Thomas Fairfax (q.v.) was directed to his assistance and Byron began the siege of Nantwich (q.v.).

MILITIA. *See* TRAINED BANDS.

MILITIA BILL. *See* MILITIA ORDINANCE.

MILITIA ORDINANCE. In the days after the attempted arrest of the Five Members (q.v.) in January 1642, suspicions about King Charles I's (q.v.) military intentions grew. Charles argued that to put down the Irish Rebellion (q.v.) he should be allowed to raise forces to go to Ireland in person. Given his attempted coup d'état, the fact that Phelim O'Neill (q.v.) and other Irish rebels claimed that the king had commissioned the Rebellion, and Charles's involvement with the Army Plot (q.v.) of 1641, opposition to the king's proposals grew. It was expected by some that if he gained an army, Charles would use it against the Parliament (q.v.) at Westminster.

Before the end of January, Parliament (q.v.) petitioned the king for control of the Trained Bands (q.v.) and the country's fortifications. Charles rejected the plea. Even so, Parliament had established a committee to discuss military affairs and in February a second proposal was put to the king and again rejected. Stronger measures were urged and a Militia Bill was drafted for discussion with the king, giving to Parliament the power to appoint lord lieutenants (q.v.), thereby controlling the Trained Bands. On 2 March negotiations between the king and Parliament broke down and Parliament passed the bill as an Ordinance. This was in effect a major diminution of kingly powers, as military might was a mark of kingship and the use of the ordinance effectively removed Charles from executive power. In normal circumstances any bill required the monarch's signature before becoming an act and therefore law. An ordinance was used in its place if the monarch was judged incapable of acting effectively, for instance, if he or she was abroad, but also if judged incompetent.

With the Militia Ordinance, Parliament took control of appointing the military commanders in each county, the lord lieutenants, and slowly over the next two months new appointees took up their posts and by summer were mustering the Trained Bands. This latter prompted the king into issuing the Commissions of Array (q.v.).

MILLENARIANISM. Broadly, this entailed a belief in the millennium, the 1000-year reign of Christ and his saints; it was a a general belief that united all Christian worship. By the First Civil War (q.v.), however, certain groups were expecting an imminent millennium and identified the Civil Wars or the wars across Europe as the last battle between Christ and Antichrist, which would herald the millennium. Writers such as Hansard Knollys (q.v.) suggested that the riots of 1641 were in effect the early warning of such an event. Millenarian beliefs did not lead all to expect an imminent second coming, although the Fifth Monarchists (q.v.) did. Others, including Oliver Cromwell (q.v.), did believe that England should be made ready for the millennium, something that influenced some Protectorate (q.v.) legislation.

MONCK, GEORGE, LATER DUKE OF ALBEMARLE (1606–1670). A Devon man who had seen service on the continent before 1639, Monck fought at the Battle of Newburn (q.v.). He then served in Ireland, fighting at the Battle of Kilrush. In 1643, after the Cessation (q.v.), he was shipped to England and fought at the Battle of Nantwich (q.v.), where he was captured and imprisoned in the Tower of London.

In 1646 he enlisted to fight again in Ireland, this time for Parliament (q.v.). There he fought in Ulster (q.v.) alongside Robert Monro (q.v.), until Monro sided with the Engagement (q.v.). Monck was involved in local settlements with Owen Roe O'Neill (q.v.) as the latter battled to retain his position within the Catholic Confederation of Kilkenny (q.v.) and Monck himself bought time. Monck was important in the conquest of Ulster after O'Neill's death. In 1650, Oliver Cromwell (q.v.) had Monck join his campaign against Scotland. Monck fought at the Battle of Dunbar (q.v.) in 1650 and from 1651–52 was commander in chief in Scotland, overseeing the defeat of the royalist (q.v.) forces.

He briefly served as a general-at-sea in the war against the Dutch in 1653, before again taking command in Scotland, where he remained until 1660. After the fall of the Protectorate (q.v.), Monck held discussions with several political factions including the royalists. In January 1660 he led an army into England publicly professing to bring stability to the political process, but his negotiations with the exiled Charles II (q.v.) had paved the way for a Restoration (q.v.). For his service he was created duke of Albemarle amongst other honours and remained commander in chief until his death in 1670.

MONRO, SIR GEORGE (?–1693). A nephew of Robert Monro (q.v.), Sir George also learned the military profession in Europe. Monro served in Ireland from 1644. He sided with the Engagers (q.v.) and led 3,000 men from Ulster (q.v.) in the Second Civil War (q.v.). Although these forces were to the rear of the marquis of Hamilton's (q.v.) army, they were not defeated in the campaign in Lancashire but instead retreated into Scotland. In the 1650s he was involved in some royalist (q.v.) plots. In the Restoration he became a member of the Estates (qq.v.).

MONRO, MAJOR GENERAL ROBERT (?–1680). Monro fought with the Swedish army during the 1630s and returned to Scotland to join the Covenanter Army (q.v.). He was appointed commander of the Scottish forces in Ulster (q.v.) in April 1642. Having defeated Sir Phelim O'Neill (q.v.) in Down at the end of April, his forces stormed and sacked Newry in May, where they committed atrocities against the people of the town. Monro controlled County Antrim until 1646. Monro refused to acknowledge the Cessation (q.v.) of 1643 between the English and Irish forces under the earl of Ormond (q.v.), and the Catholic Confederation of Kilkenny (q.v.). He defeated attempts by the earl of Castlehaven and Owen Roe O'Neill (qq.v.) to enter his territory in July and August 1644. Monro remained secure until his defeat at the Battle of Benburb (q.v.) in June 1646. When the defeat was not exploited by his enemies, Monro was able to regroup in Antrim, although his army remained shattered.

In 1648 Monro joined the Engager (q.v.) attempt to restore Charles I (q.v.), but was arrested by George Monck (q.v.) and sent to England as a prisoner. He was released in 1654, and lived the rest of his life in Ireland.

MONTGOMERY, BATTLE OF. Fought on 18 September 1644. In mid-summer 1644 the parliamentarians (q.v.) began to make inroads into central Wales. Sir Thomas Myddleton (q.v.), from bases in the West Midlands, had attempted to encroach on Wales after the capture of Oswestry in Shropshire, but failed in his first attempt. By September 1644 he was again on the offensive with the assistance of Sir William Brereton (q.v.). On September 18 the largest pitched battle of the war in Wales was fought near Montgomery, a former royalist (q.v.) garrison under Lord Herbert of Cherbury. The garrison had been handed to the parliamentarians on 8 September. Myddleton fought off a royalist (q.v.) army consisting of Welsh, Irish, and English forces under Lord Byron (q.v.), which had been besieging the castle.

The parliamentarian victory enabled a wedge to be driven between North and South Wales and the erosion of the royalist hold on mid-Wales. Conflicts over resources meant that this was a slow process, but by the end of 1644 the major garrisons in central Wales were in parliamentarian hands. It was with some truth that Archbishop Williams saw Montgomery as a Welsh Marston Moor (q.v.).

MONTHLIE MAINTENANCE. This was a tax established in Scotland during 1639 to pay for the Army of the Solemn League and Covenant (q.v.). Effectively this levy continued to fund the wars in which Scotland was embroiled between then and 1653. The levy was renewed in 1643 to cover commitments in Ulster (q.v.), although much of the income was diverted to support the army sent into England in early 1644. The month-lie maintenance consisted of two parts: a forced loan set in 1644 at £800,000 Scots (c.£66,000 sterling), and a tax of £100,000 Scots (c.£8,333 sterling). At the lowest level the tax was collected by factors in rural areas and by baillies in towns, and paid to the subcollectors of the County War Committees.

MONTHLY PAY. To pay for the New Model Army, Parliament (qq.v.) instituted the monthly pay. This levy replaced the weekly assessment (q.v.) and was levied only on the counties Parliament controlled in spring 1645. This ensured that the money raised would cover the cost of the army. The monthly pay was constantly renewed into the 1650s to pay for the army.

MONTROSE, JAMES GRAHAM, EARL AND LATER MARQUIS OF MONTROSE (1612–1650). In 1639 Montrose was the principal Covenanter (q.v.) general in the north-east of Scotland, where he defeated and captured the royalist (q.v.) marquis of Huntly (q.v.). Montrose opposed the ambitions of the marquis of Argyll (q.v.), which he believed were subverting the Covenanter cause. Even so, he led forces in the Second Bishop's War (q.v.), but began to contact King Charles I (q.v.) later in 1640. This correspondence was intercepted the following year and, during the king's stay in Edinburgh in summer 1641, Montrose was imprisoned, not being released until Charles had returned to England.

During the First Civil War (q.v.) Montrose suggested that he lead a royalist (q.v.) rising in Scotland, especially once the Covenanters had shown themselves willing to join the parliamentarian (q.v.) side. Although Queen Henrietta Maria (q.v.) encouraged him, Charles I still preferred to trust the marquis of Hamilton (q.v.), who had led the king to believe that he could win over the Scottish government, until the treaty between Scotland and Parliament (q.v.) negotiated by John Pym (q.v.) had been made public. In August 1644, after the royalist collapse in the north of England, Montrose, with two disguised companions, returned to Scotland and joined with Alasdair MacColla (q.v.).

Together, MacColla and Montrose, with an army of only around 4,000, defeated the Covenanter forces at the Battles of Tippemuir, Inverlochy, Justice Mills, Auldearn, Bridge of Alford, and Kilsyth (qq.v.). However, as Montrose awaited the meeting of the Estates (q.v.), which he had summoned to Glasgow, a section of the Army of the Solemn League and Covenant (q.v.) under David Leslie (q.v.) returned to Scotland from England and defeated the royalist Scots and Irish at the Battle of Philliphaugh (q.v.) in September 1645. From then on Montrose's campaigns were guerrilla wars in the Highlands (q.v.). He escaped to the continent in 1646.

In 1649 Montrose offered to raise a mercenary force for Charles I (q.v.) in Sweden and Denmark. Communications between Montrose and Charles broke down, and believing him lost or incapable of raising the men promised, Charles abjured him when he signed the Engagement (q.v.) in order to win Scottish support for his attempt to win the throne. Montrose landed in Orkney in December 1649. He was defeated and captured on the mainland at Invercarron. On 25 May 1650, he was executed by the vengeful Covenanters, who had never forgiven him for his abandonment of their cause in 1641 nor the defeats he had inflicted on them in 1644–45. Ironically he and they were really once again on the same side.

MUNRO, MAJOR GENERAL ROBERT. *See* MONRO, MAJOR GENERAL ROBERT.

MUNRO, SIR GEORGE. *See* MONRO, SIR GEORGE.

MUSKET. *See* FIRELOCK; MATCHLOCK.

MY ONE FLESH. A name adopted by the London Ranters (q.v.) to describe themselves. It related to the belief that Christ was present in every person.

MYDDLETON, SIR THOMAS (1586–1666). Of Denbighshire in North Wales, Myddleton was educated at Oxford University and the Inns of Court. He represented Weymouth in James VI and I's last Parliament (q.v.) and Denbigh in Charles I's (q.v.) first Parliament and throughout the 1640s. In 1643 he was appointed major general of North Wales by Parliament and made inroads into his home county against Lord Capel's (q.v.) forces in the autumn. The landings of the troops from Ireland following the Cessation (q.v.) forced him to retreat from North Wales.

In the late summer of 1644 Myddleton again attempted to divide the royalist (q.v.) hold on Wales, and in September with Sir William Brereton (q.v.) defeated the royalists at the Battle of Montgomery (q.v.). Myddleton thereafter campaigned in mid-Wales, but his progress was slow without the resources necessary, which were directed instead towards Brereton's campaigns around Chester (q.v.) and on the fringes of North Wales.

After the Second Civil War (q.v.), Myddleton led the defence of North Wales against the rising of Sir John Owen (q.v.) and John, Lord Byron (q.v.). On 1 October Myddleton defeated the royalists on Anglesey. Later, Myddleton's loyalty wavered, and in 1659 he led a rising in support of Charles I (q.v.), but was defeated by John Lambert (q.v.).

⇜ **N** ⇜

NAGS HEAD. A pub on The Strand, London, where the Levellers (q.v.) met. Discussions with Henry Ireton (q.v.) and army officers were held there on 15 November 1648. These meetings led to the drafting of the second *Agreement of the People* (q.v.) at Westminster (q.v.) the following month.

NANTWICH, THE BATTLE OF. Fought on 25 January 1644. This Cheshire market town was the site of Sir William Brereton's (q.v.) victory over Sir Thomas Aston's royalist (qq.v.) forces on 25 January 1643. This victory limited the royalist hold on the county to the county town. Nantwich had become the refuge for Sir William Brereton's parliamentarian (q.v.) forces in December 1643 after they had been driven out of North Wales and onto the defensive by John Lord Byron (q.v.). Byron's army had been reinforced by soldiers from Ireland brought over to Wales and England after the Cessation (q.v.). A siege followed, but Brereton himself had escaped to Lancashire, where he solicited help. Sir Thomas Fairfax (q.v.) marched his small forces from Lincolnshire through the heart of the marquis of Newcastle's (q.v.) territory and arrived in the region by 24 January. He and Brereton marched through deep snows to reach Nantwich. Byron attempted to intercept their approach, but was defeated during a sudden thaw that destroyed his plans to block the parliamentarians' approach. On 25 January there was a running battle between Acton and Nantwich. Nantwich was relieved and a major army from Ireland, on which the royalists had placed high hopes, scattered. A large number of royalist officers, including George Monck (q.v.), was captured.

NASEBY, BATTLE OF. Fought on 14 June 1645. For two weeks after King Charles I (q.v.) had stormed Leicester (q.v.), the royalist (q.v.) forces had remained in the south-east Midlands. In the meantime, the New Model Army (q.v.), which had been besieging Oxford (q.v.), had been freed from the overweening control of the Committee of Both Kingdoms (q.v.). Immediately its commander, Sir Thomas Fairfax (q.v.), turned towards the king's army and a pursuit through Northamptonshire, in which the king failed to shake off his enemies, ended on the Northamptonshire/Leicestershire border. On the morning of 14 June Fairfax's army observed the king's army drawn up in a strong position south of Market Harborough. The king then shifted westwards and southwards towards the New Model camped north of Naseby village. The New Model had overnight been put into a position that was so strong that it was unlikely that it would be attacked, and so Fairfax had shifted westwards too.

At around 10 A.M., the king's army began an advance on the New Model across Broadmoor. The king's army was somewhat fewer than 8,000 strong and Prince Rupert (q.v.), amongst others, had advised withdrawing to gain time to get reinforcements from Lord Goring (q.v.) and some of the Midland garrisons. The New Model was around 14,000 strong and to attack it uphill appeared an unwise decision, but an aggressive attitude had inspired some of the royalist council of war and the king was influenced by this. The overwhelming superiority in numbers resulted in the royalist left wing of Horse (q.v.) under Sir Marmaduke Langdale (q.v.) being overrun by only a portion of Oliver Cromwell's (q.v.) men on the parliamentarian (q.v.) right wing. On the opposite flank, although Henry Ireton's (q.v.) Horse was defeated by a charge led by Prince Rupert and Prince Maurice (q.v.), Parliament's larger numbers meant that significant sections were untouched.

In the centre, the royalist Foot (q.v.) under Sir Jacob Astley (q.v.) had made headway against the New Model Foot, but eventually it began to lose momentum in the face of overwhelming numbers. Sections of the New Model's flanks turned inwards and began to encircle the royalist centre. The king's attempt to lead an attack with his reserve was frustrated by his attendants. The princes had led their victorious Horse off the field and only returned belatedly from an attack on the parliamentarian reserve and baggage. Their appearance was too late to turn the fortunes of the battle and they could only provide cover for the retreat that had already begun.

Naseby was a catastrophe for the royalist cause: The king's principal army had been defeated, large numbers of veterans were killed or captured, and the king's correspondence taken. The latter revealed the king's negotiations with the Catholic Confederation of Kilkenny (q.v.), and handed Parliament an important propaganda weapon, enabling his enemies to accuse the king of planning to bring foreign troops onto English soil. The king's army regrouped en route for the West Midlands, but it was clear that major work had to be undertaken to create a new effective field army.

NATIONAL COVENANT. In the debate over the nature of the kirk in 1637, Charles I (qq.v.) refused to accept the Supplication and Complaint (q.v.) in which the Presbyterians protested the nature of the Prayer Book (q.v.) imposed upon their church. Charles also suggested that the leaders of his opponents be charged with treason. In response, Alexander Henderson and Archibald Johnston of Wariston (qq.v.) and others drafted the National Covenant. This was based upon a 1581 oath that bound the Scots to defend their kirk against its enemies. The Covenant sought to do the same.

In many ways the National Covenant was fairly conservative: such bonds were not uncommon, and keeping the kirk as it had been established was the asserted aim. However, the document was also radical in that it suggested certain illegal things that James VI and Charles I had done to alter kirk structures, and also in that the kirk was to be effectively defended not just against a vague collection of enemies such as foreign Roman Catholic (q.v.) nations, but against the lawful king of Scotland.

The National Covenant was first signed by the nobility at St Giles in Edinburgh on 28 February 1638. On successive days it was circulated throughout the city and then into the entire country. The Covenant became the focal point of opposition to the king's religious policy and later to his political control of the Scottish government also. It was signed by men and women of all social classes in Scotland and its adherents became known as Covenanters (q.v.). In 1643, during negotiations with the Parliament (q.v.) at Westminster, the signing of the Covenant by the English and Welsh became part of the condition for the alliance of Parliament and Scotland, and the resulting treaty was known as the Solemn League and Covenant (q.v.).

NATIONAL OATH. An oath imposed by Parliament (q.v.) on 5 April 1645 in areas recently captured from the royalists (q.v.). The purpose was to begin the process of finding those who had collaborated with the royalists. The oath required the taker to swear that he or she had not given aid to the royalists besides payment of compulsory taxes.

NAVY. Despite Charles I (q.v.) having redeveloped the navy during the 1630s through the income generated by ship money (q.v.), its loyalties at the outset of the First Civil War (q.v.) were parliamentarian (q.v.). The royalists (q.v.) had to build up a naval force comprising privateers and captured ships. This became easier once Bristol (q.v.) had fallen into their hands. The privateers ensured royalist communications with France and other states in Europe and allowed for the interruption of coastal trade around Britain and Ireland. The parliamentarian (q.v.) fleet, led by the earl of Warwick (q.v.), enabled Parliament (q.v.) to gain early superiority at sea and to mount joint-forces campaigns, especially in the south-west, and blockades of royalist ports.

In the Second Civil War (q.v.) several sections of the fleet joined the royalist cause, and although some of these were persuaded to rejoin Parliament, the royalists were able to develop a navy that was led by Prince Rupert and Prince Maurice (qq.v.).

NAVY COMMITTEE. This body established in the autumn of 1642 consisted of 18 members drawn from both houses of Parliament (q.v.). It was the successor to the commissioners established that summer to replace King Charles I's (q.v.) Navy Board.

NAYLOR, JAMES (?1617–1660). A parliamentarian (q.v.) soldier who served in John Lambert's Horse (qq.v.). In 1651 Naylor became a Quaker (q.v.). He preached in the north of England in 1652–53 and was imprisoned for a time. In 1655 he was in London building up a following that then progressed to the west, via Launceston and Exeter. On Palm Sunday 1656, he and seven women entered Bristol (q.v.) in the mode of Christ entering Jerusalem. For this he was arrested and sent to London. His case became the first major test of Protectorate (q.v.) blasphemy legislation and prompted major discussions in Parliament (q.v.). Although some demanded his execution, Naylor was pilloried in London and Bristol, branded with the letter "B" for blasphemer, had his tongue bored, and was imprisoned. He was released in 1659 and thereafter preached in the north-west.

NEEDHAM, MARCHMONT (1620–1678). Needham was the editor of *Mercurius Britannicus* (q.v.) between 1643 and 1646. He had been a chorister at All Souls College, Oxford (q.v.) before the Civil Wars. He saw his main aim as editor as the refutation of the contents of the royalist (q.v.) newsbook *Mercurius Rusticus* (q.v.). His diatribes against King Charles I (q.v.) led to his arrest by Parliament (q.v.). By 1647 he had begun to support the king and published *Mercurius Pragmaticus* on his behalf. In 1649 he was arrested for his attacks on Parliament. From 1650 onwards he edited the official newsbook, *Mercurius Politicus* (q.v.), and the *Public Intelligencer*. At the Restoration (q.v.) Needham had to flee abroad, but was pardoned and allowed to return. He then took up a career but continued to write and publish into the 1670s.

NEW ENGLISH. The name applied to English colonists who had settled in Ireland from the late sixteenth century onwards. This distinguished them from the Old English (q.v.) families who had been in Ireland since the twelfth century onwards.

NEW MODEL ARMY. By the end of 1644, to some parliamentarians (q.v.) it had become clear that a great number of opportunities had been lost. Parliament (q.v.) had won battles including Marston Moor (q.v.), which had seen royalist (q.v.) control of the north collapse, but the Second Battle of Newbury (q.v.)—when they had cornered the royalists—had seen them humiliated and disorganised. In the fall of 1644, political and religious arguments had surfaced in Parliament as Oliver Cromwell (q.v.), lieutenant general of the Eastern Association (q.v.) army, had been accused by his commander, the earl of Manchester (q.v.), of ineptitude and of religious radicalism. The result was the Self Denying Ordinance (q.v.), which would in effect dramatically alter military leadership in England and Wales. The wider debates resulted in the call to remodel the three principal parliamentarian armies: the earl of Essex's, Sir William Waller's, and the earl of Manchester's (qq.v.). In any case, the Self Denying Ordinance would deprive all three of their commands.

The new army would consist of 12 regiments of Foot (q.v.) numbering 14,400 men; the Horse (q.v.) would consist of 6,000 men in 12 regiments; and there would be a regiment of 1,000 dragoons (q.v.) and a reorganised train of artillery. The Horse, dragoons, and artillery were easily assembled, even if initially some regiments wished to retain their original commanders and stay in their own armies. The Foot was a different issue: the three armies together did not contain enough for the proposed regiments. Recruitment was difficult, and was to continue for some time after the New Model took the field in the spring of 1645. Sir Thomas Fairfax (q.v.) was named lord general of the army, Henry Ireton (q.v.) commissary general, Sir Philip Skippon (q.v.) major general in charge of the Foot, and eventually, despite being effectively debarred from command by the Self Denying Ordinance, Oliver Cromwell was confirmed as lieutenant general commanding the Horse. The New Model was to remain the principal, but not the only, parliamentarian army from then on, becoming the basis for the standing army retained by Charles II (q.v.) after the Restoration (q.v.).

NEWARK, BATTLES OF. This market town on the border of Nottinghamshire and Lincolnshire was a major royalist (q.v.) garrison from the end of 1642 until May 1646. The town straddled a major road north to south and protected crossings on the navigable River Trent. Parliament (q.v.) made three attempts to capture Newark: at the end of February 1643 under Sir Thomas Ballard; in March 1644 under Sir John Meldrum (q.v.); and finally from November 1645 to May 1646 under Sydenham Poyntz (q.v.) in conjunction with the Army of the Solemn League and Covenant (q.v.) under the earl of Leven (q.v.). The first siege collapsed when attempted storms failed. The second was broken at the Battle of Newark by Lord Loughborough and Prince Rupert (qq.v.) on 21 March 1644. The third siege only ended when King Charles I (q.v.), who had surrendered to the Scots at nearby Southwell, ordered the governor, Lord Belasyse (q.v.), to surrender on 6 May 1646.

NEWBURN, BATTLE OF. Fought on 28 August 1640. This was the only major battle during the Bishop's Wars (q.v.). In 1640, with the renewal of war, the Scottish Army of the Covenant (q.v.) crossed the border on 20 August. The Scots bypassed Berwick on Tweed and advanced on the English and Welsh army based along the River Tyne, defending the western approaches to Newcastle upon Tyne (q.v.).

Alexander Leslie (q.v.) headed for the crossing at Newburn where a 4,500-strong detachment of King Charles I's (q.v.) forces were led by Lord Conway. Leslie arrived there on 27 August with over 12,000 men. The Scots opened the battle in the early afternoon of 28 August with heavy concentrated fire on the English and Welsh positions, which were protected only by hastily thrown-up earthworks. When the forward sections of the king's army began to retreat, Leslie pushed his Horse (q.v.)

over the river. When Conway launched a counterattack with his Horse, it was met with concentrated musket (q.v.) and artillery fire but succeeded in temporarily slowing the Scottish Horse's advance. In the wake of the Scottish Horse, however, 10,000 Foot (q.v.) soldiers began to ford the river and the king's army was overwhelmed. The defeat left Newcastle open to attack and on the next day the town was abandoned and surrendered. The king's army fled southwards, leaving the Scots to occupy the north-eastern counties.

NEWBURY, FIRST BATTLE OF. Fought on 20 September 1643. After relieving Gloucester (q.v.), the earl of Essex (q.v.) began to return to London. King Charles I (q.v.) and his army immediately gave chase, but Essex avoided the royalist (q.v.) army by taking a more southerly route to London. Even so, by 18 September the king's leading forces under Prince Rupert (q.v.) had gotten ahead of Essex's army and forced it to a halt at Hungerford. Two days later the king's army had placed itself between Essex and London, just as it had almost a year earlier at Edgehill (q.v.).

The king's army was drawn up south and west of Newbury in a line from the Newbury to Kintbury road to close by the river Endbourne where most of the Horse (q.v.) was mustered. Essex, approaching from the west, drove into the centre of the field and captured Round Hill, which dominated the field. The royalists spent much energy in trying to shift the London Trained Bands (q.v.) from the hill, and during this fight Lord Falkland (q.v.) was killed. Rupert drove back the parliamentarian (q.v.) forces from Wash Common south of Round Hill, but Sir Philip Skippon (q.v.) brought the parliamentarian artillery from behind the hill and battered the royalist centre, achieving the effect of halting its actions and relieving pressure on the Trained Bands on Round Hill.

Fighting continued into the night, but the king's army withdrew before morning, leaving Essex the road to London. The royalists undoubtedly had lost, the army had been seriously mauled, and its ammunition exhausted. Moreover, it had lost the campaign, failing to capture Gloucester in the first place and then compounding this by failing to defeat the earl of Essex at Newbury.

NEWBURY, SECOND BATTLE OF. Fought on 27 October 1644. In the wake of the catastrophe at the Battle of Lostwithiel (q.v.), the earl of Essex (q.v.) reformed his partially disarmed army, but lacking confidence in his abilities, Parliament (q.v.) decided to amalgamate all of its main field armies. Accordingly, the earl of Manchester (q.v.) was ordered to bring the Eastern Association (q.v.) Army to the Thames Valley. Sir William Waller (q.v.) was also ordered to join the earls. The plan was to encroach on King

Charles's (q.v.) capital at Oxford (q.v.). Meanwhile, the king, still buoyed by his successes in the west, was determined to strengthen his satellite garrisons. In late October he marched to Donington Castle (q.v.), and as his army camped south of the castle and north of Newbury, the combined parliamentarian (q.v.) armies approached. On 26 October a complex strategy was devised. Sir William Waller's forces were detached to march in a loop north of the king's army, designed to bring it to the rear of the king's army, which faced west towards the rest of the parliamentarian forces.

The plan was for the two forces to launch a coordinated attack on the outnumbered royalists. Early on 27 October, Manchester launched an attack on Shaw House. The house fronted the royalist (q.v.) army where the defence was led by Sir George Lisle (q.v.), and the attack was supposed to be a diversion to draw attention from Waller's approach. This failed, and Prince Maurice (q.v.) attacked Waller as he approached. Despite this, Waller's attack drove towards the royalist centre. After the initial attacks on Shaw House, however, Manchester halted his attacks. Waller's attack halted when the Horse (q.v.), under Oliver Cromwell (q.v.) and Sir William Balfour, was defeated by the earl of Cleveland, Sir Henry Bennet, and Lord Goring (q.v.). Manchester launched an attack belatedly but was driven back by the defenders of Shaw House.

The king had engendered a crisis in Parliament's armies. They failed to defeat his outnumbered forces and he had marched away under the very noses of the parliamentarian generals. More damning, the king returned on 9 November and removed the artillery he had deposited in Donington after the battle. The parliamentarians, still in the area, were unable to impede him. The crisis led to a battle between Cromwell and Manchester and to the Self Denying Ordinance (q.v.) and eventually to the creation of the New Model Army (q.v.).

NEWCASTLE EMLYN, BATTLE OF. Fought on 23 April 1645. As part of his attempt to destroy the royalist (q.v.) hold on Pembrokeshire, Rowland Laugharne (q.v.) laid siege to Newcastle Emlyn. He was attacked there and defeated by the royalist general of South Wales, Charles Gerrard (q.v.). Gerrard's victory enabled him to drive through the county and capture Haverfordwest. Gerrard almost destroyed this parliamentarian (q.v.) stronghold in June. The royalist resurgence in this area ended when Laugharne defeated them at the Battle of Colby Moor (q.v.) in August.

NEWCASTLE, MARGARET CAVENDISH, MARCHIONESS AND LATER DUCHESS OF (1624–1674). From the Colchester Lucases, Margaret was the sister of Sir Charles Lucas (q.v.), the royalist (q.v.) general. In 1643 Margaret became a lady-in-waiting to Queen Henrietta Maria (q.v.) and went into exile with her in 1644. In Paris, Margaret met the exiled marquis of Newcastle (q.v.), a much older man, and they married in April 1645. Margaret was a writer of poetry, drama, philosophy, and biography. Her works were published from 1653 onwards when she published *Poems and Fancies* and *Philosophical Fancies* during a visit to England to try and secure compounding (q.v.) terms for her husband. In 1656 she published her autobiography, *Natures Pictures Drawn By Fancies Pencil to the Life*.

Her attempt to secure her husband's estates failed and together they lived in Amsterdam for the rest of the 1650s. Margaret continued to publish work after the Restoration (q.v.), and was the first woman to visit the Royal Society in connection with her own scientific considerations. Margaret had affected a particular style of dress that attracted critical comment from male and female commentators, and her plays, performed in London, were likewise criticised. In 1667, partly fuelled by her anger at what she perceived to be the ill-treatment meted out to her husband, she published a biography of him.

NEWCASTLE UPON TYNE. This major northern port was captured by the Scots during the first Bishop's War (q.v.) following the Battle of Newburn (q.v.). The Covenanter (q.v.) Army remained in occupation until the summer of 1641. In the First Civil War (q.v.) the Scots besieged the town from February 1644 until 14 October, when it was taken by storm. Upon his surrender to the Scots at Newark (q.v.), King Charles I (q.v.) was taken to Newcastle where negotiations began, culminating in the Newcastle Propositions (q.v.). The Scots, in frustration with the king's intransigence, abandoned the king there to representatives of the English and Welsh Parliament (q.v.) at the end of January 1647.

NEWCASTLE UPON TYNE, PROPOSITIONS OF. During King Charles I's (q.v.) captivity, representatives of the Edinburgh Estates (q.v.) and the English and Welsh Parliament (q.v.) negotiated with the king. The Westminster Parliament's proposals, presented in June 1646, were known as the Newcastle Propositions. The central tenets of the proposals were that the king would acquiesce to the establishment of a Presbyterian (q.v.) church system in England and Wales; that he would hand over control of the militia (q.v.) for 20 years to Parliament; the annulment of peerages created since 1642; and the prohibition from pardon for a long list of royalists (q.v.). The king could not stomach Presbyterianism, which he saw as the product of rebellion, and objected to the other three main points, thus ensuring that the propositions failed to provide the basis for peace.

NEWCASTLE, WILLIAM CAVENDISH, EARL, MARQUIS AND LATER DUKE OF (1593–1676). A writer and owner of massive estates in the north-east and Midlands, the earl of Newcastle served in the Bishop's Wars (q.v.) and as tutor to Prince Charles (q.v.) from 1637–41. In the First Civil War (q.v.) he was given command in the north-east, but after the failure of the earl of Cumberland to hold Yorkshire, Newcastle was given command of England north of the Trent and over Lincolnshire and East Anglia. By the summer of 1643, after defeating Lord Fairfax (q.v.), he controlled the north-east down to the Trent and could assist Henry Hastings (q.v.) in the Midlands. He was created marquis in October 1643. Newcastle did not ensure the complete defeat of the Yorkshire parliamentarians (q.v.), failing to capture their base at Hull (q.v.) in the fall of 1643.

From January until April 1644 he was in command of the attempt to destroy the Army of the Solemn League and Covenant (q.v.). After the Battle of Selby (q.v.), Newcastle had to retreat to York (q.v.), where he was besieged for 11 weeks by the Scots, Lord Fairfax, and the Eastern Association (q.v.) Army. When Prince Rupert (q.v.) relieved York on 1 July, Newcastle advised against pursuing the three armies, but was overruled. He took his forces out of York and joined the Prince at the Battle of Marston Moor (q.v.), where they were defeated. After the defeat Newcastle returned to York and then went on to Scarborough (q.v.), where he took ship for Europe.

The marquis lived in France and Holland for the next 16 years. Successive administrations during the 1640s and 1650s refused to allow him to compound (q.v.) for his estates. Whilst in exile in France he met and married Margaret Lucas, sister of Sir Charles Lucas (q.v.). The marchioness of Newcastle (q.v.) shared her husband's interests in writing as well as his exile. The couple returned to England at the Restoration (q.v.). Newcastle played no role in the Restoration government, but was important in the reconstruction of local government in the Midlands whilst rebuilding his vast estates. He attempted to save his old enemy John Hutchinson (q.v.) from persecution in 1663. He was created a duke in 1665.

NEWPORT, TREATY OF. This was the final attempt by sections of the Parliament (q.v.) at Westminster to come to terms with King Charles I (q.v.) and is named after Newport, Isle of Man. This was largely an attempt by the Presbyterians (q.v.) in Parliament who had overturned the Vote of No Addresses (q.v.) to forestall a revolution by the New Model Army (q.v.), which was beginning to call Charles a "man of blood" (q.v.). The king would not agree to Parliament's terms, only offering a limited experiment with Presbyterianism (q.v.) and ceding control of the militia (q.v.) for 10 years. Charles was already pinning hopes on an alliance in Ireland between the marquis of Ormond (q.v.) and the Catholic Confederation of Kilkenny (q.v.) and as a result the talks collapsed, and the way opened for the more radical proposals of Henry Ireton (q.v.) and the army.

NEWSBOOKS. The 1640s saw growth in the production of newspapers. By the middle of the First Civil War (q.v.) there was a paper available almost every day. These dealt, often on a day-to-day basis, with the events of the war. The royalist papers *Mercurius Aulicus* and *Mercurius Rusticus* (qq.v.) were official productions based in Oxford (q.v.). In London a wide range of papers was produced, reflecting differing perspectives based on religious and political standpoints. *See also Mercurius Britannicus*, *Mercurius Politicus*, and *Perfect Diurnal*.

NEUTERS. Individual neutrals who in England or Wales sided with neither Parliament nor the royalists (qq.v.). Both sides regarded them as the enemy and treated them as malignants (q.v.). The Clubmen (q.v.) were armed and influential neutrals who appeared from 1644 onwards.

NICHOLAS, SIR EDWARD (1593–1669). An Oxford University graduate who served the duke of Buckingham and sat as M.P. in the 1620s for Winchelsea and later Dover. In 1641 Nicholas became secretary of state to Charles I (q.v.) and served at Oxford (q.v.) throughout the First Civil War (q.v.). He was a negotiator at the Treaty of Uxbridge (q.v.) and later was involved in negotiating the surrender of Oxford at the end of the war. After initially being kept away from the centre of power in France and Holland, in 1654 Nicholas served Charles II (q.v.) in exile through Queen Henrietta Maria's (q.v.) influence. This continued until 1662, when he retired through ill health.

NINETEEN PROPOSITIONS. This set of proposals was Parliament's (q.v.) attempt to set forth its terms for ending the division in government in the summer of 1642. The Propositions, presented on 1 June, required Charles I (q.v.) to renounce the supporters gathered around him at York (q.v.), and to agree to further limitations on the power of the monarch. The militia (q.v.) was to be in Parliament's hands, as were the education and marriages of the royal children. Government and legal offices were to be filled by appointees approved of by Parliament. Laws against Roman Catholics (q.v.) were to be enacted thoroughly and Catholic peers banned from the House of Lords (q.v.). Parliament also demanded the right to direct foreign policy. The king rejected the proposals. Parliament, knowing that he would do so, had already declared itself to be sovereign during the king's absence. The tenets of the Nineteen Propositions were to appear as the basis for subsequent peace negotiations: the Oxford Treaty, the Uxbridge Treaty, and the Newcastle Propositions (qq.v.).

NORMAN YOKE. This was the belief expressed by Levellers and Diggers (qq.v.) alike that the unequal and oppressive political and social structures of English society derived from the imposition of an alien regime at the Norman conquest of the eleventh century.

NORTHAMPTON, SPENCER COMPTON, EARL OF (1601–1643). Compton accompanied the future King Charles I (q.v.) to Spain in 1623 in his attempt to marry the infanta. He succeeded to the title in 1630 and became lord lieutenant (q.v.) of Warwickshire. Northampton served in the European wars during the 1630s. In 1640 Northampton raised forces in Warwickshire as principal member of the county's Commission of Array (q.v.) and battled with the parliamentarian Lord Brooke (qq.v.) for control of the county throughout the summer. On being driven out, he joined the royalist Horse (qq.v.) under Prince Rupert (q.v.) and fought at the Battles of Powick Bridge and Edgehill (qq.v.).

In the spring of 1643, Northampton was given the task of taking control of Warwickshire after Brooke had gone north to besiege Lichfield (q.v.). After Brooke's death and the fall of Lichfield, Northampton entered Staffordshire and joined with Henry Hastings (q.v.) in trying to reestablish control of the county. They attacked Sir John Gell and Sir William Brereton (qq.v.) at the Battle of Hopton Heath (q.v.) as the parliamentarians (q.v.) prepared to attack Stafford. The royalists won the battle but Northampton was killed.

NORTHERN ARMY. The forces led by the earl of Newcastle (q.v.) and raised in the north-east and Yorkshire. The army disintegrated after the Battle of Marston Moor (q.v.), but the Northern Horse (q.v.) remained as a coherent unit.

NORTHERN ASSOCIATION. Parliament's associated counties of Northumberland, Westmoreland, Cumberland, Lancashire, Yorkshire, and from 1644, Nottinghamshire. The association only became effective after the Battle of Marston Moor (q.v.), when the royalist Northern Army (qq.v.) was defeated. The association and its army were led by Lord Fairfax (q.v.) and later by John Lambert (q.v.); by 1645 the army was commanded by Sydenham Poyntz (q.v.) and operating in the Midlands. From 1645–46 the Northern Association army was involved in the siege of Newark (q.v.). The forces were disbanded from late 1647 onwards.

NORTHERN HORSE. This was originally part of the Northern Army (q.v.) under the earl of Newcastle (q.v.). In April 1644 the Horse (q.v.), under Lord Goring (q.v.), was sent out of Yorkshire to avoid being bottled up in York (q.v.) when the earl became besieged there by the Army of the Solemn League and Covenant and Lord Fairfax (qq.v.). It camped in Nottinghamshire until late May, when it joined with Prince Rupert (q.v.) in the campaign to relieve York. The Northern Horse met with initial success at the Battle of Marston Moor (q.v.) before being defeated by Sir Thomas Fairfax (q.v.). After making its way south following the battle, the Northern Horse served with the Oxford Field Army (q.v.) and, following Goring's promotion, was led by Sir Marmaduke Langdale (q.v.). In early 1645 Langdale led the Horse on a dramatic ride to relieve Pontefract (q.v.), and on the way it fought the Battle of Melton Mowbray (q.v.). The Northern Horse served at the Battle of Naseby (q.v.) and later that summer made a dramatic but eventually futile attempt to march through the north to reach the marquis of Montrose (q.v.). Under the leadership of Lord Digby (q.v.), the Northern Horse was defeated at Carlisle.

NORTHUMBERLAND, SIR ALGERNON PERCY, 10TH EARL OF NORTHUMBERLAND (1602–1668). An experienced M.P. of the 1620s, Northumberland became lord high admiral in 1638 and commander of all forces south of the Trent during the First Bishop's War (q.v.). However, he became an opponent of King Charles I (q.v.) in the next two years and in 1642 blocked the king's attempt to take control of the navy (q.v.). When the king ordered Northumberland to appoint Sir John Pennington (q.v.) as his deputy, Northumberland instead appointed the earl of Warwick (q.v.), another of the king's opponents, who took charge of the navy by 2 July, thus ensuring its future loyalties.

Northumberland served on the executive committees of Parliament, the Committee of Safety and later the Committee of Both Kingdoms (qq.v.). Parliament appointed him governor of the king's captive children in 1645. In 1648 Northumberland led the Newport Treaty (q.v.) negotiations and later opposed the trial of the king. During the Commonwealth and Protectorate (qq.v.) Northumberland went into political retirement. At the Restoration (q.v.) he was appointed to the Privy Council (q.v.).

NORWICH, GEORGE GORING, EARL OF (?1583–1663). Goring accompanied Queen Henrietta Maria (q.v.) to France in 1642 and returned with her in February 1643. In 1644 he was created earl of Norwich after again serving in France, negotiating for military aid from Cardinal Mazarin. He remained abroad until 1647 when, under cover of returning to compound (q.v.) for his estates, he returned to raise rebellion in Kent. In May 1648 he began the rising in what became part of the main English contribution to the Second Civil War (q.v.). After defeat at the Battle of Maidstone (q.v.), Norwich led a small band of armed rebels over the Thames to join the rebels in Essex. There, he joined Lord Loughborough, Lord Capel, Sir George Lisle, and Sir Charles Lucas (qq.v.). Together with their forces they took control of Colchester (q.v.), where they were besieged by Lord Fairfax (q.v.) for 11 weeks. Norwich was tried by the High Court of Justice (q.v.) in 1649, and whilst Capel was executed, Norwich escaped death by one vote. During the 1650s he lived mainly abroad but negotiated with Edward Sexby and the Levellers (qq.v.) in the hope of gaining their support for Charles II (q.v.). He received a pension at the Restoration (q.v.). Norwich was the father of George, Lord Goring (q.v.).

NORWICH RISING (1648). At Christmas 1647 the mayor of Norwich was petitioned to allow Christmas celebrations, which had been banned, in the town. He refused to sanction celebrations, but did nothing to prevent those that happened on Christmas day. For this he was summoned to London by Parliament (q.v.). On 23 April 1648, as he was being escorted to London, a crowd closed the gates to prevent his guards leaving. A major riot developed as the crowd attacked the homes of aldermen and the county committee's (q.v.) meeting room. When troops arrived, fighting developed and the county magazine blew up, killing about 40 people. The rioters were not all royalists (q.v.) although attempts were made to portray them as such, it was more likely an expression of anger at the postwar committee-led regime.

NOTTINGHAM. This county town remained a parliamentarian (q.v.) garrison from the outset of the First Civil War (q.v.). The garrison in the castle and town was commanded by John Hutchinson (q.v.). The history of its defence was covered by Hutchinson's wife, Lucy Hutchinson (q.v.), in her biography of her husband. The town was attacked on a number of occasions, notably by Queen Henrietta Maria's (q.v.) army and Henry Hastings (q.v.) in June 1643, and by Hastings (by this time Lord Loughborough) and Sir Richard Byron (q.v.) in January 1644.

NULL AND VOID ORDINANCE. This was the end of the attempt by the Presbyterians in Parliament (qq.v.) to undo all legislation passed by the Independents (q.v.) in Parliament. Presbyterians dominated affairs after 26 July when prominent Independents fled to the New Model Army (q.v.) following attacks made on them at Westminster (q.v.) by pro-Presbyterian mobs. When the army occupied London on 6 August, the ordinances passed since 26 July were declared Null and Void by the Independent-led House of Commons (q.v.).

⇜ O ⇝

OKEY, COLONEL JOHN (1606–1662). A son of a drayman, Okey served in the parliamentarian (q.v.) forces in the First Civil War (q.v.). When the New Model Army (q.v.) was formed, Okey was appointed colonel of the regiment of dragoons (q.v.). At the Battle of Naseby (q.v.) his regiment poured fire on Prince Rupert's (q.v.) wing as it charged Henry Ireton (q.v.). Later in the battle, Okey mounted his men and led them in a charge on the flank of the royalist Foot (qq.v.).

In 1649 Okey sat as a commissioner of the High Court of Justice (q.v.) at the trial of Charles I (q.v.). For his role in the regicide (he had also worked on the subcommittee that directed the execution) he was not covered by the Act of Indemnity and Oblivion at the Restoration (q.v.) and was arrested in Holland in 1662. He was returned to London, tried, and executed.

OLD ENGLISH. The name for English families that had settled in Ireland from the twelfth century until the Reformation. Many of these families were Catholic (q.v.), and by the seventeenth century they were being excluded from the government of Ireland.

O'MORE, RORY (?–c.1652). A County Kildare landowner who became a prominent leader in the early stages of the Ulster Rising, O'More has been identified as the instigator of the rising. He held meetings in Dublin (q.v.) with fellow conspirators, including Sir Phelim O'Neill (q.v.), during the March 1640 session of the Dublin Parliament (q.v.). He was central to the plan that materialised by September 1641 to seize Ulster (q.v.) strongholds and Dublin Castle. Once the rising was underway, O'More led military forces against the Dublin government. He defeated a force at Julianstown in December 1641. He was also central to the forging of an alliance between the Old English (q.v.) and the Irish rebels at the Hill of Crofty (q.v.) in the same month. In 1643 O'More was involved in the negotiations that led to the Cessation (q.v.).

ONE AND ALL CAMPAIGN. In the wake of the Lostwithiel (q.v.) campaign, Charles I (q.v.) sought to mobilise popular opinion behind his cause. By getting the freeholders of the south-west to form into units—led by gentlemen—that marched on London with his forces, he hoped thereby to pressure Parliament (q.v.) into peace negotiations. There was some petitioning and discussions were held in Somerset, where a petition was drafted; but in Wiltshire and Dorset the king's call went unheeded. The king then changed tack, suggesting that freeholder pressure could be applied through petitions addressed to Parliament instead. This became the One and All campaign. The campaign failed to excite much royalist (q.v.) support; instead, it inspired countywide discussions on ending the war through a negotiated settlement. Disorderly conduct by the royalist military in Worcestershire ended any good will towards the king and inspired neutralist sentiment, which became evinced through the club movement. *See also* Clubmen.

O'NEILL, HENRY ROE (?–1650). Son of Owen Roe O'Neill (q.v.), Henry joined his father's forces in Ireland in 1643. He served in his father's campaigns, including the campaign under the command of the earl of Castlehaven (q.v.) in 1644 and at the Battle of Benburb (q.v.) in 1646. He was a candidate to succeed to his father's command of the Army of Ulster (q.v.) after the latter's death in 1649. He served instead with the chosen successor, Ever MacMahon, Bishop of Clogher and was present at the defeat at Scariffhollis (q.v.). He was captured and executed by Sir Charles Coote (q.v.), an act rendered more cruel by the fact that only Henry's father's agreement with Coote a year earlier had saved the Protestant general from complete defeat.

O'NEILL, OWEN ROE (early 1580s–1649). The heir to the Irish or Ulster (q.v.) title of O'Neill and the anglicized title of earl of Tyrone, Owen Roe served with the Spanish army from 1604 onwards in the wake of the Nine Years War, which his uncle Hugh O'Neill, earl of Tyrone, had waged against Elizabeth I. From 1606 he was fighting the Protestant Dutch in the Netherlands. His uncle's flight to Europe in 1607 effectively made Owen Roe an exile. He continued to serve in the Spanish army in Europe; for eight years he was governor of Rheinberg. During the same period his relationship with Phelim O'Neill (q.v.), from a rival sept to Owen Roe, declined when Phelim returned to Ireland with the blessings of England. The Anglo–Irish Thomas Preston (q.v.) was alienated by O'Neill's emphasis on the Gaelic Irish contingent in command of the Irish forces in Europe. Attempts to persuade Spain to send forces to Ireland failed to materialise and Owen Roe continued to serve in Europe through the 1630s.

By 1641 O'Neill was involved in discussions with the leaders of the Gaelic Irish community, which included his rival Sir Phelim O'Neill, during which time the last of the direct heirs of his uncle died, leaving him as the successor to the titles. On the outbreak of the Irish Rebellion (q.v.) O'Neill determined to go to Ireland. He laid down his command in the Netherlands and secretly sailed for Ireland, landing on 8 July 1642, at Doe Castle, County Donegal. Almost immediately he was appointed lord general in Ulster; his cousin Phelim O'Neill ceded his military command and became lord president of the province.

O'Neill's relations with the Catholic Confederation of Kilkenny (q.v.) were problematic. He was outside the Anglo–Irish/Gaelic Irish alliance that furthered the Rebellion, representing as he did the exiled Gaelic faction that had lost their estates, as opposed to the allied groups that had retained theirs by working with the English regime. As a result, limitations were placed on O'Neill's power. His army was poorly supported by Kilkenny (q.v.) and in 1644 when a major campaign against Robert Monro (q.v.) was launched, O'Neill was put under the command of the Earl of Castlehaven (q.v.).

Only with the arrival of the papal nuncio, Cardinal Rinuccini (q.v.), did O'Neill receive political and practical support, which enabled effective action. His victory at the Battle of Benburb (q.v.) was largely made possible because of this. Neither Rinuccini's support, nor victory ended the distrust of O'Neill felt by the Confederation. By 1647, following Lord Inchiquin's (q.v.) membership in the Confederation, Rinuccini and O'Neill became politically isolated. The other provincial generals, Lord Taffe (Munster) and Thomas Preston (Leinster), attacked the isolated O'Neill and for some months civil war reigned within the Confederation. O'Neill left the Confederation and fought independently in Ulster during 1648–49, making expedient alliances with the Scots and even with Michael Jones (q.v.) in Dublin (q.v.). In late 1649 O'Neill threw his weight behind the renewed alliance with the marquis of Ormond (q.v.) and rejoined the Confederation. However, illness and death prevented him from making an effective contribution to the war against the Parliament (q.v.) at Westminster.

O'NEILL, SIR PHELIM (?–1653). Cousin to Owen Roe O'Neill (q.v.), Phelim was a rival to the titles of O'Neill and Tyrone. He had served in the Spanish forces in Europe, but had been allowed to return to Ireland by the government. Even though no longer dispossessed of his lands, Phelim did feel dispossessed of his political power, particularly by the influx of New English (q.v.) landowners who were beginning to dominate the political landscape. In the wake of the Scottish Revolution, he and others discussed ways of altering the political balance in Ireland. Frustrated by the failure of Charles I or the Parliament (qq.v.) at Westminster to allow political change in Ireland, O'Neill became prominent in the leadership of the Ulster (q.v.) rising. It was he who on 22–23 October swept through central Ulster taking control of prominent strongholds and towns for which he claimed to have the authority of the king. It was also to be he who bore the onslaught of the Scottish invasion of May 1642.

On the arrival of Owen Roe O'Neill, Sir Phelim handed over military command and accepted the lord presidency of Ulster. From then on he spent more time at Kilkenny (q.v.) than in Ulster. In 1646 he became reconciled with Owen Roe and fought at the Battle of Benburb (q.v.). By 1647, however, encouraged by his wife, Louise, the daughter of Thomas Preston (q.v.), Phelim abandoned Owen Roe and sided with his enemies. By 1649 this act ensured that he would not succeed to Owen Roe's command at his death, for a clause in Owen Roe's personal agreement with the marquis of Ormond (q.v.) excluded anyone from command who had turned against Owen Roe.

Phelim O'Neill continued to serve the Confederation of Kilkenny (q.v.) for the rest of the war. In 1650 he was present at the defeat of the Ulster Army at Scariffhollis (q.v.). In February 1653 he was captured and became the victim of a prominent state trial, the point of which was to demonstrate that the commission from Charles I that Phelim O'Neill claimed to have in 1641 had been real. He was hanged, drawn, and quartered on 10 March 1653.

ORDINANCE. A piece of legislation that had passed through both houses of Parliament (q.v.) but that was given executive force without the monarch's signature. This was originally intended as a temporary expedient in the monarch's absence or illness, after which the ordinance would be signed and become an act. Parliament began to issue ordinances in March 1642, the first being the Militia Ordinance (q.v.). This became the standard legislative instrument of Parliament until 1649, when it began to use the term "act" to describe its legislation.

ORMOND, JAMES BUTLER, 12TH EARL AND 1ST MARQUIS AND 1ST DUKE OF ORMOND (1610–1688). Although he belonged to a prominent Old English (q.v.) family of midland Ireland, Ormond was brought up as a ward of James VI and I and in the charge of the Archbishop of Canterbury. Therefore, unlike his family, he was raised as a Protestant. During the 1630s he sided with the administration of Sir Thomas Wentworth (q.v.), with whom he became friendly, and during the Bishop's Wars (q.v.) served as lieutenant general of the Irish Army, which he had worked hard to reform. He was prominent in the 1640 Dublin Parliament (q.v.) in pressing the four subsidies through the Lords. Almost as soon as the session was over, however, Ormond withdrew to his castle at Kilkenny (q.v.) and remained there throughout the summer. He did not attend the June session of Parliament, which witnessed the beginning of the unravelling of Wentworth's regime, and he certainly doubted the effectiveness of King Charles I's (q.v.) strategy against the Covenanters (q.v.). He strenuously avoided taking up the post of captain general delegated to him by Wentworth, aware no doubt that Wentworth's political position and person were now in danger.

Ormond retained command of the armed forces during the disbandment of the army in 1641 and, upon the outbreak of the Ulster Rising (q.v.), took up command of the Dublin (q.v.) administration's forces. He defeated the rebels at Kilrush and, for a time, limited incursions into Leinster. The increasing organisation of the Catholic (q.v.) forces in the form of the establishment of the Catholic Confederation of Kilkenny (q.v.) and the war in England and Wales left Ormond and the English forces isolated. Through the agency of members of his family in the Confederation government, Ormond was persuaded that a truce was a practical solution to the Irish wars, and in September the Cessation (q.v.) came into being allowing Ormond to return troops to Wales and England.

Ormond's resolute attempts to deny the Confederation full religious freedom in any full treaty was undermined by Charles I, who had employed the earl of Glamorgan (q.v.) to negotiate separately a more liberal treaty. When Ormond arrested Glamorgan following accidental disclosure of the treaty, Charles was forced to renounce it. With the king's defeat in the First Civil War (q.v.) Ormond's purpose in Ireland came to an end and in 1647 he signed away Dublin and his command to Michael Jones (q.v.), who was sent over by the Parliament (q.v.) at Westminster.

In 1648, with the king's authority, Ormond was given the new commission of lord lieutenant of Ireland by Queen Henrietta Maria (q.v.). He returned to Ireland and recommenced discussions with the Confederation and with the isolated Owen Roe O'Neill (q.v.). By 1649 an alliance of all anti–Westminster Parliament forces had been assembled. Although it was numerically superior to the New Model Army (q.v.) contingents led by Jones, then Oliver Cromwell, and later Henry Ireton (qq.v.), the fact that the alliance was formed of such disparate forces appears to have been fatal. Jones defeated Ormond at the Battle of Rathmines (q.v.) in August 1649 and then Cromwell picked off strongholds one by one in 1649–50. At the end of 1650 Ormond left Ireland, handing the deputyship to the earl of Clanricarde (q.v.). During the 1650s Ormond worked to bring down the Protectorate (q.v.), and at the Restoration (q.v.) he was made a duke. He served as lord lieutenant of Ireland from 1661–67 and again from 1671–78. He founded the Royal Military Hospital at Kilmainham.

OVERTON, RICHARD (?–1664). Overton was a pamphleteer as early as 1642, when he used the press to attack Roman Catholics (q.v.) and the Anglican episcopacy (q.v.). During the First Civil War (q.v.) he began to attack Presbyterianism (q.v.) as it became dominant within Parliament (q.v.) and at the Westminster Council of Divines. He began issuing tracts attacking Presbyterianism under the pseudonym Martin Marpriest (q.v.). At this time he also worked with William Walwyn and John Lilburne (qq.v.), using the same press for their works. This effectively brought together the prominent Leveller (q.v.) theorists.

In 1649 Overton may have drafted *The Hunting of the Foxes from Newmarket to Triploe heath to Whitehall by five small Beagles (late of the army)*, an attack on the grandees' (q.v.) betrayal of the rank and file of the army. For this, Overton, Lilburne, Walwyn, and treasurer Thomas Prince were arrested and imprisoned in the Tower. *See also The Hunting of the Foxes.*

OVERTON, COLONEL ROBERT (?1609–1668). An East Riding Yorkshireman, Overton took up a command of Lord Fairfax's (q.v.) army during the First Civil War (q.v.). He fought at the Battle of Marston Moor (q.v.) and in 1647 became governor of Hull (q.v.). Overton was a Fifth Monarchist (q.v.). In 1650 he served at Dunbar (q.v.) and later as governor of Edinburgh. After another spell as governor of Hull in 1653–54, he was again sent to Scotland. There Overton was arrested on the orders of Oliver Cromwell (q.v.) and sent to London, where he was imprisoned in the Tower before being sent to prison on Jersey. He was only released in 1659 by Richard Cromwell (q.v.). He was again given the governorship of Hull; he used his authority to ban George Monck (q.v.) from Hull in 1660 because he did not bear "the image of Christ." From London, Monck ordered Overton to hand Hull to Thomas, Lord Fairfax (q.v.) and summoned him to London for opposing a restoration (q.v.) of the monarchy. When Charles II returned to power, Overton was arrested, although he was covered by the Pardon and Oblivion Act (q.v.). He was imprisoned first in the Tower, then at Chepstow, and finally again on Jersey, where he died.

OWEN, SIR JOHN (1600–1666). A royalist (q.v.) officer throughout the First Civil War (q.v.), he rose to the rank of major general (q.v.). Owen held Conway Castle until 18 November 1646. In 1648 he led the royalist forces in north Wales but was defeated by Thomas Myddleton at the Battle of Y Dalar Hir (q.v.) on 5 June. Owen was captured, but this did not quell the rising as attempts were made to rescue him from imprisonment at Denbigh. For this activity Owen became one of the Seven Great

Delinquents at the end of the Second Civil War (q.v.). Along with five of the other great delinquents, he was brought to trial in 1649 before the High Court of Justice (q.v.). Only Owen and Lord Norwich (q.v.) had their lives spared. Owen remained in prison until 1655.

OXFORD. A county town and centre of learning, Oxford became the capital of King Charles I's (q.v.) forces in November 1642. The university colleges in the town were turned to military and governmental use and the town was ringed by fortifications. In 1643 the earl of Essex (q.v.) directed military operations in the Thames Valley aimed at closing in on Oxford. In 1644 he did the same thing again in conjunction with Sir William Waller (q.v.). When the king broke out with the Oxford Field Army (q.v.), however, the parliamentarian (q.v.) campaign ended in acrimony. The New Model Army (q.v.) besieged the town in May–June 1645. Following the king's capture of Leicester (q.v.), Sir Thomas Fairfax (q.v.) abandoned the siege and marched northwards to take on the king. The city was besieged again from spring 1646 until June, when it surrendered on 13 July.

OXFORD FIELD ARMY. This was the army forged originally in September–October 1642 by Charles I (q.v.) and that fought at the Battle of Edgehill (q.v.). From November 1642 this army was based at Oxford (q.v.). The army generally fought in the south, the South Midlands, and the south-west. In 1644, however, it marched into the Midlands and captured Leicester (q.v.), but was defeated at the Battle of Naseby (q.v.) a fortnight later. In 1645 the army was again in the Midlands during the summer and fall. It also served in South Wales, in the Marcher counties (q.v.), and also made a lightening march into Eastern Association (q.v.) territory. The remnants of the army surrendered at Oxford in July 1646.

OXFORD PARLIAMENT. In late 1643 Charles I (q.v.) summoned those members excluded from the Parliament (q.v.) at Westminster from 1642–43 to meet at Oxford (q.v.). This alternative parliament sat from the following January in Christchurch College. Around one-third of the House of Commons (q.v.) was on the king's side, although about 57 were unable to attend the Oxford sessions because they were on active service, and there was a majority of the Lords (q.v.). The Oxford Parliament was not particularly tractable. Whilst many members had been reluctant to go along the path of the Westminster Parliament, many of them had been critics of Charles's government before 1642. They now questioned the cost of the war effort and the organisation of the army. The Parliament did establish an excise tax (q.v.). The Parliament sat until March 1645, but the king eventually dismissed it when it began to involve itself in the proposed settlements known as the Treaty of Uxbridge (q.v.).

OXFORD, TREATY OF. In the wake of the disappointing autumn campaigns of 1642, Parliament (q.v.) opened negotiations with the king in January 1643 and sent commissioners to Oxford (q.v.). Parliament stuck rigidly to the sense of the Nineteen Propositions (q.v.) by demanding control of the militia (q.v.), the punishment of Charles I's (q.v.) supporters, and prosecution of Roman Catholics (q.v.). Charles wanted all forts and ports handed over to him, and for Parliament to be moved to a neutral place. The terms were incompatible and probably offered without sincerity by both sides. Charles was elated by news coming in from the provinces concerning royalist (q.v.) successes and began to believe in victory. John Pym (q.v.) knew that the king was plotting to get help from Ireland, which would be a propaganda victory for Parliament and might bring the Scots closer to an alliance with Parliament. The negotiations ended in March 1643.

⤙ **P** ⤘

PALE, THE. The name given to the area of Ireland, particularly that around Dublin (q.v.), where English administration was in place. In the Civil War period the Pale no longer had any real meaning but was used to describe the area over which the earl of Ormond (q.v.) had control during 1643–46.

PAPISTS. This name was used by Protestants of all complexions to describe all Roman Catholics (q.v.) and the Irish in rebellion. It could also be used by parliamentarians (q.v.) as a label for royalists (q.v.) in order to suggest that they were Roman Catholics.

PARDON AND OBLIVION ACT. An act of 1 December 1651, passed by the Commonwealth Parliament (qq.v.) to stop the process of sequestration (q.v.) from being applied to any new cases. It therefore suggested that any as yet undeclared or unexposed act in support of the royalists (q.v.) was pardoned and forgotten.

PARKER, HENRY (1604–1652). Educated at Oxford University, Parker was a barrister who was appointed secretary to the earl of Essex's parliamentarian (qq.v.) army in 1642. Parker believed that political power ascended from the people rather than that it descended from God. Parker published a series of pamphlets espousing this theory, including one on King Charles I's (q.v.) rejection of the Nineteen Propositions (q.v.), *Observations upon some of His Majesty's late Answers and Expresses*. In 1645, having published a justification of Parliament's (q.v.) role in government, *Jus Populi*, in the previous year, Parker was appointed secretary to the House of Commons (q.v.).

PARLIAMENT (ENGLISH AND WELSH). Originally founded in the mid-thirteenth century, by the fourteenth century the Parliament at Westminster (q.v.) had matured into two houses, the Lords (q.v.), comprised of hereditary peers, and the Commons (q.v.), comprised of elected members representing counties and some boroughs. As a result of the union of England and Wales (1530s–1540s), the Commons was expanded to include Welsh members. Despite the efforts of earlier monarchs, the role of Parliament in government increased and it was crucially important in establishing the Reformation in England and Wales during the reigns of Henry VIII and Elizabeth I. Even by the seventeenth century, however, its role in government was still subject to the will of the monarch, although Parliament's necessary part in approving taxation ensured its continued role and existence. The House of Lords sat in the Palace of Westminster; the Commons met in St Stephen's Chapel.

Charles I's (q.v.) poor relationships with his 1620s Parliaments influenced his decision to minimise its role in government, and inspired his Personal Rule (q.v.) of the 1630s. Nevertheless, the gentry—who normally participated in Parliament and its elections—as well as a wider body of the people regarded Parliament as an essential safeguard against bad monarchical government; throughout the 1630s there were calls for elections. When Charles called Parliament in April 1640, he mistakenly believed that he could manipulate it to support his war against Scotland. His dissolution of the Short Parliament (q.v.) demonstrated his folly and, in the wake of defeat by the Scots that summer, he had little choice but to summon Parliament again.

During the Civil War period Parliament underwent many changes, most notably the abolition of the House of Lords in 1649. Various attempts were made to remodel Parliament during the Commonwealth and Protectorate (qq.v.), and an upper house was reintroduced as a result of the Humble Petition and Advice (q.v.) of 1657. The remains of the Long Parliament, or Rump Parliament (qq.v.), were recalled in 1659 and eventually oversaw the Restoration (q.v.).

PARLIAMENT (IRISH). Like its counterpart in England, the Irish Parliament, which sat in Dublin (q.v.), was founded in the thirteenth century; it represented English interests in Ireland. By the fourteenth century Parliament consisted of two houses: the Lords (q.v.), comprised of hereditary peers, and the Commons (q.v.), comprised of elected members from the Pale (q.v.) counties and anglicized boroughs.

In 1495 the lord deputy of Ireland, Sir Edward Poyning, established a law by which bills for the Irish Parliament had to be approved of by the king and his Privy Council (q.v.) before they could be debated in Parliament. Resentment over Poyning's Law was one of the grievances in Parliament in 1640–41. By 1640 Parliament was effectively dominated by the New English (q.v.), increasingly excluding not only the Gaelic Irish, but also the Old English (q.v.) interests. This caused grievances that were expressed in 1640–41 through the defiance of the lord lieutenant, Sir Thomas Wentworth (q.v.); later these grievances formed the basis for the Irish Rebellion (q.v.). The General Assembly of the Catholic Confederation of Kilkenny (q.v.) was modelled on the Dublin Parliament. In the 1650s Parliament was abolished as Irish representation was absorbed into the Protectorate (q.v.) Parliaments at Westminster, England. An Irish Parliament met again from 1661.

PARLIAMENT (SCOTTISH). *See* ESTATES.

PARLIAMENTARIAN. A reference to supporters of and things pertaining to the English and Welsh Parliament (q.v.) during the period 1640–49. The term is generally applied to England and Wales, although forces in Ireland, under Lord Inchiquin (q.v.) from 1644–48 and under Michael Jones (q.v.) from 1647–49 and Oliver Cromwell and Henry Ireton (qq.v.) from 1649–50, could also be labelled as parliamentarian.

PARLIAMENTARIANISM. This is a belief in the aims of, and support for, the English and Welsh Parliament (q.v.) during the period 1640–49.

PEACE(ABLE) ARMY. In the wake of the Battle of Naseby (q.v.), Charles I (q.v.) went into South Wales to try and raise new forces in Monmouth and Glamorgan. The Glamorgan commissioners of array (q.v.) instead suggested that they raise a county-based force to serve against the Army of the Solemn League and Covenant (q.v.), which by the end of July 1645 was in Herefordshire. Charles was almost powerless to object. When he went to Cardiff on 29 July he was met by 4,000 armed men who demanded to choose their own officers and to maintain autonomy from the king's forces. They also demanded reduced taxes. They called themselves the Peace or Peaceable army. The Peace Army was formed through a combination of popular revulsion towards the king's war effort and the local gentry's attempts to retain control over their county. As the royalists (q.v.) were at that time being defeated in south-west Wales, Charles was forced to accede to the Peace Army's demands and began to replace local governors with its nominees.

Only when the Scots withdrew from Hereford was the royalist Marmaduke Langdale (q.v.) able to force the Peace Army to disband and to co-opt 1,000 of its soldiers into the royalist army. This proved a temporary respite and, as soon as the royalists left the area, the Peace Army reformed and joined the parliamentarians (q.v.) in reducing the royalist hold on South Wales.

PEACE PARTY. In the Parliament (q.v.) at Westminster, three broad and flexible groupings developed during the First Civil War (q.v.): the War Party (q.v.), the Peace Party, and the Middle Group (q.v.). These terms are generally modern epithets. The Peace Party was in favour of opening negotiations with the king regardless of Parliament's military position in order to secure a negotiated settlement at the earliest opportunity. If a leader can be identified for this group, then it was Denzil Holles (q.v.). The Peace Party opposed the negotiations with the Scots that opened in 1643 and disliked the establishment of the Committee of Both Kingdoms (q.v.). These parties were not homogenous and many members of the War Party also objected to the involvement of the Scots in English affairs.

PEMBROKE, PHILIP HERBERT, EARL OF, AND EARL OF MONTGOMERY (1584–1650). A former favourite and privy counsellor (q.v.) of James VI and I, Pembroke's hatred for Thomas Wentworth, earl of Strafford (q.v.) ended his position as a favourite of Charles I (q.v.). A period of imprisonment in the Tower served to enhance his radicalism and, during the First Civil War (q.v.), Pembroke served on several committees, including the Committee of Safety (q.v.). He was a commissioner at the Treaties of Oxford and Uxbridge (qq.v.); in 1648 he was a commissioner sent to negotiate with Charles I during the Newport Treaty (q.v.) discussions. Pembroke accepted the abolition of the House of Lords (q.v.) in 1649 and got himself elected as an M.P. for Buckinghamshire. He also took up a seat on the first Council of State (q.v.).

PENNINGTON, ISAAC (1587–1660). A London M.P. in the Short and Long Parliaments (qq.v.), Pennington was important in raising finance for Parliament's forces in the First Civil War (q.v.). He was the leading opponent of the royalist (q.v.) faction in the City of London council. Pennington served on the High Court of Justice (q.v.), which tried Charles I (q.v.).

PENRUDDOCK'S RISING. Colonel John Penruddock was a former royalist (q.v.) officer from Compton Chamberlayne in Wiltshire who was part of a set of large-scale plans to rise up against the Protectorate (q.v.) in March 1655. The Sealed Knot (q.v.) had planned a series of risings from Newcastle in the north, through Yorkshire, and down to the west coast. However, Oliver Cromwell (q.v.) had learned about much of the plan and the ringleaders were arrested and the principal targets of the rebellion reinforced. Many of the planned risings did not occur and the one arranged for the site of the Battle of Marston Moor (q.v.) collapsed in confusion.

On the other hand, Penruddock's rebellion began on schedule: several hundred troopers seized Salisbury on 12 March 1655 and arrested two judges and the sheriff. For two days the royalists roamed the region, proclaiming Charles Stuart (q.v.) king and trying to raise support. On 14 March the rebels were defeated at South Molton and most were captured. Penruddock and several other leading figures were tried for treason and executed. The failure of the rebellion was in part due to the way in which the people of the south-west seemed determined to support the Protectorate against rebellious royalists.

PERFECT DIURNAL, THE. A London newsbook (q.v.) edited by Samuel Peeke. Information for the paper was provided by the Parliament's (q.v.) secretary John Rushworth. In 1649 Rushworth took up the editorship of the newsbook.

PERSONAL RULE. This denotes the period between 2 March 1629, when Charles I (q.v.) dissolved Parliament (q.v.), and 13 April 1640, when the Short Parliament (q.v.) met. The period was characterised by Charles's effort to govern through a strengthened Privy Council (q.v.) and by his attempt to finance government through a series of archaic taxes, including ship money (q.v.), to circumvent the need for a Parliament, which normally regulated taxation. Religious reform under Archbishop William Laud (q.v.) was also prevalent during this period: church courts were reinvigorated to enforce conformity in liturgy and the churches had railed-off altars to replace simple communion tables. There were frequent calls for a Parliament during this period, but Charles was able to ignore them until the financial necessities of the first Bishop's War (q.v.) forced him to summon what became the Short Parliament.

The name "Personal Rule" is really very Anglocentric even if it embraces Wales also. In Scotland and Ireland, Parliaments were called during the 1630s by Charles. To a great extent these were managed by the king and his counsellors, including Sir Thomas Wentworth (q.v.) in

Ireland, but they only masked opposition to Charles's policies, rather than ending it. The Scottish Estates (q.v.) met in 1638 during the political crisis that led to the first Bishop's War and in 1640 an Irish Parliament (q.v.) in Dublin (q.v.) sat in March, before that at Westminster (q.v.). Nevertheless, in all four nations the king's agents were active in trying to maximise income and unify forms and structures of religious worship.

PETERS, HUGH (1598–1660). Peters was an Oxford University graduate who took up a ministry in Salem, Massachusetts, after living in London and Holland. Peters was involved in the establishment of a colony in Connecticut. Whilst in Massachusetts he attacked political intervention in religious affairs. He returned to England in 1641. He regularly preached for the army as a chaplain and supported the Independents (q.v.). He was involved in the trial and execution of Charles I (q.v.) in 1649. Later that year he accompanied Oliver Cromwell (q.v.) in Ireland. By 1651 he was back in England and was present at the Battle of Worcester (q.v.). Peters was a preacher at Westminster (q.v.) during the 1650s, but disappeared from public life after Cromwell's death. At the Restoration (q.v.) Peters was arrested and executed for his role in Charles I's execution.

PETITION OF OFFICERS AND SOLDIERS OF THE ARMY. This petition was drafted at Saffron Walden, Essex, by the soldiers of the New Model Army (q.v.). It was a complaint about Parliament's (q.v.) failure to pay the troops. The petition had political aims as well, relating to religious freedom, freedom of Parliament, and the liberty of the people. These were edited out by officers and the petition, read in Parliament on 27 March 1647, called for indemnity for actions committed during the First Civil War (q.v.), payment of arrears, no conscription for volunteer soldiers into the proposed army for Ireland, and no compulsory service in the Foot for Horse (qq.v.) troopers. There was also a demand for compensation for widows, orphans, and maimed soldiers. The petition angered the Presbyterian (q.v.) section of the House of Commons (q.v.), particularly Denzil Holles (q.v.), who suggested that the petition was treasonous. Sir Thomas Fairfax (q.v.) was ordered to suppress the petition. This conflict represented the opening of a breach between the Presbyterians and the army, and also inspired the development of links between the soldiers and the Levellers (q.v.).

PETITION OF RIGHT. This was a document drafted in 1628 by Sir Edward Coke to be presented to Charles I (q.v.) as a supplication relating to taxation and property rights. The immediate spur was twofold. Since 1626 Charles had imposed a series of extraordinary levies on the country, a benevolence and a forced loan (q.v.); he had also proposed levies of the coastal-defence tax, ship money (q.v.). At the same time, the campaigns in support of the French Protestant Huguenots had entailed the free-quarter or unpaid billeting (q.v.) of troops and sailors along the south coast of England. The Petition of Right was in fact a forcible statement of the principles by which Parliament (q.v.) played a central role in taxation policy and on the invasion of property represented by billeting.

The king had little choice but to acknowledge that the petition was justified, but attempted to sign it without using the formal phraseology appended to such documents. This was suspected of being a means by which he could challenge the petition's authority at a later date, and the petition was returned for the correct wording. The Petition of Right had limited immediate effect as the king dissolved Parliament on 2 March, thus beginning the Personal Rule (q.v.) and his searches for alternative funding that did not require parliamentary approval. Nevertheless, the petition became accepted as the standard precedent for taxation procedure and was used as such by the king's opponents in the Hampden (q.v.) case and again in 1640.

PETITIONS OF WOMEN. Late March 1649 was marked by widescale arrests of Levellers (q.v.) and the execution of the Leveller soldier, Robert Lockyer (q.v.) in April. In response, female Levellers, including Elizabeth Lilburne and Katherine Chidley (qq.v.), organised a petition through the established Leveller network in London, ward by ward and parish by parish. The first petition was presented to Parliament (q.v.) on 25 April. The petition as well as the women were spurned and told to "meddle with your huswifery." Chidley drafted a second petition that embraced wider aims than the first, tackling the ignorance of women's role in society as expressed in the contemptuous injunction about housewifery. Chidley pointed out that women had an "interest in Christ" equal to men and equal interest in the "liberties and securities contained in the Petition of Right" (q.v.). The second petition had the signatures of 10,000 women, but was again rejected by Parliament.

PHILLIPHAUGH, BATTLE OF. Fought on 13 September 1645. After defeating the Covenanters (q.v.) at the Battle of Kilsyth (q.v.), the earl of Montrose (q.v.) summoned the Estates (q.v.) to Glasgow. His forces camped in the Lowlands between Glasgow and Edinburgh, whilst principal figures from the government made their way to pay court to Montrose. However, a section of the Army of the Solemn League and Covenant (q.v.) was sent back to Scotland from England under David Leslie (q.v.) and had reached Berwick by 6 September.

On 12 September, Montrose, with only 700 men, set off towards Leslie believing that new recruits would join him. At Kelso Montrose learned that he had been tricked and withdrew towards Philliphaugh. Whereas Montrose believed Leslie to be still near Berwick, he was in fact already approaching Philliphaugh too. By the time Montrose arrived on 13 September, the royalist Foot (q.v.) had been defeated and most of them captured and subsequently murdered by order of the Estates commissioners with Leslie. Philliphaugh wiped out Montrose's victories of the past year and thereafter the royalist (q.v.) campaigns in Scotland were reduced to guerrilla operations in the Highlands (q.v.).

PIKE. A pike was an 18-foot-long ash staff topped with a diamond-section-shaped steel point. The pike head was attached to the staff with two two-foot-long steel straps to prevent the head being cut off by a sword stroke. Pikes were wielded by the strongest men in a company of Foot (q.v.). There should have been a ratio of one pikeman to every two musketeers. In line formation the pikemen were drawn up in the centre of a company. When under attack from Horse (q.v.), the pikes formed a protective circle known as a hedgehog, with the musketeers sheltering under the pikes.

PISTOL. A short-barrelled handgun carried by officers and the Horse (q.v.). Pistols employed firelock- or wheellock-firing (qq.v.) mechanisms, making them suitable for use by mounted soldiers.

PLYMOUTH. As with Portsmouth (q.v.), Plymouth remained in parliamentarian (q.v.) hands throughout the First Civil War (q.v.), enabling supplies to be landed there for Parliament's (q.v.) forces in the south-western campaigns. On 30 September 1643, the port was besieged by Prince Maurice (q.v.). The siege lasted until 22 December. The town was blockaded thereafter and nearby Weymouth occupied by royalists (q.v.) until the Lostwithiel (q.v.) campaign. From the autumn of 1644 until early 1645, Sir Richard Grenvile (q.v.) besieged the port again, but failed in an attempt to storm it and was driven away.

POLL TAX. Originally a mediaeval personal tax on men and women, but used again in 1641 to raise the money lost by the abolition of ship money (q.v.).

PONTEFRACT CASTLE. An important fortress in south Yorkshire on the main route south and north. The castle was garrisoned by royalists (q.v.) in December 1642. After the Battle of Marston Moor (q.v.) the castle remained one of the scattered royalist holdings in the north, but was besieged from August 1644 onwards. The castle was the target of Sir Marmaduke Langdale's (q.v.) dramatic march northwards with the Northern Horse (q.v.) in February 1645 when he set out to relieve the siege. Langdale defeated the besiegers on 1 March and brought supplies to the castle. The castle was soon besieged again and surrendered on 21 July 1645.

During the Second Civil War (q.v.) royalist forces seized the castle on 8 June 1648, but were quickly besieged. In early August an attempt to kidnap the commander of the besieging forces, the Leveller Colonel Thomas Rainborough (qq.v.), went wrong and the colonel was killed. Oliver Cromwell (q.v.) took over the siege on 8 August and stayed there during the political struggles in London that culminated in Pride's Purge (q.v.). The castle held out until after Cromwell returned to London and, after the execution of Charles I (q.v.), declared itself in the name of his son Charles II (q.v.). John Lambert (q.v.) brought the siege to an end on 22 March 1649.

PORTER, ENDYMION (1587–1649). Poet and father of George Porter (q.v.), he lived much of his early life in Spain, as a result of which he played a role in Charles I's (q.v.) attempt, whilst still Prince of Wales, to marry the Spanish infanta. He was one of the principal men who assisted in the development of the royal art collection. Porter wrote verse and was associated with leading poets, including Robert Herrick and William D'Avenant (q.v.). In 1640 he was elected to sit in the Long Parliament (q.v.) for Droitwich. He opposed the Act of Attainder (q.v.) against the earl of Strafford (q.v.). In 1642 he left London with Charles I, for which he was expelled from Parliament (q.v.). Porter was suspected of being involved in a "popish plot" and thus exempted from pardon by the Oxford Treaty and the Uxbridge Treaty (qq.v.). He left England in 1645, only returning to compound (q.v.) in 1649, just before his death.

PORTER, MAJOR GENERAL GEORGE (?1622–1683). Eldest son of Endymion Porter (q.v.), and brother-in-law to George Lord Goring (q.v.). Porter served as major general of Horse in the Northern Horse (qq.v.). In March 1644 Porter was in charge of the Horse in Yorkshire whilst his commander, the marquis of Newcastle (q.v.), attempted to halt the advance of the Army of the Solemn League and Covenant (q.v.) into north-east England. He proved of little assistance to John Belasyse (q.v.) in the attempts to retake Bradford (q.v.) during March. He then took his Horse southwards to assist in the attempt to rescue Newark. In the wake of the Battle of Newark (q.v.), where his forces played an ineffective part, he lingered in the North Midlands and failed to join Belasyse at the Battle of Selby (q.v.) despite orders from Lord Loughborough (q.v.) to the contrary. Porter was captured at the Battle of Marston Moor (q.v.), but exchanged, whereupon he joined his brother-in-law, Goring, playing an ineffective role in the preamble to the Battle of Langport (q.v.). By the end of 1645 Porter had laid down his arms. During the 1650s Porter was involved in plots aimed at a restoration of the monarchy. At the Restoration (q.v.) he became a member of the queen's court.

PORTSMOUTH. Lord Goring's (q.v.) part in the Army Plot (q.v.) had been to hold Portsmouth in the king's name, but when he betrayed the plot he remained governor. On 2 August 1642, he declared for King Charles I (q.v.), but after a brief siege handed the town to Sir William Waller (q.v.) on 7 September. Portsmouth remained a parliamentarian (q.v.) garrison throughout the First Civil War (q.v.). The defeated forces of the earl of Essex (q.v.) rendezvoused there after the Battle of Lostwithiel (q.v.).

POWELL, VAVASOUR (1617–1670). A Welsh itinerant evangelist who, at the outbreak of the First Civil War (q.v.), travelled to London to preach in the city. In 1646 Powell returned to Wales, where he formed a band of preachers who travelled the country. He worked with the Commission for the Better Propagation of the Gospel in Wales (q.v.) through the 1650s. Powell opposed the creation of the Protectorate (q.v.) and became a critic of Oliver Cromwell (q.v.). Powell sympathised with the Baptists (q.v.) but his style also influenced George Fox (q.v.). After the Restoration, (q.v.) the government arrested him and he was imprisoned for most of the last 10 years of his life.

POWICK BRIDGE, BATTLE OF. Fought on 23 September 1642. Sir John Byron (q.v.) was escorting a collection of silver plate from the Oxford (q.v.) Colleges to King Charles I's (q.v.) army at Shrewsbury in mid-September. Prince Rupert (q.v.) and a section of the royalist Horse (qq.v.) marched south to Worcester (q.v.) to meet the convoy. A detachment of the earl of Essex's (q.v.) parliamentarian (q.v.) army under Colonel John Brown was sent to try and intercept Byron. Prince Rupert and the royalist Horse (q.v.) camped south of Worcester (q.v.) near the bridge over the River Teme at Powick when Brown arrived. Brown crossed the river, and Rupert allowed him to form up on the north bank before attacking his forces. An all-out charge defeated the standing parliamentarians, although some troops under Sir Nathaniel Fiennes (q.v.) managed a counterattack. This battle was the first significant conflict in the war, and Rupert's success marked the beginning of his reputation as a feared commander.

POYER, JOHN (?–1649). Poyer was a member of the Pembroke urban gentry and was mayor in 1642. He took service, first as a captain in the parliamentarian (q.v.) forces, and held the town during the First Civil War (q.v.) after recapturing it from the royalists (q.v.) in 1643. Poyer was of great assistance to his brother-in-law Rowland Laugharne's (q.v.) campaigns in South and West Wales. In 1648 Poyer felt aggrieved at the special treatment meted out to the New Model Army (q.v.) whilst his pay and that of his soldiers in Pembroke Castle was in arrears. He was also being accused by political opponents in Pembroke of corruption and when, in February 1648, he was ordered to hand over the castle to a garrison from the New Model, he refused. He and Laugharne then went into rebellion against Parliament (q.v.) in what became the first upsurge of the Second Civil War (q.v.). On 10 April 1648, Poyer openly declared for Charles I (q.v.). The rebellion in South Wales was defeated by Oliver Cromwell (q.v.) by July 11, when Poyer surrendered Pembroke. In 1649 Poyer was tried, alongside Lord Capel, the duke of Hamilton, John Owen, and the earl of Norwich (qq.v.), and executed.

POYNTZ, SYDENHAM. A professional soldier with European experience, Poyntz returned to England in 1645, where he was appointed commander of the Northern Association (q.v.) army by Lord Fairfax (q.v.). In 1645 he commanded the forces at Rowton Heath (q.v.), which defeated Charles I (q.v.). In the autumn of 1645, Poyntz led the Northern Association army into Nottinghamshire, where he captured Shelford House before besieging Newark (q.v.). His army was joined there by the Army of the Solemn League and Covenant (q.v.). In January 1646 Poyntz's forces captured Belvoir Castle.

In 1647 Poyntz was seen by Presbyterians (q.v.) in Parliament (q.v.) as a likely opponent of the Independents (q.v.) and their supporters in the New Model Army (q.v.). Before Poyntz could act on the Presbyterian's behalf, his own soldiers arrested him and sent him under escort to Sir Thomas Fairfax (q.v.). Poyntz was released and made his way to London, but on the failure of the attempt to oppose the New Model he left the country for Holland. In 1650 he joined Lord Willoughby (q.v.) in the Barbados Colony. He later moved to Virginia.

PRESBYTERIAN. A Presbyterian church system, such as the Scottish kirk (q.v.), did not depend on the apostolic succession, the laying on of hands at ordination that linked the minister of the Anglican church or the Roman Catholic (q.v.) priest to the founders of the Christian church. Nor did it have a hierarchy imposed and controlled from above through bishops and archbishops. Instead, authority within the church was theoretically derived from the ministers and elders of the church, electing their local organisations, the presbyteries, which in turn chose the members of the regional bodies, the synods, which in turn sent representatives to the central body, the General Assembly.

The Presbyterian church was also intended to be free of monarchical control; there was to be a separation of church and state and the monarch was to be a member of the church on an equal footing with other members. In reality, the kirk was a compromise body that contained bishops as well. Whilst in the wake of the First Civil War (q.v.) there was an attempt to set up a national church in England and Wales along Presbyterian lines, it failed to materialise fully because of opposition from significant elements in the army, and after Pride's Purge (q.v.), opposition was also found in Parliament (q.v.). The principal liturgy, the *Directory of Public Worship* (q.v.), imposed on parishes from 1644 onwards, was a Presbyterian document.

PRESBYTERIANS. This term had several meanings during the period. It could simply refer to the adherents of the Presbyterian Scottish kirk (qq.v.), or it could refer to those in England and Wales who wished to introduce such a system. In England it could also refer to those supporters of Presbyterianism who were keen to have the Scots enter the First Civil War (q.v.) on the side of Parliament (q.v.). By the end of this war the Presbyterians were in control of the House of Commons (q.v.). This led to conflict with the New Model Army (q.v.) in the summer of 1647 because the army contained a significant number of Independents (q.v.) who opposed the imposition of any national church.

PRESTON, BATTLE OF. Fought on 17 August 1648. One of the conditions of the Engagement (q.v.) was for the Scots to send an army into England. In April 1648 some English forces under Marmaduke Langdale (q.v.) marched from Scotland to capture Berwick and Carlisle. There was then a pause that allowed the New Model Army (q.v.) to deal with risings in Kent and Essex and those in Wales. In July the marquis of Hamilton (q.v.) led an army of 12,000 down the west coast of England. He proceeded so slowly that Oliver Cromwell (q.v.) was able to force the surrender of Pembroke Castle and march north before Hamilton left Kendal.

As the Scottish Foot (q.v.) moved through Preston on 17 August, Cromwell and John Lambert (q.v.) attacked the rearguard under Langdale. After a vicious fight, Langdale was pushed aside and Cromwell attacked the Scots in Preston itself, driving them across the rivers Darwen and Ribble. Many of the Scottish Foot were captured in the town as Hamilton rode south to bring back to Preston the Horse (q.v.), which was stretched out along the roads between it and Wigan. The commander of the Horse, John Middleton (q.v.), had in fact turned northwards to rejoin the army but took a different road to Hamilton. The two commanders passed in the night and Middleton rode straight into the victorious New Model Horse. Middleton extricated himself and rejoined Hamilton on Wigan Moor the following day, and they continued their march to Warrington, pursued by Cromwell.

PRESTON, SIR THOMAS (1585–1655). The young Preston left Ireland in the wake of the Nine Years' War and was educated in the Spanish Netherlands. He, along with Owen Roe O'Neill (q.v.), served in the Spanish Wars against the Dutch and again in the Thirty Years War. Preston returned to Ireland in the early stages of the Rebellion of 1641. After the formation of the Catholic Confederation of Kilkenny (q.v.), Preston was appointed commander of the Leinster Army (q.v.). By the spring of 1643 he cleared the earl of Ormond's (q.v.) garrisons from Queen's County and, despite being defeated at Old Ross in March, began to restrict Ormond's operations to the enclave around Dublin (q.v.).

Throughout the war Preston maintained a damaging antipathy towards Owen Roe O'Neill, based on their rival political and religious interests. O'Neill represented the dispossessed Gaelic Catholics, Preston the Old English (q.v.), who were more willing to compromise with Charles I (q.v.) on religious issues.

In 1645 Preston was directed to attack Munster where Lord Inchiquin (q.v.) had renewed the war following his change of sides. Preston and the earl of Castlehaven closed in on the principal forts, Preston capturing Dungannon in March. the campaign ended when the Confederation's logistics collapsed, leaving Preston and Castlehaven to withdraw from attacking the coastal strongholds, including Youghal (q.v.) in September. In the following year Preston campaigned in Connacht and captured Roscommon. Later in the year he and Owen Roe O'Neill were engaged in besieging Ormond in Dublin after the failure of peace negotiations. The siege failed because the two commanders could not work together. Preston also attempted to negotiate with Ormond during the siege. In November the two armies returned to quarters. In August 1647 Michael Jones (q.v.) and his forces defeated Preston at the Battle of Dungan's Hill (q.v.), destroying his army.

In 1648 Preston was engaged in attempting to destroy O'Neill's forces, rather than limit the successes of Michael Jones in Leinster. The following year, Preston, Taffe, and Inchiquin, who had now joined the alliance of royalists (q.v) and Confederation forces, attacked Dublin. The Confederation army was defeated at the Battle of Rathmines (q.v.) in August. In 1649 Preston successfully held Waterford against Henry

Ireton (q.v.), for which he was created Viscount Tara in 1650. As the war in Ireland drew to a close Preston escaped to the continent, where he died.

PRIDE, COLONEL THOMAS (?–1658). Pride took service in Parliament's (q.v.) armies as a captain during the First Civil War (q.v.). By 1645 he commanded a regiment in the New Model Army (q.v.) at the Battle of Naseby (q.v.). In 1648 Pride was associated with the Independents (q.v.) and, with Lord Grey of Groby (q.v.), stood at the door of the House of Commons (q.v.) on 6 December 1648 and stopped Presbyterian (q.v.) members from entering the house, in what became known as Pride's Purge (q.v.). Pride was a commissioner at the trial of Charles I (q.v.) and signed the death warrant. In the 1650s Pride stayed with the army, serving at the Battles of Dunbar and Worcester (qq.v.). Under the Humble Petition and Advice (q.v.) constitution, Pride took a seat in the Upper House.

PRIDE'S PURGE. At the end of the Second Civil War (q.v.) demands for bringing Charles I (q.v.) to trial grew in the army and amongst the Independents (q.v.). In Parliament (q.v.) the Presbyterian (q.v.) majority instead overturned the Vote of No Addresses (q.v.) and reopened negotiations with the king. Although the Treaty of Newport (q.v.) discussions ended in failure in late October, Parliament was opposed to the army's treatment of the king and objected to his seizure from the Isle of Wight on 5 December. On the following day, Colonel Thomas Pride and Lord Grey of Groby stood at the doors of the House of Commons (qq.v.) excluding Presbyterian M.P.s. Some 186 were excluded, 41 were arrested, and 56 stayed away. Purged of the Presbyterians, the Independent-dominated house proceeded to discuss the proposed trial of the king.

PRIVY COUNCIL. The executive of government in the four nations; there was one in Edinburgh for Scotland, Dublin (q.v.) for Ireland, and one in Westminster (q.v.) for England and Wales. These were bodies of men—generally drawn from the aristocracy and the upper echelons of the church—who effected government. The membership of each body was chosen by the monarch, although in Ireland the lord deputy or lord lieutenant was involved in selection.

PROPOSITIONS FOR MONEY AND PLATE. In June 1642 Parliament (q.v.) established a Militia Committee at Westminster (q.v.) and it tackled the question of funding the forces that Parliament intended to muster by drafting the Propositions for Money and Plate. This collection of cash and silver was intended for centralised use, but many counties made it clear that funds raised would be used for county defence.

PROTECTORATE. The Protectorate was the name given to the government of the four nations after late 1653, when the Instrument of Government (q.v.) was put in place. It lasted until the fall of Richard Cromwell (q.v.) in 1659. The head of state was known as the lord protector (q.v.) and was filled by two men: Oliver Cromwell (q.v.) (1653–58) and his son Richard (1658–59).

PROTESTATION RETURNS. These were the returns of signatures gathered on the National Oath (q.v.) in 1641 on a parish-by-parish basis.

PROTESTERS. *See* REMONSTRANTS.

PRYNNE, WILLIAM (1600–1669). Prynne was an Oxford-educated barrister who began to write pamphlets attacking arminianism from 1627. In 1634 Prynne was sentenced to have his ears cropped, to be imprisoned for the rest of his life, and fined £5,000 for publishing *Histriomastix* two years earlier, an attack on the court of Charles I (q.v.) in which he particularly castigated Queen Henrietta Maria (q.v.) for her appearance in masques. Prynne continued to write in prison and in 1637 was tried again and, alongside Henry Burton and John Bastwicke (qq.v.), pilloried and had the rest of his ears cropped. In 1640 Parliament (q.v.) declared his sentences illegal and he was released. During the First Civil War (q.v.) Prynne was a parliamentarian (q.v.), but he developed a hatred towards the Independents (q.v.) that equalled his hatred of the episcopacy and the Presbyterians (qq.v.). He began to attack the New Model Army (q.v.) in print in 1647 and was arrested at Pride's Purge (q.v.) in 1648. Prynne was imprisoned for three years during the Commonwealth (q.v.) for refusing to recognise its legality. He also attacked Oliver Cromwell and the Protectorate (qq.v.) during the 1650s. In 1660 he welcomed the Restoration (q.v.) but soon began to object to Charles II's (q.v.) religious and civil policies. He was appointed keeper of the records in the Tower of London.

PURITANS. A much-abused term during the Civil War period and afterwards. Originally Puritans were those people who sought to reform the Churches of England, Wales, and Ireland, beyond the achievements of the sixteenth-century Reformation. They sought to purify the churches of the taints of Roman Catholicism (q.v.) still present in structure and liturgy. Most of these Puritans were content to see reform from within. However, James VI and I's drive for greater conformity pushed some of the Puritans out of the Church of England and into limited separatism. Other groups emigrated to the more reformed churches in Protestant Europe, or from the 1620s onwards to the colonies in America. The accession of Charles I (q.v.) saw further restrictions on Puritans and a dashing of their hopes for reform. Archbishop William Laud's (q.v.) antipathy and persecution of Puritans, most notably William Prynne, John Bastwicke, and Henry Burton (qq.v.), drove many of them further away from the church and into separatism. Moreover, during this period the term "Puritan" began to be used to describe a much broader group of people. Indeed, it could be applied to anyone who opposed the actions of the king and his government. This resulted in the terms "parliamentarian" and "roundhead" (qq.v.) becoming used as if they were synonymous with "Puritan."

Historians have seen Puritanism as being many things: As an ideology of the capitalist classes, bonding them together in opposition to the feudal restraints on trade and providing them with a creed that stressed the godliness of labour. Others have seen Puritanism as a doctrine of liberty, associated with the development of parliamentary democracy. Neither of these ideas has fully explained the nature or importance of Puritanism in the history of the Civil War period. It is certain that Puritans were important in the development of opposition to Charles I's religious policies, but they were insufficiently central to fully explain the impetus of opposition expressed during 1640–42 across the British Isles. As a term, "Puritan" is clearly ineffective as a label for the strands of religious perspectives within England and Wales that could create no single system to replace the Churches of England, Wales, and Ireland.

PUTNEY DEBATES. This meeting between the General Council of the Army (q.v.), the agitators (q.v.), and representatives of the Levellers (q.v.) was held in and around St Mary's Church, Putney, from 20 October through 11 November 1647. The meeting was called to discuss *The Case of the Army Truly Stated* (q.v.), but the Levellers produced the *Agreement of the People* (q.v.) and discussions also took place on this constitutional document. The first part of the discussions centred on whether the army could really discuss wide-ranging issues such as the change in the form of government proposed in the *Agreement* given its engagements to defend Parliament (q.v.). The debate then switched to the franchise proposals in the *Agreement* and Henry Ireton (q.v.) attacked the notion that all men should have a vote, arguing that an elector must have a fixed interest, that is, property, before he could be said to be a freeborn Englishman, a voter. Colonel Thomas Rainborough (q.v.), who was imbued with some aspects of Leveller thought, argued that everyone bound by a government should have a say in its election.

The Putney Debates were the first time that democratic issues were debated in such an open forum in Britain. They also clearly showed the gulf between Levellers, agitators, and the army grandees (q.v.). Agreement centred on the idea that the indigent and servants be excluded from the vote, but this could have effectively withheld the vote from any man who received a wage. By 1 November discussion moved to the position of the monarch, with some of the Levellers arguing that Charles I (q.v.) be left out of the constitutional arrangements until after the *Agreement* was in place, but others, including agitator Edward Sexby (q.v.), argued that Charles I should be brought to trial. For the first 10 days of November these discussions continued, with the grandees trying to close the discussion of the king's position, but with the meeting being constantly brought back to that issue.

The meeting was broken up on 11 November with the receipt of the news that Charles I had escaped from captivity in Hampton Court (q.v.). The Levellers, not happy with the failure to fully adopt the *Agreement*, intended to gain the support of the rank and file at several rendezvous over the following days, most notably at Corkbush Field (q.v.).

PYM, JOHN (1584–1643). Pym was a former Oxford University and Middle Temple student who, during the 1620s, became an important speaker in the House of Commons (q.v.). He opposed the actions of the duke of Buckingham and was central to attempts to impeach him just before his murder. During the Personal Rule (q.v.), Pym was involved with companies developed to ease emigration to the Puritan (q.v.) colonies in America. In the Short Parliament (q.v.) it was Pym who encapsulated the principles of opposition to Charles I (q.v.) under the three headings of religion, breaches of parliamentary privilege, and taxation. During the Long Parliament (q.v.) Pym quickly established himself as a leading figure in the Commons, supported by his sponsor the earl of Bedford in the Lords (q.v.). He was instrumental in the impeachments (q.v.) of the earl of Strafford and Archbishop William Laud (qq.v.).

In the summer of 1641 Pym tried to keep up the momentum of reform after the successes of eradicating many of the instruments of government associated with the Personal Rule. This pressure lapsed somewhat until after the Irish Rebellion (q.v.), however, when Pym drafted the Grand Remonstrance (q.v.). In January 1642 Pym was named as one of the Five Members (q.v.) the king sought to arrest.

Pym remained central to Parliamentary business during 1642 and 1643, directing the work of setting up financial and military administration. During 1643 he also began to negotiate with the Scots and was successful in drawing them into the war with the agreement known as the Solemn League and Covenant (q.v.). Shortly after this was successfully concluded, Pym died of bowel cancer on 8 December 1643. The nature of his death was used by royalists (q.v.) to symbolise his political corruption. Pym steered Parliament by remaining at the head of the Middle Group (q.v.), which lent its support to the other factions, the War Party and the Peace Party (q.v.), on particular issues rather than wholeheartedly siding with either.

↩ Q ↩

QUAKERS. Formally known as the Society of Friends, the Quakers came into existence during the 1650s. The name "Quakers" appears to come from their visible shaking when filled with the holy spirit. The Quakers did not hold with any form of structured service, believing that there was no intermediary between the individual and God. Their meetings were therefore unstructured and the speakers were those who felt that God was speaking through them. The Quakers also held that there was no authority except that derived from God, and that social distinctions were not so ordained. The Quakers regarded women as equal to men, many of their early tracts were written by women, and much of their early missionary work on both sides of the Atlantic was undertaken by women. Their refusal to accept social distinctions was visibly demonstrated by their refusal to remove their hats to those normally regarded as social betters, and orally demonstrated by their reference to everyone by the equalising "thou." This opened the Quakers to concerted abuse as they seemed to attack the very foundations of society, something the revolution had not done. The Quakers were the most feared of the religious sects in the 1650s because of their social views. For many the example of John Naylor (q.v.) summed up the dangers of this social and religious revolution: although other Quakers, such as Elizabeth Hooton and George Fox (q.v.), behaved differently they were still imprisoned.

At the Restoration (q.v.) the Quakers, despite Fox having met Charles II (q.v.), were persecuted even more viciously and attempts were made to associate them with several plots. This obliged them to take up the stance of pacifism. Their refusal to fight even when being attacked savagely at their meeting places began to win them some grudging respect. In the American colonies, to which many emigrated, the Quakers were equally feared and persecuted until William Penn negotiated the creation of Pennsylvania colony, where they would be safe from persecution.

QUARTER. The practise of granting life to an enemy soldier upon his capture. On some occasions quarter was not granted, such as at the capture of Shelford in Nottinghamshire in October 1645, or after 1643 to any

Irishmen captured in arms in the service of Charles I (q.v.) in England or Wales.

QUARTER SESSIONS. The general courts held in each English county four times a year, dealing with minor crimes and passing more severe cases onto the biannual assizes. These courts were generally suspended during the war, although in some counties, such as Cornwall, they were continued.

QUARTERMASTER. A noncommissioned rank in the army. There was one quartermaster per regiment of Foot (q.v.) and one to each troop of Horse (q.v.). The main responsibility of the quartermaster was to find lodgings for soldiers whilst in garrisons or on campaign. Quartermasters were also used to collect taxation in England and Wales.

⇜ R ⇝

RAIN(S)BOROUGH (OR RAINBOROW), COLONEL THOMAS (?–1648). Rainborough served as a colonel in the New Model Army (q.v.), but at the outset of the Second Civil War (q.v.) was given a naval command, which proved disastrous. By the end of the war he was in command at the siege of Pontefract (q.v.). Rainborough moved to centre stage in October 1648 at the Putney Debates (q.v.). He seems to have attached himself to Leveller (q.v.) principles possibly from personal grievance rather than deeper associations. During a debate on 29 October, Rainborough, with these words declared himself in favour of manhood suffrage: "For really I think that the poorest he that is in England hath a life to live, as the greatest he; and therefore truly sir I think it's clear that every man that is to live under a government ought first by his own consent to put himself under that government." Although he later agreed to a more limited system during the debates, Rainborough remained a problem for the grandees (q.v.). On 29 October 1648, the royalists (q.v.) at Pontefract bungled an attempt to kidnap Rainborough, and in the ensuing fight he was killed.

RANTER. An antinomian group that developed in the late 1640s, the Ranters rejected formal church structure and common morality, arguing that as God was within every human being, nothing that the elect could do was sinful. Therefore, there was no need for social institutions like marriage, or sins like blasphemy. This led to law breaking and to sexual license. To the outsiders this aspect of their faith became a dominating impression and the Ranters were regarded as frightening and dangerous. Women, such as Mary Middleton and Anna Trapnel, were prominent in the movement and were the centre of many Ranter groups in London. Lawrence Clarkson was one of the prominent male Ranters. The short life of the movement has led to several historians questioning the existence of a movement at all. There have been suggestions that there was only a small core of men and women who held these doctrines and who published them, but that there was nothing that would constitute a movement of church. Other historians argue that the publications do exhibit a consistent set of doctrines and thus indicate the existence of a coherent movement.

RATHMINES, BATTLE OF. The marquis of Ormond (q.v.) launched a new siege on Dublin (q.v.) with royalist (q.v.) forces and the Catholic Confederation of Kilkenny (q.v.) on 19 June 1648. The garrisons of Drogheda (q.v.), Dundalk, Newry, and Trim had been captured by Lord Inchiquin (q.v.), and his forces joined Ormond in July. Most of Ormond's army was based south of the River Liffey and centred on Rathmines. By 26 July the parliamentarian (q.v.) forces in the city under Michael Jones (q.v.) had been reinforced by sections of the New Model Army (q.v.) sent over from England in advance of the main body led by Oliver Cromwell (q.v.). Ormond switched tactics trying to cut off Jones's grazing areas south of the city. If this were successful, Ormond would press on to the deep-water port at Ringsend to deny English reinforcements a harbour. On 2 August this plan was to be effected by establishing a fort at Baggotrath Castle, and troops were sent to build a fort in the early hours of the morning. By daybreak the fort was hardly begun and Jones attacked the advanced enemy.

Jones's attack drove the allied forces from Baggotrath, and on through Donnybrook. Ormond had, on realising that the fort had not been built as quickly as he desired, moved his whole army down towards Baggotrath. He made the troops at the castle his right wing, brought Inchiquin's men forward as a centre, and had the rest of the forces at Rathmines assemble as the left wing. However, Jones capitalised on his success at Baggotrath and pressed on towards Rathmines itself. Ormond tried to hold the centre but the forces detailed to watch the left flank allowed Jones's Horse (q.v.) to advance up the line of the River Dodder and thus reach Ormond's rear. The centre of Ormond's force collapsed and the left, still some way to the rear, on realising that the ring and centre had gone, began to melt away and surrender to Jones's forces bearing down on them. The defeat was complete, the siege ended, and any chance gone of preventing the New Model Army (q.v.) from landing at Ringsend.

RECRUITER ELECTIONS. These were elections held principally in 1645 and 1646 to fill up the seats in the English and Welsh Parliament (q.v.) left vacant by death and the expulsion of royalist (q.v.) M.P.s during the First Civil War (q.v.). The term was a royalist one.

RED HILL, BATTLE OF. Fought on 15 September 1648. In the Second Civil War (q.v.), Anglesey was held for the royalists (q.v.) by Lord Bulkeley. After their defeat at the Battle of Y Dalar Hir (q.v.), royalists from north Wales fled to the island. They were quickly followed by parliamentarians (q.v.) who defeated them at Red Hill and took over the island.

REFORMADOES. Generally the term applied to reformed regiments, bodies of discharged officers, or those whose original regiments had been disbanded. There were large numbers of reformadoes in London at the end of 1641 following the disbanding of the army after peace with Scotland. Many of these were recruited as cavaliers (q.v.) by Thomas Lunsford (q.v.) and fought against the roundheads (q.v.) at the end of December. In 1647, as the conflict between the Presbyterian (q.v.) faction in Parliament (q.v.) and the New Model Army (q.v.) developed, the Presbyterians sought to create an army out of the reformadoes in London. These reformadoes were from regiments disbanded when the New Model Army was created or following the end of the First Civil War (q.v.). The advance of the New Model on London that summer ended these attempts to create and anti-army force.

REGICIDES. These were the 59 signatories of the death warrant authorising the execution of Charles I (q.v.), including John Bradshaw, Lord Grey of Groby, Oliver Cromwell, Henry Ireton, John Hutchinson, and John Downes (qq.v.). The term also applied to the three men charged with overseeing the execution—Colonel Francis Hacker (q.v.), Colonel Hercules Hunkes, and Colonel Robert Phayre—and to Daniel Axtell, who commanded the guards at the trial. The regicides were to be excepted from pardon at the Restoration (q.v.) when 41 were still alive. The coffins of Bradshaw, Cromwell, and Ireton were exhumed and their bodies displayed and dismembered.

Axtell and Hacker were executed, although Phayre and Hunkes managed to use influence to win reprieve. Hutchinson died in prison for alleged complicity in plots after the Restoration; nine of the other signatories were hanged, drawn and quartered.

REMONSTRANTS. After the defeat at the Battle of Dunbar (q.v.), sections of the Kirk Party (q.v.) known as the Resolutioners (q.v.), under the leadership of the marquis of Argyll (q.v.), prepared to create a new army by allowing former Engagers (q.v.) and former royalists (q.v.) to enlist, whereas they had been previously prohibited from doing so. The Remonstrants were those who believed that this would compromise the cause of the National Covenant (q.v.) and they questioned the nature of the alliance with Charles II (q.v.), who they suspected of not having signed the Covenant with pure motives. They took their name from the Western Remonstrance, which they issued in the wake of Dunbar, and had supporters in both the kirk and the Estates (qq.v.). These deep and seemingly unbridgeable divisions lessened the effectiveness of Scottish opposition to England's invasion during the 1650s. The Remonstrants were also to become known as the Protesters (q.v.).

REPUBLIC. A state governed by elected representatives of the people rather than a nonelected monarchy or oligarchy. The term was applied to England and Wales from May 1649, following the execution of Charles I (q.v.), and then, after the wars against Scotland and Ireland ended in 1652–53, these two states were absorbed into the "British" Republic. The Republic embraced two periods: the Commonwealth (q.v.), namely, the rule of the remains of the Long Parliament (q.v.), and the Protectorate (q.v.) of Oliver Cromwell and Richard Cromwell (qq.v.), who were both unelected. The Republic ended in May 1660 with the Restoration of Charles II (qq.v.).

RESOLUTIONERS. After the defeat at the Battle of Dunbar (q.v.), the marquis of Argyll (q.v.) and a section of the Kirk Party (q.v.) saw that the only chance of defeating the New Model Army (q.v.) lay in broadening the support for Charles II (q.v.). Previously excluded groups—royalists and Engagers (qq.v.)—were allowed to enlist in the reformed army. Argyll's group became known as the Resolutioners. The Resolutioners were able to dominate the General Assembly in the early 1650s, but the rifts between them and the Remonstrants (q.v.) who opposed them weakened Scotland's opposition to English invasion during 1651–53.

RESTORATION, THE. This label covers the return of the monarchy to the three kingdoms of England (and Wales), Scotland, and Ireland in May 1660 in the person of Charles II (q.v.). The name is also applied to the recreation of the separate states and the disestablishment of the union of the four nations, and the reestablishment of the Church of England, the Church of Wales, and the Church of Ireland. The Restoration was brought about by the failure of attempts to find solutions to the problem of governance after the collapse of the Protectorate (q.v.) and the return of the

Rump Parliament (q.v.). Failure to create a balance between the civil government and the army resulted in a power vacuum for several months. In the winter of 1659, George Monck's (q.v.) use of the Scottish-based regiments provided the military muscle needed for the Rump to call for a convention Parliament, which invited Charles Stuart to return.

RINUCCINI, GIOVANNI BATTISTA. Born in Florence, Rinuccini was educated by Jesuits and rose to become Archbishop of Fermo. In 1645 Pope Innocent X sent Rinuccini to Ireland as a nuncio to conserve and restore the Catholic (q.v.) faith, which meant adopting a hard line against any attempts to reduce the position of the church in treaties made between the Catholic Confederation of Kilkenny and the marquis of Ormond (qq.v.). Rinuccini spent four months in France on the way to Ireland in negotiation with Queen Henrietta Maria (q.v.) and did not arrive in Ireland until 21 October 1645.

Rinuccini supported the Catholic Irish faction at Kilkenny (q.v.) and their general in the field, Owen Roe O'Neill (q.v.). He urged the Irish government not to agree to any terms that diminished the Catholic church and thus opposed the open negotiations with Ormond and distrusted the intentions of the secret treaty being negotiated with the earl of Glamorgan (q.v.). Arms and weapons that Rinuccini brought to Ireland were sent to O'Neill's army and allowed him to go onto the offensive and led to the Battle of Benburb (q.v.). Rinuccini's hard-line support for the Irish faction led to difficulties in the government that drove a wedge between them and the Old English (q.v.) Catholics who favoured a treaty with Ormond. When the Confederation published its treaty with Ormond in August 1646, Rinuccini issued a declaration of excommunication to all those who signed it or worked towards its acceptance. Under Rinuccini's influence the Supreme Council was reconstructed and the so-called Ormondists driven out.

By the spring of 1647, however, the nuncio's power was on the wane; although the treaty had been dropped, the excommunications were repudiated. In May 1648, when Lord Inchiquin (q.v.) changed sides again and joined the Confederation, Rinuccini tried to block his acceptance by the Kilkenny government. When he failed, the nuncio, whose relationship with O'Neill was now soured, decided that as he could no longer influence policy, he should leave Ireland, which he finally did in early 1649.

RIPPLE FIELD, BATTLE OF. Fought on 13 April 1643. During Sir William Waller's (q.v.) campaign against royalists (q.v.) in the Marcher counties (q.v.), he pressed across the border into Wales following his victory at the Battle of Highnam (q.v.). Prince Maurice (q.v.) and Sir

Richard Cave closed in on him, causing Waller to retreat into Gloucestershire. The royalists pursued him into the Forest of Dean, where they defeated him at Ripple Field, almost destroying his army, but severely denting Waller's reputation.

ROMAN CATHOLIC. *See* CATHOLIC.

ROOT AND BRANCH PETITION. On 11 November 1640, a petition signed by 15,000 Londoners was presented to Parliament (q.v.). The majority of its 28 clauses referred to religion. This became known as the Root and Branch Petition because of its demands that episcopacy (q.v.) be removed from the church root and branch. The episcopacy was seen as the route through which Roman Catholicism (q.v.) could invade the English Church. The Petition was liked by many who wished to reform the church, and the Scots approved of its aims. It was received coolly in Parliament, however, because it was by no means certain that complete reform was necessary once the agents of church government, including Archbishop William Laud (q.v.), had been removed from power. The demand that the bishops all be removed was left aside until the end of 1641.

ROUNDHEAD. This name was applied to supporters of the English and Welsh Parliament (q.v.) in England and Wales during the period 1642 to 1651. It could still be applied to supporters of the Commonwealth and the Protectorate (qq.v.) during the 1650s. The name was applied to the New Model Army (q.v.) in Scotland and Ireland from 1649 during the army's incursions into those countries. The name originated as a class-based insult. It is thought that it originally applied to the shaven heads of the London apprentices involved in the riots and demonstrations in London in late December 1641. The name was then extended to all supporters of Parliament in an attempt to associate the parliamentarian (q.v.) movement with disorder and with lower class origins. Unlike the term "cavalier" (q.v.), which the royalists (q.v.) themselves adopted, parliamentarians did not used the term "roundhead" themselves. There were vain attempts to convert the word to "soundhead."

ROUNDWAY DOWN, BATTLE OF. Fought on 13 July 1644. After the defeat at Lansdown (q.v.), and the injuries suffered after the battle, Sir Ralph Hopton (q.v.) retreated to Devizes, closely pursued by Sir William Waller (q.v.). By 11 July the town was encircled, but Prince Maurice and Lord Hertford (qq.v.) had led a small party of Horse (q.v.) out towards the royalist (q.v.) capital at Oxford (q.v.) to fetch help. A relief force under Henry Wilmot (q.v.) had already set out towards Devizes when Maurice and Hertford arrived and without rest they turned around to follow it. On 12 July the two royalists caught up with Wilmot at Marlborough. On 13 July Waller prepared to launch his attack on Devizes.

The royalist Horse arrived on Roundway Down north-west of Devizes and to the north of Waller and sent a message to Hopton urging him to attack Waller's forces once gunfire was heard from the Down. Wilmot attacked quickly, despite being heavily outnumbered, as he feared the initiative would pass to Waller, who had over 4,500 Horse and Foot (q.v.) on the field. The message to Hopton had been intercepted, and so Wilmot's initial charge was unsupported. Nevertheless, it was so effective that the charge precipitated the collapse of the parliamentarian (q.v.) army. Waller's Horse fled the field, many ending up in a crumpled heap at the foot of a steep hill (now known as Bloody Ditch), to the rear of their initial position. Hopton's Foot emerged from the town and drove off Waller's Foot. This was the second army Parliament had lost in the west in two months, the other being the earl of Stamford's (q.v.) at the Battle of Stratton (q.v.), and the royalists were able to dominate the area. Waller fled to Gloucester and then on to London; the royalists occupied Bath and moved on to attack Bristol (q.v.).

ROUS, FRANCIS (1579–1659). Rous was an M.P. for Truro in Devon and also an author, whose book *Oile of Scorpions* (1623) suggested that various calamities, such as plague and death, then afflicting England should serve as a warning of the need for political and religious reform. He was the half-brother of John Pym (q.v.), and in the Short Parliament (q.v.) it was Rous who began the attack on the Personal Rule (q.v.), enabling Pym to identify the three evils afflicting the country in his speech of 17 April 1640. Rous continued to serve in Parliament (q.v.) throughout the 1640s and became a supporter of the Independents (q.v.). During the 1650s he wrote pamphlets arguing that the Commonwealth (q.v.) had received divine favour shown by the victories bestowed on its forces. He went on to serve as speaker of the Commonwealth Parliament of 1649–53.

ROWTON HEATH, BATTLE OF. Fought on 23 September 1645. Having been denied the support from South Wales that he had expected following the creation of the Peace(able) Army (q.v.), and having heard that Prince Rupert (q.v.) had surrendered Bristol (q.v.), King Charles I (q.v.) left the west. He turned towards Chester, where he hoped that an Irish army would be landed following the earl of Glamorgan's (q.v.) treaty with the Catholic Confederation of Kilkenny (q.v.). The king hoped to end Sir William Brereton's and Michael Jones's (qq.v.) siege of the port. On 22 September the king forced his way into Chester.

On 23 September Sir Marmaduke Langdale (q.v.) crossed the River Dee to attack Michael Jones. However, in Langdale's rear was the parliamentarian Northern Association (qq.v.) army under Sydenham Poyntz (q.v.). Langdale turned to face Poyntz's forces and defeated them as they tried to make it towards Jones in the Chester suburbs. However, Jones sent musketeers to Poyntz's aid and they enabled Poyntz to launch a counterattack, which forced Langdale to retreat towards Chester. The king tried to send troops out of Chester to reinforce Langdale but they were hemmed into the suburbs, where protracted street fighting developed. As Langdale's men crushed into the same streets the confusion added to the scale of the defeat and large numbers of the royalist Horse (q.q.v) were picked off by Jones's musketeers in the narrow confines of suburban Chester. In the wake of the defeat of his army, Charles left Chester and sought refuge in Wales.

ROYALIST. The name applied to supporters of King Charles I and his son Charles II (qq.v.) throughout the period 1642–60. The name was current in all four nations during this period. *See also* Cavalier.

RUMP PARLIAMENT. A derogatory term applied to the remains of the Long Parliament (q.v.) summoned to reassemble in May 1659 after the collapse of Richard Cromwell's Protectorate (qq.v.). The term appears only to have been used in popular parlance after the Parliament, having been dismissed again by the army in October 1659, was reassembled at the end of December 1659. The term referred to fact that of the 78 M.P.s still eligible to sit after death and the purges of 1648–53 had reduced their number, only 65 did so. The term has been applied by some historians to the Commonwealth (q.v.) Parliament of 1649–53 as well as that of 1659–60.

RUPERT, PRINCE (1619–1682). A nephew of Charles I (q.v.), the son of the king's sister Queen Elizabeth of Bohemia, Rupert served in the Protestant forces in Europe in the 1630s and was captured at the Battle of Eiberg in 1638. He spent three years in prison before being ransomed by Charles I. In 1642 he arrived in England with his younger brother, Prince Maurice (q.v.). Charles I appointed him general of Horse (q.v.) and in this role the prince was in action from mid-August onwards. During September Rupert and the Horse patrolled the Midlands between the king's forces and those of the earl of Essex's parliamentarian (qq.v.) army. On 23 September 1642 the first major clash between the two armies at the Battle of Powick Bridge (q.v.) was won by Rupert. At the Battle of Edgehill (q.v.) Rupert's devastating charge drove the parliamentarian left flank from the field. A flaw in Rupert's tactics was revealed, however: his own forces became so disordered by such a charge that they too took some time to be reorganised and useful again.

Rupert played an important role in many of the major battles of the First Civil War (q.v.), including the Battle of Chalgrove Field, the First Battle of Newbury, and the Battle of Newark (qq.v.) in 1644. In May of that year he left his base in the Marcher counties (q.v.), where he had been reorganising the royalist (q.v.) war effort to launch a campaign to rescue the marquis of Newcastle (q.v.), who was trapped in York (q.v.). This latter campaign ended in Rupert's defeat at the Battle of Marston Moor (q.v.). In the late summer Rupert was appointed commander-in-chief of the king's army but set about strengthening the royalist hold on Bristol (q.v.) and the west.

In 1645 Rupert, Prince Maurice, and Lord Loughborough (q.v.) worked to try and regain control of the northern Wales marches south of Cheshire, a campaign they were all deflected from when the king marched out of Oxford (q.v.) to mount an attack on the forces besieging Chester (q.v.). After the siege of Chester ended as the king marched in its direction, the army turned on Leicester (q.v.), which was captured at the end of May. A bare fortnight later, Rupert, as commander of the army, was defeated at the Battle of Naseby (q.v.) by Sir Thomas Fairfax and the New Model Army (qq.v.). In the wake of this defeat Rupert returned to Bristol, but surrendered the port in September. For this defeat the king dismissed him, although a court-martial cleared Rupert of any wrong-doing. Rupert and Maurice went into exile in Europe.

During the Second Civil War (q.v.) Rupert served in the small royalist fleet, a role that he was to continue into the 1650s. Rupert returned to England at the Restoration (q.v.). He did not become involved in government, although he was a stockholder in colonial ventures, especially the Hudson's Bay Company, which took over land named after the prince. Rupert also became an experimental scientist, a member of the Royal Society, the inventor of an early form of bullet-proof glass, and a developer of surgical instruments.

RUSHWORTH, JOHN (1612–1690). Rushworth served as secretary to the New Model Army (q.v.) during the First Civil War (q.v.) and afterwards. In 1650 he became Oliver Cromwell's (q.v.) secretary. Rushworth collected parliamentary papers covering the periods of the First and Second Civil Wars (qq.v.) and these were published in seven volumes as the *Historical Collections of Private Passages of State* between 1659 and 1701. The first volume was dedicated to Richard Cromwell (q.v.) and Rushworth, whilst professing to be editing an impartial collection, was attacked for his support of and association with the Republican cause.

⤳ S ⤶

ST FAGANS, BATTLE OF. Fought on 8 May 1648. In the wake of the rebellion led by Rowland Laugharne and John Poyer (qq.v.) in south-west Wales in 1648, they and royalists (q.v.) who joined their rebellion formed an army. Parliament (q.v.) sent a part of the New Model Army (q.v.) under Colonel Thomas Horton into south Wales to deal with the rebellion, after forces under Adjutant General Fleming had been defeated. Horton's troops met with the rebels at St Fagans in the largest pitched battle in Wales. Despite the hasty construction of the rebel army and its uncomfortable amalgamation of former parliamentarian Presbyterians (qq.v.) and royalists, the battle was a long and hard one. Eventually, Horton won and his victory ensured that the rebellion would be restricted to south-west Wales. The rebel leaders were penned into Pembroke as further sections of the New Model Army under Oliver Cromwell (q.v.) approached.

ST JOHN, OLIVER (?1598–1673). St John defended John Hampden (q.v.) in his case against ship money (q.v.) in 1637. He was identified with King Charles I's (q.v.) opponents in 1640 when he launched the attack on ship money. In 1641, he was part of the attempt to build bridges between the king and his opponents when he was appointed solicitor general despite his support of the attack on the earl of Strafford (q.v.). During the First Civil War (q.v.) St. John became the parliamentarian (q.v.) attorney general and served as a commissioner at the Treaty of Uxbridge (q.v.). During 1648–49 he refused to serve at the trial of Charles I. St John served in the governments of the Protectorate (q.v.) in the 1650s and on the Council of State (q.v.) just before the Restoration (q.v.). He escaped punishment in the 1660s but, on being barred permanently from office, he left the country in 1662.

ST NEOTS, BATTLE OF. Fought on 9 July 1648. In the wake of the royalist (q.v.) risings in the south-east during the Second Civil War (q.v.), rebels from Surrey fled north and were caught at St Neots, Huntingdonshire, by forces led by Colonel Adrian Scrope. In the defeat the royalist leader, the earl of Holland (q.v.), was captured.

SAINTS. The term "saints" implied the "elect" or those, in Calvinist theology, predestined to salvation. During the Civil War period the term became attached to the godly members of the New Model Army (q.v.), which was said to be doing God's work. It later applied to those whom it was hoped were carrying out a godly reformation of the four nations during the Republic (q.v.).

SAYE AND SELE, WILLIAM FIENNES, VISCOUNT (1582–1662). By opposing the forced loans (q.v.) of the 1620s and approving of the Petition of Right (q.v.) in 1629, Saye and Sele became an important opponent of Charles I (q.v.). Saye and Sele was heavily involved in colonising Connecticut and New Hampshire and helped establish the Providence Island Company with Lord Brooke and John Pym (qq.v.) to facilitate emigration by those alienated from the church by Charles I's religious policies. In 1639 Saye and Sele and Lord Brooke refused to take the oath imposed during the war with Scotland and thus became the centre of opposition to the war. In 1641 Charles I took him into the government as part of the attempt to build bridges between himself and his opponents. During the First Civil War (q.v.) Saye and Sele was a member of the Committee of Safety (q.v.) and participated in the Westminster Assembly (q.v.). In 1648 he tried to get Charles I to come to terms with Parliament (q.v.). At the Restoration (q.v.) Saye and Sele was appointed to the Privy Council (q.v.).

SCARAMPI, PIER FRANCESCO. Scarampi was appointed by Pope Urban VIII as the Vatican's representative to the Catholic Confederation of Kilkenny (q.v.) in the summer of 1643. He encouraged the Confederation to try and secure open religious freedom for Ireland's Roman Catholics (q.v.) in their negotiations with the earl of Ormond (q.v.). In 1645 Scarampi was replaced by Giovanni Battista Rinuccini (q.v.), the nuncio of the new pope, Innocent X.

SCARBOROUGH. This Yorkshire port was held by parliamentarian (q.v.) forces under Sir Hugh Cholmeley from the beginning of the First Civil War (q.v.) until Queen Henrietta Maria (q.v.) landed at Bridlington (q.v.). She persuaded Cholmeley to change sides and the town became an important port for the royalist (q.v.) forces based in Yorkshire and as a source of customs income. After the Battle of Marston Moor (q.v.) the port was besieged by parliamentarians, initially led by Sir John Meldrum (q.v.), who was killed during the siege. The port surrendered on 22 July 1645. In the Second Civil War (q.v.) Scarborough's governor, Michael Boynton, followed Cholmeley's example and changed sides. The port was again besieged, resisting Parliament's (q.v.) army until 19 December 1648.

SCARRIFFHOLLIS, BATTLE OF. Fought on 21 June 1650. The Ulster Army (q.v.), led by Ever MacMahon, Bishop of Clogher after Owen Roe O'Neill's (q.v.) death, had set about reconquering the west of Ulster (q.v.) in early 1650, but by the summer it had been cornered in Donegal by Sir Charles Coote (q.v.). Coote defeated Clogher's army at Scarriffhollis and set about executing the leaders of the army, including O'Neill's son Henry O'Neill (q.v.). Clogher was captured later and hanged. The defeat destroyed the last field army that the Catholic Confederation of Kilkenny or the marquis of Ormond (qq.v.) could muster. Indeed, the battle at Scarriffhollis marked the effective end of the war in Ireland outside the province of Connaght.

SEACROFT MOOR, BATTLE OF. Fought on 30 March 1643. After Lord Goring (q.v.) had returned to England with Queen Henrietta Maria (q.v.), the earl of Newcastle (q.v.) appointed him commander of the Horse (q.v.). In March, Goring led the Horse in attacks on the parliamentarians under Sir Thomas Fairfax (qq.v.) as they moved from Selby into the West Riding of Yorkshire. Goring caught and defeated Fairfax on Seacroft Moor and drove the parliamentarians to seek refuge in Leeds.

SEALED KNOT. A royalist (q.v.) secret organisation of the 1650s whose six members included Lord Belasyse and Lord Loughborough (qq.v.). The Knot attempted to coordinate the actions of royalists aiming to restore the monarchy. The Knot was cautious in its approach, awaiting instability in the Republican regime as a prerequisite for successful action. It spent 1654 in laying plans for a rebellion across Britain and condemned actions such as Penruddock's Rebellion (q.v.) in the spring of 1655 as ill considered.

SECOND CIVIL WAR. The period of warfare and rebellion in England and Wales began with the revolt of John Poyer and Rowland Laugharne (qq.v.) on south Wales and ended with the defeat of the north Wales rebellion of John Byron (q.v.) during 1648. The main military action centred on the invasion of England by the duke of Hamilton and the Engager (qq.v.) army. The war also embraced the Kentish Rebellion (q.v.), the sieges of Cochester, Scarborough, and Pontefract (qq.v.), and the Battles of St Fagans and Preston (qq.v.).

SEEKERS. A religious sect that appeared in the wake of the Civil Wars in England. The seekers questioned the validity of the scriptures and advocated searching their own consciences and divining their relationship with God through contemplation. In the 1650s many of the Seekers were absorbed into the Quaker (q.v.) movement.

SELBY, BATTLE OF. Fought on 11 April 1644. Whilst he was in the north-east attempting to slow the advance of the Army of the Solemn League and Covenant (q.v.), the earl of Newcastle (q.v.) left John Belasyse (q.v.) in command of the forces in Yorkshire. Belasyse faced a difficult task, trying to hem in the parliamentarians (q.v.) at Hull (q.v.) and prevent the renaissance of their fortunes in the West Riding of Yorkshire. To try and drive a wedge between these two areas, Belasyse placed himself at Selby, south of York. Here, however, he was trapped on 11 April when Lord Fairfax (q.v.), united with his son, Sir Thomas Fairfax, and Sir John Meldrum (qq.v.) at Ferrybridge and launched an attack on Selby. As the three sections of the parliamentarian army pressed into the town the royalists (q.v.) were trapped in the streets. Half of the Yorkshire royalist forces were destroyed and Belasyse was captured. The consequences were immense: Newcastle was forced to retreat into York (q.v.) where he was soon besieged by the Scots, the Fairfaxes, and eventually the Eastern Association (q.v.) forces under the earl of Manchester (q.v.). The siege led to the march of Prince Rupert (q.v.) into the area and culminated with the Battle of Marston Moor (q.v.).

SELF DENYING ORDINANCE. In the wake of the disappointing campaigns in late 1644, arguments broke out among the commanders of Parliament's (q.v.) forces. The earl of Manchester, a Presbyterian (qq.v.), accused Oliver Cromwell, an Independent (qq.v.), of breeding radical dissent in the army, after Cromwell and Sir William Waller (q.v.) had blamed Manchester for the disaster at the Second Battle of Newbury (q.v.). Manchester was backed by the Scots, who resented the way in which Cromwell's role at the Battle of Marston Moor (q.v.) had been played up at the expense of David Leslie (q.v.) and who also accused Cromwell of filling the army with Independents.

The results of an investigation into the autumn campaigns were announced by Zouch Tate (q.v.) on 9 December. Chief amongst the problems were "pride and covetousness." Cromwell quickly agreed with the findings, possibly to fend off further attacks on both his religion and his own lacklustre performance at Newbury. Zouch Tate's solution was a Self Denying Ordinance, by which everyone was to eschew personal ambitions, and through which one could no longer serve as a member of Parliament and retain a military command. As peers could not resign their place in the Lords (q.v.), however, the Self Denying Ordinance automatically deprived peers, such as the earl of Manchester and the earl of Essex (q.v.), of military command. This resulted in strenuous opposition to the bill from the House of Lords, which blocked it until April 1645. By this time the New Model Army (q.v.) had been created, effectively dissolving both the earls' armies in any case.

SEQUESTRATION. In early 1643 both sides in England and Wales adopted sequestration as one of the means of funding the war. Parliament (q.v.) quickly adopted the expedient of taking over a delinquent's (q.v.)

estate and managing it through subcommittees in each county, collecting rents and selling timber and produce. Out of this income was paid an allowance to the delinquent's dependents; the rest was used to fund the war effort. Although the royalists (q.v.) eventually adopted the same system, they had begun by trying to sell off enemy estates. This did not meet with success as very few people were prepared to risk buying such property when a royalist victory was far from assured.

SEXBY, EDWARD (?–1658). Sexby served in Oliver Cromwell's (q.v.) regiment of Horse (q.v.) from 1643 onwards. He became a prominent opponent of the disbanding of the army during the summer of 1647, campaigning for soldiers' rights to back pay. He participated in the Putney Debates (q.v.). In 1649 Sexby raised a regiment of his own, but in 1651 he was cashiered because of his radical stance. Sexby opposed the Protectorate (q.v.) and proposed assassinating Oliver Cromwell in a pamphlet entitled *Killing No Murder*. He died in the Tower of London.

SHERBURN IN ELMET, BATTLE OF. Fought on 15 October 1645. During the dramatic ride north led by Lord Digby, the Northern Horse (qq.v.) captured the parliamentarian (q.v.) garrison of Sherburn in Elmet. Digby was attempting to get to Scotland to join with the marquis of Montrose (q.v.). The victory was short-lived, however, as Colonel Copely arrived with fresh troops and drove Digby and the Horse out of town. The defeat led to the Northern Horse being chased northwards in a pursuit that was only to end with its defeat on Carlisle sands.

SHIP MONEY. Ship money was an emergency tax levied on coastal counties to pay for naval defence in times of war. Charles I (q.v.) extended the levy to cover all counties in England and Wales in 1636. It soon became clear that the tax was being regarded by the king as an ordinary levy, collected year after year. All counties were given an annual sum to pay based on the cost of building, equipping, and manning one or more warships. The tax was levied on a broader range of people than that usually covered by subsidies (q.v.). Ship money became one of the most disliked features of the Personal Rule (q.v.) and it was challenged in the courts by John Hampden (q.v.) and his defence lawyer, Oliver St John (q.v.), in 1637. Although the king won the case, five of the 12 judges had decided in favour of Hampden and many took this as a moral victory. Opposition to the levy was stepped up after the case, and quarter sessions (q.v.) courts in the country were faced with increasing numbers of defaulters. The levy was attacked in the Short Parliament (q.v.) and abolished by the Long Parliament (q.v.).

SHORT PARLIAMENT. In order to finance a second war against Scotland, Charles I (q.v.) called a Parliament (q.v.) to meet in April 1640, thereby ending the Personal Rule (q.v.). He had hoped that the Irish Parliament (q.v.), managed by the earl of Strafford (q.v.), which had met in March and offered four subsidies (q.v.) to the king, would encourage the cooperation of the English and Welsh Parliament. Instead, when the Parliament met on 13 April, the M.P.s began to attack the features of the Personal Rule, including ship money (q.v.), and refused to discuss raising money until their grievances were answered. Attempts by the king to change the course of discussions only succeeded in angering Parliament more. On 5 May Charles dissolved the Parliament.

SKIPPON, PHILIP (?–1660). Having served in the European wars in the 1620s and 1630s, Skippon was in London by 1639 and in 1642 was appointed by Parliament (q.v.) to command the London Trained Bands (q.v.). During the First Civil War (q.v.) Skippon served as major general (q.v.) to the earl of Essex (q.v.); in 1643 he fought at Reading and Gloucester (q.v.) and the First Battle of Newbury (q.v.). In 1644 Skippon led Essex's Foot (q.v.) during the disastrous Lostwithiel (q.v.) campaign. When his commander fled the scene by boat, Skippon was left to surrender the Foot to the royalists (q.v.) on 2 September. He fought at the Second Battle of Newbury (q.v.) and in 1645 was appointed commander of the New Model Army's (q.v.) Foot. Skippon was badly wounded at the Battle of Naseby (q.v.), but organised the siege of Oxford (q.v.) later that year.

In 1647 Parliament appointed Skippon to lead the new army being assembled for Ireland, although he was broadly sympathetic towards the soldiers and the agitators (q.v.) in the New Model Army. Nevertheless, he was given command of the London forces during the Second Civil War (q.v.). During the Republic (q.v.), Skippon served on several Councils of State (q.v.). In 1656 he served as one of the major generals (q.v.), and was responsible for London. He was an M.P. in the first Protectorate (q.v.) Parliament and later a member of Oliver Cromwell's Upper House. In 1659 Skippon was appointed again to command the London forces by the Rump Parliament (q.v.).

SLIGO. This port on the west coast of Ireland was held by Catholic Confederation of Kilkenny (q.v.) forces from the end of 1642 when it was taken by Tahg O'Connor Sligo. In June 1645 Sir Charles Coote (q.v.), having announced his rejection of the Cessation (q.v.), went on the offensive in North Connaght. That month he captured Sligo and massacred the garrison. Fighting continued in the area and during one of the skirmishes, Malachy O'Queely, Archbishop of Tuam, was killed and the terms of the earl of Glamorgan's (q.v.) treaty were found on his body. In 1649 Sligo was captured by the Confederation and royalist (q.v.) forces. The garrison established in 1649 remained in the town until it surrendered to the English forces in 1652.

SLINGSBY, SIR HENRY (1602–1658). Sir Henry Slingsby served in the English and Welsh forces in the first Bishop's War (q.v.). Slingsby sat as M.P. for Knaresborough in the Long Parliament (q.v.), but left his seat in 1642 to raise a regiment of Foot (q.v.) for Charles I (q.v.). From 1643 until the surrender of York (q.v.) Slingsby served in the Northern Army (q.v.). He moved to the Oxford Field Army (q.v.) in 1644 and accompanied Charles I when he fled Oxford for Newark (q.v.) in disguise in 1646. Slingsby wrote a diary of the First Civil War (q.v.), which was first published in 1806. Slingsby refused to comply with any of the Republican governments during the 1650s and, in 1658, was accused of treason on spurious grounds and executed. His shirt, bloodstained from execution, is housed at Knaresborough castle.

SOLEMN LEAGUE AND COVENANT. Essentially the treaty between the Estates and the Long Parliament (qq.v.) signed in September 1643. This treaty had been engineered by John Pym (q.v.) with the aim of securing military aid for the parliamentarian (q.v.) cause in England and Wales. Pym had tried to convince the Scots that Charles I (q.v.) might secure the help of the Irish rebels against Scotland; and, in Edinburgh, the Cessation (q.v.) of September 1643 seemed to be proof of this. By the terms of the treaty the Scots were to send a 20,000-strong Army of the Solemn League and Covenant (q.v.) into England. In return, the Long Parliament promised to raise a levy to pay the Scots forces, to demolish the episcopacy (q.v.) of the church in England, and host a debate at Westminster (q.v.) on the future of the English and Welsh church.

SOURTON DOWN, BATTLE OF. Fought on 25–26 April 1643. As Sir Ralph Hopton (q.v.) advanced into Devon, his forces were intercepted by part of the earl of Stamford's (q.v.) army, led by James Chudleigh. Hopton's 3,600 men were caught in the night on Sourton Down near Okehampton by Chudleigh's small party of Horse (q.v.). The surprised royalists (q.v.) were defeated and driven back, leaving behind 1,000 muskets (q.v.) and Hopton's portmanteau with the names of local royalists inside.

SPRIGG, JOSHUA (1618–1684). An Oxford University-educated divine in the employ of Sir Thomas Fairfax (q.v.), who published *Anglia Rediviva* in 1647. This tract dealt with the victories of Parliament's (q.v.)

armies and thus pleased both Parliament and Fairfax, the commander of the New Model Army (q.v.), Parliament's principal army. Despite opposing, as did Fairfax, the execution of Charles I (q.v.), Sprigg was appointed fellow and bursar of All Soul's College, Oxford University, a post from which he retired at the Restoration (q.v.).

STAMFORD, HENRY GREY, EARL OF (?1599–1673). Stamford was a long-standing opponent of the Hastings family's hegemony in Leicestershire in the seventeenth century. When Parliament (q.v.) removed the earl of Huntingdon, the head of the Hastings family, from his place as lord lieutenant (q.v.) of the county with the Militia Ordinance (q.v.) in 1642, it appointed Stamford in his place. Although the earl combated Huntingdon's royalist (q.v.) son's, Henry Hastings's (q.v.), attempts to take over the military forces in the county during the ensuing summer, it was in the south-west where Stamford saw the most action during the First Civil War (q.v.). The earl had early successes against the royalists led by Sir Ralph Hopton (q.v.), but his truce in the spring of 1643 was heavily criticised at Westminster (q.v.) and when his army was decisively defeated at the Battle of Stratton (q.v.), Stamford retired from military service. Stamford's sympathy with his cause waned over the years; in 1645 he assaulted Sir Arthur Hesilrige (q.v.) at Westminster. He also opposed the actions of his son, Lord Grey, in 1648 and remained distant from the Republic (q.v.). In 1660 Stamford was in favour of the Restoration (q.v.).

STAPLEFORD, SIR PHILIP (1603–1647). A Yorkshire parliamentarian (q.v.) and M.P. for Boroughbridge, Stapleford served in the army of the earl of Essex (q.v.) during the First Civil War (q.v.). After the formation of the New Model Army (q.v.), Stapleford was appointed to the Committee of Both Kingdoms (q.v.). In 1647 Stapleford, a Presbyterian (q.v.), was identified as a leading opponent of the New Model Army and was one of the Eleven Members (q.v.) excluded from Parliament (q.v.) when the army advanced on London during the summer.

STAR CHAMBER. This was a prerogative court consisting of members of the Privy Council (q.v.) and the two chief justices. The court dealt with public-order offences, but by 1640 had been used by Charles I (q.v.) to enforce unpopular laws and religious changes. As a result, the court became one of the most hated features of the Personal Rule (q.v.). It was abolished by the Long Parliament (q.v.) in 1641.

STOW ON THE WOLD, BATTLE OF. Fought on 21 March 1646. During the autumn of 1645 and winter of 1646, Lord Astley (q.v.) had been attempting to strengthen the royalist (q.v.) position in the northern Welsh marches. His aim had been to ensure control of the region in preparation for the arrival of troops from Ireland following the earl of Glamorgan's (q.v.) treaty. When Chester fell in February 1646, the chances of landing troops in the area diminished, and when Glamorgan's treaty fell through, Astley's mission was at an end. He then gathered 3,000 troops and they marched to join the Oxford Field Army (q.v.). However, he was followed by Sir William Brereton (q.v.) and as he left Worcester (q.v.), Astley was defeated at Stow on the Wold. The battle is generally considered the last pitched battle of the First Civil War (q.v.) in England.

STRAFFORD, THOMAS WENTWORTH, EARL OF (1593–1641). An opponent of Charles I 's (q.v.) government during the 1620s, Wentworth was incorporated into the government in 1628 and became fundamental to the government of the Personal Rule (q.v.). In the early 1630s Wentworth was appointed lord president of the Council of the North, where he made use of the Star Chamber (q.v.) to prosecute opponents. In 1632 he was appointed lord deputy of Ireland. In Ireland, Wentworth set out to reinvigorate royal government and create income for the crown. He also began to bring the Irish Protestant church into line with Archbishop William Laud's (q.v.) reforms in England and Wales. His government in Ireland met with mixed success, but it created a great deal of opposition from several factions. Outwardly his regime looked stable until he left for England in March 1640 to attend the Short Parliament (q.v.). In his absence his management of the March Irish Parliament (q.v.) was questioned and the subsidies that he had persuaded it to vote on were dramatically reduced in value. In the summer, Wentworth wanted a full-scale invasion of Scotland and promised an Irish army for use against the Scots. He was then named earl of Strafford.

On the defeat of the English and Welsh forces at the Battle of Newburn (q.v.), campaigns in the four nations against Strafford were united. By the end of 1640 he had been impeached (q.v.) by the Long Parliament (q.v.) and a committee considered charges of treason and tyranny from across Britain and Ireland. In March 1641 Strafford was brought to trial. The case against him was very weak and Strafford was able to defend himself with ease. To prevent his escape, a Bill of Attainder (q.v.) was drafted that required only suspicion of guilt to serve as proof. Strafford was sentenced to death and Charles I, afraid of mob riots and that the queen might be impeached if he did not comply, signed the death warrant. On 11 May 1641, Strafford was beheaded at Tower Hill.

STRATTON, BATTLE OF. Fought on 15 May 1643. Following the defeat of Sir Ralph Hopton (q.v.) at the Battle of Sourton Down (q.v.), the earl of Stamford (q.v.) moved in to defeat the royalists (q.v.). Stamford had almost double Hopton's numbers, and as he sent out a party to prevent Hopton from recruiting, the earl drew his men up on a hill near Stratton. Although the hill appeared unassailable, Hopton attacked the parliamentarians (q.v.) in a three-pronged advance. Eventually all three sections forced their way onto the hill and defeated the earl's forces, effectively ending his military career.

STRODE, WILLIAM (?1599–1645). As one of the men who held Speaker John Finch (q.v.) in his seat at the end of the 1629 Parliament (q.v.), Strode was imprisoned until 1640 when he was released by the Long Parliament (q.v.). After his release and election to Parliament, he was a vigorous opponent of Charles I (q.v.). Strode was an important figure in the prosecution of the earl of Strafford (q.v.) in 1642 and one of the Five Members (q.v.) the king attempted to arrest on 5 January 1642. Strode was buried in Westminster Abbey in 1645, but his body was dug up after the Restoration (q.v.).

STUART, CHARLES. *See* CHARLES II.

STURMINSTER NEWTON, BATTLE OF. Fought on 29 June 1645. Edward Massey's (q.v.) Western Army was attacked by Clubmen (q.v.) in Dorset. The Clubmen had been provided with weapons by George, Lord Goring (q.v.), who had hoped to win all the county's Clubmen to the royalist (q.v.) cause. Massey was worsted and withdrew from the area. When Sir Thomas Fairfax (q.v.) and the New Model Army (q.v.) arrived in the area a week later, however, Fairfax managed to convince the Clubmen that King Charles I (q.v.) intended to bring Roman Catholic (q.v.) Irish troops into the country, and the Clubmen abandoned their royalist leanings.

SUBSIDIES. Ordinary taxation in England, Ireland, and Wales instituted by the Tudor monarchs. By the mid-seventeenth century the income from an English subsidy had fallen from a level of £140,000 to £55,000 and to have any real purpose they had to be collected in multiples instead of singly. As subsidies were collected with the authority of Parliament (q.v.), Charles I (q.v.) had no access to this form of income in England or Wales during the Personal Rule (q.v.). Four subsidies were voted by the Irish Parliament (q.v.) of March 1640, which act the earl of Strafford (q.v.) hoped to encourage in the forthcoming Parliament in England (the Short Parliament [q.v.]).

SYMONDS, RICHARD (1617–1692). Symonds was an antiquarian and an officer in Prince Rupert's Horse (qq.v.). On campaigns he took the time to visit churches and note memorials; he compiled lists of the officers in regiments he encountered as well as their colors. He kept both a diary and a notebook that have survived and provide useful source material. He travelled through Europe after the Civil Wars.

ᔐ T ᔐ

TABLES. The Scottish term for a committee, roughly analogous to a board in English. Tables were established as the executive bodies of the Estates (q.v.) during 1637–39. There were initially four tables, one representing each of the groups in the Estates: the burgess, the lairds, the clergy, and the aristocracy. The principal table, the fifth table, acted as an executive committee with representatives from the others sitting on it. The fifth table was eventually replaced by the Committee of Estates (q.v.).

TATE, ZOUCH (1606–1650). An M.P. in the Long Parliament (q.v.), Tate led a committee that reported on the poor performance of the parliamentarian (q.v.) armies at the Second Battle of Newbury (q.v.). It was Tate who suggested that commanders and M.P.s should eschew personal interests for the good of the parliamentarian cause: This gave rise to the Self Denying Ordinance (q.v.).

TAUNTON. A Somerset town held by royalists (q.v.) from 5 June 1645, until it fell to a surprise attack on 10 July 1644, during the earl of Essex's Lostwithiel (qq.v.) campaign. Repeated attempts to recapture the town failed and in 1645 Lord Goring's (q.v.) departure from the Oxford Field Army (q.v.) weakened the royalist forces before the Battle of Naseby (q.v.).

TEN PROPOSITIONS. A series of proposals drafted by John Pym (q.v.) and presented to Charles I (q.v.) in June 1641. The proposals called on Charles to delay his planned journey to Scotland so that a series of bills could be passed by Parliament (q.v.). The proposals also called for the army to be reduced in size, and for Queen Henrietta Maria (q.v.) to be deprived of her Roman Catholic (q.v.) advisors. The proposals further demanded that no ambassadors of the pope be admitted to the country and that Roman Catholics should be banned from the court. The king rejected the proposals and went to Scotland as planned, but elements from the proposals reappeared in the Grand Remonstrance and the Nineteen Propositions (qq.v.) of 1642.

THIRD CIVIL WAR. A term used to describe the war of 1650–51 between the Republic (q.v.) and the Scottish and royalist (q.v.) forces of Charles II (q.v.). The war embraced the invasion of Scotland, the Battle of Dunbar (q.v.) in 1650, Charles II's (q.v.) invasion of England, and the Battle of Worcester (q.v.) in 1651.

THOMASON, GEORGE (?–1666). A bookseller and publisher from St Paul's Churchyard, London, Thomason collected copies of many of the pamphlets and books published from 1641 until the Restoration (q.v.). His collections number around 23,000 volumes, which eventually made their way to the British Library and are known as the Thomason Tracts.

THOMPSON, CORNET JAMES (?–1649). Younger brother of William Thompson, James Thompson was one of the three soldiers shot at Burford (q.v.) for his part in the mutiny on 15 May 1649.

THOMPSON, WILLIAM (?–1649). A Leveller (q.v.) who wrote *England's Freedom, Soldiers Rights* in the wake of the Corkbush Field (q.v.) mutiny of 1647. In 1649 Thompson wrote *England's Standard Advanced*, which called for a mutiny against the grandees (q.v.) and so was involved in the mutiny of May of that year. Thompson became the focus of a rising around Banbury that proclaimed the third *Agreement of the People* (q.v.). His group made their way to the centre of the Burford mutiny (q.v.) and, when the mutineers were attacked, Thompson escaped with some followers. The mutineers made it to Northampton where they released prisoners and redistributed excise (q.v.) money to the poor. A party from the army followed Thompson's men and they were caught near Wellingborough and in the ensuing fight Thompson was killed. Thompson was called captain at various times during the period but he was not a member of the army.

THURLOE, JOHN (1616–1668). Thurloe was educated at Lincolns Inn and worked for Oliver St John (q.v.). He served as M.P. for Ely and later Cambridge University in the Protectorate Parliaments (qq.v.) of 1654, 1656, and 1659. As a member of the Council of State (q.v.) and secretary of state, Thurloe assembled an excellent intelligence service that kept track of royalist (q.v.) plots and outwitted the Sealed Knot (q.v.) throughout the 1650s. At the Restoration (q.v.) Thurloe was accused of treason but imprisoned only briefly.

TIPPEMUIR, BATTLE OF. Fought on 1 September 1644. The marquis of Montrose's (q.v.) forces attacked the local Covenanter (q.v.) forces under Lord Lothian in this, the first pitched battle of Montrose's Scottish campaign. Montrose's Irish and Highland (q.v.) army made a rapid attack on Lothian's forces, which quickly broke the spirit of the Covenanters, who fled. The victorious royalists (q.v.) then took their revenge on their enemies and slaughtered many of them as they fled along the road to Perth.

TONBRIDGE, BATTLE OF. Fought on 23 July 1643. A small-scale fight that ended attempts by royalists (q.v.) to establish a foothold in the county of Kent when royalists were defeated by a parliamentarian (q.v.) force.

TORRINGTON, BATTLE OF. Fought on 16 February 1646. Ralph, Lord Hopton (q.v.) was called out of semi-retirement to take command of the Western royalists (q.v.) early in 1646. To try to take pressure of the royalists besieged in Exeter, Hopton moved his forces into the town of Torrington. Sir Thomas Fairfax (q.v.) and the New Model Army (q.v.) attacked Hopton and, after fierce fighting and the destruction of the town's church, which had been a magazine, the royalists were defeated and their cause in the west destroyed.

TRAINED BANDS. In the years before the Civil Wars, England and Wales had no standing armies. Instead, local part-time soldiers were organised on a county basis. These forces, called trained bands, comprised landholders drawn from each village and town within the shire. The Trained Bands were under the command of the lord lieutenants (q.v.) and trained by muster masters at regular sessions. Apart from the London Trained Bands, which fought in campaigns in the south of England, most of these levies proved unreliable during the early stages of the First Civil War (q.v.). Members of the bands held a variety of loyalties: royalist, parliamentarian (qq.v.), and localist. As a result, the trained bands often refused to serve either side.

TRIENNIAL ACTS. The first triennial act was passed in Scotland and provided for the calling of the Estates (q.v.) every three years whether or not the monarch willed it to be called. The second triennial act was passed in England in February 1641 and made the same form of provision for Parliament (q.v.). This latter act was accompanied by the Act against the Dissolution of Parliament (q.v.), which made it impossible for the monarch to dismiss the Long Parliament (q.v.). Both Triennial Acts were repealed at the Restoration (q.v.).

TRUE LEVELLERS. *See* DIGGERS.

TRUE LEVELLERS' STANDARD ADVANCED, THE. Perhaps the seminal tract of the Diggers (q.v.) or True Levellers, the *True Levellers' Standard Advanced* was written by Gerrard Winstanley and William Everard (qq.v.). The tract set out the principle by which the Diggers sought to have land held in common. It stated that God had given dominion over the animals to mankind, but not over other human beings. Men and women should only have wealth or an income derived from work they themselves had done. All this would be put into practise by the Diggers on St George's Hill and elsewhere so as to teach by example.

TUNNAGE AND POUNDAGE. A tax on wine and customs taxes traditionally allowed to the monarch by Parliament (q.v.) and granted for his or her lifetime. In 1625 Parliament decided to grant these taxes to Charles I (q.v.) only for a year at a time. In the wake of his difficult relationships with his early Parliaments, Charles I collected the taxes anyway.

TURNHAM GREEN, BATTLE OF. Fought on 13 November 1642. Following the Battle of Edgehill, Charles I (q.v.) and his army advanced on London via Oxford (q.v.). On 12 November his forces closed in on the capital and clashed at Brentford (q.v.) with sections of the earl of Essex's (q.v.) army, Lord Brooke's, Denzil Holles's, and John Hampden's (qq.v.) regiments in particular. On 13 November the king's army pushed on through the town towards London. Essex's army was by now supported by the London Trained Bands (q.v.) under Philip Skippon (q.v.) and armed Londoners, a total of 24,000. Alongside the armed forces were crowds of unarmed men and women with food and other supplies. The king arrived at Turnham Green with only 12,000 men and did not attack the massive forces ranged against him. Instead, for a day the two armies stood facing each other, until at nightfall the king withdrew towards Oxford. This was the closest Charles and his army got to London during the First Civil War (q.v.), and his retreat marked the point at which it was clear that the war would not be over quickly.

TWSYDEN, SIR ROGER (1597–1672). Sir Roger refused to pay ship money (q.v.) during the 1630s and opposed the levy during the Short Parliament (q.v.) of 1640. Twsyden's opposition was fairly mild, however, and as the Long Parliament (q.v.) pressed on with its dramatic reforms of government, he drifted to Charles I's (q.v.) side. In 1642 he was embroiled with Justice Malet's Kentish Petition (q.v.), which called for moderation and accommodation between Parliament (q.v.) and the king. For his part in this act Twsyden was arrested, then bailed, but arrested again on being caught attempting to leave the country. Twsyden's Kentish estates were placed under sequestration (q.v.) in 1643. During the 1650s he returned to his home estates and lived a scholarly life. At the Restoration (q.v.) he was made a deputy lieutenant but remained distant from the new regime.

TYLDESLEY, SIR THOMAS (1612–1651). Tyldesley was a Roman Catholic (q.v.) veteran of the wars in Europe and in 1642 raised regiments in Lancashire for Charles I (q.v.). He led these regiments at the Battle of Edgehill (q.v.). He became attached to the army of Queen Henrietta Maria (q.v.) in 1643 and stormed Burton on Trent in June that year. After service with the Oxford Field Army (q.v.), in 1643–44, Tyldesley was appointed governor of Lichfield (q.v.) after the death of Richard Bagot (q.v.), displacing Harvey Bagot. In the Second Civil War (q.v.) Tyldesley was involved in the fighting in the north-west and was captured at Appleby. A convinced royalist (q.v.), Tyldesley joined the earl of Derby's (q.v.) rising in 1651 but was killed at the Battle of Wigan Lane (q.v.).

U

ULSTER. One of the four provinces of Ireland and the last to undergo thorough colonisation. The Irish Rebellion (q.v.) broke out in the province on 22 October 1641, led by principal members of the Gaelic Irish.

ULSTER, ARMY OF. Forces raised in the province of Ulster (q.v.) by Sir Phelim O'Neill (q.v.) in 1641–42. From 1642 the army was commanded by Owen Roe O'Neill (q.v.), until 1649. The Bishop of Clogher took command after Owen Roe O'Neill's death. The army was destroyed at the Battle of Scarriffhollis (q.v.) in 1650.

UPTON ON SEVERN. On 2 September 1651, as the Republican army began to surround the royalist (q.v.) and Scottish armies at Worcester (q.v.), a skirmish broke out in the village of Upton. Royalist forces under Edward Massey (q.v.) attempted to hold the bridge across the Severn. Victory enabled Oliver Cromwell (q.v.) to cross to the west bank of the River Severn and encircle the city. Massey was captured in the fight.

URRY, SIR JOHN (?–1650). Born in Pitfichie in Aberdeenshire, Urry served in European wars before enlisting in the Covenanter Army (q.v.). In 1641 he was recruited by those plotting to overturn the leadership of the marquis of Argyll and the marquis of Hamilton (qq.v.), but he betrayed the plot, which became known as the "Incident" (q.v.). In 1642 he fought at the Battle of Edgehill (q.v.) for Parliament (q.v.), but in spring 1643 he deserted to Charles I (q.v.) and gave away the route of a supply convoy. Prince Rupert (q.v.) led an attack on the convoy, which resulted in the Battle of Chalgrove Field (q.v.) and the death of John Hampden (q.v.).

In 1644 Urry fought at the Battle of Marston Moor (q.v.) and was captured. He changed sides again and accompanied William Baillie (q.v.) to Scotland and campaigned against the earl of Montrose (q.v.). Urry's forces were defeated by Montrose at the Battle of Auldearn (q.v.). By the Second Civil War, Urry had changed sides again, and was then an Engager (q.v.) who was present at the Battle of Preston (q.v.). Urry escaped to Europe and in 1650 joined Montrose in his attempt to land royalist forces in north Scotland. Urry was captured at Carbisdale (q.v.) and executed at Edinburgh.

USSHER, JAMES. *See* ARMAGH, ARCHBISHOP OF.

UXBRIDGE, TREATY OF. Discussions were held between the representatives of King Charles I (q.v.) and those of the English and Welsh Parliament (q.v.) and the Scottish commissioners at Uxbridge in February 1645. The discussions concentrated on the reform of the church in England and Wales, the control of the armed forces, and the future of Ireland. Three days were set aside for each of these issues. The king had a few major successes in southern England, especially the Battle of Lostwithiel (q.v.) and his rescue of the garrison at Donnington (q.v.), and despite his complete loss of control in the north of England after the Battle of Marston Moor (q.v.), Charles was receiving promising news from the earl of Montrose (q.v.) in Scotland. This encouraged him in his obstinacy towards any notion of compromise on any issue. Parliament was placing its faith in the creation of a New Model Army (q.v.) and was in no mood for compromise either. Some of the parliamentarian (q.v.) commissioners at Uxbridge let it be known that they feared the extremists (meaning the Independents and the War Party [qq.v.] in Parliament) might gain control of the House of Commons (q.v.) if peace was not made at Uxbridge. The discussions failed to reach agreement on any of the main issues and on 22 February 1645 the talks ended.

∽ **V** ∽

VALENTINE, BENJAMIN (?–1652). In the House of Commons (q.v.) on 2 March 1629, Valentine was one of the M.P.s who held Speaker Sir John Finch (q.v.) in his chair whilst Sir John Eliot (q.v.) read a series of resolutions against Charles I's (q.v.) government. For this he was imprisoned for 11 years. He was only released by the Long Parliament (q.v.), of which he was elected a member.

VANE, SIR HENRY (1589–1655). Father of Sir Henry, the younger. He served as a member of the royal household and as a member of Charles I's (q.v.) government. In the Short Parliament (q.v.) he worked on the king's behalf although he was already estranged from elements of royal policy, most notably the Bishop's Wars (q.v.). In the trial against the earl of Strafford (q.v.), Vane gave evidence against the earl. Vane remained part of Charles I' Privy Council (q.v.) until November 1641, when he was dismissed from all of his posts. During the First Civil War (q.v.) Vane served on the Committee of Both Kingdoms (q.v.). He remained an active parliamentarian (q.v.) and was an M.P. in the 1654 Protectorate Parliament (qq.v.).

VANE, SIR HENRY (1613–1662). Son of Sir Henry Vane, the elder (q.v.), Vane served as governor of the Massachusetts colony in 1636–37 but returned to England in 1640 to be elected M.P. for Hull (q.v.) in both the Short Parliament and the Long Parliament (qq.v.). In 1641 he assisted in the trial of the earl of Strafford (q.v.) by using his father's Privy Council (q.v.) papers to suggest that Strafford intended to bring an Irish army to England to use against the king's enemies there. During the First Civil War (q.v.) Vane was influential in Parliament (q.v.) and was involved in the negotiations that brought about the Solemn League and Covenant (q.v.) and was involved in the Treaty of Uxbridge (q.v.); although he was not himself a Presbyterian (q.v.) he favoured toleration. He served as secretary to the navy from 1642 until 1650. Vane did not become involved with the trial of Charles I, but he did serve in Commonwealth and Protectorate (qq.v.) Parliaments. Vane was also the author of several religious tracts. It was Vane who was at the centre of the crisis that brought about the end of the Protectorate of Richard Cromwell (q.v.). He was executed at the Restoration (q.v.).

VENNER, THOMAS (?–1661). A cooper who had spent some time in Massachusetts, by the 1650s Venner was a London-based Fifth Monarchist (q.v.). In order to bring about the millennium, Venner was to have led a rising in 1657 but was captured before it began and imprisoned until 1659. In January 1661 Venner's church sought again to bring about the millennium, and on 6 January seized St Paul's Cathedral. After several days of fighting against the London Trained Bands (q.v.), Venner was captured and later executed. The rising provided a pretext for the arrest of many dissenters, especially Quakers (q.v.), by the government.

VERNEY, SIR EDMUND (1590–1642). Verney accompanied the future Charles I (q.v.) to Spain in 1623 in pursuit of a Spanish marriage. Verney served in the Parliament (q.v.) at Westminster in the 1620s and again in the Short and Long Parliaments (qq.v.), where he began to oppose some of the practices of the Personal Rule (q.v.). When the First Civil War (q.v.) began, however, Verney declared himself loyal to the king and enlisted. He was killed at the Battle of Edgehill (q.v.) in 1642 whilst carrying the royal standard.

VERNEY, SIR EDMUND (1616–1649). Son of the elder Sir Edmund Verney (q.v.), Sir Edmund served in the English and Welsh Army in the Bishop's Wars (q.v.), and then in Ireland after the Irish Rebellion (q.v.). In 1644, having returned to England, he was knighted and served in Chester before going into exile on the continent. In 1649 he went into service in Ireland with the marquis of Ormond (q.v.). He was killed at Drogheda (q.v.) in September of that year.

VERNEY, SIR RALPH (1613–1696). Son of the elder Sir Edmund Verney (q.v.), Ralph Verney served in the Parliament (q.v.) at Westminster in the early stages of the First Civil War (q.v.) but withdrew abroad after the signing of the Solemn League and Covenant (q.v.). He returned to England in 1653, but was suspected of being actively opposed to the Protectorate (q.v.) and was imprisoned in 1655. Verney returned to a parliamentary career in 1680, having being knighted after the Restoration (q.v.).

VICARS, JOHN (1580–1652). A Presbyterian (q.v.) author who sought to demonstrate that the parliamentarian (q.v.) victory in the First Civil War (q.v.) was due to the will of God. He wrote pamphlets to that end entitled *Jehovah Jireh* in 1644 and *Gods Arke* in 1646.

VOTE OF NO ADDRESSES. Following the escape of Charles I (q.v.) from Hampton Court (q.v.) in November 1647, there was increasing pressure to end any further negotiations with him. He had already rejected the Newcastle Propositions and the Heads of the Proposals (q.v.). Unbeknownst to Parliament (q.v.), the king had signed the Engagement (q.v.) with Scottish commissioners. On 3 January 1648, by 191 votes to 41, Parliament passed a bill ending negotiations and the Lords (q.v.), having heard of the Engagement, joined in. Nevertheless, the Four Bills (q.v.) were presented to the king during the Second Civil War (q.v.) and in August the Vote of No Addresses was rescinded to prepared the way for the Treaty of Newport (q.v.).

☙ W ☙

WAKEFIELD, BATTLE OF. Fought on 21 May 1643. A brief, desperate battle in which the town was surprised and captured by Sir Thomas Fairfax's (q.v.) West Yorkshire Parliamentarians (q.v.). George, Lord Goring (q.v.), the commander of the Northern Army (q.v.) Horse (q.v.), was captured.

WALLER, SIR EDMUND (1606–1687). Waller was a poet and an M.P. throughout the 1620s and again in the Long Parliament (q.v.). He opposed the developing radicalism of the Parliament (q.v.) but remained a member of it until 1643. He was appointed to be a commissioner at the Treaty of Oxford (q.v.) at which time he became embroiled in a plot to raise royalist (q.v.) forces in London. He betrayed his fellow plotters, but was imprisoned in the Tower of London and then banished.

Oliver Cromwell (q.v.) sought Waller's pardon in 1651, which allowed him to return to England. He served in the government and wrote verses supporting the Protectorate (q.v.). In 1660, however, he turned his poetic talents to the service of the Restoration (q.v.) and resumed his career as an M.P. in 1661 and continued to sit in the House of Commons (q.v.) until his death.

WALLER, SIR HARDRESS (1604–1666). A settler in Ireland with estates at Castletown, County Limerick, Waller took service with the English forces during the Irish Rebellion (q.v.). In 1644 he was governor of Cork but went to England in 1645 and became a colonel in the New Model Army (q.v.). In 1649 Waller served on the High Court of Justice (q.v.) and signed Charles I's (q.v.) death warrant. During 1650–51 Waller served in Ireland, for which he received more estates in Limerick (q.v.). At the Restoration (q.v.), Waller was tried as a regicide (q.v.) and imprisoned for the rest of his life.

WALLER, SIR WILLIAM (?1597–1668). Waller was a friend of Ralph (later Lord) Hopton (q.v.) and they fought together in Europe as part of Queen Elizabeth of Bohemia's army at the Battle of the White Mountain. Waller, however, took the side of Parliament (q.v.), in which he was M.P. for Andover, in the First Civil War (q.v.), whilst his erstwhile friend became a royalist (q.v.). Waller quickly achieved a series of victories against the royalist forces in the south of England, capturing Portsmouth, Winchester, Arundel, and Chichester, earning for himself the name "William the Conqueror."

In 1643 he turned his attention to the southern Marches (q.v.), capturing Hereford and defeating royalist forces at the Battle of Highnam (q.v.). At the Battle of Ripple Field (q.v.), however, Prince Maurice (q.v.) defeated Waller's army. In the south-west, fighting his old friend Hopton, Waller seemed to return to form, defeating the royalists at the Battle of Lansdown (q.v.). This victory was quickly followed by the disaster at the Battle of Roundway Down (q.v.), however. Waller then had to raise a new army in London, with which he defeated the royalist attempt to take control of the southern approaches to London in the fall of 1643 and spring of 1644. Waller defeated Hopton and Lord Forth (q.v.) at the Battle of Cheriton (q.v.) in March 1644.

In the summer, Waller and his rival, the earl of Essex (q.v.), joined in a campaign to put pressure on Oxford (q.v.), but when King Charles I (q.v.) broke out of the city, Waller followed him whilst Essex set off into the south-west. As Waller pursued the king across the Midlands, Charles turned on him at Cropredy Bridge (q.v.) and defeated him. Once again Waller's army was destroyed.

Having raised yet another force, Waller was involved in the second Battle of Newbury (q.v.). After the subsequent inquiry, the Self Denying Ordinance (q.v.) deprived Waller of his command. Waller now became a leader of the Presbyterians (q.v.) in the House of Commons (q.v.). In 1647 Waller was involved in the attempts to raise forces for Ireland and thereby identified as an enemy of the New Model Army (q.v.). As the army advanced on London, Waller and others, identified as the Eleven Members (q.v.), left the House. Waller went abroad, but returned in 1648. He was excluded from Parliament and arrested at Pride's Purge (q.v.). Waller remained in prison for three years. In 1658 he was again arrested, but released after being interviewed by Oliver Cromwell (q.v.). Waller was allowed into the Parliament.

WALLER'S PLOT. The plot was named after Sir Edmund Waller (q.v.), who became embroiled in the plot in early 1643 whilst a commissioner at the Treaty of Oxford (q.v.). The plan was to proclaim a Commission of Array (q.v.) in London, but it was betrayed by Waller's Presbyterian (q.v.) sister. To save his own life, Waller gave away the names of the other principal figures.

WALWYN, WILLIAM. A principal Leveller (q.v.) and silk trader of London, Walwyn was an advocate of religious toleration and responded to Thomas Edward's *Gangraena* (qq.v.). Walwyn favoured the abolition of tithes, a subject about which he wrote in *The Ordinance for Tithes Discounted*. In 1646 Walwyn worked with Richard Overton (q.v.) on drafting *A Remonstrance of Many Thousand Citizens*. Walwyn was also responsible for the Large Petition (q.v.) in 1647. He was also involved in drafting the *Agreement of the People* (q.v.). In 1649 he was arrested with other Leveller leaders, arrests that prompted the Petition of Women (q.v.). Walwyn wrote numerous tracts arguing for his release. He was released from prison at the end of the year and then disappeared into obscurity.

WAR PARTY. As Parliament (q.v.) fragmented into factions, two major groups, a War Party and a Peace Party (q.v.) were formed, although neither really constituted a political party. The War Party was concerned with winning the war so as to open negotiations with King Charles I (q.v.) from a position of strength. In order to achieve this the Party was at first supportive of the Scots' involvement in the war and getting rid of the earl of Essex (q.v.). Oliver Cromwell (q.v.) was associated with this group, but, demonstrating the fragility of the term "party," opposed the involvement of the Scots.

WARDS, COURT OF. A court derived from a mediaeval prerogative court that administered the estates of tenants in chief passed into royal hands whilst held by a minor. The court usually sold off the guardianship of the landholder and the administration for ready money. Relatives were favoured purchasers. The system was open to abuse, however, as the estates of the minor could be exploited by the appointed guardian. In 1640 Parliament (q.v.) professed an interest in abolishing the court as it was perceived as having been abused by Charles I (q.v.) as a source of income during the Personal Rule (q.v.). The appointment of Lord Saye and Sele (q.v.) as master of the court in 1641 and the onset of war saved it until 1646, however.

WARE, MUTINY. *See* CORKBUSH FIELD.

WARRINGTON. *See* WINWICK, BATTLE OF.

WARWICK, ROBERT RICH, EARL OF (1587–1658). Warwick became alienated from court politics during the reign of Charles I (q.v.), refusing to pay the forced loan (q.v.) of 1626 or ship money (q.v.) in the 1630s. Warwick was heavily involved in establishing colonial settlements in Massachusetts and Connecticut. In 1642 he was appointed commander of the English and Welsh fleet by Parliament (q.v.). He also held an appointment as head of a committee examining the government of the colonies, however, and became involved in establishing the Rhode Island Colony in 1645. He was able to reorganise the parliamentarian navy (qq.v.) after a large part of it deserted to the royalists (q.v.) in the Second Civil War (q.v.). Although his grandson Robert married Oliver Cromwell's (q.v.) daughter, Warwick remained aloof from government in the 1650s.

WARWICK, SIR PHILIP (1609–1683). Warwick served as secretary to Lord Treasurer Juxon (q.v.) during the 1630s and sat in the Long Parliament (q.v.) for Radnor. He opposed the Bill of Attainder (q.v.) enacted on the earl of Strafford (q.v.). He remained a member of the house until 1644, when he went to sit in the Oxford Parliament (q.v.). Warwick became Charles I's (q.v.) secretary in 1646 during the king's captivity. In 1649 he compounded (q.v.) for his estate. In 1655, in the aftermath of Penruddock's (q.v.) Rising, Warwick was arrested. At the Restoration (q.v.) Warwick was knighted and took up his Parliamentary career again. He worked in the Treasury with the earl of Southampton during the 1660s.

WATERFORD. One of the major ports of the Catholic Confederation of Kilkenny (q.v.) from which Protestants were expelled in 1642. The port was significant for trade and communications with Catholic (q.v.) powers in Europe. In 1649 the port was in the hands of the alliance between the Confederation and the marquis of Ormond (q.v.). After Oliver Cromwell and the New Model Army (qq.v.) had stormed Wexford (q.v.), Waterford braced itself for a siege. The port held out until August 1650, when it surrendered to Henry Ireton (q.v.).

WEEKLY ASSESSMENT. This levy formed the main parliamentarian (q.v.) levy from late 1642 until it was replaced by the monthly tax (q.v.) in early 1645. The money was collected throughout the areas of England and Wales controlled by Parliament (q.v.) from anyone who rented property and had beasts on the village or town pastures. The rate of the levies was based on proportional assessments (q.v.) used to collect ship money (q.v.), although the amounts were higher and could be collected in the form of cash and supplies. Weekly assessment levies were similar to the levies of contribution collected by royalists (qq.v.).

WENTWORTH, THOMAS, VISCOUNT. *See* STRAFFORD, EARL OF.

WESTMINSTER. Adjacent to London, Westminster was the seat of government in England, where both the Palace of Westminster, where Parliament (q.v.) met, and the Palace of Whitehall, where the monarch lived, were situated.

WESTMINSTER ASSEMBLY OF DIVINES. Established in July 1643 to debate the future of the Protestant church in England and Wales, the Assembly was supposed to embrace all facets of the Protestant faith in the countries. The vast majority of Episcopalians stayed away from the

Assembly, however, and left it to be dominated by English Presbyterians (q.v.). The Presbyterian dominance was enhanced after the Solemn League and Covenant (q.v.), when Scottish representatives, including Robert Baillie (q.v.), attended. In January 1645 the assembly's liturgy, the *Directory of Public Worship* (q.v.), was published by Parliament (q.v.), establishing a basis for Presbyterian worship in England and Wales. The Assembly won few supporters outside of the English Presbyterians; the Independents (q.v.) disliked its advocacy of Presbyterian worship and the Scots regarded it as weak and ineffectual.

WEXFORD. An important asset to the Catholic Confederation of Kilkenny (q.v.), the port of Wexford, like Waterford (q.v.), was important for communications with Roman Catholic (q.v.) Europe. In 1649 the port was held by an English garrison as part of the confederation's alliance with the marquis of Ormond (q.v.) and was a base for royalist (q.v.) ships attacking English and Welsh vessels. On 12 October Oliver Cromwell and the New Model Army (qq.v.) stormed the town. The initial storm was followed by slaughter inside the town, not only of the garrison but also of civilians; as many as 300 were killed on boats in the harbour that were sunk as they tried to escape.

WHALLEY, BATTLE OF. Fought on 20 April 1643, this battle refers to two related skirmishes in Lancashire between the forces of the earl of Derby (q.v.) and his parliamentarian (q.v.) enemies. In an attempt to defeat a newly raised parliamentarian force, Derby attacked Ralph Assheton, M.P. at Whalley Abbey. His advance party was stopped by musket fire and driven back. As the royalists (q.v.) retreated, local people joined with Assheton's men and advanced on Derby's main body, which ran. This spelled the end of Derby's attempt to hold the county and the royalist presence diminished, leaving only Lathom House (q.v.) as a significant, but isolated, royalist stronghold. Derby himself crossed the Pennines to Yorkshire in a vain attempt to gain aid, and then left for the Isle of Man to secure his hold on the island. His wife Charlotte, Countess of Derby (q.v.), was left in command at Lathom.

WHEELLOCK. A name appended to small arms (usually pistols [q.v.]) in which the charge is ignited by lowering a flint into contact with a spinning rough-surfaced wheel. This action created a spark, which ignited the charge. The wheel was powered by a clockwork and had to be wound with a spanner, making it slow to prepare. As the mechanism was expensive and had no need of a lighted match, it was carried by Horse (q.v.) troopers and officers.

WHIGGAMORE RAID. The defeat of the Engagers (q.v.) at the Battle of Preston (q.v.) in 1648 was greeted with joy by more radical Covenanters (q.v.) in Scotland who had not approved of the Engagement (q.v.) with Charles I (q.v.). A popular rising against the Engagers broke out in southwest Scotland, and the marquis of Argyll and Lord Leven (qq.v.) led attempts to overthrow the Engager government. Although both armed attempts were defeated, the Engagers' success was short lived as Oliver Cromwell (q.v.) and his section of the New Model Army (q.v.) approached Scotland. Cromwell enabled Argyll to form a new government excluding the Engagers, who had sided with the king.

WHITECOATS. Nickname given to the earl of Newcastle's (q.v.) regiment of Foot (q.v.), which from the outset of the First Civil War (q.v.) was issued undyed white cloth for its uniforms.

WHITELOCKE, BULSTRODE (1605–1675). A diarist whose record of the Civil War period is a valuable source for historians. Whitelocke was an M.P. in the 1620s as well as in the Long Parliament (q.v.). In 1648 he was appointed one of three commissioners of the Great Seal, and asked to consider the nature of King Charles I's (q.v.) trial. He declined to take part in the trial, but served on the Council of State (q.v.) during the Commonwealth (q.v.). He served as an ambassador to Sweden during 1653–54 and as an M.P. in Protectorate Parliaments (q.v.). Whitelocke urged Oliver Cromwell (q.v.) to accept the title of king in 1657. After the fall of Richard Cromwell (q.v.), Whitelocke served as president of the Council of State. At the Restoration (q.v.) Whitelocke was left unmolested.

WIGAN LANE, BATTLE OF. Fought on 25 August 1651. As Charles II (q.v.) marched his Anglo-Scottish Army south through western England, the earl of Derby (q.v.) raised men in Lancashire and on the Isle of Man to support his cause. As Charles fortified himself in Worcester (q.v.), Derby began marching his forces southwards in the king's wake. At Wigan Lane, between Wigan and Warrington (q.v.), Derby was ambushed and defeated. In the wake of the battle, Derby was captured and later executed.

WILDMAN, JOHN (1621–1693). Wildman served in the New Model Army (q.v.). At the Putney Debates (q.v.) in October and November 1647 Wildman was prominent amongst the Agitators (q.v.) present. His radicalism led to imprisonment in 1648, but by 1649 he was serving in Ireland. He was arrested again during the Protectorate (q.v.) for plotting against the government. During the Restoration (q.v.) years, he worked with opponents of Charles II (q.v.) and James, Duke of York. He was knighted in 1692 by William III.

WILLIAMS, JOHN. *See* YORK, ARCHBISHOP OF.

WILLYS, SIR RICHARD (1614–1690). A Cambridgeshireman with European military experience, Willys entered King Charles I's (q.v.) service during the Bishop's Wars (q.v.). At the Battle of Edgehill (q.v.) he was a major in Lord Grandison's Horse (q.v.). In 1643 he was major general (q.v.) in Lord Capel's (q.v.) army. He was captured in fighting in Cheshire in January 1644. He was exchanged later that year and was appointed governor of Newark (q.v.) after Sir Richard Byron's (q.v.) defeat at Denton. After Prince Rupert (q.v.) had surrendered Bristol (q.v.) and forced the king to grant him a court-martial at Newark, the king dismissed Willys from his post, as he saw him as one of Rupert's protégés.

Willys went into exile and stayed out of the country until 1652, by which time he was a member of the Sealed Knot (q.v.), the secret royalist (q.v.) organisation aimed at restoring the monarchy. It would seem that Willys also cooperated with the Protectorate (q.v.), however; he certainly played a double game and was often accused of being half-hearted towards the prospect of a royalist rising. At the Restoration (q.v.) Willys went into obscurity, living on his Cambridgeshire estates until 1690.

WILMOT, HENRY, LORD (?1612–1658). Wilmot served in the Dutch forces during the 1630s but had returned to England by the second Bishop's War (q.v.), when he served as commissary-general for the Horse (q.v.). He sat as an M.P. in the Long Parliament (q.v.), but was expelled for involvement with the Army Plot (q.v.). During the First Civil War (q.v.), Wilmot served with the Oxford Field Army (q.v.) and was ennobled in 1643. During the 1644 campaign in the south-west of England, when he was lieutenant general in command of the Horse, Wilmot made overtures towards the earl of Essex (q.v.). Wilmot seems to have been convinced that the war was futile and ruinous and suggested that he and Essex unite and force peace on both Charles I and Parliament (qq.v.). Essex rejected the suggestion, and the king had Wilmot arrested. At this, the royalist (q.v.) Horse regiments protested, and the king allowed them to petition Essex for an end to the war. This came to naught. Wilmot went into exile and was replaced by George, Lord Goring (q.v.).

In 1650 Wilmot, who had served Charles II (q.v.) since the previous year, went into Scotland with the king. After the Battle of Worcester (q.v.), Wilmot accompanied the king in his escape from England. In 1652 he was created earl of Rochester and worked with secret royalist organisations until his death.

WINCEBY, BATTLE OF. Fought on 11 October 1643. Following the Battle of Horncastle, the earl of Manchester's (q.v.) army pressed on towards Old Bolingbroke in Lincolnshire. At Winceby, Manchester's Horse (q.v.), under Oliver Cromwell (q.v.), came across a force of royalists (q.v.). Cromwell, and Sir Thomas Fairfax (q.v.) with his Yorkshire Horse, attacked and quickly routed the royalist before Manchester's Foot (q.v.) had even reached the field. The defeat prompted the earl of Newcastle (q.v.) to bring his forces down into Lincolnshire to redress the situation.

WINCHESTER, SIR JOHN PAULET, MARQUIS OF (1598–1675). A Roman Catholic (q.v.) and close friend of Queen Henrietta Maria (q.v.), Winchester was one of the richest men in England. Much of his money was directed to the royalist (q.v.) cause during the First Civil War (q.v.). His principal seat, Basing House (q.v.), was a royalist garrison until it was stormed by Oliver Cromwell (q.v.) in 1645. Winchester was held in the Tower for many years, and although he regained his estates at the Restoration (q.v.), he never received financial recompense in full.

WINDEBANK, SIR FRANCIS (1582–1646). A secretary of state in Charles I's Personal Rule (qq.v.), Windebank was associated with secret negotiations with Roman Catholic (q.v.) powers in Europe. Windebank was an M.P. in both the Short Parliament and the Long Parliament (qq.v.). He was held under suspicion because of his religion and his political dealings, and in December 1640 he fled the country at the same time as John, Lord Finch (q.v.).

WINSTANLEY, GERRARD (?1609–?). Winstanley emerged in March 1649 as a principal figure at the St George's Hill Digger (q.v.) colony. Winstanley was the author, with William Everard (q.v.), of *The True Leveller's Standard Advanced* (q.v.), which set forth the Digger position. He was also the author of poetry and songs on Digger themes, including *The Digger's Mirth*. Winstanley derived his egalitarian ideas from the Bible, suggesting that the rural communal life he advocated was how Eden would have been if not for the Fall from Grace. Winstanley believed that in a society free from property ownership there would be no need for lawyers or magistrates, as most litigation concerned property disputes. Once the colonies disappeared, Winstanley moved in religious sects, and was possibly a founding influence on the Quakers (q.v.).

WINWICK, BATTLE OF. Fought on 19 August 1648. As the Engager (q.v.) army fled southwards after the Battle of Preston (q.v.), they were pursued by a section of the New Model Army (q.v.). As the main Engager force made it to Warrington, a small detachment defended the rear at Winwick. This limited force held Oliver Cromwell (q.v.) back for several hours before being driven back on Warrington. Attempts to hold the Mersey Bridges at Warrington failed when large numbers of the soldiers surrendered to the New Model Army.

WORCESTER. Worcester was the site of one of the earliest conflicts of the First Civil War (q.v.) when the Battle of Powick Bridge (q.v.) was fought just south of the city. Thereafter the city was occupied, first, by the parliamentarian (q.v.) forces, but for most of the war the city remained a royalist (q.v.) garrison until 23 July 1646. On 22 August 1651, Charles II (q.v.) and his Scottish army arrived in the town and were quickly besieged by Oliver Cromwell (q.v.). Some of the earliest fighting at the Battle of Worcester on 3 September occurred at Powick Bridge and the Republic's (q.v.) army forced their way across the River Teme. Cromwell attacked from the south and east of the city, and as he did so the two wings of his army, on opposite banks of the Severn, became separated. Charles saw this split develop and launched an attack. He and the second Duke of Hamilton (q.v.) tried to drive a wedge between the two Parliamentarian wings and managed briefly to do so. Cromwell had to leave his command on the left and recross the River Severn with his own regiment of Horse (q.v.). He gathered the remains of the right wing and launched a counterattack. This attack succeeded in driving the royalists from their positions and back into the city. Panic spread through the royalist forces as the defeated Horse crowded back into the city. As Charles Fleetwood (q.v.) led forces across the meadows to cut off a royalist retreat towards Wales, Charles made his escape from the city with sections of the Horse, leaving the Foot (q.v.) to surrender in the town. Cromwell called the Battle of Worcester the "crowning mercy" and English observers declared that the war had begun and ended at Worcester.

WORCESTER, HENRY SOMERSET, MARQUIS OF (1577–1646). Perhaps the richest man in England and Wales. He was suspected of being at the centre of Roman Catholic (q.v.) plots in Wales during the early 1640s. He put much of his fortune at King Charles I's (q.v.) disposal during the First Civil War (q.v.). For this and the fortification of his castle at Raglan, he was created a marquis in 1643. He was captured at Raglan when the garrison surrendered in 1646. He died in captivity in London.

WORTLEY, SIR FRANCIS (1592–1652). A Yorkshireman who drew his sword in public at York (q.v.) swearing to defend King Charles I (q.v.), Wortley kept up his brash behaviour by being the first man to raise Horse (q.v.) for the royalist (q.v.) cause. He led his forces southwards in late 1642 and came into conflict with Sir John Gell (q.v.) in Derbyshire and then the Moorlanders in Staffordshire en route. Wortley was captured in 1644 and remained in prison until his death.

WORTLEY, FRANCIS (1620–1665). Son of Sir Francis Wortley (q.v.), Wortley raised a regiment of dragoons (q.v.), which served in Henry Hastings's (q.v.) army in 1643. Wortley was fined at the end of the First Civil War (q.v.), but was still active as a royalist (q.v.) conspirator in the 1650s.

↩ Y ↪

Y DALAR HIR, BATTLE OF. Fought on 5 June 1648. Sir John Owen (q.v.) led the North Wales royalists (q.v.) in the Second Civil War (q.v.) and stood against some of the prominent parliamentarians (q.v.) who had fought in the region during the First Civil War (q.v.). His attempt to take on one of these, Sir Thomas Myddleton (q.v.), resulted in the Battle at Y Dalar Hir in Caernarfonshire. Owen's men were defeated. Although it is probable that fewer than 500 men were involved, the battle effectively ended the royalist attempt to raise the north of the country against Parliament (q.v.).

YORK. Second city in England, York became the headquarters of King Charles I's (q.v.) government after he had left London in January 1642. Charles established himself in the King's Manor, seat of the Council of the North. From here the king launched his attacks on Hull (q.v.) in the spring and summer of that year. His attempts to rally support at nearby Heworth Moor on 3 June failed because a large contingent of opponents led by Lord Fairfax and his son Sir Thomas Fairfax (qq.v.) presented a petition calling for peace.

After the king's departure from York in August 1642, the city became the headquarters of the local royalists (q.v.), and after the earl of Newcastle (q.v.) had taken command in the north, the city became a regional capital. At the end of April 1644 the city was besieged by the Army of the Solemn League and Covenant (q.v.) and the Fairfaxes' forces. In May these two armies were joined by the earl of Manchester and the Eastern Association Army (qq.v.). The siege lasted 11 weeks until Prince Rupert (q.v.) relieved the city on 1 July. Following Prince Rupert's defeat at the Battle of Marston Moor (q.v.) the next day, however, the city fell under siege again and surrendered on 17 July. Thereafter, York became the headquarters of Lord Fairfax and of the Northern Association (q.v.).

YORK, JOHN WILLIAMS, ARCHBISHOP OF (1582–1650). Williams, whilst Bishop of Lincoln, opposed some the activities of Archbishop William Laud (q.v.) and was imprisoned from 1637 to 1640. When released, he chaired the Long Parliament's (q.v.) committee investigating innovations in the church. In 1641 he was appointed Archbishop of York by Charles I (q.v.), probably as a conciliatory measure. He was of little material aid to the Yorkshire royalists (q.v.) in 1642, instead moving to his native North Wales to fortify Conwy for the king. By 1645, after the Battle of Montgomery (q.v.) had convinced him that the royalist side was losing the war, Williams negotiated a local cessation. Sir John Owen (q.v.) repudiated the treaty and took over Conwy.

YOUGHAL. An important port on the south Cork coast, Youghal was occupied from the beginning of the Irish Rebellion (q.v.) by Protestant forces. On 26 July 1644, Lord Broghill (q.v.) ordered all Roman Catholics (q.v.) living in the town to leave. The town was part of Lord Inchiquin's (q.v.) territory when he sided with the English Parliament (q.v.) that year, and it also went over to the alliance of the marquis of Ormond and the Catholic Confederation of Kilkenny (qq.v.) with Inchiquin in 1648. The town was surrendered to Oliver Cromwell's (q.v.) army in 1649 after the siege of Wexford (q.v.).

Bibliography

Introduction

The Civil War and Republican period in the history of the four nations of the British Isles is one of the most vibrant periods of study. It has lent itself to many radical and conservative forms of interpretation over the past 350 years. As a result, the terminology used to describe the period has changed many times. In part this is reflected in the titles of the articles and books listed here. The reader will be confronted with a catalogue of terms that include: the Civil War, the Great Rebellion, the English Civil War, the British Civil Wars, the English Revolution, and so on. The naming of the period following the Civil Wars themselves is likewise problematic. There is the English Republic, the British Republic, the Commonwealth, and the Protectorate to contend with.

This problem with naming began right away. Whereas "civil war" was reasonably apolitical, the changes of fortune in the immediate decades made other names problematic. Contemporaries used terms like "rebellion" after the Restoration to suggest that the events of 1637–1660 were something of an aberration from the normal pattern of a monarchical state. Indeed, the Republic was ignored by the monarchy itself, which commenced the dating of Charles II's reign from the moment of his father's death on the scaffold, 30 January 1649. Later, however, the gap between Charles I's death and the return of Charles II in May 1660 was recognised by the use of the term "interregnum." Again, this is a term that could only be applied after the Restoration. The term "revolution" came into common usage in the nineteenth century to describe the dramatic impulse to the period provided by the Puritan movement. Revolution subsequently became associated with the Marxist approach, which identified the period as one in which the vestiges of a feudal–monarchical state were overturned by a modern state open to the influence and control of the capitalist wealth producers hitherto largely excluded from access to power. This approach has been considerably developed within the last quarter of the twentieth century in response to serious challenges that sought to present the period as a "hiccough" with neither long-term causes nor little deep or lasting effect. For an examination of the changing contexts of these debates, consult R. C. Richardson's *The Debate on the English Revolution* (London: Routledge, 1988). This text does not fully address the newly explored implications that gender had on the period.

It is a difficult task to break down a bibliography for this period and the categories that follow are in no way definitive, nor are they wholly suitable. The diversities of approach that have been incorporated within single texts have resulted in contentious categorisation. Thus, it is possible to argue that the works cited in section V.A of the bibliography by Andrew Coleby or Stephen Roberts are less about the particular regions they explore than about the national implications of the revolution. Similarly, whilst J. P. Kenyon's *The Civil Wars of England* may appear to be a text on the military wars, it is far more broad-ranging than a true military history might be, although its inclusion in section III remains contentious. Similarly, a good case could be made for including John Morrill's *Revolt of the Provinces* in section V, but it remains in section II, as it includes evidence from several areas in both England and Wales.

Section I comprises a collection of varied and useful primary sources for examining the period in the words of those who lived through it. There are official documents such as the *Journals of the House of Commons* and the *Calendar of State Papers Domestic*, and the papers of individuals from many walks of life—M.P.s and ministers of the church included. Section II serves a dual purpose. It includes texts that provide background material for anyone approaching the period for the first time and who is in need of context. It also provides material that will explain the context of issues raised in later sections. Therefore, if reading from later sections raises questions about the nature of, say, Scottish Highland culture, then works dealing with this in a general and a specific way can be found in section II. Section III offers a comprehensive grouping reflecting the intermingling of religious, political, and some military issues in the Civil War and Republican period, and will provide the bulk of reading material. Section IV caters more specifically to those with an interest in the general military history of the period, although some of these texts extend beyond purely military issues. It will also be necessary to approach this section in conjunction with section V, which also contains articles and books on military matters as they reflect local issues. Section V demonstrates the importance of local studies in this period. Readers who have used Anthony Fletcher's *The Outbreak of the English Civil War* (section III) will have been made aware of this fact. Readers will also notice that this field of study is more developed with regard to England than elsewhere. The splendid History and Society series produced by Geography Publications is making inroads to offset this state of affairs for Ireland, but the lack of local approaches to Scottish history in the period is much regretted. The same is true of the lack of modern studies of Wales's local history.

Those who wish to begin reading the history of the period for the first time can find introductory texts in most sections of the bibliography. For the history of the four nations, the best starting points are those texts that most provide a complete general context, such as Hugh Kearney's *The British Isles: A History of Four Nations*. There are several books that can then be used to explore the immediate context; in themselves they are good guides to further reading, such as G. Jenkins's *The Foundations of Modern Wales* or Nicholas Canny's *From Reformation to Restoration: Ireland, 1534–1660*. The first chapter of David Stevenson's *Highland Warrior* makes an excellent introduction to Scottish culture and society. There are many books providing a way into the Civil Wars themselves, including Martyn Bennett's *The Civil Wars 1637–1653* and *The English Civil War 1640–1649* or Peter Gaunt's *The British Wars*. Progress can then be made through Ann Hughes's *The Causes of the English Civil War*, and so on. For a still-challenging examination of the radical consequences of the wars, the reader will still find interest in Christopher Hill's *The World Turned Upside Down*, although a fascinating later perspective can be found in Brian Manning's *1649 Crisis of the Revolution*.

The military history of the wars can be followed through a variety of accessible texts in sections IV and V, such as J. P. Kenyon's *The Civil Wars of England*, David Stevenson's *Highland Warrior*, David Scott's essay on the wars in Ireland in Jane Ohlmeyer's *Ireland From Independence to Occupation*, and Norman Tucker's *North Wales in the Civil War*. These lead on towards examining the war in particular areas through the texts in section V. Section I contains many valuable sources for examining the wars and revolution through contemporary papers, but it is recommended that these be explored after becoming familiar with the general secondary texts. One way of exploring what some contemporaries thought of the wars could be through Charles Carlton's *Going to the Wars: The Experience of the British Civil Wars, 1638–1651*, which cites many contemporary accounts.

The bibliography is organized as follows:

I. Printed Primary Sources for the Period 1637–1660

II. General Background Texts: The Histories of the Four Nations

III. Political and Religious Histories of the Civil War and the Republican Period

I. Printed Primary Sources for the Period 1637–1660

Ashburnham, John. *A Narrative of His Attendance on King Charles*. London: Payne and Foss, 1830.

Ashcroft, M. Y., ed. *Scarborough Records, 1600–1640*. Northallerton: North Yorkshire Record Office, 1991.

———, ed. *Scarborough Records, 1641–60*. Northallerton: North Yorkshire Record Office, 1991.

Baillie, Robert (ed. D. Laing). *The Letters and Journals of Robert Baillie, A.M. 1637–1662*, 3 vols. Edinburgh: Bannatyne Club, 1841–42.

Baker, W. T., ed. *Records of the Borough of Nottingham 1625–1702*. Nottingham: Nottingham Corporation, 1900.

Baxter, Richard (ed. N. H. Keeble). *The Autobiography of Richard Baxter*. London: Dent, 1974, 1985.

Bennett, Martyn, ed. *A Nottinghamshire Village in War and Peace: The Accounts of the Constables of Upton 1640–60*. Nottingham: Thoroton Society, 1995.

Birch, John (eds. J. and T. W. Webb). *Military Memoirs of Colonel John Birch*. London: Camden Society, 1873.

Bond, S. M., ed. *The Chamber Order Book of Worcester, 1602–1650*. Worcester: Worcestershire Historical Society, 1974.

Bonsey, C., and J. G. Jenkins, eds. *Ship Money Papers and Richard Greville's Notebook*. Buckingham: Buckinghamshire Record Society, 1965.

Calendar of State Papers: Domestic, Charles I. Liechtenstein: Kraus Reprint, 1967.

Calendar of State Papers Relating to Ireland in the Reign of Charles I, 1633–47. London: HMSO, 1901.

Calendar of State Papers Relating to Ireland in the Reign of Charles I, 1647–60. London: HMSO, 1903.

Calendar of Wynn of Gwydir Papers, 1515–1690. Aberystwyth: National Library of Wales, 1926.

Caulfield, R., ed. *The Council Book of the Corporation of Youghal*. Guilford: n.p., 1878.

Charles, B. J., ed. *Calendar of the Records of the Borough of Haverfordwest, 1539–1660*. Cardiff: University of Wales Press, 1967.

Clanricarde, Earl of (ed. J. Lowe). *Letter-Book of the Earl of Clanricarde 1642–47*. Dublin: Irish Manuscripts Commission, 1983.

Clarendon, Earl of (ed. W. H. Mackay). *The History of the Rebellion and Civil Wars in England*. Oxford: Clarendon Press, 1888.

Coates, W. H., A. S. Young, and V. F. Snow, eds. *The Private Journals of the Long Parliament*. New Haven, CT: Yale University Press, 1982.

Cope, E. S., and W. H. Coates, eds. *Proceedings of the Short Parliament of 1640*. London: Royal Historical Society, 1977.

Cranford, J. (printer). *The Souldiers Catechisme Composed for the Parliaments Army, 1644*. London: Cresset Press, n.d.

Cromwell, Oliver (ed. I. Roots). *Speeches of Oliver Cromwell*. London: Dent, 1989.

——— (ed. T. Carlyle). *Oliver Cromwell's Letters and Speeches*, 3d ed. London: Ward Lock and Co., n.d.

Dickenson, W. C., and G. Donaldson, eds. *A Source Book of Scottish History, 1567–1707*, Vol. 3. Edinburgh: Nelson, 1954.

Erickson, J., ed. *The Journal of the House of Commons, 1547–1900*. New York: Readex Microprint, 1964.

Everitt-Green, M., ed. *Calendar of the Committee for Compounding*. Liechtenstein: Kraus Reprint, 1967.

———. *Calendar of the Committee for the Advance of Money*. Liechtenstein: Kraus Reprint, 1967.

Firth, C. H., ed. Journal of Prince Rupert's Marches. *English Historical Review* XIII, 1899.

Firth, C. H., and R. S. Rait, eds. *Acts and Ordinances of the Interregnum*. London: HMSO, 1911.

Fitzpatrick, T., ed. *The Bloody Bridge and Other Papers Relating to the Insurrection of 1641*. Dublin: Sealy, Bryers and Walker, 1903.

Fleming, D. H. Scotland's Supplication and Complaint against the Book of Common Prayer (otherwise Laud's Liturgy), the Book of Canons and the Prelates, 18 October 1637. *Proceedings of the Society of Antiquaries of Scotland* LX, 1923.

Gardiner, Samuel R., ed. *The Constitutional Documents of the Puritan Revolution*. Oxford: Clarendon Press, 1889.

Gibson, J. S. W., and E. R. C. Brinkworth, ed. *Banbury Corporation Records, Tudor and Stuart*. Banbury: Banbury Historical Society, 1977.

Gilbert, J. T., ed. *A Contemporary History of Affairs in Ireland from 1641–1652*, 3 vol. Dublin: Irish Archaeological and Celtic Society, 1879–80.

Graham, E., H. Hinds, E. Hobby, and H. Wilcox, eds. *Her Own Life: Autobiographical writings by Seventeenth-Century English Women*. London: Routledge, 1989.

Historical Manuscripts Commission. *Third Report*. London: HMSO, 1872.

———. *Thirteenth Report*. London: HMSO, 1891.

———. *Fourteenth Report*. London: HMSO, 1895.

———. *Report on the Manuscripts of the Marquis of Ormonde*. London: HMSO, 1899.

———. *Report on the Manuscripts of the Marquis of Ormonde, New Series*. London: HMSO, 1902.

———. *Report on Franciscan Manuscripts*. Dublin: HMSO, 1906.

———. *Report on Manuscripts in Various Collections*, vol. 7. London: HMSO, 1914.

———. *Report on the Records of the Borough of Exeter*. London: HMSO, 1916.

———. *Report on the Papers of Reginald Rawdon Hastings*. London: HMSO, 1930.

Hobson, M. G., and H. E. Salter, ed. *Oxford Council Acts, 1626–1665*. Oxford: Oxford University Press, 1933.

Hogan, J., ed. *Letters and Papers Relating to the Irish Rebellion*. Dublin: Stationery Office, 1930.

Holmes, Clive, ed. *The Suffolk Committees for Scandelous Ministers, 1644–46*. Ipswich: Suffolk Records Society, 1970.

Hope, Thomas. *A Diary of the Public Correspondence of Sir Thomas Hope of Craighall, Bt, 1633–1645*. Edinburgh: Bannatyne Club, 1843.

Howells, B. E., ed. *A Calendar of Letters Relating to North Wales, 1533–c.1700*. Cardiff: University of Wales Press, 1967.

Hutchinson, Lucy. *Memoirs of the Life of Colonel Hutchinson*. London: Longman, Orme, Rees, and Brown, 1806.

Jansson, Maija, ed. *Two Diaries of the Long Parliament*. Stroud: Sutton, 1984.

Jenning, B., ed. *Louvain Papers, 1606–1827*. Dublin: Irish Manuscripts Commission, 1968.

Johnston of Wariston, Archibald (ed. G. H. Paul, D. H. Fleming, and J. D. Ogilvie). *Diary of Sir Archibald Johnston of Wariston*, 3 vol. Edinburgh: Scottish History Society Publications, Vol. LXI, 1911; Second Series, XVIII, 1919; Third Series, XXIV, 1940.

Johnson, D. A., and D. G. Vaisey, ed. *Staffordshire and the Great Rebellion*. Stafford: Staffordshireshire County Council, 1964.

Lockyer, Roger. *The Trial of Charles I*. London: Folio Society,1959.

Kenyon, John P., ed. *The Stuart Constitution*, 2d ed. Cambridge: Cambridge University Press, 1986.

Luke, Sir Samuel (ed. I. G. Phillips). *Journal of Sir Samuel Luke*, 3 vol. Oxford: Oxfordshire Record Society, 1950–53.

MacTavish, D. C., ed. *Minutes of the Synod of Argyll 1639–1651. Minutes of the Synod of Argyll, 1652–1661*. Publications of the Scottish History Society, Series Three, Vols. XXXVII and XXXVIII. Edinburgh. Edinburgh University Press, 1943, 1944.

Marwick, J. D., ed. *Extracts of the Records of the Burgh of Glasgow, 1630–1662*. Glasgow: Scottish Burgh Record Society, 1881.

Morton, A. L. *Freedom in Arms: A Selection of Leveller Writings*. London: Lawrence and Wishart, 1975.

Newcastle, Margaret Cavendish, Duchess of (ed. C. H. Firth). *Memoirs of William Cavendish Duke of Newcastle and Margaret His Wife*. London: Routledge, n.d.

Nicholson, J., ed. *Minutebook kept by the War Committee of the Covenanters in the Stewartry of Kircudbright 1640–41*. Kirkudbright: Nicholson, 1855.

Pennington, D. H., and Ivan Roots, ed. *The Committee at Stafford*. Stafford: Staffordshire Historical Collections, 1957.

Prall, Stuart, ed. *The Puritan Revolution: A Documentary History*. London: Routledge and Kegan Paul, 1968.

Razzell, E., and P. Razell, ed. *The English Civil War: A Contemporary Account* (The papers of the Venetian Ambassadors, 1625–1675), 5 vol. London: Caliban, 1996.

Roy, Ian, ed. *The Royalist Ordinance Papers*. Oxford: Oxfordshire Record Society, 1964.

Rushworth, John, ed. *Historical Collections*, 7 vol. London: n.p., 1657–1701.

Stevenson, David. *The Government of Scotland under the Covenanters, 1637–1651*. Edinburgh: Scottish History Society, 1982.

Stewart, J., ed. *Extracts from the Council Register of the Burgh of Aberdeen*, 2 vol. Edinburgh: Scottish Burgh Record Society, 1871–72.

———. *Minutes of the Committee for the Loan Monies and Taxations of the Shire of Aberdeen*. Edinburgh: Spalding Club Miscellany, Vol. III, 1846.

Stocks, H. E., ed. *Records of the Borough of Leicester, 1603–89*. Cambridge: Cambridge University Press, 1923.

Symonds, Richard (ed. C. E. Long). *Diary of the Marches of the Royal Army*. London: Camden Society, 1859.

Taylor, L. B., ed. *Aberdeen Council Letters*, vol. 2. Oxford: Oxford University Press, 1950.

Terry, C. S., ed. *Papers Relating to the Army of the Solemn League and Covenant. 1643–47*, 2 vol. Edinburgh: Edinburgh University Press, 1917.

Verney, F. P., ed. *Memoirs of the Verney Family during the Civil War*. London: Tabard Press, 1970.

Whitlock, Bulstrode. *Memorials of English Affairs from the Beginning of the Reign of Charles I to the Restoration of Charles II*. Oxford: Oxford University Press, 1853.

Wilson, J., ed. *Buckinghamshire Contributions for Ireland 1642 and Richard Greville's Military Accounts 1642–45*. Buckingham: Buckinghamshire Record Society, 1983.

Wood, H., ed. *A Guide to the Records Deposited in the Public Record Office of Ireland*. Dublin: HMSO, 1919.

Wood, M., ed. *Extracts from the Records of the Burgh of Edinburgh*, 2 vol. Edinburgh: Oliver and Boyd, 1936, 1938.

II. General Background Texts: The Histories of the Four Nations

Bardon, Jonothan. *A History of Ulster*. Belfast: Blackstaff, 1992.

Bossy, J. *The English Catholic Community*. London: Darton, Longman and Todd, 1975.

Brown, Keith M. *Kingdom or Province: Scotland and the Regal Union*. London: Macmillan, 1992.

Cain, T. G. S., and K. Robinson. *Into Another Mould, Change and Continuity in English Culture 1625–1700*. London: Routledge, 1992.

Canny, Nicholas. *From Reformation to Restoration, Ireland 1534–1660*. Dublin: Helicon, 1987.

Cliffe, J. T. *The Yorkshire Gentry*. London: Athlone Press, 1969.

———. *The Puritan Gentry*. London: Routledge and Kegan Paul, 1984.

Collinson, Patrick. *The Birthpangs of Protestant England*. London: Macmillan, 1988.

Cope, Esther. *Politics without Parliaments*. London: Allan and Unwin, 1987.

Corish, Patrick. *The Catholic Community in the Seventeenth and Eighteenth Century*. Dublin: Helicon, 1981.

Crawford, Patricia. *Denzil, First Lord Holles*. London: Royal Historical Society, 1979.

Cronne, H. A., T. W. Moody, and D. B. Quinn, ed. *Essays in British and Irish History in Honour of James Eadie Todd*. London: Frederick Muller, 1949.

Cust, Richard, and Ann Hughes. ed. *Conflict in Early Stuart England*. London: Longman, 1989.

Donaldson, Gordon. *Scotland: James V–James VII*. Edinburgh: Mercat Press, 1990 (originally published in 1965).

Edwards, Ruth D. *An Atlas of Irish History*. London: Routledge, 1973 (reprinted 1991).

Erickson, Amy-Louise. *Women and Property in Early Modern England*. London: Routledge 1993.

Fitzpatrick, Brendan. *Seventeenth Century Ireland: The War of Religions*. Dublin: Gill and Macmillan, 1988.

Ford, A. *The Protestant Reformation in Ireland, 1590–1641*. Dublin: Four Courts Press, 1997.

Ford, A., J. McGuire, and K. Milne, ed. *As By Law Established: The Church of Ireland Since the Reformation*. Dublin: Lilliput Press, 1995.

Ford, B. *Seventeenth Century Britain: The Cambridge Cultural History*. Cambridge: Cambridge University Press, 1992.

Gillespie, Raymond. *The Transformation of the Irish Economy, 1550–1700*. Dublin: Economic and Social History Society of Ireland, 1991.

Herlihy, K., ed. *The Irish Dissenting Tradition, 1570–1750*. Dublin: Four Courts Press, 1995.

Hobby, Elaine. *Virtue of Necessity, English Women's Writing 1649–88*. London: Virago, 1988.

Houston, R. A., and I. D. Whyte, ed. *Scottish Society, 1500–1800*. Cambridge: Cambridge University Press,1989.

Jenkins, Geraint. *Protestant Dissenters in Wales*. Cardiff: University of Wales Press, 1992.

———. *The Foundations of Modern Wales*. Oxford: Oxford University Press, 1987.

Jones, J. G. *Early Modern Wales*. London: Macmillan, 1994.

Kearney, Hugh F. *The British Isles: A History of Four Nations*. Cambridge: Cambridge University Press, 1993.

Kenyon, John P. *Stuart England*, 2d ed. Harmondsworth: Penguin, 1985.

Lockyer, Roger. *The Early Stuarts*. London: Longman, 1989.

MacCurtain, Margaret, and Mary O'Dowd, ed. *Women in Early Modern Ireland*. Edinburgh: Edinburgh University Press, 1991.

Mitchison, Rosalind. *Lordship to Patronage Scotland, 1603–1745*. Edinburgh: Edinburgh University Press, 1983.

Moody, T. W., F. X. Martin, and F. J. Byrne, ed. *A New History of Ireland*, Vol. III. Oxford: Oxford University Press, 1976.

Potter, Lois. *Secret Rites and Secret Writing: Royalist Literature, 1641–1660*. Cambridge: Cambridge University Press, 1989.

Quintrell, Brian. *Charles I*. London: Longman, 1993.

Rees, W. *An Historical Atlas of Wales From Early to Modern Times*. London: Faber and Faber, 1951.

Reeve, J. *Charles I and the Road to Personal Rule*. Cambridge: Cambridge University Press, 1989.

Stone, Lawrence. *The Crisis of the Aristocracy*. Oxford: Clarendon Press, 1965.

Whyte, Ian D. *Agriculture and Society in Seventeenth Century Scotland*. Edinburgh: John Donald, 1979.

Williams, Glanmor. *Renewal and Reformation: Wales, c.1415–1642*. Oxford: Oxford University Press,1993.

Withers, C. J. *Gaelic Scotland: The Transformation of a Cultural Region*. London: Routledge, 1988.

III. Political and Religious Histories of the Civil War and the Republican Period

Adair, John. *By the Sword Divided*. London: Century Press, 1983.

Adamson, J. S. A., The Baronial Context of the English Civil War. *Transactions of the Royal Historical Society* 40, 1990.

Ashton, Robert. *The English Civil War Conservatism and Revolution*. London: Weindenfield and Nicholson, 1978.

———. *Counter Revolution: The Second Civil War and its Origins*. New Haven, CT: Yale University Press, 1994.

Aylmer, Gerald E. *The Interregnum: The Quest for a Settlement*. London: Macmillan, 1972.

———. *The Levellers in the English Revolution*. London: Thames and Hudson, 1975.

———. *Rebellion or Revolution: England from Civil War to Restoration*. Oxford: Oxford University Press, 1986.

Barnard, T. C. Crises of Identity Among Irish Protestants, 1641–85. *Past and Present* 127, May 1990.

———. *The English Republic*, 2d ed. London: Longman, 1997.

Baskerville, S. Blood Guilt in the English Revolution. *Seventeenth Century* VIII(2), Autumn 1993.

———. *Not Peace But a Sword: The Political Theory of the English Revolution*. London: Routledge, 1993.

Bennett, Martyn. *The English Civil War*. London: Longman, 1995.

———. *The Civil Wars in Britain and Ireland*. Oxford: Blackwell, 1997.

———. *The Civil Wars, 1637–1653*. Stroud: Sutton, 1998.

Bernard, G. W. The Church of England, c.1529–c.1642. *History* 75(224), June 1990.

Birkenhead, Earl of. *Strafford*. London: Hutchinson, 1938.

Bone, Quentin. *Henrietta Maria, Queen of the Cavaliers*. Urbana: University of Illinois Press, 1972.

Braddick, Michael. Popular Politics and Public Policy: The Excise Riot at Smithfield in February 1647 and its Aftermath. *Historical Journal* 34(3), 1991.

Bradley, I. Gerrard Winstanley, England's Pioneer Green. *History Today* 39, 1989.

Brunton, D., and D. H. Pennington. *Members of the Long Parliament.* Cambridge, MA: Harvard University Press, 1954.

Canny, Nicholas. The Ideology of English Colonisation from Ireland to America. *William and Mary Quarterly* 30, 1973.

————. Protestants, Planters and Apartheid. *Irish Historical Studies* XXV(98), November 1986.

Cope, Esther S. Dame Eleanor Davies, Never Soe Mad a Ladie? *Huntingdon Quarterly* 50(2), Spring 1987.

Cotton, A. B. Cromwell and the Self Denying Ordinance. *History* LXII, 1977.

Cregan, D. F. The Confederate Catholics of Ireland: The Personnel of the Confederation. *Irish Historical Studies* XXIX(116), November 1995.

Davis, J. C. *Fear, Myth and History: The Ranters and the Historians.* Cambridge: Cambridge University Press, 1986.

————. Fear, Myth and the Furore: Reappraising the Ranters. *Past and Present* 129, November 1990.

Donaghan, Barbara. Codes and Conduct in the English Civil War. *Past and Present* 118, February 1988.

Donald, Peter. *An Uncouncelled King: Charles I and the Scottish Troubles, 1637–41.* Cambridge: Cambridge University Press, 1990.

Durston, Christopher. "Let Ireland be Quiet": Opposition in England to the Cromwellian Conquest of Ireland. *History Workshop Journal* 21, Spring 1986.

————. Signs and Wonders and the English Civil War. *History Today* 37, October 1987.

————. *The Family in the English Revolution.* Oxford: Blackwell, 1989.

Eley, G., and W. Hunt, ed. *Reviving the English Revolution: Reflections and Elaborations on the work of Christopher Hill.* London: Verso, 1988.

Ensberg, J. Royalist Finances during the English Civil War. *Scandinavian Economic History Review* 14(2), 1966.

Firth, C. H. *Oliver Cromwell, and the Rule of the Puritans.* Oxford: Oxford University Press, 1900.

————. Ballards on the Bishop's Wars, 1638–1640. *Scottish Historical Review* III (11), April 1906.

————. *The House of Lords during the Civil War.* London: Longman, 1910.

Fletcher, Anthony. *The Outbreak of the English Civil War.* London: Arnold, 1981.

Friedman, Jerome. *Miracles and the Pulp Press during the English Revolution.* London: University College London Press, 1993.

Gardiner, Samuel R. *History of the Great Civil War,* 4 vol. (originally published 1893). Adelstrop: Windrush Press, 1987 and 1991.

————. *History of the Commonwealth and Protectorate, 1649–1656,* 4 vol. (originally published 1903). Adelstrop: Windrush Press, 1988.

Gaunt, Peter. *Oliver Cromwell.* Oxford: Blackwell, 1996.

————. *The British Civil Wars.* Oxford: Blackwell, 1997.

Gregg, Pauline. *Freeborn John: A Biography of John Lilburne.* London: Harrap, 1961.

Hainsworth, R. *The Swordsmen in Power: War and Politics under the English Republic.* Stroud: Sutton, 1997.

Hardacre, P. *The Royalists during the Puritan Revolution*. The Hague: Martinus Nijhoff, 1956.

Harrington, Peter. *Archaeology of the English Civil War*. Princes Risborough: Shire, 1992.

Hazlett, H. The Financing of the British Armies in Ireland: 1641–49. *Irish Historical Studies* 1, 1938.

Hibbard, Caroline. Charles I and the Popish Plot. Chapel Hill: University of North Carolina, 1983.

Hill, Christopher. *The World Turned Upside Down* (originally published 1972). Harmondswort: Penguin, 1975.

———. *God's Englishman: Oliver Cromwell and the English Revolution*. (originally published 1970). Harmondsworth: Penguin, 1979.

———. *The English Revolution* (originally published 1940). London: Lawrence and Wishart, 1979.

———. *Puritanism and Revolution* (originally published 1958). Harmondsworth: Peregrine, 1986.

———. *The English Bible and the Seventeenth Century Revolution*. London: Allen Lane, 1993.

Hughes, Ann. The King, the Parliament and the Localities during the English Civil War. *Journal of British Studies* 24, April 1985.

———. *The Causes of the English Civil War*. London: Macmillan, 1992.

Hutton, Ronald E. The Structure of the Royalist Party. *Historical Journal* 23(3), 1981.

———. *The Restoration: A Political and Religious History of England and Wales*. Oxford: Clarendon Press, 1985.

———. *Charles II, King of England Scotland and Ireland*. Oxford: Oxford University Press, 1989.

———. *The British Republic*. London: Macmillan, 1990.

Ives, W. *The English Revolution, 1600–1660*. London: Arnold, 1968.

Jones, C., M. Newitt, and S. Roberts. *Politics and People in Revolutionary England: Essays in Honour of Ivan Roots*. Oxford: Blackwell, 1986.

Kaplan, L. Steps to War: Scots and Parliament, 1642–43. *Journal of British Studies* IX, 1970.

Kearney, Hugh F. *Stafford in Ireland: A Study of Absolutism* (originally published 1959). Cambridge: Cambridge University Press, 1989.

Kelsey, Sean. *Inventing a Republic: The Political Culture of the English Commonwealth, 1649–1653*. Manchester: Manchester University Press, 1997.

Kenyon, John P. *The Civil Wars of England*. London: Weidenfield and Nicholson, 1988.

Kenyon, T. *Utopian Communism and Political Thought in Early Modern England*. London: Pinter, 1989.

Laurence, Ann. Women's Work and the English Civil War. *History Today* 42, 1992.

Lee, Maurice. *The Road to Revolution: Scotland under Charles I 1625–1637*. Chicago: University of Illinois Press, 1985.

MacInnes, Allan I. *Charles I and the Making of the Covenanting Movement, 1625–1641*. Edinburgh: John Donald, 1991.

Mack, Phyllis. Women as Prophets during the English Civil War. *Feminist Studies* 8(1), 1982.

McArthur, E. A. Women Petitioners and the Long Parliament. *English Historical Review* XXIV, 1909.

McElligott, J. *Cromwell: Our Chief of Enemies*. Dundalk: Dundalgan Press, 1994.

McGregor, J. F., and B. Reay, ed. *Radical Religion in the English Revolution*. Oxford: Oxford University Press, 1984.

McKenny, K. Charles II's Irish Cavaliers: The 1649 Officers and the Restoration Land Settlement. *Irish Historical Studies* XXVIII(112), November 1993.

Malcolm, Joyce L. *Caesar's Due: Loyalty and King Charles, 1642–1646*. London: Royal Historical Society, 1983.

Manning, Brian, ed. *Politics, Religion and the English Civil War*. London: Edward Arnold, 1973.

———. *The English People and the English, 1640–1649*. London: Heineman, 1976.

———. *1649: The Crisis of the English Revolution*. London: Bookmarks, 1992.

Morrill, John S. *The Revolt of the Provinces*. London: Longman, 1976.

———. *The Nature of the English Revolution*. London: Longman, 1993.

Morrill, John S., ed. *Reactions to the English Civil War*. London: Macmillan, 1982.

———. *Oliver Cromwell and the English Revolution*. London: Longman, 1990.

———. *The Scottish National Covenant in its British Context*. Edinburgh: Edinburgh University Press, 1990.

———. *The Impact of the English Civil War*. London: Collins and Brown, 1991.

———. *Revolution and Restoration: England in the 1650s*. London: Collins and Brown, 1992.

Newman, Peter R. The Royalist Officer Corp as a Reflection of the Social Structure. *Historical Journal* 26(4), 1983.

———. *Companion to the English Civil Wars*. London: Facts on File, 1990.

Ohlmeyer, Jane. The Marquis of Antrim: A Stuart Turn-kilt? *History Today* 43, 1993.

———. *Civil War and Restoration in the Three Stuart Kingdoms: The Career of Randal MacDonnell, Marquis of Antrim, 1609–1683*. Cambridge: Cambridge University Press, 1993.

Ohlmeyer, Jane, ed. *Ireland, From Independence to Occupation, 1641–60*. Cambridge: Cambridge University Press, 1995.

Parry, R. H. *The English Civil War and After, 1642–1658*. London: Macmillan, 1970.

Percival-Maxwell, M. The Ulster Rising of 1641 and the Depositions. *Irish Historical Studies* XXI (82), September 1978.

———. *The Outbreak of the Irish Rebellion of 1641*. Dublin: Gill and Macmillan, 1994.

Porter, Stephen. The Fire-Raid in the English Civil War. *War and Society* 2(2), September 1984.

———. *Destruction in the English Civil Wars*. Stroud: Sutton, 1994.

Richardson, R. C., ed. *The Debate on the English Revolution Revisited*. London: Routledge, 1988.

———. *Town and Countryside in the English Revolution*. Manchester: Manchester University Press, 1992.

Ridley, J. *The Roundheads*. London: Constable, 1970.

Ridsdill-Smith, G., M. Toynbee, and P. Young. *Leaders of the Civil Wars*. Kineton: Roundwood Press, 1977.

Roy, I. England Turned Germany? The Aftermath of the Civil War in its European Context. *Transactions of the Royal Historical Society* 5(28), 1978.

Russell, Conrad. Why Did Charles I fight the Civil War? *History Today* 34, 1984.

———. The British Background to the Irish Rebellion of 1641. *Historical Research* 61(145), 1988.

———. *The Causes of the English Civil War*. Oxford: Oxford University Press, 1990.

———. *The Fall of the British Monarchies, 1637–42*. Oxford: Oxford University Press, 1991.

———. The Scottish Party in English Parliaments, 1640–42 or the Myth of the English Revolution. *Historical Research* 66(159), 1993.

Russell, Conrad, ed. *The Origins of the English Civil War*. London: Methuen, 1973.

Sanderson, J. *But the Peoples' Creatures: The Philosophical Basis of the English Civil War*. Manchester: Manchester University Press, 1989.

Sharpe, Kevin. *The Personal Rule of Charles II*. New Haven, CT: Yale University Press, 1992.

Shaw, H. *The Levellers*. London: Longman, 1968.

Sommerville, J. P. *Politics and Ideology in England, 1603–40*. London: Longman, 1986.

Stevenson, David. The Financing of the Cause of the Covenanters, 1638–51. *Scottish Historical Review* LI, 1972.

———. *The Scottish Revolution, 1637–44*. Newton Abbot: David and Charles, 1973.

———. *Revolution and Counter-Revolution in Scotland, 1644–1651*. London: Royal Historical Society, 1977.

———. *The Covenanters*. Edinburgh: Saltire Society, 1988.

———. *Highland Warrior: Alasdair MacColla and the Civil Wars* (originally published 1980). Edinburgh: Saltire Society, 1994.

Stewart, D. The Aberdeen Doctors and the Covenant. *Records of the Scottish Church History Society* XXII, 1984.

Stone, Lawrence. *The Causes of the English Revolution*. London: Routledge and Kegan Paul, 1977.

Tanner, J. R. *The English Constitutional Conflicts of the Seventeenth Century, 1603–1689*. Cambridge: Cambridge University Press, 1962.

Trease, Geoffrey. *Portrait of a Cavalier, William Cavendish, First Duke of Newcastle*. London: Macmillan, 1979.

Underdown, David. *Royalist Conspiracy in England*. New Haven, CT: Yale University Press, 1960.

———. *A Freeborn People: Politics and the Nation in Seventeenth Century England*. Oxford: Oxford University Press, 1996.

Wedgwood, C. V. *Thomas Wentworth: First Earl of Strafford. A Revaluation*. London: Jonathan Cape, 1961.

———. *The King's Peace* (originally published 1955). Harmondsworth: Penguin, 1983.

————. *The King's War* (originally published 1958). Harmondsworth: Penguin, 1983.

————. *The Trial of Charles I* (originally published 1964). Harmondsworth: Penguin, 1983.

Woolrych, Austin. The Cromwellian Protectorate: A Military Dictatorship. *History* 75(224), June 1990.

Wormald, Jenny, ed. *Court, Kirk and Community*. London: Edward Arnold, 1981.

————. *Scotland Revisited*. London: Collins and Brown, 1991.

Young, John R., ed. *The Scottish Parliament*. Edinburgh: Edinburgh University Press, 1996.

————. *Celtic Dimensions of the British Civil Wars*. Edinburgh: John Donald, 1997.

IV. Military History

Adair, John. *Cheriton, 1644, the Campaign and the Battle*. Kineton: Roundwood Press, 1973.

Anderson, M. S. *War and Society in Europe of the Old Regime, 1618–1789*. Leicester: Leicester University Press, 1988.

Ashley, Maurice. *The Battle of Naseby and the Fall of King Charles I*. Stroud: Sutton, 1992.

Bennett, Martyn. *Travellers' Guide to the Battlefields of the English Civil War*. Exeter: Webb and Bower, 1990.

Blackmore, David. *Arms and Armour of the English Civil War*. London: Royal Armouries, 1990.

Capp, Bernard. *Cromwell's Navy*. Oxford: Clarendon Press, 1989.

Carlton, Charles. *Going to the Wars: The Experience of the British Civil Wars, 1638–1651*. London: Routledge, 1992.

Casaway, Jerold I. *Owen Roe O'Neill and the Struggle for Catholic Ireland*. Philadelphia: University of Pennsylvania Press, 1984.

Firth, C. H. *Cromwell's Army* (originally published 1902). London: Greenhill, 1992.

Fissel, Mark. *The Bishops' Wars: Charles I's Campaigns against Scotland*. Cambridge: Cambridge University Press, 1994.

Gentles, Ian. *The New Model Army in England, Ireland and Scotland, 1645–1653*. Oxford: Blackwell, 1992.

Gratton, Malcolm. The Military Career of Richard, Lord Molyneux, c.1623–54. *Transactions of the Lancashire and Cheshire Historical Society* 134, 1984.

Hutton, Ronald E. *The Royalist War Effort*. London: Longman, 1982.

Malcolm, J. L. A King in Search of Soldiers: Charles I in 1642. *Historical Journal* 21(2), 1978.

Newman, Peter R. *The Battle of Marston Moor*. Chichester: Anthony Bird, 1981.

————. *Royalist Officers in England and Wales, 1642–60*. New York: Garland, 1981.

————. *Atlas of the English Civil War*. London: Croom Helm, 1985.

————. *The Old Service: Royalist Regimental Colonels and the Civil War, 1642–46*. Manchester: Manchester University Press, 1993.

Wanklyn, Malcolm, and Peter Young. A King in Search of Soldiers: Charles I in 1642: A Rejoinder. *Historical Journal* 24(1), 1981.

Woolrych, Austin. *Battles of the English Civil War*. London: Pan, 1966.

Young, Peter. *Edgehill 1642: The Campaign and the Battle*. Kineton: Roundway Press, 1967.

———. *Marston Moor 1644: The Campaign and the Battle*. Kineton: Roundway Press, 1970.

———. *Naseby 1645: The Campaign and the Battle*. London: Century, 1985.

Young, Peter, ed. *Newark upon Trent, the Civil War Siegeworks*. London: HMSO, 1964.

V. Local Studies

A. England

Atkin, M., and M. Laughton. *Gloucester and the Civil War*. Stroud: Sutton, 1992.

Beats, L. The East Midland Association, 1642–44. *Midland History* IV, 1978.

Bennett, Martyn. *Lord Loughborough, Ashby de la Zouch and the English Civil War*. Ashby-de-la-Zouch: Ashby Museum, 1984.

———. Leicestershire's Royalist Officers and Their War-Effort in the County, 1642–46. *Transactions of the Leicestershire Archaeological and Historical Society* LIX, 1984–85.

———. Contribution and Assessment: Financial Exactions in the First Civil War 1642–46. *War and Society* 5(1), 1986.

———. Between Scylla and Charybdis: The Creation of Rival Administrations at the Beginning of the English Civil War. *Local Historian* 22(4), 1992.

———. "My Plundered Townes, My Houses Devastation": The Civil War and North Midlands' Life, 1642–1646. *Midland History* XXII, 1997.

Blackwood, B. G. *The Lancashire Gentry and the Great Rebellion, 1640–1660*. Manchester: Chetham Society, 1978.

Brighton, J. T. *Royalists and Roundheads in Derbyshire*. Bakewell: Bakewell and District Historical Society, 1981.

Coate, M. *Cornwall in the Great Civil War* (originally published 1933). Truro: Bradford Barton, 1963.

Coleby, A. M. *Central Government and the Localities, Hampshire, 1649–1689*. Cambridge: Cambridge University Press, 1987.

Duffin, A. *Faction and Faith: Politics and Religion in the Cornish Gentry Before the Civil War*. Exeter: Exeter University Press, 1996.

Eales, J. *Puritans and Roundheads: The Harleys of Bampton Bryan and the Outbreak of the English Civil War*. Cambridge: Cambridge University Press, 1990.

Everritt, Alan. *The Local Community and the Great Rebellion*. London: Historical Association, 1969.

———. *The Community of Kent and the Great Rebellion, 1640–1660*. Leicester: Leicester University, 1973.

Fleming, D. Faction and Civil War in Leicestershire. *Transactions of the Leicestershire Archaeological and Historical Society* LVII, 1981–82.

Garner, A. A. *Boston and the Great Civil War*. Boston: Richard Key, 1972.

Gentles, Ian. *The Purchasers of Northamptonshire Crown Lands, 1649–1660*. *Midland History* III(3), Spring 1976.

Gillet, E., and K. A. MacMahon. *A History of Hull*. Oxford: Oxford University Press, 1980.

Gladwish, P. The Herefordshire Clubmen: A Reassessment. *Midland History* X, 1985.

Gruenfelder, J. K. The Electoral Influence of the Earls of Huntingdon, 1603–40. *Transactions of the Leicestershire Archaeological and Historical Society* L, 1974–75.

Guttery, D. R. *The Great Civil War in Midland Parishes: The People Pay*. Birmingham: Cornish Bros., 1950.

Holmes, Clive. *The Eastern Association in the English Civil War*. Cambridge: Cambridge University Press, 1974.

———. *Seventeenth Century Lincolnshire*. Lincoln: History of Lincoln Committee, 1980.

Hughes, Ann. Warwickshire on the Eve of Civil War: A County Community? *Midland History* VII, 1982.

———. *Politics, Society and Civil War in Warwickshire*. Cambridge: Cambridge University Press, 1987.

Hutton, Ronald E. The Worcestershire Clubmen in the English Civil War. *Midland History* V, 1979–80.

———. The Failure of the Lancashire Cavaliers. *Transactions of the Lancashire and Cheshire Historical Society* 129, 1980.

Ketton-Cremer, R. W. *Norfolk in the Civil War*. Hamden: Archon, 1970.

Lindley, Keith. *Fenland Riots and the English Revolution*. London: Heinemann, 1982.

Liu, T. *Puritan London: A Study of Religion and Society in the City Parishes*. Newark: University of Delaware Press, 1986.

Morrill, John, ed. *Cheshire 1630–1660*. Oxford: Oxford University Press, 1974.

Newman, Peter R. Catholic Royalist Activists in the North, 1642–46. *Recusant History* 14(1), 1977.

———. Catholic Royalists of Northern England. *Northern History* XV, 1979.

———. The Defeat of John Belasyse: Civil War in Yorkshire January–April 1644. *Yorkshire Archaeological Journal* CII, 1980.

O'Riordan, C. Thomas Ellison, the Hixon Estate and the Civil War. *Durham County Local History Society Bulletin* 39, December 1987.

Osborne, S. The War, the People, and the Absence of Clubmen in the Midlands, 1642–46. *Midland History* XIX, 1994.

Porter, Stephen. *London and the Civil War*. London: Macmillan, 1996.

Roberts, A. The Depredations of the Civil War in South-West Leicestershire. *Leicestershire Historian* 3(4), 1985–86.

Roberts, S. K. *Recovery and Restoration in and English County Devon Local Administration*. Exeter: University of Exeter, 1985.

Seaver, P. *Wallington's World: A Puritan Artisan in Seventeenth Century London*. Stanford, CA: Stanford University Press, 1985.

Seddon, P. The Nottinghamshire Elections for the Short Parliament of 1640. *Transactions of the Thoroton Society of Nottinghamshire* LXXXIV, 1976.

Sherwood, R. E. *The Civil War in the Midlands*. Stroud: Sutton, 1992.

Spence, R. T. *Skipton Castle in the Great Civil War*. Skipton: Skipton Castle, 1992.

Stone, Brian. *Derbyshire in the Civil War*. Cromford: Scarthin Books, 1992.

Tennant, Phillip. *Edgehill and Beyond: The People's War in the South Midlands, 1641–45*. Stroud: Sutton, 1992.

———. *The Civil War in Stratford upon Avon: Conflict and Community in South Warwickshire, 1642–1646*. Stroud: Sutton, 1996.

Toynebee, M. *Strangers in Oxford: A Sidelight on the Civil War*. Chichester: Phillimore, 1973.

Underdown, David. *Somerset in the Civil War and Interregnum*. Newton Abbot: David and Charles, 1973.

———. *Revel, Riot and Rebellion: Popular Politics and Culture in England, 1603–60*. Oxford: Clarendon Press, 1985.

———. *Fire from Heaven: Life in an English Town in the Seventeenth Century*. London: HarperCollins, 1992.

Wanklyn, Malcolm. Royalist Strategy in the South of England, 1642–44. *Southern History*, 1982.

Warner, Tim. *Newark: Civil War and Siegeworks*. Nottingham: Nottinghamshire County Council, 1992.

Wenham, P. *The Great and Close Siege of York*. Kineton: Roundway Press, 1970 (now reprinted as *The Siege of York*. York: Jonson, 1994).

Wood, A. C. *Nottinghamshire in Civil War* (originally published 1937). Wakefield: S. R. Reprint, 1971.

Woods, T. P. *Prelude to Civil War*. Salisbury: Russell Publishing, 1980.

Woolfe, M. *Gentry Leaders in Peace and War: The Gentry Governors of Devon in the Early Seventeenth Century*. Exeter: Exeter University Press, 1997.

Wroughton, John. *A Community at War: The Civil War in Bath and North Somerset*. Bath: Lansdown Press, 1992.

B. Ireland

Berresford-Ellis, P. *Hell or Connaught! The Cromwellian Colonisation of Ireland, 1652–1660* (originally published 1975). Belfast: Blackstaff Press, 1991.

Gillespie, Raymond. *Colonial Ulster: The Settlement of East Ulster, 1600–1641*. Cork: Cork University Press, 1985.

———. Mayo and the Rising of 1641. *Cathair Na Mart* 5, 1985.

Gillespie, Raymond, ed. *Cavan: Essays on the History of an Irish County*. Blackrock: Irish Academic Press, 1995.

Gilligan, H. A. *The Port of Dublin*. Dublin: Gill and Macmillan, 1989.

Jordan, D. E. *Land and Popular Politics in Ireland, County Mayo from the Plantation to the Land War*. Cambridge: Cambridge University Press, 1994.

MacCuarta, B., ed. *Ulster 1641: Aspects of the Rising*. Belfast: Institute of Irish Studies, 1993.

Moran, G., and Raymond Gillespie, ed. *Galway: History and Society*. Dublin: Geography Publications, 1996.

Nolan, W., and T. C. McGrath, ed. *Tipperary: History and Society*. Dublin: Geography Publications, 1985.

Nolan, W., and K. Whelan, ed. *Kilkenny: History and Society*. Dublin: Geography Publications, 1990.

Nolan, W., and T. P. Power, ed. *Waterford: History and Society*. Dublin: Geography Publications 1992.

Nolan, W., L. Roynayne, and M. Dunleavy, ed. *Donegal: History and Society*. Dublin: Geography Publications, 1995.

O'Dowd, M. *Power Politics and Land: Early Modern Sligo 1568–1688*. Belfast: Institute of Irish Studies, 1991.

O'Flanaghan, P., and C. P. Buttimer. *Cork: History and Society*. Dublin: Geography Publications, 1993.

Stevenson, J. *Two Centuries of Life in Down* (originally published 1920). Belfast: Whiterow Press, 1990.

Whelan, K., ed. *Wexford: History and Society*. Dublin: Geography Publications, 1987.

C. Scotland

McKerral, A. *Kintyre in the Seventeenth Century*. Edinburgh: Oliver and Boyd, 1948.

Makey, W. H. Elders of Stow Liberton, Canongate and St Cuthbert's in the Mid-Seventeenth Century. *Records of the Scottish Church History Society* XVII, 1969.

D. Wales

Dodd, A. H. Wales and the Second Bishop's War. *Bulletin of the Board of Celtic Studies* XII, 1948.

———. Anglesey in the Civil War. *Transactions of the Anglesey Antiquarian Society*, 1952.

———. Civil War in East Denbighshire. *Transactions of the Denbighshire Historical Society* 3, 1954.

Dore, R. N. Sir Thomas Myddleton's Attempted Conquest of Powys, 1644–45. *Montgomeryshire Collections* 57, 1961.

Dore, R. N., and J. Lowe. The Battle of Nantwich. *Transactions of the Lancashire and Cheshire Historical Society* 71, 1961.

Eames, A. Seapower and Caernarvonshire, 1642–60. *Transactions of Caernarvonshire History Society* 16, 1955.

Jones, E. D. Gentry of South-West Wales in the Civil War. *National Library of Wales Journal* 11, 1959.

Jones, J. G. Caernarfonshire Administration: Activities of the Justices of the Peace. *Welsh Historical Review* V, 1970.

———. Aspects of Local Government in Pre-Restoration Caernarfonshire. *Transactions of the Caernarfonshire Historical Society* 33, 1972.

Lloyd, H. A. *Gentry of South West Wales, 1540–1640*. Cardiff: University of Wales Press, 1968.

Raymond, S. A. Glamorganshire Commissioners of Array, 1642–46. *Morgannwg* 24, 1980.

Rees, F. Breconshire during the Civil War. *Brycheiniog* 8, 1962.

Tucker, N. Rupert's Letters to Anglesey and Other Civil War Correspondence. *Transactions of the Anglesey Antiquarian Society*, 1958.

Williams, P. The Attack on the Council of the Marches, 1603–42. *Transactions of the Cymmrddorion Society*, 1961.

About the Author

MARTYN BENNETT (B.A. [Hons.], Ph.D., Loughborough University) is a Reader in History at Nottingham Trent University. He is a Fellow of the Royal Historical Society. He has been the leader of the History Subject-Group at the university since 1994. Dr. Bennett lectures on Early Modern British, Irish, and American History. He has worked on local aspects of the Civil Wars within each of the four nations of the British Isles for 20 years. This work has resulted in six books on the subject, including the local study, *A Nottinghamshire Village in War and Peace: The Accounts of the Constables of Upton 1640–60*. Published in 1995, this volume is an edited collection of papers covering the war and revolution in east Nottinghamshire. Another of his more recent works is entitled *The Civil Wars in Britain and Ireland*, published in 1997. His research on the war and the use of constables' accounts have been published in national and international journals.